Executing Data Quality Projects

In Praise of Executing Data Quality Projects

Danette's book takes a pragmatic and practical approach to achieving the desired state of data quality within an organization. It is a "must-read" for any organization starting out on the road to data quality.

— Susan Stewart Goubeaux, Director, Business Intelligence, FHLBanks, Office of Finance

"Data quality" has become one of those hackneyed phrases in our industry that everyone supports, but only a few organizations have achieved to the degree they need to move forward in their industries. What is required is a guide to explain to the business people who want better data just how to get it. This book is just such a guide. While the individual steps should not be a great surprise, her organization makes them immediately actionable to a degree previous books have not. In short, this is definitely required reading for anyone embarking on a data quality project.

— David Hay, President, Essential Strategies

Danette has taken what has previously been presented in the abstract and made an excellent, concrete guide toward improving data quality.

— John Ladley, President, IMCue Solutions

Using this methodology, you will never lose your way on your data quality project! This book is peppered with tips, guidelines, templates, cross-references, and callout icons. Plus, there are many easy-to-follow examples for the most common types of data quality projects.

— Larissa T. Moss, President, Method Focus Inc.

This book presents a valuable reference for not just data professionals, but also project managers and business representatives interested in or responsible for establishing, maintaining, and/or improving data and information quality. What sets this book apart from others in the field is the business impact-driven approach to assessing and improving data quality, and the specific steps and techniques it provides every step of the way.

— Mehmet Orun, Senior Manager and Principal Architect, Data Services Center of Excellence, Fortune 250 Company

Comprehensive is the first word I would use to describe this book. It addresses so many nuances of every aspect of data quality assessment and improvement—things that would go unmentioned by more superficial treatments. Bravo!

— Michael Scofield, Manager, Data Asset Development, ESRI, Inc.

This book is a "must-own" for business and technical data quality managers and practitioners. Danette clearly demonstrates where her process will add value to quality projects that stand-alone or as the backbone of a successful data integration effort.

— Robert S. Seiner, KIK Consulting & Educational Services, LLC; The Data Administration Newsletter, LLC

Danette's writing style is appropriate for her audience, the content is superb, and her Ten Steps approach is clear and easy to follow but comprehensive. This is an excellent book and I would think it will be an essential reference for any effort in data quality.

— Anne Marie Smith, Ph.D., Director of Education and Principal Consultant, EWSolutions, Inc.

Danette has compiled a valuable toolkit for managing information quality improvement projects. Her clear, concise definitions of concepts also make it a nice primer on the principles of information quality for data professionals, business managers, or students. I would recommend this practical handbook to anyone embarking on an information quality project.

— Eva Smith, MSIM, CCP, CDMP, Instructor, Computer Information Systems

No two data quality projects are the same. Some are large efforts focused entirely on improving some quality aspect of information. Others are subprojects within other efforts, such as a data migration. Still others are led by a few individuals trying to make a difference as they perform their everyday activities. What I like about McGilvray's Ten Steps approach is that it can serve any of these situations. This book provides a structured, easy-to-understand, and easy-to-govern methodology that you can apply to the degree that is appropriate for you.

— Gwen Thomas, President, The Data Governance Institute

Executing Data Quality Projects

Ten Steps to Quality Data and Trusted Information™

Danette McGilvray

AMSTERDAM • BOSTON • HEIDELBERG • LONDON
NEW YORK • OXFORD • PARIS • SAN DIEGO
SAN FRANCISCO • SINGAPORE • SYDNEY • TOKYO
Morgan Kaufmann is an imprint of Elsevier

MORGAN KAUFMANN PUBLISHERS

Morgan Kaufmann Publishers is an imprint of Elsevier.
30 Corporate Drive, Suite 400, Burlington, MA 01803

This book is printed on acid-free paper.

Library of Congress Cataloging-in-Publication Data
McGilvray, Danette.
  Executing data quality projects : ten steps to quality data and trusted information /
Danette McGilvray.
      p. cm.
  Includes bibliographical references and index.
  ISBN 978-0-12-374369-5 (alk. paper)
 1. Information technology—Management. 2. Electronic data processing—Quality
  control. I. Title.
  HD30.2.M397 2008
  658.4'04—dc22   2008013824

For information on all Morgan Kaufmann publications,
visit our Web site at *www.mkp.com* or *www.books.elsevier.com*.

Printed and bound in the United Kingdom
Transferred to Digital Printing, 2010

**Working together to grow
libraries in developing countries**

www.elsevier.com | www.bookaid.org | www.sabre.org

ELSEVIER   BOOK AID
            International   Sabre Foundation

To Jeff

Now voyager, sail thou forth to seek and find.
– Walt Whitman

Contents

ACKNOWLEDGMENTS   xi

INTRODUCTION   xiii
    The Reason for This Book   xiii
    Intended Audiences   xiv
    Structure of This Book   xv
    How to Use This Book   xvii

CHAPTER 1   **Overview**   **2**
    The Impact of Information and Data Quality   4
    About the Methodology: Concepts and Steps   6
    Approaches to Data Quality in Projects   9
    Engaging Management   12

CHAPTER 2   **Key Concepts**   **14**
    Introduction   16
    The Framework for Information Quality   16
    The Information Life Cycle   23
    Data Quality Dimensions   30
    Business Impact Techniques   35
    Data Categories   39
    Data Specifications   45
    Data Governance and Data Stewardship   52
    The Information and Data Quality Improvement Cycle   54
    The Ten Steps Process   57
    Best Practices and Guidelines   59

CHAPTER 3   **The Ten Steps Process**   **62**
    Introduction   64
    Step 1   **Define Business Need and Approach**   **66**
        Introduction   66
    Step 1.1   Prioritize the Business Issue 69
    Step 1.2   Plan the Project   72
    Step 2   **Analyze Information Environment**   **76**
        Introduction   76
    Step 2.1   Understand Relevant Requirements   82
    Step 2.2   Understand Relevant Data and Specifications 84
    Step 2.3   Understand Relevant Technology   90
    Step 2.4   Understand Relevant Processes   93
    Step 2.5   Understand Relevant People/Organizations   98
    Step 2.6   Define the Information Life Cycle   102
    Step 2.7   Design Data Capture and Assessment Plan   105

Step 3	**Assess Data Quality**	**108**
	Introduction	108
Step 3.1	Data Specifications	114
Step 3.2	Data Integrity Fundamentals	118
Step 3.3	Duplication	128
Step 3.4	Accuracy	134
Step 3.5	Consistency and Synchronization	140
Step 3.6	Timeliness and Availability	143
Step 3.7	Ease of Use and Maintainability	147
Step 3.8	Data Coverage	149
Step 3.9	Presentation Quality	151
Step 3.10	Perception, Relevance, and Trust	155
Step 3.11	Data Decay	159
Step 3.12	Transactability	161
Step 4	**Assess Business Impact**	**163**
	Introduction	163
Step 4.1	Anecdotes	167
Step 4.2	Usage	173
Step 4.3	Five "Whys" for Business Impact	175
Step 4.4	Benefit versus Cost Matrix	177
Step 4.5	Ranking and Prioritization	181
Step 4.6	Process Impact	186
Step 4.7	Cost of Low-Quality Data	189
Step 4.8	Cost–Benefit Analysis	195
Step 5	**Identify Root Causes**	**198**
	Introduction	198
Step 5.1	Five "Whys" for Root Cause	201
Step 5.2	Track and Trace	203
Step 5.3	Cause-and-Effect/Fishbone Diagram	204
Step 6	**Develop Improvement Plans**	**208**
Step 7	**Prevent Future Data Errors**	**213**
Step 8	**Correct Current Data Errors**	**218**
Step 9	**Implement Controls**	**222**
Step 10	**Communicate Actions and Results**	**227**
	The Ten Steps Process Summary	**233**
CHAPTER 4	**Structuring Your Project**	**238**
	Projects and The Ten Steps	240
	Data Quality Project Roles	252
	Project Timing	253
CHAPTER 5	**Other Techniques and Tools**	**256**
	Introduction	258
	Information Life Cycle Approaches	258
	Capture Data	263
	Analyze and Document Results	263

	Metrics	269
	Data Quality Tools	271
	The Ten Steps and Six Sigma	277
CHAPTER 6	A Few Final Words	278
APPENDIX	Quick References	282
	The Framework for Information Quality	284
	The POSMAD Interaction Matrix in Detail	286
	POSMAD Phases and Activities	288
	Data Quality Dimensions	289
	Business Impact Techniques	290
	Overview of The Ten Steps Process	291
	Definitions of Data Categories	293
GLOSSARY		295
BIBLIOGRAPHY		303
LIST OF FIGURES, TABLES, AND TEMPLATES		307
INDEX		311
ABOUT THE AUTHOR		334

Acknowledgments

I now have a better appreciation for the long lists of people who authors' acknowledge. Writing a book is definitely not a one-person effort and this book is no exception.

To Judy Kincaid, who unknowingly started me on the path of information quality. Many years ago she called me into her office and asked me to work with Larry English, who was to come to Hewlett-Packard to consult on information quality. She felt that by working with him the knowledge we gained would not leave the company when he was no longer there. Her words were, "It will be full time this week and then taper off after that." Thanks to Judy that assignment turned the course of my career and more than fifteen years later I'm still working on information quality full time!

I owe a debt of gratitude to Larry English who provided my initial education in information quality, mentored me through my first project, and brings visibility to this important topic.

Special thanks to Mehmet Orun, Wonna Mark, Sonja Bock, Rachel Haverstick, and Mary Nelson for their feedback, time, and expertise when I was creating the first fully written version of my methodology. Their knowledge, probing questions, thoughtful comments, and insight shaped that version and provided the foundation for this book. Without their efforts this book would not have been possible.

Thanks to those who reviewed the original proposal, or the detailed manuscript, or spent time discussing and providing input for specific sections of the book—David Hay, Mehmet Orun, Eva Smith, Gwen Thomas, Michael Scofield, Anne Marie Smith, Lwanga Yonke, Larissa Moss, Tom Redman, Susan Goubeaux, Andres Perez, Jack Olson, Ron Ross, David Plotkin, Beth Hatcher, Mary Levins, Dee Dee Lozier—and to those who chose to remain anonymous. Your honest comments for improvement and encouragement regarding what worked have made this a much better book.

Thanks to those over the years who have put into practice or supported the ideas presented here as sponsors, project managers, team members, and practitioners in various organizations. Unfortunately, there is not room to name you all individually, but thanks to you the knowledge gained and practices evolved from those experiences are being used to help others on their information quality journey.

To those who have attended my workshops and courses—thanks for your participation and willingness to share ideas, lessons learned, and successes. Your enthusiastic feedback and response provided motivation for me to write this book.

To the many leaders in this and related fields who have taken the time to write or teach so that I and others can learn. One look at the bibliography shows the extent of my appreciation to those who have made that effort; I have certainly been the beneficiary of their work. Special thanks to Tom Redman, David Loshin, Larissa Moss, Graeme Simsion, Peter Aiken, David Hay, Martin Eppler, Richard Wang, John Zachman, Michael Brackett, John Ladley, Len Silverston, and Larry English.

In addition, my thanks to those who lead professional associations, provide the venues for me to teach or publish, or offer behind-the-scenes advice and support. Although I cannot name all the individuals involved, I would like to recognize Tony Shaw and all those at Wilshire Conferences, all those at TDWI, Jeremy Hall and all those at IRM UK, those involved with IAIDQ and DAMA International, Mary Jo Nott, Robert S. Seiner, Larissa Moss, Sharon Adams, Roger Brothers, John Hill, Ken Rhodes, and Harry Zoccoli.

To my colleagues at Morgan Kaufmann, my appreciation for their excellent work—particularly Nate McFadden for his guidance and insight, and Denise Penrose, Mary James, Marilyn E. Rash, Dianne Wood, Jodie Allen, and the production team who finished making this book a reality.

To the teachers in the Logan City School District and Utah State University, where I received the education that created opportunities that have led me where I am today.

To Keith and Myrtle Munk. I was fortunate to have parents who stressed education, encouraged my activities, and always believed in me—even when I did not believe in myself. I am lucky to be part of a large extended family and a network of friends who provide fun, laughter, and lots of loving support—the reasons for working hard and what makes life worthwhile.

To my daughter, Tiffani Taggart, and my late son, Jason Taggart—they were the motivation for me to keep going even when times were tough.

The most special appreciation goes to my husband, Jeff McGilvray, for his unwavering love, encouragement, and support. None of this could have happened without you.

Introduction

Only four types of organizations need to worry about data quality:
Those that care about their customers,
Those that care about profit and loss,
Those that care about their employees, and
Those that care about their futures.

– Thomas C. Redman (2006)

The Reason for This Book

Information is currency. In today's world of instant global communication and trends that turn on a dime, up-to-date and reliable information is essential to effective competition. Whether it is market research, patent applications, manufacturing improvement metrics, taking sales orders, or receiving payments, information is as essential to the *functioning* of a business as it is to providing that business with a *competitive edge*.

Information quality contributes to that edge by delivering the right information, at the right time, in the right place, to the right people. Human beings cannot make *effective* business decisions with flawed, incomplete, or misleading data. Humans need information they can trust to be correct and current if they are to do the work that furthers business goals and objectives.

The *right* information can help inventory managers keep the supply chain lean, help CEOs make long-term plans for growth based on accurate and dependable performance measures, help social services identify high-risk youth who need their help, and instill trust in voters that election results are accurate. Understanding the quality of the information can allow decision makers to account for the impact of poor-quality data.

The *wrong* information can make the difference between a satisfied customer and a frustrated customer, or several thousand frustrated customers. In some cases, incorrect information can make the difference between life and death. Even if the stakes are not as high as that, poor-quality data impact the health of any organization. Lost business, magnified by the effects of wrong information propagated throughout information systems, can lead to millions of dollars in lost revenue. Businesses must use sound practices for improving information quality and reducing error to prevent loss of business and to produce *satisfied customers*. Every organization—for-profit, nonprofit, government, educational institutions—depends on information to support its customers and whatever the organization provides.

This book provides a systematic approach for improving and creating data and information quality within any business. It explains a methodology that combines a *conceptual framework* for understanding information quality with the *techniques, tools,* and *instructions* for improving and creating information quality. The *Framework for Information Quality* is the conceptual framework and *The Ten Steps* are the processes for implementing its concepts.

The methodology can be applied in the following ways by choosing the appropriate steps, activities, processes, and techniques:

For information quality-focused projects, such as a data quality assessment of a particular database or assessing the business impact of an issue that is the result of poor-quality data with the goal of identifying root causes and implementing improvements.

In the course of daily work whenever you are responsible for managing data quality or the work you do impacts data quality.

To integrate specific data quality activities into other projects and methodologies. For example, Enterprise Resource Planning (ERP) migration, building a data warehouse, or other application development and implementation.

The methodology can also form a foundation to create your own improvement methodology or to integrate data quality activities into a company's standard project life cycle or software/solution development life cycle.

Every company is different, yet the underlying approach to data quality described in the pages that follow applies to all companies and all types of data, whether finance, research, development, procurement, manufacturing, sales and marketing, order management, human resources, and so on. It applies to numerous types of organizations—businesses and corporations of all sizes, educational institutions, government agencies, and nonprofit and charitable organizations—because all depend on information to succeed.

Intended Audiences

Are you:

- An individual contributor or practitioner?
- A member of a project team?
- A project manager?

Do you find yourself in any of the following types of situations?

- Poor-quality data are causing issues for the organization, but no one is sure of their real impact and how much should be invested in dealing with those issues.

- Your company is implementing (or has implemented) an ERP application. Poor-quality data are having an impact on project timelines and are hampering the migration and test results. Once in production, confidence in the information is low and data previously used by one business function are being used in end-to-end processes, with poor results.

- Your new application development project goes live on time, maybe even under budget; the user-acceptance tests are complete and the solution is being used. A few months later, however, complaints start to surface. Additional staff is needed to handle data quality and reconciliation needs. It is discovered that the final solution did not have all the information those involved need to make decisions. Or worse, incorrect information is presented to decision makers leading to costly mistakes.

- Because of mergers and acquisitions, your company is starting a project to integrate data from the acquired companies. The project team has a tight schedule, yet you already know there are quality issues with the data to be integrated.

- The organization has invested heavily in purchasing data from external sources but cannot depend on its quality to meet business needs.

- The data warehouse has been in production for more than a year. Users from the business intelligence group don't trust the reports, complain about the quality, and are reverting to their own spreadsheets for verification.

- The company invested in a major master data clean-up project, such as customer, vendor, employee, or product. A few years later another clean-up project is started because the data quality declined and is causing issues for the business.

- Your organization has purchased a data quality tool, but doesn't know how to best implement it and use it effectively.

- You are involved in a Six Sigma project at the company and need more help regarding the information and data aspects of the project.

- Managing data quality is an important part of your daily responsibilities.

If these situations sound familiar, *this book is for you!* Whether you are just starting a project or are already in production, it is not unusual to find that information quality issues prevent the company from realizing the full benefit of its investment in the projects. The business therefore does not receive the expected improvements to operations, decision-making and business intelligence processes, and customer satisfaction.

There is hope! Although problems with data and information quality can seem urgent and overwhelming, an iterative information quality process of accountability, root cause analysis, prevention, ongoing monitoring, continuous improvement, and communication makes the issues solvable. Here you will learn processes, techniques, and ideas to address the data quality challenges. The same techniques and tools presented in this book can also be used during system development and implementation projects to prevent or minimize data quality challenges from the beginning.

This book has what you need to address information improvement at every stage—from an initial assessment project to fine-tuning current information processes to developing and implementing IT solutions that produce the most current, most relevant information to use.

Structure of This Book

This book describes a methodology, *Ten Steps to Quality Data and Trusted Information*™, which consists of a framework, concepts, and processes for improving and creating information and data quality.

The Ten Steps are concrete instructions for executing information and data quality improvement projects. The steps combine Data Quality Dimensions (aspects or features of information used for defining, measuring, and managing data) with Business Impact Techniques (qualitative and quantitative techniques for analyzing the impact of data quality issues). Performing the first steps in the process help present a picture of the current state of data and information quality in the business or organization and produce a convincing rationale for pursuing data and information quality. Subsequent steps address the business needs revealed by the picture of the current state of information quality. The descriptions of The Ten Steps process include templates, examples, and advice for executing them, with the goal of reaching a future state of excellence in information quality and information processes.

To implement The Ten Steps effectively, it is necessary to understand some key concepts about information and data quality; for this reason, several of the concepts are presented first. The Framework for Information Quality (FIQ) provides the conceptual foundation for understanding the components necessary for information quality. The framework includes the very important Information Life Cycle, which brings insight into the life of information as it is created, applied, stored, maintained, and ultimately disposed. The groundwork is also laid by defining other concepts such as the data quality dimensions, business impact techniques, data categories (groupings of data with common characteristics or features such as reference, master, transactional, and metadata),

data specifications (standards, models, business rules, metadata, and reference data), data governance and stewardship, and best practices and guidelines for implementation.

Main Sections

This book contains the following main sections:

Chapter 1, Overview—a summary of the information and data quality approach.

Chapter 2, Key Concepts—the philosophy and fundamental concepts that are integral components of the methodology and on which The Ten Steps process is built.

Chapter 3, The Ten Steps Process—the process flow, instructions, advice, examples, and templates for completing information and data quality improvement projects.

Chapter 4, Structuring Your Project—advice about approaches to data quality projects, timing, and assembling a team. Use this chapter to help structure your information and data quality improvement project.

Chapter 5, Other Techniques and Tools—techniques that can be applied in various ways throughout the methodology.

Chapter 6, A Few Final Words—a summary of the other chapters and some words of encouragement.

Appendix, Quick References—this section pulls together materials that were presented throughout the book into an easy-to-read reference format.

Glossary—an alphabetical list of terms discussed in the book together with their meanings.

Bibliography—the list of books, articles, and websites used during the writing of the book.

Conventions

Italicized text is used to indicate references to the steps and important words or concepts in this book (e.g., *Step 1—Define Business Need and Approach*). The list that follows contains a description of the callout icons you will see in boxes at various places within the text.

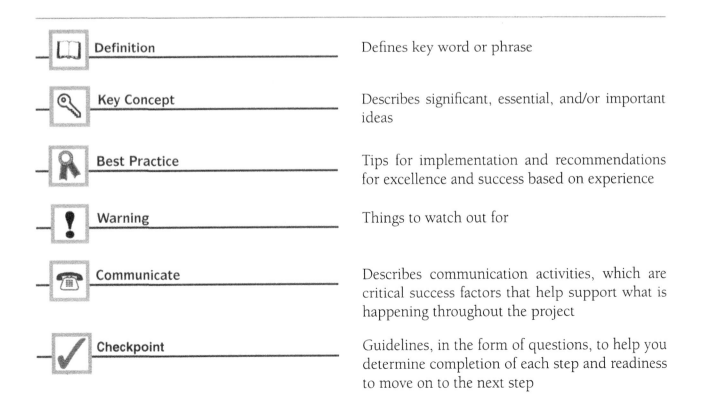

Definition	Defines key word or phrase
Key Concept	Describes significant, essential, and/or important ideas
Best Practice	Tips for implementation and recommendations for excellence and success based on experience
Warning	Things to watch out for
Communicate	Describes communication activities, which are critical success factors that help support what is happening throughout the project
Checkpoint	Guidelines, in the form of questions, to help you determine completion of each step and readiness to move on to the next step

How to Use This Book

The goal of this book is to teach the basic concepts of information quality and to provide enough specific step-by-step instructions so that you can improve and create quality information.

In today's fast-moving world, readers need to be able to get information and find what they need quickly. This book's format is conducive to reading front to back, but also to quickly finding items of particular interest at any point in time. It is expected that the book will be used as a reference guide, with the reader returning to it when new data quality situations arise. For example, here are two common laments:

- "We know data quality is important, but we don't know how to get started."
- "Some of us know data quality is important, but we don't know how to show the value of information quality."

What's here will help anyone who is responsible for the quality of data and information: program managers, project managers, practitioners, individual contributors, and internal and external consultants. Practitioner job titles include data analysts, business analysts, developers, database administrators, subject-matter experts, information consumers or knowledge workers, data modelers, and data stewards. This book also provides techniques for assessing business impact that can be used to show the importance of information quality.

This book operates under the "just enough" principle. Readers are given just enough background on the underlying concepts to understand the components necessary for information quality and to provide the foundation for the instructions. The step-by-step instructions provide just enough structure for readers to understand what needs to be done and why. The methodology is designed for the users in a way that allows them to pick and choose the steps applicable to their specific projects. The beauty of the approach is that it provides just enough structure to know how to proceed, but enough flexibility so that those using it can also incorporate their own data quality improvement knowledge, tools, and techniques.

When the words *business* or *company* or *organization* are used, it means any type of organization that uses data and information to support its goals. For-profit corporations are obvious, but it also means other organizations such as government, nonprofits, and educational institutions. Many of the examples center around customer information because that is familiar to most people and can be used to easily illustrate the concepts and techniques. *Customer* means whoever uses what an organization provides. However, what is presented here applies to all types of information (e.g., customer, employee, product, sales and marketing, manufacturing, research) in any industry (e.g., high tech, financial services, insurance, biotech, retail, manufacturing). All organizations depend on quality information to support whatever they provide.

This approach is not specific to, nor does it require, any particular data quality software (e.g., data profiling or cleansing tools), but the methodology can be used to help implement these tools more effectively if they are available to you.

The companion website for this book—*www.books.elsevier.com/companions/9780123743695*—contains more information, including links to additional resources.

Project Managers

For this group, the following will provide background so that you can help set up a data quality project and make good judgments about which data quality activities are needed to achieve the project's goals. Read the Introduction and Chapters 1 and 2. After doing so, you will understand the

Data Quality Dimensions and Business Impact Techniques so that you and your team can make good decisions about which to use to achieve goals.

In addition, read the first few pages at the beginning of each of the steps in Chapter 3, focusing on the Step Summary tables and the sections on Business Benefit and Context. Next, read Chapter 4 for information on resources and other valuable information about setting up a project.

Project managers don't need to know the same level of detail as team members. But you do need to understand enough about the data quality approach so that you can support data quality, whether in the form of a focused data quality project or data quality activities integrated into another project plan or methodology. Project managers influence the priority of team members' time. Your support is required to confirm that data quality is appropriately incorporated and implemented into a project—which will greatly increase your chance of success.

Individual Contributors and Practitioners

The detail in this book is for you! You are the ones who will implement what is needed for success. Become familiar with its contents. The information is presented in a logical format, from concepts to more specific detail, as you move through the book. You may not need to read it cover to cover, but know what is included and then use it as a reference as various data quality situations arise.

All the information in Chapter 2, Key Concepts, is provided as a basis of education. These underlying concepts will help you understand the necessary information quality components and provide the foundation for the step-by-step instructions in The Ten Steps process. The steps are the how-to for information quality and are designed so that you can pick and choose those steps that are applicable to your projects and/or issues.

Even with the how-to, it is expected that you will combine the concepts and the instructions to make good judgments as to how to best apply them to *your* particular situation. Key to success is the ability to select the relevant steps *and* determine the right level of detail needed to address a specific situation. The methodology presented in this book provides enough structure so that you know how to proceed, but enough flexibility so that you can incorporate your own knowledge, tools, and techniques into the process.

Of course, the support of management, along with appropriate investments in time, money, and people, are essential for success. Use the ideas here to help explain information quality and gain management support. You will need it. Ultimately, however, this book is for you—the individual contributors and practitioners who are chartered to make data quality a reality!

There are numerous situations where this methodology can be applied. Use what you learn here as a starting point to get going, bring value to your organization, and enjoy the journey!

Executing Data Quality Projects

Chapter 1

Overview

If the state of quality of your company's products and services was the same level of quality as the data in your databases, would your company survive or go out of business?

— Larry English

A corollary: *If the state of quality of your company's data was the same level of quality as your company's products and services, how much more profitable would your company be?*

— Mehmet Orun

In This Chapter

The Impact of Information and Data Quality   4

About the Methodology: Concepts and Steps   6

Approaches to Data Quality in Projects   9

Engaging Management   12

The Impact of Information and Data Quality

Information quality problems and their impact are all around us: A customer does not receive an order because of incorrect shipping information; products are sold below cost because of wrong discount rates; a manufacturing line is stopped because parts were not ordered—the result of inaccurate inventory information; a well-known U.S. senator is stopped at an airport (twice) because his name is on a government "Do not fly" list; many communities cannot run an election with results that people trust; financial reform has created new legislation such as Sarbanes–Oxley.[1]

Information is not simply data, strings of numbers, lists of addresses, or test results stored in a computer. Information is the product of business processes and is continuously used and reused by them. However, it takes human beings to bring information to its *real-world* context and give it meaning. Every day human beings use information to make decisions, complete transactions, and carry out all the other activities that make a business run. Applications come and applications go, but the information in those applications lives on.

That's where information quality comes into play. *Effective* business decisions and actions can only be made when based on high-quality information—the key here being *effective*. Yes, business decisions are based all the time on poor-quality data, but *effective* business decisions cannot be made with flawed, incomplete, or misleading data. People need information they can trust to be correct and current if they are to do the work that furthers business goals and objectives.

A firm's basis for competition . . . has changed from tangible products to intangible information. A firm's information represents the firm's collective knowledge used to produce and deliver products and services to consumers. Quality information is increasingly recognized as the most valuable asset of the firm. Firms are grappling with how to capitalize on information and knowledge. Companies are striving, more often silently, to remedy business impacts rooted in poor quality information and knowledge.

– Kuan-Tsae Huang, Yang W. Lee, and Richard Y. Wang[2]

Tom Redman says it well:

The costs of poor quality are enormous. Some costs, such as added expense and lost customers, are relatively easy to spot, if the organization looks. We suggest (based on a small number of careful, but proprietary studies), as a working figure, that these costs are roughly 10 percent of revenue for a typical organization. . . . This figure does not include other costs, such as bad decisions and low morale, that are harder to measure but even more important.[3]

What is the cost to a company of the sales rep, publicly announced to have won the top sales award for the year along with the trip to Hawaii, only to have it rescinded a few days later because the sales data were wrong? Does

---

[1]The Sarbanes–Oxley Act of 2002 was enacted in the United States with the purpose of protecting investors by improving the accuracy and reliability of corporate disclosures.
[2]Kuan-Tsae Huang, Yang W. Lee, and Richard Y. Wang, *Quality Information and Knowledge* (Prentice Hall PTR, 1999), p. 2.
[3]Tom Redman, *Data Quality: The Field Guide* (Digital Press, 2001), p. 3.

the resulting embarrassment and low morale influence that sales rep's productivity and therefore sales, or even his decision to stay with the company? What is the cost to the embassy whose name was splashed across the front pages of a major U.S. city's newspaper when its visa applications containing sensitive personal and business information, such as Social Security numbers and strategic business plans, were found thrown in an open dumpster instead of being properly disposed of? Does the resulting lack of trust in the management of that information influence another company's decision to do business in that country?

What Is Information Quality?

Information quality is the degree to which information and data[4] can be a trusted source for any and/or all required uses. Simply put, it is having the right information, at the right time and place, for the right people to use to run the business,

 Definition

Information quality is the degree to which information and data can be a trusted source for any and/or all required uses. It is having the right set of correct information, at the right time, in the right place, for the right people to use to make decisions, to run the business, to serve customers, and to achieve company goals.

serve customers, and achieve company goals. Quality information is also fit for its purpose—the level of quality supports all of its uses.

Where Do Information Quality Problems Come From?

Information quality problems may be caused by human, process, or system issues. They are not restricted to older or particular types of systems. Although everyone is aware that data cause problems from time to time, it may be difficult to perceive the extent to which these problems affect the business. Some normal business activities are indicative of data quality problems[5]:

- Correction activities
- Rework
- Reprocessing orders
- Handling returns
- Dealing with customer complaints

Many of these activities do not appear to be associated with information quality, when in fact they are. Since processes and functions are distributed across an organization and many people, the cost and scope of data quality problems are often not visible.

Business processes create, update, and delete data in addition to applying information in many ways. Information technology (IT) teams are responsible for the quality of the *systems* that store and move the data, but they cannot be held completely responsible for the *content*. Both IT and the business must share

---

[4]*Data* are known facts or other items of interest to the business; *information* refers to facts within context. Examples of data are "01/16/2008" and "752-5914"; an example of information is "Order #752-5914 was shipped on 01/16/2008." While there are academic differences between the two concepts, this approach does not generally differentiate between data and information. (There are a few exceptions, which are noted in the book.) Some organizations respond to "data quality," others to "information quality." It may also vary with whomever you are speaking with. I tend to use *information* when talking to businesspeople, and *data* when discussing more detailed issues with those in IT or others responsible for the data. Use the term that will be most effective for you.

[5]Jack E. Olsen has an excellent discussion of reasons for and impacts of data quality problems in his book *Data Profiling: The Accuracy Dimension* (Morgan Kaufmann, 2003), pp. 13–16.

in insisting on clearly articulated requirements, strict testing of systems, and the development of quality processes for data management.

The Information Quality Challenge

I believe that two major trends have created an environment where information quality is getting more of the attention it deserves. One is the increasing number of legal and regulatory data quality requirements. The need for and benefits from information quality have always been there and ready for any organization who invests in it. But human nature being what it is, the threat of bad publicity and high fines and the risk of a CEO going to jail have created the motivation to actually do something about data quality.

The second reason is based on the need for business to see information brought together in new ways. Examples include the need to see what top customers are doing across the enterprise through CRM (Customer Relationship Management), to have data available for decision support through business intelligence and data warehousing, to streamline business processes and information through ERP (Enterprise Resource Planning), and to deal with the high rate of mergers and acquisitions, which require the integration of data from different companies.

All these initiatives require data integration—bringing together data from two or more different sources and combining them in such a way that new and better uses can be made of the resulting information. Data that previously fulfilled the needs of one particular functional area in the business are now being combined with data from other functional areas—often with very poor results. We have different business uses for the same information; different platforms, systems, databases, and applications;

different types of data (customer, vendor, manufacturing, finance, etc.); different data structures, definitions, and standards; and data, processes, and technology customized to fit the business, geography, or application. These are the challenges of the current environment.

What we need is the ability to share information with our customers and with each other across the company. We need the ability to find what we need, when we need it, and to be able to trust it when we get it. What is required for that to happen? We must consciously manage information as a resource (a source of help) and as an asset (a source drawn on by a company for making profit). We must have information that is real (an accurate reflection of the real world), recent (up to date), and relevant (that our business and customers need and care about).

This book is here to help.

About the Methodology: Concepts and Steps

"Doctor, my left arm hurts!" The doctor puts your arm in a sling, gives you an aspirin, and tells you to go home. But what if you were having a heart attack? You would expect the doctor to diagnose your condition and take emergency measures to save your life. After you were stabilized you would expect the doctor to run tests, get to the root cause of the heart attack, and recommend measures to correct any damage done (if possible) and prevent another attack from occurring. The doctor would have you come in for periodic tests and follow-up to assess your condition and determine if other measures needed to be taken.

This seems like common sense when talking about our health. But when it comes to data and information, how often do we address the immediate business problem, then go for the "easy fix" (the aspirin and sling) and expect that to take care of our problems? No tests or assessments are run to determine the location or magnitude of the problems, no root cause analysis is performed, and no preventive measures are put into place. And then we are surprised when problems appear and reappear!

This book describes a methodology, *Ten Steps to Quality Data and Trusted Information*, that represents a systematic approach to improving and creating data and information quality. The methodology combines a conceptual framework for understanding information quality and The Ten Steps process, which provides instructions, techniques, and best practices. The methodology is for practical use—put it to work to create and improve the quality of information in your business and to establish continuous improvement through better information management.

Just as with your own health, you can use the methodology presented in this book to prevent data quality "health" problems and to assess and take action if they appear. This book provides processes, activities, and techniques that will improve your company's information quality health. Think of it as your "wellness" program for data and information.

The Ten Steps Process

The Ten Steps are explicit instructions for planning and executing information quality improvement projects with detailed examples, templates, techniques, and advice. They combine data quality dimensions and business impact techniques to present a picture of the current state of data and

information quality in your business. Data quality dimensions are facets of data quality you can use to measure and manage your data and information quality—which can only be improved if they can be measured. You will choose the data quality dimensions to measure and manage that best address your business needs.

Business impact techniques are quantitative and qualitative techniques for assessing the impact of your information quality on the business. Using them answers the questions "What is the impact of the data quality issues" and "Why should I care?" Results from assessing business impact are used to establish the business case for information quality. They are also used to gain support for and help determine the optimal level of investment in it. Following the assessments of quality and/or business impact, root cause analysis is conducted and appropriate actions for preventing and correcting data quality issues are put into place. Communication is critical to the success of any data quality effort, so it too is one of the Ten Steps that takes place throughout the life of every project.

All of the information contained in The Ten Steps is "how-to." But just as you want a doctor who understands the theories and concepts of medicine so that specific actions can be correctly applied to your medical concerns, you also need to understand information quality basics so that the "how-to" can be properly applied in the many different situations that arise in your company. For that reason, the key concepts are presented first in this book, followed by The Ten Steps process.

The Key Concepts

The key concepts provide the foundation for understanding what information quality is and what is required to achieve it. They include the Framework for Information Quality, the Information Life Cycle, and the Information and Data Quality Improvement Cycle.

The Ten Steps process describes how to implement the key concepts. Just as with your own health, you can use the methodology presented in this book to prevent data quality "health" problems and to assess and treat them.

The Framework for Information Quality (FIQ) establishes the conceptual structure for understanding the components that contribute to quality. It helps you understand an existing complex environment that creates information quality problems. The concepts from the framework can also be used when developing an environment that will produce high-quality data.

The Information Life Cycle provides a view of how information is obtained, used, and discarded. When you use it to look at your information, you can see how quality information affects business processes during all phases in the life of information. By managing information as a resource throughout its life cycle, you can maximize its value to the business.

The Information and Data Quality Improvement Cycle explains the assessment, awareness, and action cycle as it leads to continuous quality improvement, for which The Ten Steps process provides concrete directions for execution.

Additional key concepts discussed include data categories (groupings of data with common characteristics or features such as reference data, master data, transactional data, and metadata), data specifications (data standards, data models, business rules, metadata, and reference data), data governance and stewardship, and best practices and guidelines for implementation. Other concepts introduced as key concepts, detailed in later chapters, include data quality dimensions, business impact techniques, and The Ten Steps process.

Additional Material

If you haven't already done so, please read the Introduction. It contains useful background to help you make use of this book. Once you become familiar with The Ten Steps, Chapter 4 provides additional detail to the discussion on projects begun in this chapter. Techniques that can be used in several places throughout the methodology are included in Chapter 5.

The Appendix contains at-a-glance references for some of the concepts presented in the book. These are great for keeping close at hand (on your office or cube wall) to provide a quick reference for ideas that have been explained more thoroughly in the chapters that follow. Of course, the usual List of Figures, Glossary, Bibliography, and Index provide additional ways to help you find what you are looking for and where to go for more information.

A Word about Terminology

The full Ten Steps methodology consists of key concepts (outlined in Chapter 2) and The Ten Steps process—that is, Steps 1 to 10 (detailed in Chapter 3). For brevity I use the term "Ten Steps" to refer to the methodology (whose full name is *Ten Steps to Quality Data and Trusted Information*) and the phrase "The Ten Steps process" to refer to the steps themselves (the names of which appear in italic wherever they appear in the book). The point to remember is that the methodology is not just about The Ten Steps process, but is also about the key data quality concepts that underlie them.

Definition

In this book, a **project** is defined as any significant effort that makes use of the methodology.

Approaches to Data Quality in Projects

In this book, a *project* is any significant effort that makes use of The Ten Steps methodology. A project team can consist of a single person or a group of people. A project can focus solely on data quality improvement, or it can be data quality tasks integrated into another project or methodology (e.g., new application development or data migration or integration such as in a data warehouse or ERP implementation). A project can be the conscious application of specific steps in the methodology by an individual to solve an issue within his or her area of responsibility.

It has been briefly explained that The Ten Steps process has explicit instructions for planning and executing information quality improvement projects with detailed examples, templates, techniques, and advice. The process is intended to be flexible so that you can use those steps and activities applicable to your needs and situation. I want to introduce you to some of the ways the Ten Steps can be used now—even though you only know them at a high level. (More detail on applying The Ten Steps process to projects is provided in Chapter 4—but do read Chapter 3 first.)

What is useful to know at this point is that The Ten Steps process is designed to be used by projects in a pick-and-choose manner. That is, use the steps in different combinations to initiate projects with different approaches or to engage the process at different levels of detail. To make the methodology more accessible no matter where you are in your data quality journey, use these simple guidelines:

- Pick and choose the steps to structure a project that fits your situation. You don't have to use all of them.
- Any of the steps can be carried out at varying levels of detail. You make the choice as to which fits your needs.
- Use your knowledge of the key concepts to help you choose the steps and level of detail when implementing them.

Project Approaches

The methodology can be used in many different business situations (data quality improvement, data warehouse development, ERP migration, etc.). You may be trying to have data quality activities integrated into any of these types of projects, and the projects may be at different stages of completion. For example, before obtaining full management sponsorship, you may need to build a business case for data quality. Or a specific data quality problem may have already been identified and the need is to determine business impact or find root causes and implement solutions. In any of these examples different steps and activities in The Ten Steps process can be used to address what is needed now. Some typical approaches to applying the methodology are described in the following sections. Remember, you can use these approaches whether you are an individual or a member of a project team.

Establish Business Case

An Establish Business Case approach may be an exploratory assessment or a quick proof of concept assessing quality on a very limited set of data. As an individual, you can implement a brief project that will help you make a business case for further data quality improvements. If you already have a specific data quality problem, you may just want to assess the business impact of that problem without further quality assessment.

Use the methodology to think through the problem, understand the information environment at a very high level, and write a few queries against the data. Use some of the less complicated or less time-consuming business impact techniques to quickly demonstrate the business impact of the data quality problems you discover. Decide if there is a need for in-depth efforts to deal with data quality.

An Establish Business Case project may extend over a few days or weeks with one person doing the bulk of the work while enlisting help from colleagues (e.g., to gain access to data or determine business impact).

Establish Data Quality Baseline

An Establish Data Quality Baseline approach is used when the business has committed to improving data quality and there is support for a project team and resources. The project team will be looking at data in a single database or comparing them across databases. The data quality assessment will take longer here than in Establish Business Case. The goal is not just to uncover problems but to determine which ones are worth addressing, to identify the root causes for the high-priority issues, and to develop realistic action plans for improvement. The project may include purchasing and/or using some data quality tools for profiling or cleansing.

Often those who can correct the data errors found or implement the recommended improvements are not those on the project team. In this case, a new project is needed to implement improvement plans recommended by the baseline project.

Determine Root Causes

A Determine Root Causes approach is used when you already know the data quality issues and have decided that the impact of those issues warrants further investigation into their root causes. This may take the form of a focused workshop or a series of workshops that use techniques from the methodology for determining root causes. Once the causes are uncovered, this project should include developing specific recommendations for addressing them. The end result will be to find owners and gain commitment to implement the improvements.

Implement Improvements

An Implement Improvements approach executes the recommendations developed when the data quality assessment and business impact analysis have generated a data quality improvement plan. Or the recommendations may be data quality improvements suggested by another project. Many companies have resources dedicated to correcting data errors—but with no attention to preventing them. Correcting errors is an important part of improvement, particularly if the data errors are causing critical business problems. (For example, a product cannot be shipped and the problem is traced back to faulty master data.) However, spending the majority of resource time on correction with little or no time on prevention is a common pitfall and will only lead to more time wasted fixing more problems in the future.

It is equally important to ensure that data errors are prevented. Some of the prevention activities will warrant a project (e.g., to define and document data standards); others may be specific actions (e.g., to assign new quality-related responsibilities to an existing team and complete the associated training). Some recommendations will go to the business to improve its processes (e.g., to collect information needed or to educate and reward sales reps for synchronizing customer information from their handheld devices with the central database on a weekly basis).

Implement Ongoing Monitoring and Metrics

An Implement Ongoing Monitoring and Metrics approach focuses on instituting operational processes for monitoring, evaluating, and reporting results. When designing and implementing your control processes, remember to include actions for addressing issues found—both to correct current errors and to prevent future ones. It is less expensive and more efficient to incorporate monitoring and metrics during the initial system implementation.

Make use of the results from Establish Data Quality Baseline, if done, as part of your monitoring to provide the baseline metrics for tracking data quality improvement. Any data quality assessment will reveal many data quality issues—some big, some small, some important, some not. You may need to assess business impact to determine the data with high business value and therefore whose quality is worth tracking on a regular basis. The monitoring should also show if prevention improvements put into place are achieving the desired results.

Address Data Quality as an Individual

You as an individual may be assigned to address data quality by yourself. If so, any of the project situations just described could apply to you. Even without a project team, you may need to establish a business case, do an initial assessment or implement monitoring on a focused

set of data, put into operation a specific data quality improvement, or address other information quality issues. As an individual you will still need to apply good project management processes (e.g., you have to handle your scope carefully, and you still need management support, even if only from your direct superior). Also, you will still need to decide which steps to incorporate, communicate effectively, and consult with other knowledgeable sources to meet your project goals.

In some circumstances you will simply find techniques that are useful to incorporate into your everyday processes. In all cases, you will be required to make good decisions to apply the key concepts and The Ten Steps process to your particular situation. Everything in this book can help you as an individual contributor—it will just be implemented in a more abbreviated fashion than if you had a project team.

Integrate Data Quality Activities into Other Projects and Methodologies

You can combine The Ten Steps concepts and techniques with your company's favored project management style. Many data quality activities can and should be included in the various phases of a project life cycle and can also be integrated into a third-party methodology such as a vendor's ERP migration program. Building a new application, migrating data from existing applications to new ones, and making process improvements are other examples of where data quality activities can benefit a project. For example, you can improve the quality of, and decrease the time needed to complete, source-to-target mappings or institute data clean-up as part of any migration project.

Careful planning at the beginning of a project will guarantee that appropriate data quality activities are fully integrated into it. The earlier that data quality is incorporated into the project, the better. But even if you are engaging the project later in its timeline, adding in suitable data quality activities can still significantly contribute to its success.

Engaging Management

Support from the right level of management and suitable investments in time, money, and people are essential for success. While the critical topic of obtaining management support is far too broad for the scope of this book, the following suggestions are presented to stimulate your thinking about how you can engage your management.[6]

Best-Case Scenario—Engage the CEO. In the best-case scenario, the CEO of your company will be completely convinced of the need to improve information and data quality, and will allocate resources to support the culture-change activities that are necessary to create an environment that supports continuous quality improvement.

Right Level of Management—Not everyone who initiates an information and data quality improvement project has access to the CEO. The Establish Business Case approach, for example, is designed so that an individual can initiate the project and use it to gain support from management and team members. A successful project can be a significant victory for a department, and engaging the right level of management is necessary to make a project successful.

Using the Methodology—Use the results of the appropriate business impact techniques from Step 4 to show the importance of information

quality and to gain support for your information quality improvement project. You can also incorporate ideas from *Step 10—Communicate Actions and Results* to help you engage managers in the information improvement process. Prepare managers for expected levels of resource commitment by communicating the business need and the improvement plan. This will increase the likelihood that you will receive the time, money, and participation needed. Likewise, provide regular status reports to managers and other working groups to enable them to see progress and continue to champion your project, and to prevent conflicting or duplicated work.

Communication Techniques—The ideas presented in *Step 10—Communicate Actions and Results* (see Chapter 3) will help you optimize communication of important data quality concepts and project progress. Use those ideas to plan your communication strategy. Of course, communication goes two ways and it is vital to open a dialogue, get feedback, gauge reaction, and gain trust.

Know Your Audience—Knowing your audience's goals, values, and success criteria are some of the best ways to help you communicate effectively. Various audience groups need different communication formats and different levels of detail.

Right-Size the Message—Even though you may be excited about your improvement project, your management audience rarely needs to hear the details of your data profiling or the impressive way in which you can now merge records to decrease redundancy. What they want to hear is that the improvement is working and that it is going to positively impact their work. Right-size the message to emphasize the topics that are most important to them.

---

[6] I'm indebted to Rachel Haverstick for her assistance in expressing these important ideas.

Repeat—Repeat your project goals and review the milestones. Repeating your goals is especially important for communicating with managers, who need to be able to perceive the essentials of a project and track its pace and resource usage.

Broaden the Scope—Be alert for opportunities to communicate your project goals and the information quality key concepts to a broader audience. The famous "elevator pitch" (a 30- to 60-second summary) is a good technique for communicating to new audiences outside of a formal presentation. Also consider creating a four-slide project summary to make available in other presentations, such as department meetings or quarterly updates.

Manager as Resource—Your manager can be a valuable networking resource, so keeping her or him informed performs double duty—ensuring support for your project and connecting you to other projects or efforts with which you can collaborate on shared goals.

Chapter 2

Key Concepts

He who loves practice without theory is like the sailor who boards ship without a rudder and compass and never knows where he may cast.

– Leonardo da Vinci

In This Chapter

Introduction	16
The Framework for Information Quality	16
The Information Life Cycle	23
Data Quality Dimensions	30
Business Impact Techniques	35
Data Categories	39
Data Specifications	45
Data Governance and Data Stewardship	52
The Information and Data Quality Improvement Cycle	54
The Ten Steps Process	57
Best Practices and Guidelines	59

Introduction

This chapter discusses a number of concepts that are important to understand so that you can better implement The Ten Steps process. The Ten Steps provide practices for assessing, improving, implementing, and creating quality data. The concepts provide the background about information quality and the components necessary for it. These concepts are not unnecessary theory with no practical application to reality. Understanding them will help you decide which activities from The Ten Steps process you should implement. In many cases concepts from the steps can be used immediately to analyze and better understand your particular data quality situations.

Think of it this way: If you are going on a road trip to an unfamiliar area of the country, you look at a map. The map can be a paper copy you unfold and consult as you continue your journey, or you might enter coordinates into a GPS system. Either way, there are basics about the map or the GPS that you need to know in order to understand what they are telling you. A legend shows various symbols on the map and their descriptions; such things as types of roads, route symbols, sites of interest, hospitals, and scale help interpret what you see.

Similarly, the *key concepts* are broad ideas or guiding general principles that help you interpret and understand information quality. The specific activities in The Ten Steps process are based on the principles outlined in the key concepts. Just as you can better plan and carry out your trip if you understand the basic concepts of how to use a map, you will make better decisions about

Key Concept

The Framework for Information Quality (FIQ) enables organized thinking so you can effectively plan and implement improvements.

applying The Ten Steps if you understand the basic ideas presented in the key concepts.

The Framework for Information Quality

The *Framework for Information Quality (FIQ)* provides a logical structure for understanding the components that contribute to information quality. It helps you understand a complex environment that creates information quality problems. Most important, the FIQ enables organized thinking so that you can effectively plan and create quality data, and implement improvements as needed.

Think of this framework as you would the Food Pyramid,[1] which was established to improve nutrition and provide dietary guidance (Figure 2.1). The Food Pyramid comprises guidelines and a visual of the components for healthy eating and physical activity. Upon first look its meaning may not be obvious, but after a quick tutorial it is clear that the illustration provides a wealth of information that can be referenced in one glance, and additional instructions are available to describe and apply its concepts.

---

[1]The Food Pyramid was developed by the Center for Nutrition Policy and Promotion, an organization within the U.S. Department of Agriculture (*http://www.mypyramid.gov/*).

Figure 2.1 • Visualizing a plan for help: the Food Pyramid and the Framework for Information Quality.

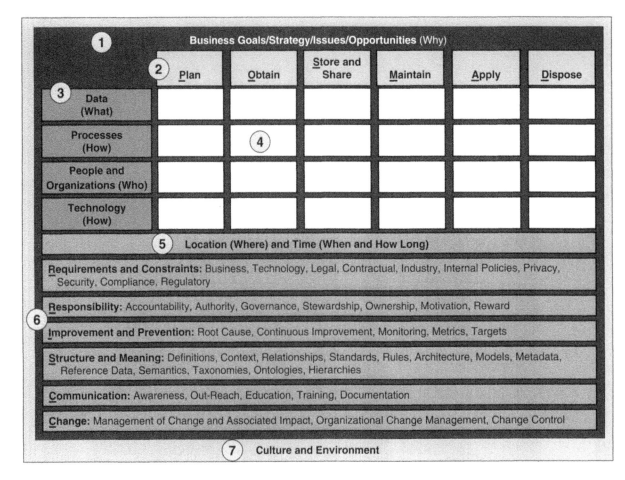

Figure 2.2 • The Framework for Information Quality.

Source: Copyright © 2005–2008 Danette McGilvray, Granite Falls Consulting, Inc.

The Food Pyramid is not one size fits all, but the basics are the same. You use what you have learned about it to make it work for you. The Food Pyramid continues to provide a useful reminder about health, nutrition, and activity.

Likewise, the FIQ (Figure 2.2) provides a visual of the components necessary for healthy information. There are seven main sections, which are described in the following section. Remember: The framework shows the *components* necessary for information quality. Later in the book you will learn about The Ten Steps, which are the *process* for implementing the FIQ concepts. You will use what you have learned from it to make The Ten Steps process work for you.

Once you understand the FIQ, it provides a helpful quick reference and you can use it as a tool for

- **Diagnosis**—Assess your practices and processes; realize where breakdowns are occurring and determine if all components necessary for information quality are present; identify which components are missing and use them as input to project priorities and initial root cause analysis.

- **Planning**—Design new processes and ensure that components impacting information quality have been addressed; determine where to invest time, money, and resources.

- **Communication**—Explain the components required for and impacting information quality.

Sections of the Framework Explained

The FIQ is easy to understand if you look at it section by section. Use the framework to provide the foundation for your use of The Ten Steps process. The framework's seven sections are described next.

1—Business Goals/Strategy/Issues/Opportunities (Why)

Business goals and strategies should drive all actions and decisions. An issue is a situation that is currently suboptimal. An opportunity is something new to be used to your advantage. Information should always start with the question, "Why is this important to the business?" This section is indicated as a sheet behind the other sections because *anything* done with information should support the business in meeting its goals.

2—The Information Life Cycle

To manage any resource, it is important to understand the idea of a *life cycle*, which refers to the process of change and development throughout the useful life of something. Any resource should be properly managed throughout its life cycle in order to get the full use and benefit from it. Use the acronym POSMAD to remember the six phases in the Information Life Cycle.

Plan—Identify objectives, plan information architecture, and develop standards and definitions; model, design, and develop applications, databases, processes, organizations, and the like. Anything done prior to a project going into production is part of the Plan stage. Of course, throughout design and development all phases of the life cycle should be accounted for so the information will be properly managed once in production.

Obtain—Data or information is acquired in some way, for example, by creating records, purchasing data, or loading external files.

Store and Share—Data are stored and made available for use. They may be stored electronically such as in databases or files; they may also be stored in hardcopy such as a paper application form that is kept in a file cabinet. Data are shared through such means as networks or email.

Maintain—Update, change, and manipulate data; cleanse and transform data; match and merge records; and so forth.

Apply—Retrieve data; use information. This includes all information usage such as completing a transaction, writing a report, making a management decision from a report, and running automated processes.

Dispose—Archive information or delete data or records.

A solid understanding of the Information Life Cycle is required for information improvement, and it will be referenced throughout The Ten Steps process. See details in the Information Life Cycle section later in this chapter.

3—Key Components

Four key components affect information throughout its life cycle. These components need to be accounted for in all of the phases in the POSMAD life cycle.

Data (What)—Known facts or other items of interest to the business.

Processes (How)—Functions, activities, actions, tasks, or procedures that touch the data or information (business processes, data management processes, processes external to the company, etc.). "Process" is the general term used here to capture activities from high-level functions describing what is to be accomplished (such as "order management" or "territory assignments"), to more detailed actions describing how it is to be accomplished (such as "create purchase order" or "close purchase order") along with inputs, outputs, and timing.

People and Organizations (Who)—Organizations, teams, roles, responsibilities, or individuals that affect or use the data or are involved with the processes. They include those who manage and support the data and those who use (apply) it. Those who use the information can be referred to as knowledge workers, information customers, or information consumers.

Technology (How)—Forms, applications, databases, files, programs, code, or media that store, share, or manipulate the data are involved with the processes, or are used by people and organizations. Technology is both high-tech such as databases and low-tech such as paper copies.

4—The Interaction Matrix

The *interaction matrix* shows the interaction between the Information Life Cycle phases and the key components of data, process, people and organizations, and technology. Through it you can understand what needs to be known for each component throughout the Information Life Cycle. See Figure 2.3 for sample questions in each cell of the matrix indicating the interaction between the life cycle phases and the key components. The questions in the interaction matrix can be used to help you understand an existing situation or to help you plan a new process or application. Use them to prompt your thinking to develop additional questions relevant to your circumstances.

5—Location (Where) and Time (When and How Long)

Always account for *location and time—where* events are happening, *when* the information will be available, and *how long* it needs to be available. For example, where are the knowledge workers and those who maintain the information located? In which time zones are they? Does this impact their ability to access the data? Are adjustments to processes needed to account for location or time? Is there a required time period for which the data must be managed before they are archived or deleted?

Note that the top half of the FIQ, along with the first bar, answers the interrogatives of who, what, how, why, where, when, and how long.[2]

6—Broad-Impact Components

Broad-impact components are additional factors that affect information quality. They are indicated as bars that span the upper sections of the interaction matrix because they should be considered throughout the information's life cycle. Lower your risk by ensuring that components have been discussed and addressed. If they are *not* addressed, you are still at risk as far as information quality is concerned. The acronym RRISCC will help you remember the categories and associated topics that describe the broad-impact components.

Requirements and Constraints—Obligations the company must meet and the information needed to support the ability of the company to meet them. These include: business, technology, legal, contractual, industry, internal policies, privacy, security, compliance, regulatory requirements.

Responsibility—Accountability, authority, governance, stewardship, ownership, motivation, reward.

Improvement and Prevention—Root cause, continuous improvement, monitoring, metrics, targets.

Structure and Meaning—Definitions, context, relationships, standards, rules, architecture, models, metadata, reference data, semantics, taxonomies, ontologies, hierarchies. Structure and Meaning provide context for the data, so we know what the data mean and therefore how best to use them.

---

[2]The Framework for Information Quality was developed independently of the Zachman Framework for Enterprise Architecture, but both address the same interrogatives.

	Plan	Obtain	Store and Share	Maintain	Apply	Dispose
Data (What)	What are the business objectives? Which data supports the business needs? What are the business rules? What are the data standards?	Which data are acquired? Which data are entered into the system—individual data elements or new records?	Which data are stored? Which data are shared? What is the key data to be backed up for rapid recovery?	Which data are updated and changed in the system? Which data will be transformed prior to migration, integration, or sharing? Which data are aggregated to support metrics or reporting?	What information is needed by the business to support transactions, metrics, compliance, requirements, decision making, automated processes, and other objectives? What information is available for use by the business?	Which data need to be archived? Which data need to be deleted?
Processes (How)	What are the high-level processes? What is the training and communication strategy?	How are data acquired from sources (internal and external)? How are data entered into the system? What are the triggers for creating new records?	What is the process for storing data? What is the process for sharing data?	How are data updated? How are data monitored to detect change? How are standards maintained? How are data change managed and impact assessed? Triggers for maintenance?	How are data used? How is information accessed and secured? How is information made available for those using it? What are the triggers for use?	How are data archived? How are data deleted? How are archive locations and processes managed? Triggers for archival? For disposition?
People and Organizations (Who)	Who identifies business objectives and assigns priorities and resources? Who develops processes, business rules, and standards? Who manages those involved in this phase?	Who acquires information from sources? Who enters new data and creates records in the system? Who manages those involved in this phase?	Who supports the storing technology? Who supports the sharing technology? Who manages those involved in this phase?	Who decides what should be updated? Who makes actual changes in the system? Who is responsible for quality? Who needs to know about changes? Who manages those involved in this phase?	Who directly accesses the data? Who uses the information? Who manages those involved in this phase?	Who sets the retention policy? Who archives the data? Who deletes the data? Who needs to be informed? Who manages those involved?
Technology (How)	What is the high-level architecture and the technology that support the business?	How is the application used to create new information and create records in the system?	What is the technology for storing the data? What is the technology for sharing the data?	How are data maintained and updated in the system?	How is information accessed to meet various business needs? How are business rules applied in the application architecture?	How are information and records deleted from system and/or archived? How are information and records archived from system?

Figure 2.3 • POSMAD interaction matrix detail—sample questions.

Source: Copyright © 2005–2008 Danette McGilvray, Granite Falls Consulting, Inc.

Communication—Awareness, outreach, education, training, documentation.

Change—Management of change and associated impact, organizational change management, change control.

7—Culture and Environment

Culture and Environment are shown as a background to all sections and all components of the FIQ. They have an impact on all aspects of your information quality work, but are often not consciously considered.

Culture—A company's attitudes, values, customs, practices, and social behavior. It includes both written (official policies, handbooks, etc.) and unwritten "ways of doing things," "how things get done," "how decisions get made," and so forth.

Environment—Conditions that surround people in your company and affect the way they work and act. Examples are financial services versus pharmaceutical; government agencies versus publicly traded companies.

This is not to say that you cannot be creative in how you approach some of your information quality work. However, you will better accomplish your goals if you understand and can work effectively within the culture and environment of your company. For example, a company that is highly regulated and is already used to following documented standard operating procedures will most likely have less difficulty accepting standardized processes to ensure information quality than will a company where everyone operates independently. Even within a company you may find differences. For example, discussing information quality with a sales team may take on a different look and feel than discussing it with an IT team.

Quick-Assessment Parameters

The FIQ concepts will be used in detail throughout The Ten Steps process. In addition, the framework can be used at a high level to quickly ascertain a situation. The FIQ provides a logical structure for understanding the components that contribute to information quality. By understanding these components (along with the details in the POSMAD interaction matrix), you can better analyze a situation or complex environment where you are having information quality problems.

Suppose someone has contacted you regarding a data quality issue. You can immediately start asking yourself (and others) questions such as:

- What is the business issue associated with this situation?
- Which phase of the information life cycle are we in and what is happening in that phase?
- Which data, specifically, are involved?
- Which processes are involved?
- Which people organizations are involved?
- Which technology is involved?
- What happened to the data in the earlier phases of the life cycle?
- How will data in the later phases of the life cycle be impacted?
- Which broad-impact components have been addressed? Which areas need further attention?

Answers to these questions will help you understand the initial business impact, determine the scope of the issue and who needs to be engaged in solving it, and uncover linkage points to other business areas and systems. You may also highlight potential root causes.

You can also use the FIQ to help when analyzing existing processes or developing new processes to ensure that you have accounted for the components that will impact data quality. Imagine how much more stable your processes would be (and how much better the resulting quality) if you could account for what was happening to your data, processes, people, and technology throughout the Information Life Cycle.

Determine the phase(s) of the Information Life Cycle that are within scope of your project. Realize that quality is affected by all phases but that real work must have manageable and specific boundaries. Of course, you cannot address everything at once and will need to prioritize your efforts. For example, one project team realized they had spent a lot of time in the Obtain phase of the framework but had not spent any time managing the Maintain phase. So they decided that their next project would focus on how they were updating and maintaining their information. Knowing the larger picture can help you put together an approach to addressing what is most important now.

The Information Life Cycle

Because the Information Life Cycle is so important to managing information quality, we will expand on the idea of the life cycle introduced earlier.

Information is a resource and is essential to performing business processes and achieving business objectives, just as money, inventory, facilities, and people are resources. Any resource should be properly managed throughout its life

---

 Key Concept

Information is a resource that should be properly managed throughout its life cycle in order to get the full use and benefit from it.

---

cycle in order to get the full use and benefit from it. In reality, you will have to make choices about which information life cycle phases you have the time and resources to address at any given time. Understanding the concept of a life cycle will help you make better choices about priority.

The Life Cycle of Any Resource

In his 1999 book, Larry English talks about a universal resource life cycle that consists of processes required to manage any resource—people, money, facilities and equipment, materials and products, and information.[3] I refer to these processes as phases. The high-level phases in the Information Life Cycle as I have applied them are described as follows[4]:

- **Plan**—You prepare for the resource.
- **Obtain**—You acquire the resource.
- **Store and Share**—You hold information about the resource electronically or in hardcopy and share it through some type of distribution method.
- **Maintain**—You ensure that the resource continues to work properly.
- **Apply**—You use the resource to accomplish your goals.
- **Dispose**—You discard the resource when it is no longer of use.

For financial resources you *plan* for capital, forecasting, and budgeting; you *obtain* financial resources by borrowing through a loan or selling stock; you *maintain* financial resources by paying interest and dividends; you *apply* financial resources by purchasing other resources; and you *dispose* of the financial resources when you pay off the loan or buy back the stock.

---

[3]Larry English, *Improving Data Warehouse and Business Information Quality* (John Wiley & Sons, 1999), pp. 200–209.

[4]Many thanks to Larry English for teaching me about the universal resource life cycle (Plan, Acquire, Maintain, Dispose, Apply). I modified the names of the life cycle phases slightly from his original, added the "Store and Share" phase, and developed the acronym POSMAD as a reminder of the Information Life Cycle phases. He provided the examples for activities within each of the phases for financial, human, and information resources.

For human resources you *plan* for staffing, skills, recruiting, and the like; you *obtain* human resources by hiring; you *maintain* human resources by providing compensation (wages and benefits) and developing skills through training; you *apply* human resources by assigning roles and responsibilities and putting skills to use; and you *dispose* of human resources through retirement or "downsizing" or through employees leaving of their own accord. Even financial and human resources have activities in the Store and Share phase, as information supporting those resources must be stored and shared in some manner.

Phases of the Information Life Cycle

The acronym POSMAD is used to help remember the six phases in the Information Life Cycle. Table 2.1 describes the phases and provides

Table 2.1 • POSMAD Information Life Cycle Phases and Activities

INFORMATION LIFE CYCLE* PHASE (POSMAD)	DEFINITION	EXAMPLE ACTIVITIES FOR INFORMATION
Plan	Prepare for the resource.	Identify objectives, plan information architecture, develop standards and definitions. When modeling, designing, and developing applications, databases, processes, organizations, etc., many activities could be considered part of the Plan phase for information.
Obtain	Acquire the resource.	Create records, purchase data, load external files, etc.
Store and Share	Hold information about the resource electronically or in hardcopy, and make it available for use through a distribution method.	Store data electronically in databases or some type of file, or store as hardcopy such as a paper application form. Share information about the resource through networks, an enterprise service bus, or email.
Maintain	Ensure that the resource continues to work properly.	Update, change, manipulate, parse, standardize, validate, or verify data; enhance or augment data; cleanse, scrub, or transform data; de-duplicate, link, or match records; merge or consolidate records, etc.
Apply	Use the resource to accomplish your goals.	Retrieve data; use information. This includes all information usage: completing a transaction, writing a report, making a management decision from information in those reports, running automated processes, etc.
Dispose	Discard the resource when it is no longer of use.	Archive information; delete data or records.

*Note: The Information Life Cycle may also be referred to as the Information Resource Life Cycle, the Data Life Cycle, the Information Value Chain, or the Information Chain.

examples of activities within each phase of the life cycle as it applies to information.

Value, Cost, and Quality and the Information Life Cycle

It is important to understand value, cost, and quality in relation to the Information Life Cycle (see Figure 2.4). Following are some key points:

- *All* phases of the Information Life Cycle have a cost.
- It is only when the resource is *applied* that the company receives value from it. If the information is what the knowledge worker expected, and is useful when applied, then it is helpful and has value to the company. If the quality is not what the knowledge worker needs, then that information has a negative impact on the business.
- Data quality is affected by activities in *all* of the phases in the life cycle.
- By viewing information as a resource, you can determine its costs and its value to the business.

While the business really only cares about the information when it wants to use it, resources should be devoted to every phase in the life cycle in order to produce the quality

Key Concept

There is an economic formula for enterprise profitability and survival. The economic formula is simple. Economic Value occurs when the benefit derived from a resource's application is greater than the costs incurred from its planning, acquisition, maintenance, and disposition.

– Larry English (1999, p. 2)

information needed. In reality, you cannot do everything at once. It may not be practical or feasible to address all phases of the life cycle at the same time. However, you should know enough about what happens in each phase and carefully consider how the information is being managed (and needs to be managed) in every phase so you can make informed decisions about investing in your information resource.

Information Is a Reusable Resource

A major difference between information as a resource and other resources is that information is *reusable. It is not consumed when used.* Once a product on the shelf is purchased by a customer,

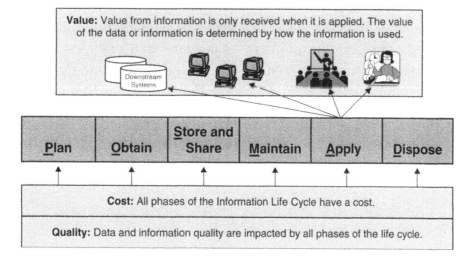

Figure 2.4 • Value, cost, and quality and the Information Life Cycle.

it is no longer available for the next customer to buy. Once materials are used to build that product, they are not available to be used in the next manufacturing cycle. What happens with information? Just because Sam runs a report on the first of the month, does the information disappear when Maria runs her report on the tenth, or when Patel accesses the information to help a customer? Of course not! When information is used it is not depleted. The implications of this difference are important:

Quality is critical—If the information is wrong, it will be used again and again—with negative results. And each time, that poor-quality information causes more cost to the company or may result in lost revenue. (More about this later.)

The value of the information increases the more it is used—Many of the costs in planning, obtaining, storing, sharing, and maintaining the information have been expended. Often with little or no incremental cost, it can be used in additional ways to help the company.

The Information Life Cycle—Not a Linear Process

We have talked about the life cycle as if in the real world these activities happen in a very clear, recognizable order. This is not the case. Figure 2.5 illustrates the phases in the Information Life Cycle. Note that the life cycle is NOT a linear process and is very iterative.

There can be multiple ways that any piece of data or set of information is obtained, maintained, applied, and disposed of. In actuality the same information can also be stored in more than one place. It is because activities in the real

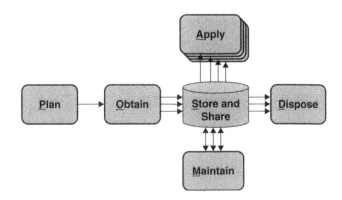

Figure 2.5 • The Information Life Cycle is not a linear process.

Source: Adapted from a figure in Larry P. English's *Improving Data Warehouse and Business Information Quality* (John Wiley & Sons, 1999), p. 203. Used with permission.

world *are* complicated and messy that knowing the Information Life Cycle is so helpful.

For example, suppose you purchase information from an external source. The data are received by your company and stored—maybe initially in a temporary staging area. The data are then filtered and checked before being loaded into the internal database. Once in the database the data are available for others to apply—some are retrieved through an application interface, or some may be shared through a mechanism called an enterprise service bus and loaded into another database where others in the company access and use them through yet another application. Data can also be maintained in various ways—by updating individual fields and records through an application interface or by receiving updates from a subsequent file sent from an external data provider.

It is easy to see how the information path quickly becomes very complicated. Applying your knowledge of the Information Life Cycle helps bring clarity to a complex situation.[5]

---

[5]Use of the POSMAD interaction matrix (see Figure 2.3, page 21) is another way of providing clarity.

Life Cycle Thinking

Using the Information Life Cycle helps you analyze and segment activities in such a way that you can look at what is happening and identify in which phase of the life cycle those activities are taking place. This knowledge helps you make decisions about what is working, what is not working, and what needs to be changed. I advocate the idea of "life cycle thinking," which can be applied in many ways. Using life cycle thinking helps you immediately start to understand (or start asking the right questions to discover) what is happening to your data from any view in your company. Let's look at a few examples.

Life Cycle Thinking at a High Level

Assume you are responsible for the customer information that supports the Sales and Marketing functions in your company. Maybe all you know right now is what your organization looks like. The head of Sales and Marketing for Europe in one global company was concerned about the quality of the customer data that supported his organization. He described his organization to me, and I drew a high-level chart on the board. The Call Center, Marketing, and Field Sales were the three main teams under the manager's geographical organization (in this case Europe Sales and Marketing). We chose to look further at the organizational structure under Marketing, which consisted of four teams—Business Intelligence, Customer Information Management, Marketing Communications, and Business Segments.

After a very brief tutorial on the Information Life Cycle, I asked which teams impacted the customer information in each of the life cycle phases: Which have input into the planning process for their customer information? Which obtain the data? Who uses or applies the customer information? Who maintains the data? Who can dispose of the data? Figure 2.6 shows the result of that 30-minute conversation. Examine it and see what you can learn about information quality—just with this amount of information and at this high level of detail.

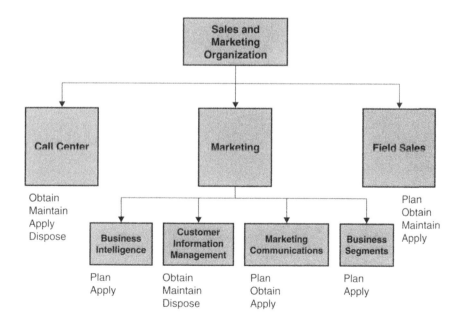

Figure 2.6 • Organization and the POSMAD life cycle.

As shown in the figure, four teams have input to the planning phase of their customer information (Business Intelligence, Marketing Communications, Business Segments, and Field Sales). The Call Center, Customer Information Management, Marketing Communications, and Field Sales all obtain this information in various ways, but only three of these teams maintain or update it. This makes sense, as often the data obtained from Marketing Communications come from field events and this team sees each customer signing in as a new one. Therefore, we can already see that to avoid duplicate customer records there needs to be a process for identifying already existing records in the customer database when adding new customer records obtained through Marketing Communications.

A potential data quality problem can be seen when asking the question, "Do all teams that obtain the data receive the same data entry training and do they have the same set of data entry standards (whether manual or automated)?"

If the answer is no, you can be sure you have a data quality problem—you just don't know yet how big it is or which pieces of data are most affected. You can also see that the Call Center obtains, maintains, applies, and disposes of the customer information, yet is not involved in the planning phase. Thus, important requirements could be missed and could impact data quality. There is more you can learn from this illustration, but it shows how you can start seeing potential impacts to data quality even at this point.

Now let's look at the life cycle from another view—that of points where the company has interaction with its customers. Figure 2.7 starts with the customer and shows multiple communication methods between the company and the customer, the storage of the customer data in the database, and the various uses of customer information. Some uses of the information include recontacting the customer. Once again, the various phases of the Information Life Cycle are indicated. Note that this time we

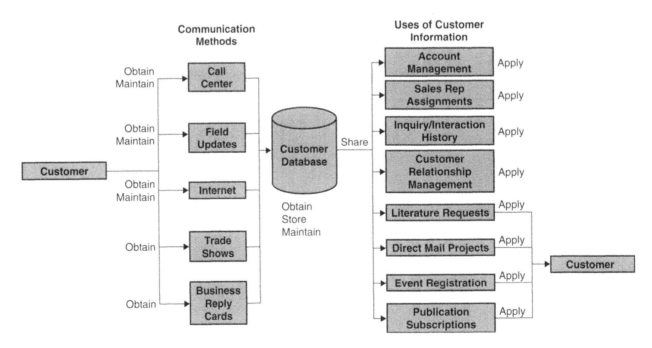

Figure 2.7 • Interactions with customers and the POSMAD life cycle.

choose not to include the Plan phase, but do include the Store and Share phase.

What can you learn from the Figure 2.7 illustration? One key lesson for the team during this exercise was seeing the list of ways their customer information was being used. If you were to ask, most would know that Account Management uses customer information and Sales Rep Assignments also rely on it. But somehow just seeing this simple list of the important ways customer information was used by Sales and Marketing almost built the business case for the data quality project.

Life Cycle Thinking at a Detailed Level
You have seen how to apply life cycle thinking at a high level. Let's go to a different level of detail. It is still life cycle thinking but from yet another view of the company—that of roles. Figure 2.8 lists roles down the first column and several business terms associated with customer information across the remaining columns. The business terms could also be known as data subject areas or data groups. Note that only three of the life cycle phases are used (Obtain, Maintain, and Apply). The team looked at each role and noted

if that role obtained, maintained, and/or applied the corresponding customer information.

Analyze each row and each column in Figure 2.8. The rows show the breadth of the data being impacted by each role. The columns show all the roles that impact a specific data group.

A question can be raised similar to the one asked when looking at POSMAD at the organizational level: "Do all roles that obtain the data receive the same training and have the same set of data entry standards?" If not, once again, there's a data quality problem, but you don't know its size or which data are most affected.

One project team knew that many departments could apply or use the same data, but they thought only one department could create or update them. Through this application of life cycle thinking they found that people in other departments actually had the ability to create and update data. The impact to data quality could immediately be seen: No consistent training or standards for entering data across the teams means poor-quality data. This information gives you the knowledge to make some educated

Roles	Business Term or Data Subject Area							
	Contact Name	Site Name	Division	Department	Address	Phone	Title	Profile
Field engineer	O, M, A	O, M, A	O, M, A	O, M, A	O, M, A	O, M, A	O, M, A	O, M, A
District manager	O, M, A	O, M, A	O, M, A	O, M, A	O, M, A	A	O, M, A	O, M, A
Customer service representatives	O, M, A	O, M, A	O, M, A	O, M, A	O, M, A	O, M, A	O, M	
Order coordinators	O, M, A	O, M, A	O, M, A	O, M, A	O, M, A	O, M, A		
Quote coordinators	O, M, A	O, M, A	O, M, A	O, M, A	O, M, A	O, M, A	O, M	
Collection coordinators	A	A	A		A			
Business center mailroom		A	A		A			
Online tech support	O, M, A	O, M, A	O, M, A	O, M, A	O, M, A	O, M, A	O, M, A	O, M, A
Sales finance		A	A		A	A		
Information management team	O, M, A	O, M, A	O, M, A	O, M, A	O, M, A	O, M, A	O, M, A	O, M, A

O = Obtains the data; M = Maintains the data; A = Uses or applies the data.

Figure 2.8 • Roles and the Information Life Cycle.

statements about your information quality and where you want to focus your efforts.

In Figure 2.8, you can also see three roles that only apply the information; they do not collect or maintain it. What often happens in that situation is that the needs of those knowledge workers are not taken into consideration when obtaining the data. For example, pharmacists at one drug store chain needed to track information about customers when there was no place to enter it on their screen. So to the end of the customer's name they added codes such as "WC" (to show the customer had Workers' Compensation) and a variety of other strange symbols that indicated things like alternate insurance, suspected of shoplifting, and whether the patient had another record under a different name. Later the mailroom created labels for an offer that was sent to customers. Complaints started coming in from those who received letters with names on the mailing label that looked like "John Smith WC ! * check Rx comments to see alternate name."

The life cycle of information is an essential component of the FIQ and will be used throughout The Ten Steps process. Use life cycle thinking—at many levels of detail—to help you manage information as a resource and improve data quality.

Data Quality Dimensions

Data quality dimensions are aspects or features of quality. They provide a way to measure and manage the quality of data and information. This section introduces you to the data quality dimensions and explains why they are important.

Definition

A **data quality dimension** provides a way to measure and manage the quality of data and information.

Key Concept

During a data quality project, you will choose to measure the data quality dimensions that best address your business needs.

Detailed instructions for assessing each dimension are found in Chapter 3 as part of The Ten Steps process in *Step 3—Assess Data Quality*. Each data quality assessment aligns with a dimension of quality (e.g., Data Integrity Fundamentals, Duplication, or Accuracy).

Reasons for Data Quality Dimensions

Each data quality dimension requires different tools, techniques, and processes to measure it. This results in varying levels of time, money, and human resources to complete the assessments. You can better scope your project by understanding the effort required to assess each of the dimensions and choosing the ones that fit your needs. Initial assessment of the data quality dimensions results in setting a baseline. Additional assessments can be built into your operational processes as part of ongoing monitoring and information improvement.

Differentiating the dimensions of quality will help you

- Match dimensions against a business need and prioritize which assessments to complete first.

- Understand what you will (and will not) get from assessing each dimension.
- Better define and manage the sequence of activities in your project plan within time and resource constraints.

Data Quality Dimensions Defined

Each of the data quality dimensions is defined in Table 2.2.

Table 2.2 • Data Quality Dimensions

No.	Dimension	Definition and Notes
1	Data Specifications	*Definition*—A measure of the existence, completeness, quality, and documentation of data standards, data models, business rules, metadata, and reference data. *Notes*—Data specifications provide the standard against which to compare data quality assessment results. They also provide instruction for manually entering data, designing data load programs, updating information, and developing applications.
2	Data Integrity Fundamentals	*Definition*—A measure of the existence, validity, structure, content, and other basic characteristics of the data. *Notes*—All other dimensions of quality build on what is learned in Data Integrity Fundamentals. This dimension includes measures of basic data quality such as completeness/fill rate, validity, lists of values and frequency distributions, patterns, ranges, maximum and minimum values, and referential integrity.
3	Duplication	*Definition*—A measure of unwanted duplication existing within or across systems for a particular field, record, or data set. *Notes*—There are many hidden costs associated with duplicate records. For example, duplicate vendor records with the same name and different addresses make it difficult to ensure that payment is sent to the correct address. When purchases by one company are associated with duplicate master records, the credit limit for that company can unknowingly be exceeded. This can expose the business to unnecessary credit risks.
4	Accuracy	*Definition*—A measure of the correctness of the content of the data (which requires an authoritative source of reference to be identified and accessible). *Notes*—Data accuracy requires comparing the data to the real-world object they represent (the authoritative source of reference). Sometimes it is not possible to access the real-world object represented by the data, and in those cases a carefully chosen substitute for it may be used as the authoritative source of reference.

(Continued)

Table 2.2 • Data Quality Dimensions (Continued)

No.	Dimension	Definition and Notes
4	Accuracy (Cont'd)	The assessment of accuracy is often a manual and time-consuming process. For example, assessing Data Integrity Fundamentals can reveal if an item number contains a valid code indicating a make or buy part, but only someone familiar with item #123 can determine if that particular item is a make item or a buy item. A data profiling tool can be used to assess Data Integrity Fundamentals and show if a customer record has a valid pattern for a zip code, but only that customer can tell you if that is his or her zip code. Likewise, profiling can show that a field in the inventory system has a value and that it is the correct data type. But only by counting products on the shelf and comparing that number to the record in the inventory system can you know if the inventory count in the database is an accurate reflection of the inventory available.
5	Consistency and Synchronization	*Definition*—A measure of the equivalence of information stored or used in various data stores, applications, and systems, and the processes for making data equivalent. *Notes*—Equivalence is the degree to which data stored in multiple places are conceptually equal. The same measures from Data Integrity Fundamentals can be used across multiple databases, and results compared for consistency.
6	Timeliness and Availability	*Definition*—A measure of the degree to which data are current and available for use as specified and in the time frame in which they are expected. *Notes*—Data values change over time, and there will always be a gap between when the real-world object changes and when the data that represent it are updated in a database and made available for knowledge workers. This assessment examines the timing of information throughout its life cycle and shows if the data are up to date and available in time to meet business needs.
7	Ease of Use and Maintainability	*Definition*—A measure of the degree to which data can be accessed and used, and the degree to which data can be updated, maintained, and managed. *Notes*—Having the data available in the database so they can be used is not the same as the *ease* with which they can be used. It is not unusual for a small team of people to work several days to pull together what appears to be a simple report. Knowing how easy (or difficult) it is to use and maintain high-priority data will help the business make better decisions on investments in managing the data.

No.	DIMENSION	DEFINITION AND NOTES
8	Data Coverage	*Definition*—A measure of the availability and comprehensiveness of data compared to the total data universe or population of interest. *Notes*—This dimension looks at how the database captures and reflects the total population of interest to the business. For example, the database should contain all customers in North and South America, but it is known that the database reflects only a portion of the company's customers. Coverage in this example is the percentage of customers actually captured in the database compared to the population of all customers that should be in it.
9	Presentation Quality	*Definition*—A measure of how information is presented to and collected from those who utilize it. Format and appearance support appropriate use of the information. *Notes*—Presentation quality affects information when it is collected *and* when it is reported. Presenting information in a way that is easy and effective from the user's perspective increases overall data quality. Presentation quality applies to user interfaces, reports, surveys, etc.
10	Perception, Relevance, and Trust	*Definition*—A measure of the perception of and confidence in the data quality; the importance, value, and relevance of the data to business needs. *Notes*—Understand which data are of most value to the business and therefore which data should have first priority in management and maintenance. Understand how knowledge workers perceive the data quality, compare perception to actual data quality assessment results, and address any gaps.
11	Data Decay	*Definition*—A measure of the rate of negative change to the data. *Notes*—Knowing data decay rates helps determine whether mechanisms should be put into place to maintain the data and what the frequency of those updates should be. Volatile data requiring a high reliability level require more frequent updates than data with a lower decay rate.
12	Transactability	*Definition*—A measure of the degree to which data will produce the desired business transaction or outcome. *Notes*—Even if the right people have defined the business requirements and prepared the data to meet them, it is important for the data to produce the expected outcome: Can the invoice be correctly generated? Can a sales order be completed?

Data Quality Dimensions Work Together

You should choose the dimensions most meaningful to your situation, but it is often hard to know how to begin. Following are a few recommendations to get you started.

If you are not sure where to start your data quality efforts, the dimension of Perception, Relevance, and Trust can provide insight into issues by surveying the knowledge workers (the information customers) and getting their point of view. Use those results to articulate the business problem and prioritize your data quality efforts.

If you already have some idea of your data quality issues, you can use any prioritization technique with which you are familiar to agree on your business needs. Once the business needs and high-priority issues have been determined, assess the data based on the recommendations outlined next.

Data Specifications are important because they provide the standard against which to compare the results of the other data quality dimensions. Collect, update, and/or document the applicable Data Specifications (data standards, data models, business rules, metadata, and reference data) as early as possible. If you don't have the Data Specifications at first, at some point in time you will have to get them.

Once you are clear on your business issues and the related data, I strongly recommend Data Integrity Fundamentals as one of the first dimensions to assess. If you don't know anything else about your data, you need to know what you learn from that dimension because it provides a snapshot of data validity, structure, and content. This assessment provides facts about data and lets you see where the problems are and the magnitude of those problems.

All other dimensions of quality build on what is learned from the Data Integrity Fundamentals. It is tempting to skip this dimension because others may seem more important. For example, if your major concern about data quality is duplicate records, you may want to jump to the Duplication dimension and skip Data Integrity Fundamentals. However, the algorithms developed in Duplication, which determine the uniqueness of a record, are based on combinations of data elements. If the input is incorrect—if those data elements do not actually contain data (e.g., have a low fill rate) or do not contain the data expected (e.g., a Social Security Number in a phone number field)—or if the quality of the data is poor (e.g., incorrect values in a state field), then the output of your de-duplication process will be incorrect. It is through Data Integrity Fundamentals that you can see the actual content of those data elements.

I learned this lesson years ago. The business was concerned about duplicates, so we went straight to determining what combination of data elements indicated a unique record. That information was critical in configuring the algorithms and thresholds for the software used to identify duplicates. We could not get valid results when trying to find duplicate records, so we went back and assessed Data Integrity Fundamentals and found that one of the fields we "knew" was essential for indicating uniqueness only had a 20 percent fill rate. That is, only 20 percent of the records had a value in that field. No wonder we could not get good results in identifying duplicates!

Once you have completed Data Integrity Fundamentals (at the appropriate level of detail for your project), choose from the other dimensions based on your business need. For example,

Consistency and Synchronization can use the same techniques used in Data Integrity Fundamentals—just use them on multiple data sets and compare results. Timeliness and Availability link closely to Consistency and Synchronization, by adding the time element to the assessment. To determine decay rates in Data Decay, you may be able to do some additional calculations on create dates and update dates after you complete the Data Integrity Fundamentals or an assessment of Accuracy. You may look at Coverage and determine that some of the issues there are the result of problems with Ease of Use and Maintainability. You may look at Presentation Quality as an aspect that relates to most of the other dimensions.

Key Considerations for Choosing Data Quality Dimensions

Here are the key considerations for choosing the data quality dimensions to assess:

- *Should* I assess the data?
  - Only spend time testing when you expect the results to give you *actionable* information related to your business needs.
- *Can* I assess the data?
  - Is it possible or practical to look at this quality dimension?
  - Sometimes you cannot assess/test the data, or the cost to do so is prohibitive.
- *Only* assess the dimensions if you can say YES to both questions.
- *Once* a data quality dimension has been assessed, the assessment results should drive improvement activities.

Business Impact Techniques

Business impact techniques are used to determine the effects of data quality on the business.

They include both qualitative and quantitative measures and also methods for prioritizing.

Whenever a data quality problem is found, the first two words usually spoken by management are "So what?" Management wants to know, "What impact does this have on the business?" and "Why does it matter?" Another way of saying it is, "What is the value of having information quality?" These are important questions. After all, no one has the money to spend on something that is not worthwhile. The business impact techniques help answer those questions and are the basis for making informed investment decisions for your information resource.

Business impact focuses on how the information is used—such as completing transactions, creating reports, making decisions, running automated processes, or providing an ongoing source of data for another downstream application such as a data warehouse. Information uses are part of the Apply phase of the Information Life Cycle POSMAD. (See The Information Life Cycle section on page 23.)

Details of the various business impact techniques are described as part of The Ten Steps process in *Step 4—Assess Business Impact.* Each business impact assessment aligns with a business impact technique (e.g., anecdotes, usage, or process impact).

 Definition

Business impact techniques use qualitative and quantitative measures for determining the effects of data quality on the business.

Key Concept

Data governance expert Tom Carlock has a nice way of expressing why knowing value is important: Value Assures Love and Understanding from Executives.

Reasons for Business Impact Techniques

Results from the business impact techniques help make the usually intangible aspects of data tangible and meaningful to those who have to make tough investment decisions. Business impact is another way of expressing the idea that there is value in having quality information. It is only by showing business impact that management can understand the value of information quality. Use results from assessing business impact to

- Establish the business case for information quality.
- Gain support for investing in information quality.
- Determine the optimal level of investment.

Table 2.3 defines each of the business impact techniques.

Table 2.3 • Business Impact Techniques Defined

No.	BUSINESS IMPACT TECHNIQUE	DEFINITION AND NOTES
1	Anecdotes	*Definition*—Collect examples or stories of the impact of poor data quality. *Notes*—Collecting stories is the easiest and most low-cost way of assessing business impact. The right story can stimulate interest and engage leadership quickly.
2	Usage	*Definition*—Inventory the current and/or future uses of the data. *Notes*—An easy way to demonstrate how important data are to a business is to list all the processes and organizations that rely on them.
3	Five "Whys" for Business Impact	*Definition*—Ask "Why" five times to get to real business impact. *Notes*—A quality technique often used in manufacturing where asking "Why" five times usually gets you to the root cause of a problem. This same technique can be used by asking "Why" five times to get to the real business impact.
4	Benefit versus Cost Matrix	*Definition*—Analyze and rate the relationship between benefits and costs of issues, recommendations, or improvements. *Notes*—This uses another standard quality technique of comparing benefits and costs. As it relates to data quality improvement, it can be used to review and prioritize alternatives and provide answers to questions such as: "On which data quality issues should we focus?" "Which data quality dimensions should we assess?" "Which recommendations resulting from a quality assessment are of most importance?" "Which improvements should we implement?"

No.	BUSINESS IMPACT TECHNIQUE	DEFINITION AND NOTES
5	Ranking and Prioritization	*Definition*—Rank the impact of missing and incorrect data on specific business processes. *Notes*—Prioritizing indicates relative importance or value. Something with a high priority, then, implicitly has a higher impact on the business. The importance of data quality will vary for different data and will vary for different usage of the same data. This technique brings together those who actually use the data to rank the effect of incorrect and missing data on their associated business processes.
6	Process Impact	*Definition*—Illustrate the effects of poor-quality data on business processes. *Notes*—Workarounds become a normal part of business processes and hide the fact that they are often a result of poor-quality data. Duplication of effort, costly problems, distractions, wasted time, and lower productivity are other effects. By showing the impact of poor-quality data on the processes, the business can make informed decisions about improving issues that were previously unclear.
7	Cost of Low-Quality Data	*Definition*—Quantify the costs and revenue impact of poor-quality data. *Notes*—Poor-quality data cost the business in many ways: waste and rework, missed revenue opportunities, lost business, etc. This technique quantifies the costs and revenue impact that may have been understood only through stories or observation.
8	Cost–Benefit Analysis	*Definition*—Compare the potential benefits of investing in data quality with anticipated costs, through an in-depth evaluation. This includes return on investment (ROI)—profit from an investment as a percentage of the amount invested. *Notes*—This technique and ROI are standard management approaches to making financial decisions. This detailed information may be required before considering or proceeding with any significant financial investment—and investments in information quality are often considerable. Management has the responsibility to determine how money is spent and will need to weigh investment options against each other.

Business Impact Techniques Work Together

Figure 2.9 shows a continuum with the relative time and effort to determine business impact for each technique, from generally less complex and taking less time (Technique 1 from Table 2.3) to more complex and taking more time (Technique 8 from Table 2.3).

The importance of being able to show business impact cannot be stressed enough. It is essential to getting any kind of support—be it time, resources, money, expertise, or anything else. What I want you to understand is that you can show business impact in a variety of ways. It does not always have to take the form of a comprehensive and time-consuming

Figure 2.9 • Relative time and effort of business impact techniques.

cost–benefit analysis or ROI (Technique 8). Much can be learned through other techniques that require less effort but can still provide enough information to make good decisions.

The techniques don't stand alone. You can easily combine ideas from the various techniques to show business impact. For example, an anecdote can be effective even without quantitative data (*Step 4.1—Anecdotes*), but you can expand on some aspect of your anecdote and bring in quantitative information as your time permits. As you assess impact using other techniques, learn how to quickly tell a story using the facts and figures you have collected.

You may complete a list of the various business processes, people, and/or applications that use data (*Step 4.2—Usage*) and then employ *Step 4.6—Process Impact* to visualize the impact of poor-quality data for one or two specific business processes. Further, you may employ the techniques in *Step 4.7—Cost of Low-Quality Data* to quantify the costs associated with those few business processes. Once you have a list of how the data are used, you can draw on *Step 4.4—Benefit versus Cost Matrix* or *Step 4.5— Ranking and Prioritization* to determine where to focus your data quality efforts.

Once you have been able to describe business impact through *Step 4.3—Five "Whys" for Business Impact* you can use other techniques to focus on that area to further quantify or visualize impact.

Sometimes a full cost–benefit analysis is required (*Step 4.8—Cost–Benefit Analysis*). It is

relatively easy to gather costs (training, software, human resources, etc.). The difficult piece as it applies to data is showing the benefit. You can draw on all of the previous techniques to help you do this. For example, even though in Step 4.7 we express the output as cost of poor-quality data, it can also be phrased as the benefit from having high-quality data. Use applicable results as input to the benefit portion of your cost–benefit analysis.

Key Considerations for Choosing Business Impact Techniques

Use the business impact techniques that best fit your situation, time, and available resources to complete the assessment. Consider the following suggestions when choosing techniques.

Remember, the continuum shows relative *effort*, not relative results—Less complex does not mean less useful results, nor does more complex mean more useful results. The reverse is also true—less complex does not necessarily mean more useful results, nor does more complex necessarily mean less useful results.

That said, it is usually a good practice to start easy and move to the more complex as needed—Almost everyone has some story to tell—they experienced it themselves or heard it from others. Something prompted you to start dealing with data quality, and that something is usually found in a situation that can be summarized and retold as an anecdote. Continue to quantify as you are able.

Determine who needs to see the business impact and for what purpose—If you are describing business impact to a business analyst or subject matter expert for the purpose of gaining their willing participation on a data quality project, then a full cost–benefit analysis is overkill. If you are just in the stage of raising awareness about data quality, anecdotes or usage may be enough. If you have progressed to the point of getting budget approval, your financial approval process may require the more time-consuming quantification techniques. But even at this stage, don't ignore the power of the other techniques.

Ask yourself if it is possible or practical to assess business impact using a particular technique with the time and resources you have available—It may be better to employ a technique against a focused scope such as a few processes or a single data set rather than to do nothing at all.

You need to show enough business impact (within a reasonable time period, using available resources) to take action and make good investment decisions—that requires some experience and experimenting to get the right balance. So use your best judgment to focus your efforts with the time and resources at hand, start moving, and adjust your approach if needed later.

Data Categories

Data categories are groupings of data with common characteristics or features. They are useful for managing the data because certain data may be treated differently based on their classification. Understanding the relationship and dependency between the different categories can help direct data quality efforts. For example, a project focused on improving master data quality may find that one of the root causes of quality problems actually comes from faulty reference data that were included in the

master data record. By being aware of the data categories, a project can save time by including key reference data as part of its initial data quality assessments. From a data governance and stewardship viewpoint (see section on this topic, pages 52–54), those responsible for creating or updating data may be very different from one data category to another.

Data Categories Example

Your company, Smith Corp., sells widgets to state and federal government agencies, commercial accounts, and educational institutions. ABC Inc. wants to purchase four Blue Widgets from you. ABC Inc. is one of your commercial customers (identified as Customer Type 03) and has been issued a customer identifier number of 9876. The Blue Widget has a product number of 90-123 and its unit price depends on customer type. ABC Inc. purchases four Blue Widgets at a unit price of $100 each (the price for a commercial customer) for a total price of $400. Figure 2.10 illustrates that transaction.

When the agent from ABC Inc. calls Smith Corp. to place an order, the Smith Corp. customer representative enters ABC Inc.'s customer number in the sales order transaction. ABC Inc.'s company name, customer type, and address are pulled into the sales order screen from its customer master record. The master data mentioned are essential to the transaction. When the product number is entered, the product description of "Blue Widget" is pulled into the sales order along with a unit price that has been derived based on the customer type. Therefore, the total price for four Blue Widgets is $400.

Let's look at the data categories included in this example. We have already mentioned that the basic customer information for ABC Inc.

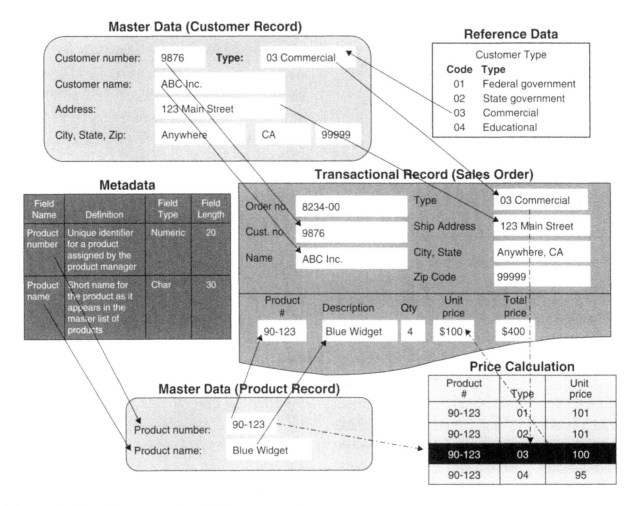

Figure 2.10 • An example of data categories.

Note: Thanks to Bruce Burton for the original inspiration behind this figure. Copyright © 2005–2008 Danette McGilvray, Granite Falls Consulting, Inc.

is contained in the customer master record. Some of the data in the master record are pulled from controlled lists of reference data. An example is customer type. Smith Corp. sells to four customer types, and the four types with associated codes are stored as a separate reference list. Other reference data associated with this customer's master record (but not shown in the figure) are the list of valid U.S. state codes, which is used when creating the address for ABC Inc. An example of reference data needed for the transaction but not pulled in through the master data are the list of shipping options available (also not shown in the figure).

Reference data are sets of values or classification schemas that are referred to by systems, applications, data stores, processes, and reports, as well as by transactional and master records. Reference data may be unique to your company (such as customer type), but can also be used by many other companies. Examples are standardized sets of codes such as currencies defined and maintained by ISO (International Standards Organization). In our example, the price calculations further emphasize the importance of high-quality reference data. If the code list is wrong, or the associated unit price is wrong, then the incorrect price will be used for that customer.

Why have the customer record and product record been classified as master data? Master data describe the people, places, and things that are involved in an organization's business. Examples include customers, products, employees, suppliers, and locations. Gwen Thomas created a ditty sung to the tune of "Yankee Doodle" that highlights master data:

Master data's all around
Embedded in transactions.
Master data are the nouns
Upon which we take action.[6]

In our example, Smith Corp. has a finite list of customers and a finite list of products that are unique to and important to it—no other company will be likely to have the very same lists. While ABC Inc. is a customer of other companies, how its data are formatted and used by Smith Corp. is unique to Smith Corp. For example, if Smith Corp. only sells to companies within the United States, it may not include address data (such as country) needed by other companies that sell outside of the United States and that also sell to ABC Inc. Addresses would be formatted differently within those companies to take international addresses into account. Likewise, Smith Corp.'s product list is unique to it, and the product master record may be structured differently from other companies' product masters.

The sales order in the example is considered transactional data. Transactional data describe an internal or external event or transaction that takes place as an organization conducts its business. Examples include sales order, invoice, purchase order, shipping document, and passport application. Transactional data are typically grouped into transactional records that include associated master and reference data. In the example, you can see that the sales order pulls data from two different master data records. It is also possible that reference data specific to the transaction are used—so not all reference data have to come through the master record.

Figure 2.10 also illustrates *metadata*, which literally means "data about data." Metadata label, describe, or characterize other data and make it easier to retrieve, interpret, or use information. The figure shows documentation defining the fields in the product master record along with the field type and field length. Several kinds of metadata are described in Table 2.4.

Metadata are critical to avoiding misunderstandings that can create data quality problems. In Figure 2.10, you can see in the master record that the field containing "Blue Widget" is called "Product Name," but the same data are labeled "Description" in the transactional record screen. In an ideal world, the data would be labeled the same wherever they are used. Unfortunately, inconsistencies such as the one in the figure are common and often lead to misuse and misunderstanding. Having clear documentation of metadata showing the fields (and their names) that are actually using the same data is important to managing those data and to understanding the impact if those fields are changed, or if the data are moved and used by other business functions and applications.

Data Categories Defined

Table 2.4 includes definitions and examples for each of the data categories discussed previously. These definitions were jointly created by the author of this book and Gwen Thomas, president of the Data Governance Institute.

---

[6]For entertainment and education, see *www.datagovernance.com* for other ideas that Gwen Thomas has set to familiar tunes.

Table 2.4 • Definitions of Data Categories

DATA CATEGORY	DEFINITION
Master Data	Master data describe the people, places, and things that are involved in an organization's business. *Examples* include people (e.g., customers, employees, vendors, suppliers), places (e.g., locations, sales territories, offices), and things (e.g., accounts, products, assets, document sets). Because these data tend to be used by multiple business processes and IT systems, standardizing master data formats and synchronizing values are critical for successful system integration. Master data tend to be grouped into master records, which may include associated reference data. An example of associated reference data is a state field within an address in a customer master record.
Transactional Data	Transactional data describe an internal or external event or transaction that takes place as an organization conducts its business. *Examples* include sales orders, invoices, purchase orders, shipping documents, passport applications, credit card payments, and insurance claims. These data are typically grouped into transactional records, which include associated master and reference data.
Reference Data	Reference data are sets of values or classification schemas that are referred to by systems, applications, data stores, processes, and reports, as well as by transactional and master records. *Examples* include lists of valid values, code lists, status codes, state abbreviations, demographic fields, flags, product types, gender, chart of accounts, and product hierarchy. Standardized reference data are key to data integration and interoperability and facilitate the sharing and reporting of information. Reference data may be used to differentiate one type of record from another for categorization and analysis, or they may be a significant fact such as country, which appears within a larger information set such as address. Organizations often create internal reference data to characterize or standardize their own information. Reference data sets are also defined by external groups, such as government or regulatory bodies, to be used by multiple organizations. For example, currency codes are defined and maintained by ISO.
Metadata	Metadata literally means "data about data." Metadata label, describe, or characterize other data and make it easier to retrieve, interpret, or use information. Technical metadata are metadata used to describe technology and data structures. Examples of technical metadata are field names, length, type, lineage, and database table layouts. Business metadata describe the nontechnical aspects of data and their usage. Examples are field definitions, report names, headings in reports and on

DATA CATEGORY	DEFINITION
Metadata (Cont'd)	Web pages, application screen names, data quality statistics, and the parties accountable for data quality for a particular field. Some organizations would classify ETL (Extract–Transform–Load) transformations as business metadata. Audit trail metadata are a specific type of metadata, typically stored in a record and protected from alteration, that capture how, when, and by whom the data were created, accessed, updated, or deleted. Audit trail metadata are used for security, compliance, or forensic purposes. Examples include timestamp, creator, create date, and update date. Although audit trail metadata are typically stored in a record, technical metadata and business metadata are usually stored separately from the data they describe.
	These are the most common types of metadata, but it could be argued that there are other types of metadata that make it easier to retrieve, interpret, or use information. The label for any metadata may not be as important as the fact that it is being deliberately used to support data goals. Any discipline or activity that uses data is likely to have associated metadata.
Additional data categories that impact how systems and databases are designed and data are used:	
Historical Data	Historical data contain significant facts, as of a certain point in time, that should not be altered except to correct an error. They are important to security and compliance. Operational systems can also contain history tables for reporting or analysis purposes. Examples include point-in-time reports, database snapshots, and version information.
Temporary Data	Temporary data are kept in memory to speed up processing. They are not viewed by humans and are used for technical purposes. Examples include a copy of a table that is created during a processing session to speed up lookups.

Source: Copyright © 2007–2008 Danette McGilvray and Gwen Thomas. Used by permission.

Your data may be categorized different from what the table describes. For example, some companies combine reference data and master data categories and call them master reference data (MRD). Sometimes it is difficult to decide whether a data set, such as a list of valid values, is only reference data or is also metadata. It has been said that one person's metadata is another person's data. No matter how data are categorized, the important point is that you are clear on what you are (and are not) addressing in data quality activities. You may find that such data quality activities should include data categories not considered previously.

Relationships between Data Categories

Figure 2.11 shows the associations between the various data categories. Note that some reference data are required to create a master data record and that master data are required to create a transactional record. Sometimes reference data specific to transactional data (and not pulled in through the master records) are needed to create a transactional record. Metadata are required to better use and understand all other data categories. From an historical data point of view, corresponding reference data may need

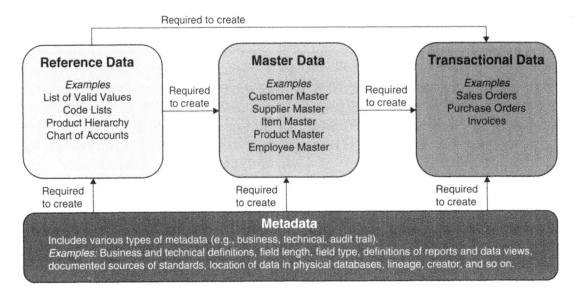

Figure 2.11 • Relationships between data categories.

to be maintained along with the master and transactional records; if not, important context and the meaning of the data may be lost. Auditors will want to know who updated the data and when—for all categories of data. That is why audit trail data are a part of metadata.

Data Categories—Why We Care

It is easy to see from the examples just given that the care given to your reference data strongly impacts the quality of your master and transactional data. Reference data are key to interoperability. The more you manage and standardize them, the more you increase your ability to share data across and outside of your company. The significance of an error in reference data has a multiplying effect as the data continue to be passed on and used by other data.

The quality of master data impacts transactional data, and the quality of metadata impacts all categories. For example, documenting definitions (metadata) improves quality because it transforms undocumented assumptions into documented and agreed-on meanings so the data can be used consistently and correctly.

As mentioned previously, your company's data are unique (master product, vendor, customer data, etc., reference data, metadata). No other organization will be likely to have the very same data list. If correct and managed conscientiously, your data provide a competitive advantage because they are *tuned for your company needs.* Imagine the cost savings and revenue potential for the company that has accurate data, can find information when needed, and trusts the information found. Quality must be managed for all data categories in order to gain that competitive advantage. Of course, you will have to prioritize your efforts, but consider all the data categories when selecting your data quality activities.

> **Definition**
>
> The term **data specifications** is used in this book to include data standards, data models, business rules, metadata, and reference data.

Data Specifications

Specifications provide the information needed to make, build, or produce something. The term "data specifications" is used in this book to include data standards, data models, business rules, metadata, and reference data. *Data specifications* can be used when building applications to ensure data quality from the beginning and to provide conditions against which to determine the level of data quality in existing applications. They provide important guidance in the same way that an architect's drawings, electrical diagrams, and other plans specify how to build a house or what should be included in it. An introduction to each of the five data specification types (data standards, data models, business rules, metadata, and reference data) follows. There are several books available on any of these types for those who would like more in-depth information.

 Definition

Data standards are rules and guidelines that govern how to name data, how to define it, how to establish valid values, and how to specify business rules.

Data Standards

The preceding box contains a definition provided by Larry English from the glossary on the IAIDQ website (*http://www.iaidq.org/main/glossary.shtml*). Examples of standards include:

Naming Conventions for Tables and Fields—An example of a naming convention is: if the data in the field contain names, the column name should include the standard abbreviation "NM" along with a descriptive word for the name type—for example, "NM_Last" or "NM_First."

Data Definitions and Conventions for Writing Business Rules—You may have a standards document that describes the minimum set of information to be defined for each field—for example, each field must be documented in the data dictionary; documentation must include the field name, description, example of data content, whether the field is mandatory or optional, and a default value (if one exists).

Establishing, Documenting, and Updating Lists of Valid Values—It is important to agree on the values that are valid for any given field. Sometimes the valid value list is developed internally, and sometimes you may use an external standard list. In any case, there should be a process that outlines how changes are made to the list and who is involved in those decisions.

Commonly Accepted Reference Values for Classification and Categorization—For example, NAICS, the North American Industry Classification System, was developed by the United States in cooperation with Canada and Mexico as the standard for use by federal statistical agencies in classifying business establishments. Use of the standard allows for a high level of comparability in business statistics among the three countries. NAICS was adopted in 1997 to replace the old SIC (Standard Industrial Classification system).[7]

This example illustrates the impact of standards on data quality: If your company was using the SIC system, did it change to NAICS? What is the standard being used now? If NAICS is being used, were all data in

---

[7]*Source:* NAICS Association, Questions and Answers (*http://www.naics.com/faq.htm#q1*).

the company updated from SIC to NAICS? How were existing SIC codes mapped and changed to NAICS? The NAICS codes can also be used as an example of reference data. The code list comprises the valid sets of values (reference data), but it is also the standard by which business establishments are classified.

Choice of Notation and Modeling Method for Data Modeling—Each data modeling method has a different emphasis and the methods are approximately interchangeable—but not quite. The modeling notation used should be based on your objective.

Data Models

A *data model* is a way of visually representing the structure of an organization's data. It is also a specification of how data is to be represented in a database—which data will be held and how they will be organized. As Simsion and Witt note in *Data Model Essentials*: "No database was ever built without at least an implicit model, just as no house was ever built without a plan" (2005, p. xxiii).

 Definition

A **data model** is a way of visually representing the structure of an organization's data. It is also a specification of how data are to be represented in a database.

The data model graphically reflects the way data are organized—and the more explicit the model the better as far as data quality is concerned. In managing data quality, it is important to understand the database that contains the data and the programs that capture, store, maintain, manipulate, transform, delete, and share them.

The terms entity and attribute are central concepts in data modeling. An *entity* is a person, place, event, thing, or concept that is of interest to the business. An entity class, also called an entity type, is a set of those things whose instances are uniquely identifiable. (Entity classes are often loosely referred to as entities.) An *attribute* is the definition of a characteristic, quality, or property of an entity class.[8] For example, "Person" and "Organization" are examples of an entity class; "John Doe" and "Smith Corp." are examples of an entity; and "First Name" and "Last Name" are attributes of "Person."

There are multiple notations for data models, but they all use a rectangular box with rounded or square corners to represent an entity class, and a line to represent a relationship between two entity classes. Notations differ in how they represent a relationship's

- "Cardinality"—how many instances of one entity class can be related to an instance of another entity class: zero, one, or many; for example, a company can have one or many Addresses.

- "Optionality"—whether an instance of one entity class exists, or whether it is necessary for there to be an instance of a related entity class; for example, "A Company must have at least one Address."

As stated before, a data model is a way of visually representing the structure of an organization's data. The view may be from various approaches. The terms most commonly used are "conceptual," "logical," and "physical" and there are multiple

---

[8]My thanks to David Hay for these definitions.

definitions for each. Table 2.5 (see pages 48–49) compares and describes those terms as used by three of the several different approaches.

In the first approach, the term *conceptual model* refers to a comprehensive view of the organization in detail. The term *logical model* is specific to a data management technology (such as a relational database or XML), and the term *physical model* describes the technology in detail (in terms of such things as table spaces, and partitions).

The second approach uses *conceptual model* to describe a high-level overview and *logical model* to describe the business. The third approach, sponsored by the Object Management Group (OMG), simply distinguishes between models that are independent of the technologies that are used to implement them and those that are specific to such technologies.

People disagree on the terminology used in Table 2.5 for the various levels of data models. It is not the purpose of this book to discuss the merits of the three approaches. It is only important to know that differences exist so when you are discussing data models and the terms are used, you can ask about and understand the definitions that apply in your environment.

Whichever terms are used, it is important to distinguish between (1) the viewing of data structures in casual terms, (2) the viewing of the fundamental structure of your data (and through that the fundamental structure of your business), and (3) the viewing of data structures that are based on technological constraints. The latter will change frequently. It is only by maintaining a solid understanding of the *nature* of the data you use that you will be able to rise above such changes and respond instead to changes in your business.

Among other things, a data model can serve as a platform for discussing—and ultimately determining—a system's scope. Separately, processes can be documented to show where they can or cannot be supported because the data do or do not exist. For the most part, business rules cannot be documented on a data model; however, they should be documented in conjunction with one.

A good data model combined with documentation of constraints at every project life cycle level of execution—database design, application interaction, and accessibility—will help produce high-quality, reusable data and prevent many postproduction data quality problems, such as redundancy, conflicting data definitions, and difficulty in sharing data across applications.

Business Rules

Ron Ross, known as the "father of business rules," describes business rules thus: "Rules serve as guides for conduct or action. Rules provide criteria for making decisions."[9]

 Definition

A **business rule** is an authoritative principle or guideline that describes business interactions and establishes rules for actions and resulting data behavior and integrity.

[9]From Ronald G. Ross, *Business Rule Concepts: Getting to the Point of Knowledge, Second Edition* (Business Rule Solutions, LLC, 2005), p. 76.

Table 2.5 • Data Model Comparison

Level	Description	First Approach Term[a,b]	Second Approach Term[c]	Third Approach Term[d]
1	This model is a sketch that includes primary entities. There are many-to-many relationships and virtually no attributes.	Context	Conceptual or Subject	Environment
2	This model describes the *semantics* of the business. The semantic data model consists of boxes representing sets of things of significance to the business ("entity classes"), such as "Person" or "Activity," and lines to describe relationships between pairs of such entity classes. It contains a more complete list of entity classes (often in a more abstract form). Nearly all attributes are shown, and many-to-many relationships may be resolved. This model contains basic and critical concepts for a given scope and is used to communicate between a data modeler and business stakeholders. It specifies data that might be held in a database, independent of the technology and the actual physical implementation that might be used. It includes both diagrams and supporting documentation.	Conceptual	Logical	Class-of-Platform (*Technology*) Independent Model
3	This model arranges data, in terms to be used by a particular data management technology, to accommodate technical constraints and expected usage. Examples might be in terms of relational tables and columns, object-oriented classes, or XML tags. Structures from model level 2 can be implemented using a database management system (DBMS), object-oriented programs, or XML schemas. But they are independent of specific database software (Oracle, DB2, etc.) or reporting tools.	Logical	Physical	Class-of-Platform (*Technology*) Specific Model, Vendor Platform Independent Model

Level	Description	First Approach Term[a,b]	Second Approach Term[c]	Third Approach Term[d]
4	This model organizes the data on one or more physical media. It is concerned with physical table spaces, disk drives, partitions, and so forth. This includes changes made to logical structures to achieve performance goals. It is embedded in a particular vendor's database management approach.	Physical		Vendor Platform Specific Model

[a]Terms as used by Graeme Simsion and Graham Witt in *Data Modeling Essentials, Third Edition* (Morgan Kaufmann, 2005), p. 17.

[b]Terms as used by David Hay in "What Exactly Is a Data Model?" DM *Review* (Vol. 13, No. 2), 2003 (*www.dmreview.com/issues/20030201/6281-1.html*).

[c]Terms as used by Steve Hoberman in "Leveraging the Industry Logical Data Model as Your Enterprise Data Model," Teradata white paper, p. 7 (*www.teradata.com/t/pdf.aspx?a=83673&b=162511*).

[d]Terms as used by Donald Chapin in "MDA Foundational Model Applied to Both the Organization and Business Application Software," Object Management Group (OMG) working paper (March 2008).

Source: Copyright © 2008 David C. Hay and Danette McGilvray. Used by permission.

For data quality, you must understand business rules and their *implications* for the constraints on the data. Therefore, my definition of a business rule as it applies to data quality is this: "A business rule is an authoritative principle or guideline that describes business interactions and establishes rules for actions and resulting data behavior and integrity." (An authoritative principle means the rule is mandatory; a guideline means the rule is optional.)

In his 2005 book *Business Rule Concepts*, Ron Ross presents samples of business rules and informally categorizes each one according to the kind of guidance it provides. The first two columns in Table 2.6 are from Ron's book. The last two have been added to illustrate the business action that should take place and to provide an example of an associated data quality check.

The data are the output of a business process, and violations of data quality checks can mean that the process is not working properly or that the rule has been incorrectly captured. Collect business rules to provide input for creating necessary data quality checks and analyzing the results of the assessments. The lack of well-documented business rules often plays a part in data quality problems.

Table 2.6 • Business Rules and Data Quality Checks

TYPE OF BUSINESS RULE*	EXAMPLE OF BUSINESS RULE*	BUSINESS ACTION	DATA QUALITY CHECK
Restriction	A customer must not place more than 3 rush orders charged to its credit account.	A service rep checks customer's credit account to determine whether number of rush orders placed exceeds 3. If yes, customer can only place a standard order.	The rule violated if: Order_Type = "Rush" and Account_Type = "Credit" and number of rush orders placed = 3.
Guideline	A customer with preferred status should have its orders filled immediately.	A service rep checks customer status. If designated as preferred ("P"), order should be shipped within 12 hours of being placed.	The guideline is violated if: Customer_Status = "P" and any ship date = Order Date + 12 hours.
Computation	A customer's annual order volume must be computed as total sales closed during the company's fiscal year.	Not applicable—based on automated calculations.	The computation is correct if: Annual_Order_Volume = Total_Sales for all quarters in fiscal year.
Inference	A customer must be considered preferred if customer places more than 5 orders over $1,000.	A service rep checks order history of customer when placing order to determine if customer is preferred.	Preference is inferred when: Sum of 5 or more customer orders > $1,000.
Timing	An order must be assigned to an expeditor if shipped but not invoiced within 72 hours.	To ensure that the business transaction is finalized, service rep checks daily "Order Transaction" report and forwards to expeditor any orders shipped but not invoiced within 72 hours.	The rule is violated if: Ship date-time = 72 hours and invoice date = null and Expeditor_ID = null.
Trigger	"Send-advance-notice" must be performed for an order when the order is shipped.	The "Send-advance-notice" is automatically generated when order is shipped.	The rule is violated if: Send_Advance_Notice = null and Order Date = not null.

*Source: Ronald G. Ross, Business Rule Concepts: Getting to the Point of Knowledge, Second Edition (Business Rule Soloutions, LLC, 2005), p. 25. Used by permission.

Metadata

Metadata are often referred to as "data about the data"—an accurate but not particularly useful definition on its own. Metadata label, describe, or characterize other data and make it easier to retrieve, interpret, or use information. Metadata were discussed in the section Data Categories earlier in this chapter and are included here because they also specify data. Examples include descriptive information about the name given to a data field, definition, lineage, domain values, context, quality, condition, characteristics, constraints, methods of change, and rules.

 **Definition**

Metadata literally means "data about data." Metadata label, describe, or characterize other data and make it easier to retrieve, interpret, or use information.

The two examples that follow help explain metadata:

Example 1—Suppose you want to buy a book from an online bookstore or find a book on the shelf in a brick-and-mortar store, but you can't remember the complete title. You can look it up by entering the author's name or the subject. Books matching the criteria will be listed on the screen. You are able to find the book you are interested in because of metadata.

Example 2—Suppose you go into the grocery store and all the cans on the shelf have an empty label. How do you know what is in them? The name of the product, the picture on the label, the distributor, the number of calories and the nutrition chart—all are metadata that describe the food in the cans. Imagine how difficult it would be to do your shopping without those metadata.[10]

Metadata are important because they

- Provide context for and aid in understanding the meaning of data.
- Facilitate discovery of relevant information.
- Organize electronic resources.
- Facilitate interoperability between systems.
- Facilitate information integration.
- Support archiving and preservation of data and information.

Refer to Table 2.4 for descriptions and examples of technical metadata, business metadata, and audit trail metadata.

Metadata can be found in physical data (contained in software and other media such as hardcopy documentation) and in the knowledge of people (such as employees, vendors, contractors, consultants, or others familiar with the company).

Reference Data

Reference data are sets of values or classification schemas that are referred to by systems, applications, data stores, processes, and reports, as well as by transactional and master records. An example of reference data is a list of valid values (often a code or abbreviation) that can be used in a particular field. Analyzing the list of values appearing in a data field, determining the frequency and validity of those values, and comparing them to associated reference data (usually stored in a separate table) are some of the most common data quality checks.

---

[10]From R. Todd Stephens, Ph.D. Used by permission.

(These checks come under the data quality dimension of Data Integrity Fundamentals. See Table 3.15 in Step 3.2 on page 123 for more information on this dimension.)

 Definition

Reference data are sets of values or classification schemas that are referred to by systems, applications, data stores, processes, and reports, as well as by transactional and master records.

For example, a list of valid values for gender could be M, F, or U, where M = Male, F = Female, U = Unknown.[11] Domain values that are defined and enforced ensure a level of data quality that would not be possible if any value was allowed in a field. The NAICS codes previously discussed are also an example of reference data. For more information on reference data, see the Data Categories section earlier in this chapter.

Data Specifications—Why We Care

You cannot ensure information or data quality unless you also manage and understand the data specifications that are needed to make, build, use, manage, or provide your information. Use data specifications when building new applications (to help ensure data quality at the beginning) and to understand what constitutes data quality for assessment purposes in existing systems. Problems with data specifications are often the cause of poor data quality. In fact, the same techniques and processes presented in this book—most often applied to master and transactional data—should also be applied to reference data and metadata. For example, a metadata repository is just another data store that can be assessed for quality, and metadata have their own information life cycle, which needs to be managed to ensure quality.

Data Governance and Data Stewardship

You live in a typical neighborhood. You know most of the people who live there. Every household maintains its home according to its own preferences—some people mow the lawn once a week; others work in their yards on a daily basis. Now imagine that everyone on the street is packing their bags and leaving their homes.

 Definition

Data governance is the organization and implementation of policies, procedures, structure, roles, and responsibilities that outline and enforce rules of engagement, decision rights, and accountabilities for the effective management of information assets.

– John Ladley, Danette McGilvray, Anne-Marie Smith, Gwen Thomas

---

[11]Some would point out that a list of gender values could also include such codes as M-F, meaning previously male, now female, or FM, meaning previously female, now male—with these values needing some type of associated date field for when the new gender took effect. In a medical setting this is critical information, but for the sake of simplicity and explanation only three codes have been included in the example. Still, this illustrates the fact that the values need to be discussed and agreed on, and must meet the needs of those using them.

All the occupants of all the houses are moving in together!

Each household brings its own ways of living, preferences, and attitudes. We can immediately see the potential for conflict. Certainly a different level of coordination and cooperation is required to live together productively and peacefully in the same house than was needed to live as neighbors in separate dwellings.

Any time your company integrates information, such as in an Enterprise Resource Planning (ERP) application or a data warehouse, it is as though all of the source systems—with their associated people, business processes, and data—are packing up and moving in together. Companies are living in a world that is much more integrated than it was in the past.

How are decisions to be made in this integrated world? In my house example, each family has its own room in one large home. Occupants of a particular room have the right to put down new flooring and decorate the way they want. However, none of them can change the plumbing or redecorate the living room (a common area for all) without the agreement of the others who live in the building. In some cases, the occupants can bestow authority on someone to make the plumbing and common-area decisions. They trust that person to make decisions for the benefit of everyone who lives in the building, and they expect to be informed of changes and to be able to raise any issues that need attention. There need to be roles, responsibilities, rules, and processes in place for managing the house. In other words, governance is required.

Data governance has been getting much attention lately. So has data stewardship. But what is governance? What is stewardship? And

what do they have to do with data quality? It is outside the scope of this book to outline "how to do data governance." But its importance to data quality requires at least a short discussion.

Data Governance versus Data Stewardship

Data governance ensures that the appropriate people representing business processes, data, and technology are involved in the decisions that affect them. Data governance provides venues for interaction and communication paths to

- Ensure appropriate representation.
- Make decisions.
- Identify and resolve issues.
- Escalate issues when necessary.
- Implement changes.
- Communicate actions.

 **Definition**

Data stewardship is an approach to data governance that formalizes accountability for managing information resources on behalf of others and for the best interests of the organization.

As noted in the previous box, data stewardship is an approach to data governance that formalizes accountability for managing information resources. I promote governance and the idea of stewardship as it relates to data and information, but I do not promote the use of "ownership." Why?

A *steward* is someone who manages something on behalf of someone else. *Owner* has two different meanings according to the *Encarta Dictionary: English (North America)*: (1) *possession*, emphasizing that somebody or something belongs to a particular person or thing and not to somebody or something else; (2) *responsibility for*, acknowledging full personal responsibility for something. Too often people act as if they "own" the data as in the first definition, which is counterproductive to the well-being of the organization. I do promote the use of "ownership" when it comes to business processes. Why?

Because it is usually used as in the second definition (i.e., to acknowledge full personal responsibility for something), and those with the authority do "own" the processes in that sense. But even though the business may "own" a process, anyone who touches the data in carrying out that process is their "steward." That is, they have to manage the data not just to meet their own immediate needs but on behalf of others in the company who also use the data or information.

So stewardship is a concept and a way of acting. A *data steward*, on the other hand, can be the name of a particular role. There is no agreed-on set of responsibilities for a data steward and there can be different types of data stewards. Some assign that title to someone who is a subject matter expert or who fixes data at the application level. Others consider the data steward to be the person who is responsible for data names, definitions, and standards. Still others assign it a strategic role with responsibility for a data subject area across business processes and applications.

As mentioned before, it is outside the scope of this book to discuss "how to implement" data governance and stewardship. (Governance and stewardship are included in the FIQ as part of "Responsibility"—the second *R* in the RRISCC broad-impact components.

See the section on the FIQ earlier in this chapter.) Therefore, what is important is that you do implement some level of data governance and stewardship; whatever roles, responsibilities, and titles are used, ensure they are meaningful and agreed on by those within the organization.

Data Governance and Data Quality

Data quality is often seen as a one-time project—"Fix the data and we're done." Even if there is awareness that data quality requires ongoing attention, the lack of formal accountability for the data is a critical component that causes many data quality initiatives to dwindle over time or fail completely. It is also the reason that many application development projects, once in production, cannot uphold the quality of data required by the business. Data governance is the missing link that provides the structure and process for making decisions about a company's data. It ensures that the appropriate people are engaged to manage information throughout its life cycle. Implementing data governance and stewardship is important for the sustainability of data quality.

The Information and Data Quality Improvement Cycle

The Information and Data Quality Improvement Cycle, shown in Figure 2.12, provides an easy way to discuss and start thinking about improvement through three high-level steps: assessment, awareness, and action. It is a modification of the familiar "Plan-Do-Check-Act" approach,[12] which allows organizations to identify and act on those issues or opportunities with the most impact on the business. The improvement cycle provides a structured approach to improvement that can be used by an individual or a team.

Assessment (looking at your actual environment and data and comparing them to requirements and expectations)

> *is key to*

Awareness (understanding the true state of your data and information, impact on the business, and root causes)

> *which leads to*

Action (prevention of future information and data quality problems in addition to correction of current data errors)

> *which is verified by*

Periodic assessments. And so the cycle continues.

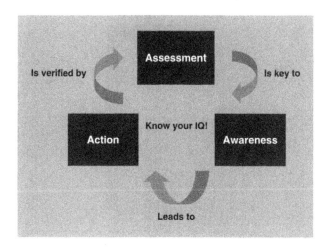

Figure 2.12 • The Information and Data Quality Improvement Cycle.

Source: Copyright © 2005–2008 Danette McGilvray, Granite Falls Consulting, Inc.

An Example of the Information and Data Quality Improvement Cycle

One company profiled the data that supported order management. Everyone "knew" there should be no open sales orders older than six months, but the data quality assessment showed open sales orders dating back several years—some older than the company itself. Financial exposure was potentially in the millions of dollars.

Because of that assessment, an investigation was launched. Some of the orders older than the company were explained as leftovers from the parent company, which the current company had left. It was found that report parameters in the Business Center were not set to catch old orders—there was no visibility to open orders older than six months, and reports used by customer service reps in the Business Center and by management contained conflicting information. In addition, they found root causes of the old orders—for example, various order management applications "talked" to each other, and during this "conversation" of sending data back and forth, flags could be missed, data could become corrupted, and so forth.

Based on this awareness, the action taken included manually closing orders in the order management system and moving to the order management history database, correcting report parameters to ensure visibility of open orders older than six months, and consolidating reports to make certain that the same information was sent to both managers and customer service reps.

---

[12]Plan-Do-Check-Act, or PDCA, is a basic technique for improving processes that was created by Walter Shewhart. It is also known as the Shewhart cycle or the Deming cycle (because W. Edwards Deming adopted it and introduced it in Japan).

So why was tracking older open sales orders so important? There was a financial impact to the company because the cost of manufacturing and selling the product or service had been incurred but the company had not been paid. And all this important work and resulting value to the company was triggered from a simple data quality assessment!

The Information and Data Quality Improvement Cycle and The Ten Steps Process

The Information and Data Quality Improvement Cycle is the basis for The Ten Steps process (see Figure 2.13). The Ten Steps process (for which an overview is provided in the next section) describes a set of methods for the continuous assessment, maintenance, and improvement of critical business information. Included are processes for

- Describing and analyzing the information environment.
- Assessing data quality.
- Determining the business impact of poor data quality.
- Identifying the root causes of data quality problems and their affect on the business.
- Correcting and preventing data defects through needed modifications to processes, people and organizational issues, and technology.

The Ten Steps are a concrete articulation of the Information and Data Quality Improvement Cycle. Like the cycle, they are iterative—when one improvement cycle is completed, start again to expand on the results.[13] (See the next figure for an illustration of this relationship.)

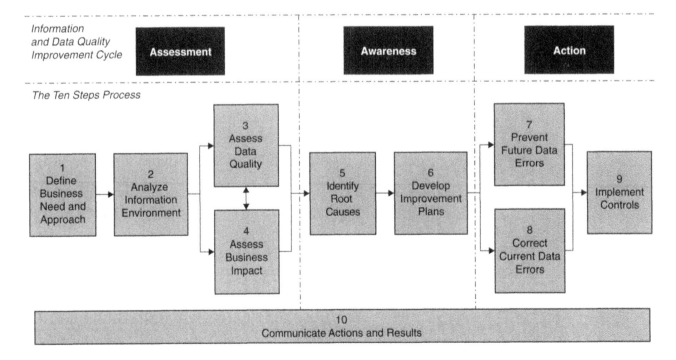

Figure 2.13 • The Information and Data Quality Improvement Cycle and The Ten Steps process.

[13]For those familiar with Six Sigma, The Ten Steps can also be understood using DMAIC. See the section The Ten Steps and Six Sigma in Chapter 5.

The Ten Steps Process

The Ten Steps process is an approach for assessing, improving, and creating information and data quality. The steps are illustrated in Figure 2.14 and described in the sidebar on the next page. Detailed processes and techniques for each of the steps can be found in Chapter 3.

The Ten Steps are concrete instructions for planning and implementing information and data quality improvement projects. Each step contains general principles, directions, advice, and examples. Steps 1 to 4 contain the essential techniques for defining the business need and assessing the current state of the data and information, as well as for communicating the importance of the current state to stakeholders. *Step 5—Identify Root Causes* is where the action begins—addressing the root cause and correcting errors, leading to improvement in both the data and the processes that produce them.

While the Ten Steps are represented by a linear progression from step to step, the process of information and data improvement is iterative—project teams can return to previous steps to enrich their work, they can choose those steps that meet the business need, and they can repeat the entire Ten Steps to support continuous information improvement. Communication is represented as a bar that runs under all of the steps and is critical for success and ongoing support throughout any project.

The Ten Steps were designed as a pick-and-choose approach where the applicable steps, activities, and techniques from the methodology can be applied at the appropriate level of detail to meet your needs.

For Information Quality–Focused Projects—such as a data quality assessment of a particular database and/or assessment of the business impact of an issue resulting from

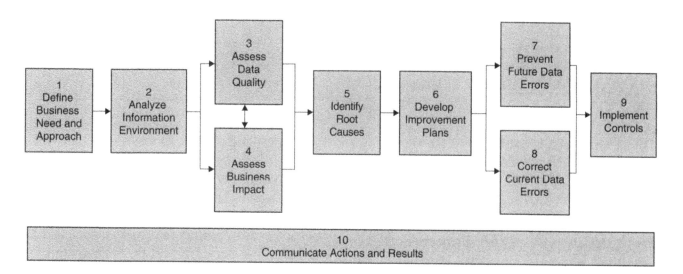

Figure 2.14 • The Ten Steps process.

Source: Copyright © 2005–2008 Danette McGilvray, Granite Falls Consulting, Inc.

The Ten Steps Process—Assessing, Improving, and Creating Information and Data Quality

1. **Define Business Need and Approach**— Define and agree on the issue, the opportunity, or the goal to guide all work done throughout the project. Refer to this step throughout the other steps in order to keep the goal at the forefront of all activities.

2. **Analyze Information Environment**—Gather, compile, and analyze information about the current situation and the information environment. Document and verify the information life cycle, which provides a basis for future steps, ensures that relevant data are being assessed, and helps discover root causes. Design the data capture and assessment plan.

3. **Assess Data Quality**—Evaluate data quality for the data quality dimensions applicable to the issue. The assessment results provide a basis for future steps, such as identifying root causes and needed improvements and data corrections.

4. **Assess Business Impact**—Using a variety of techniques, determine the impact of poor-quality data on the business. This step provides input to establish the business case for improvement, to gain support for information quality, and to determine appropriate investments in your information resource.

5. **Identify Root Causes**—Identify and prioritize the true causes of the data quality problems and develop specific recommendations for addressing them.

6. **Develop Improvement Plans**—Finalize specific recommendations for action. Develop and execute improvement plans based on recommendations.

7. **Prevent Future Data Errors**—Implement solutions that address the root causes of the data quality problems.

8. **Correct Current Data Errors**—Implement steps to make appropriate data corrections.

9. **Implement Controls**—Monitor and verify the improvements that were implemented. Maintain improved results by standardizing, documenting, and continuously monitoring successful improvements.

10. **Communicate Actions and Results**— Document and communicate the results of quality tests, improvements made, and results of those improvements. Communication is so important that it is part of every step.

---

poor data quality. For the most sustained results, the goal should be to identify root causes and implement improvements. Your project may be looking at internally and/or externally acquired data.

For Integration into Other Projects and Methodologies—for example, any ERP migration, data warehouse, or other application development project will yield better results if data quality is addressed early in the project and built into the technology, processes, and roles/responsibilities that will be part of the system once in production. Steps within the methodology can also form a foundation to create your own improvement methodology, to integrate data quality activities into your company's project life cycle, or to develop a standard process for managing externally acquired data.

For Use in Your Daily Work—where you are responsible for managing data quality or the work you do impacts data quality.

Best Practices and Guidelines

While the process flow for The Ten Steps shows a natural progression from step to step, realize that **successfully applying the methodology takes an iterative approach**. For example, project teams who are new to the quality improvement process often discover that the root causes of their issues found in *Step 5—Identify Root Causes* result in problems that are much more widespread than they had originally believed. Suddenly the *scope* of the problem broadens, and the original data quality dimension assessments seem inadequate. In this case, they can return to *Step 3—Assess Data Quality* and redo the assessment with a larger data set or choose another dimension to assess. Likewise, if the scope has broadened, they may have more information to use in a business impact technique (*Step 4—Assess Business Impact*) so that they can present the business issue and solicit more resource allocation.

The Ten Steps themselves are iterative—if a project team has made use of the applicable steps in one project, they can identify another business issue and start the improvement process again. Information quality improvement takes rework and rework—it requires a true continuous-improvement mindset to institute long-term change.

Another common scenario: It is not unusual for one project team to assess data quality and business impact, identify root causes, and develop specific recommendations for improvement. Yet it is a different team who can actually effect change and implement the improvements. A different project may be implemented that focuses just on the correction and prevention of data errors. Yet another team may be focused on implementing controls such as metrics and scorecards based on what was learned from the first team's work.

The following are additional guidelines for best results when applying The Ten Steps process.

Use This Book—This guideline is so important that it is mentioned first. While you may not read the book cover to cover or apply it all at once, understand what is included so you can reference it when needed. Expect to cross-reference the various sections regularly and use the concepts when applying the Ten Steps. Become familiar with the Framework for Information Quality and the Information Life Cycle. Reference the sections on data quality dimensions, business impact techniques, and other key concepts in this chapter, and other tools and techniques in Chapter 5, as they are integral parts of the methodology.

Project Management—Executing The Ten Steps process successfully requires use of sound project management practices. A project is defined as any use of the methodology to address a defined business issue related to information—whether by a single person or a team, as a standalone data quality improvement project, or as data quality tasks integrated into another project or methodology (e.g., as a data migration project using a third-party methodology). Even if you are an individual, you can apply good project management practices in a much more abbreviated fashion than a project manager and team would need to.

Good Judgment and Your Knowledge—The Ten Steps process is not designed as a cookbook approach with exact directions that must be applied the same way each time in order to ensure success. Its best use requires good judgment, knowledge of your business, and creativity.

Pick and Choose—The Ten Steps process is designed to be flexible. Take a pick-and-choose approach to its use and execute only those steps applicable to your project. While you should *thoughtfully consider* each of the Ten Steps, use your judgment to choose which of the steps and activities apply to *your* situation.

Level of Detail—The level of detail required for each step will vary depending on the needs of the business. Look to the business issue or opportunity to determine what is relevant and focus there. Start at a high level and work to lower levels of detail only if useful. Use the following questions to help guide your decisions about the appropriate level of detail: (1) Will the detail have a significant and demonstrable bearing on the business issue? (2) Will the detail provide evidence to prove or disprove a hypothesis about the quality or business impact of the data?

Apply Appropriately—Most of the steps can be used in some way if the project is focused on data quality improvement (assuming you stay at the appropriate level of detail). Activities from the various steps can be used in conjunction with other projects, such as integrating data in a data warehouse or migrating data to an ERP. This allows appropriate integration of data quality tasks into existing project plans or other methodologies. Many activities can also be used by an individual responsible for data quality.

Iterative Approach—As additional information is uncovered throughout the process, earlier assumptions may need to be revisited and revised. For example, it may be found that more detail is required from a previous step. Return to those activities to gather the necessary information.

Scalability—The Ten Steps process can be used for everything from a one-person, few-week project to a several-month project with a multiperson team. The issue to be addressed, the steps chosen, and the level of detail needed greatly affect the length of time and the resources required. For example, a specific step could take one person two hours to complete while the same step used in a different project could take a project team two weeks.

Reuse (80/20 Rule)—Many times the process requires information already available within your company. It may be formally documented or simply known by those who work there. Supplement existing materials with original research only as needed. For example, expect that 80 percent of what is asked for in *Step 2—Analyze the Information Environment* already exists somewhere. The value of this step is in bringing together existing knowledge in such a way that you can understand it better than you did before and make better decisions because of it. Also, *ensure that your discoveries, documentation, or updates are made available for reuse by other projects and teams.*

Use Examples as a Starting Point—Be aware that the actual output of the steps may take a different form than the examples shown. For instance, the Sample Output and Templates in *Step 2.4—Understand Relevant Processes* show two different matrices as a way of relating the processes to the data. However, the output of the step is not a matrix; it is knowledge about the processes and related data, how they interact, and how that can impact data quality. Your output may take the physical form of a matrix, a diagram, or a textual explanation. The format used should enhance understanding, in this case, of the relationship and impact of the processes and data. *It is the learning that comes out of completing the steps that is important. This applies to all steps.*

Flexibility—Successful projects require the ability to deal with continuous change and to remain open to input from many stakeholders (both within and outside the project team.)

Focus on Processes—Focus on why the problems exist, not on who is making them. "Blame the process, not the people."

Practice Makes Perfect—As with anything new, as you gain experience with the methodology (both concepts and process steps), subsequent uses of it will be easier and faster.

Tool Independent—The Ten Steps process does not require any particular vendor tool. However, there are tools on the market that can make your data quality job easier. For example, there are tools available to help with profiling, matching, parsing, standardization, enhancement, and cleansing of your data. Applying The Ten Steps process can help you more effectively make use of these tools.

Improvement Activities—Some of the improvement activities (root cause, prevention, and clean-up) can be implemented within the timeline and scope of your project. Others may generate additional activities or even separate projects.

Analyze and Document—Throughout the project be sure to capture in a central area the results of your analysis, suspected causes of issues you are finding, and suspected impact on the business. As you go through the project, you will learn more to prove or disprove your early assumptions.

Broad Data Management Perspective—Documenting your plans and results is an excellent way to enable you to retrace your steps and learn more about what worked during your improvement project. However, many information and data quality improvement projects happen in concert with company-wide improvements that may also involve change-management documentation. Keep informed by contacting other project leaders so that you can produce and share documentation with each other that you can all use to inform your projects.

Chapter 3

The Ten Steps Process

I have been impressed with the urgency of doing.
Knowledge is not enough; we must apply.
Being willing is not enough; we must do.

– Leonardo da Vinci

In This Chapter

Introduction	64
Step 1—Define Business Need and Approach	66
Step 2—Analyze Information Environment	76
Step 3—Assess Data Quality	108
Step 4—Assess Business Impact	163
Step 5—Identify Root Causes	198
Step 6—Develop Improvement Plans	208
Step 7—Prevent Future Data Errors	213
Step 8—Correct Current Data Errors	218
Step 9—Implement Controls	222
Step 10—Communicate Actions and Results	227
The Ten Steps Process Summary	233

Introduction

Remember the map example at the beginning of Chapter 2? Maps come in different levels of detail and you will use those different levels depending on your needs at a particular moment. Suppose you are driving across the country. You might start with a high-level map of the country in which you are traveling (we will use the United States for our example here). You get an idea of the layout of the country, the number of states you will travel through, and the location of the cities in the various states, and you outline a plan to drive from your current location to your final destination.

Alternatively, you may decide that with the amount of time you have for the trip driving is not the best way to get to your location, so you book an airplane flight for the first leg of the journey. Once you arrive at your destination city, the U.S. and state maps do not help you get from the airport to your hotel. A different level of detail is needed, so you look at a street-level map.

All along the way, there are a number of approaches to get to your goal. You could plan the complete trip yourself, using maps and travel books to provide necessary information. You could ask friends and family who have taken similar trips in the past for suggestions. Or you could use a travel agent to plan the complete trip or just book the transportation. Once you reach your city, you could hire a tour guide for a specific activity. You might use GPS or an online map tool to provide step-by-step driving instructions.

Think of The Ten Steps as your map (Figure 3.1). Apply them to meet your needs—with different combinations of steps and high-level or detailed instructions depending on your requirements at the time. The instructions, techniques, examples, and templates in the steps are meant to provide enough direction so you can understand your options. It is up to you to decide what is relevant and appropriate to your situation.

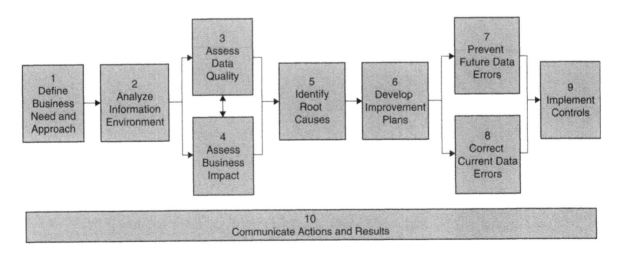

Figure 3.1 • The Ten Steps process.

Source: Copyright © 2005–2008 Danette McGilvray, Granite Falls Consulting, Inc.

The Ten Steps Conventions

As you know The Ten Steps process was introduced in Chapter 2. This chapter provides detailed instructions and examples for each of those steps. The Ten Steps conventions are described here:

You Are Here Graph—Each step (1–10) is introduced by the graph of The Ten Step process and an indication of where you are in it.

Step Summary Table—This table describes (for that step) the objective, purpose, inputs, tools and techniques, outputs, and checkpoint. See Table 3.1 for further detail.

Business Benefit and Context—This section contains background helpful for understanding the step and benefits from completing the step.

Approach—This section contains the step-by-step instructions for completing the step.

Sample Output and Templates—This section contains examples of forms and tables that projects can use to structure their own outputs.

   Note that the first five steps of The Ten Steps also contain substeps and a further detailed process flow. The substeps are also presented according to the format of Business Benefit and Context, Approach, and Sample Output and Templates.

The Step Summary Table

The steps' summary in Table 3.1 provides a quick reference to the main objectives, inputs, outputs, and checkpoints for each of the Ten Steps.

Table 3.1 • Step Summary Table Explained

< Step Name and Number >	
OBJECTIVE	**What am I trying to achieve?** Goal or intended results
PURPOSE	**Why should I do it?** Why the activity is important
INPUTS	**What do I need to perform the step?** Information needed to execute the step; inputs from other steps
TECHNIQUES AND TOOLS	**What will help me complete the process?** Techniques, tools, and practices to support or facilitate the process
OUTPUTS	**What is produced as a result of this step?** Results of the step (most steps contain examples or templates)
CHECKPOINT	**How can I tell if I'm finished or ready to move to the next step?** Guidelines to determine completeness of the step and readiness to continue to the next step

Step 1   Define Business Need and Approach

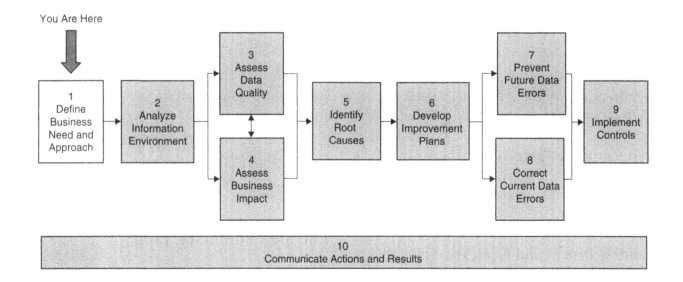

You Are Here

Introduction

The importance of this step cannot be over-stated. Business goals and strategies should drive all actions and decisions. Information-related projects should always start with the question, "Why is this important to the business?" *Anything* done with information should support the business in meeting its goals, and this step ensures that you are working on situations of importance to the business.

You may be focusing on issues (situations that are suboptimal) or opportunities (something new to be used to your advantage). This step shows how to implement the first section in the Framework for Information Quality—Business Goals/Strategy/Issues/Opportunities. (See the Framework for Information Quality section in Chapter 2.)

Businesses embarking on information and data quality improvement projects are often already aware of the issues affecting them most urgently. *Step 1.1—Prioritize the Business Issue* builds on that awareness and prioritizes the business issues or opportunities where data quality is suspected to be a major component. This is also where the information environment is described at a high level. The information environment comprises the data, processes, people/organizations, and technology associated with the issues to be addressed. *Step 1.2—Plan the Project* initiates the project to deal with the issues chosen.

Whether you are embarking on a data quality project with a team, focusing as an individual contributor on one data quality issue for which you are responsible, or integrating data quality activities into another project or methodology, this step is critical. Many a project has failed because of misunderstanding between those involved (sponsors, management, teams, business, IT, etc.). Don't let lack of clarity regarding what will be accomplished and why keep your project from succeeding.

Effective planning is essential to the successful execution of any project, and defining the business need and approach provides the necessary focus for your project activities (see Table 3.2). I'm a big believer in taking enough planning time to ensure that you are looking at those issues or opportunities worth investing in and in good project management planning.

Kimberly Wiefling, in *Scrappy Project Management™: The 12 Predictable and Avoidable Pitfalls Every Project Faces*, puts it well when she says, "Just enough planning to optimize results. Not a drop more! . . . But not a drop less either."

Table 3.2 • Step 1—Define Business Need and Approach

OBJECTIVE	• Prioritize and finalize the issues that are the focus of the project • Describe the high-level information environment—data, processes, people/organizations, and technology associated with the business situation • Plan and initiate the project using good project management practices
PURPOSE	• Ensure that the project has value to the business • Clarify the project focus and agree on expected results • Provide the initial high-level snapshot of the information environment • Establish the project and the approach for resolving issues
INPUTS	• Business issues and opportunities where quality of data/information is a component • Known or suspected data quality problems • Business needs, goals, strategies, issues, and opportunities (any knowledge to help describe the current information environment, such as organization charts, application architecture, data models)
TOOLS AND TECHNIQUES	• Interviews and research • Project management practices • Organization charts • Benefit versus Cost Matrix (see *Step 4.4—Benefit versus Cost Matrix*) • Any results from applicable strategic planning processes • Any prioritization technique that works for you • Communication plan, RACI, 30-3-30-3 of Selling Data Quality (see *Step 10—Communicate Actions and Results*)

OUTPUTS	• Clear agreement and documentation of the business issue to be addressed and the relationship to data quality
	• A description of the high-level data, processes, people, and technology related to issues
	• An appropriate project plan:
	  – New project plan, including project charter, context diagram, work breakdown structure, timeline, resource estimates (with a team or as an individual), OR
	  – Existing project plan with applicable data quality tasks integrated
	• An initial communication plan

CHECKPOINT	• Are the business issues and project objectives clearly defined, understood, and supported by management, sponsors, stakeholders, and the project team? • Are the high-level processes, data, people/organizations, and technology associated with the issue understood and documented? • Has an appropriate project plan been created, along with applicable documents such as project charter, context diagram, timeline, and work breakdown structure (e.g., task list, assigned resources, dependencies)? • Is sponsor supportive of project and have appropriate resources been committed? • If working with a team, has project been properly initiated (e.g., a project kickoff)? • Has an initial communication plan been created? • Has other communication needed at this time been completed?

Step 1.1 Prioritize the Business Issue

Business Benefit and Context

Your project should only spend time on those issues where you expect to get results worth the time and money spent. In many cases there will be several issues or opportunities from which you will have to choose. You need to prioritize where to focus your efforts. There are multiple ways to prioritize issues, and this step mentions just one. If you have a favorite technique for prioritization, use it here. If you are already very clear about the business issues or opportunities to address, you only need to document and confirm agreement on the data quality issues your project will address before devising your project plan.

Who should be involved in this step? A draft list of the issues should be created by the responsible management and project manager. (Remember, if you are working on a data quality issue yourself you are the project manager and the project team in one.) Ensure that appropriate stakeholders are engaged.

A stakeholder is a person or group with a direct interest, involvement, or investment in the information quality work. Stakeholders are those "actively involved in the project or those whose interests may be positively or negatively affected by execution or completion of the project and its deliverables."[1] For example, the person responsible for manufacturing processes would be a stakeholder for any data quality improvements that impact the supply chain. Stakeholders may also exert influence over the project and its deliverables. Examples of stakeholders include customers, project sponsors, the public, or organizations whose personnel are most directly involved in doing the work of the project.

The list of stakeholders may be long or short depending on the expected scope of the project. The point is that stakeholders must agree on the business issue that will be addressed by the data quality project.

Approach

1. List the specific issues or problems.
Focus on those data quality issues deemed critical—based on what you know at this time.

Consider issues or opportunities in the following areas:

Lost revenue and missed opportunities—where revenue could increase if the data quality issue were addressed—for example, increasing the products or services purchased because the customer information was correct and therefore more customers were able to be contacted. Put another way, the customer did not get the chance or choice of doing business with your company because they were never contacted as a result of incorrect address, phone, or email data.

Lost business—where your company once had a customer or vendor, but they chose not to do business with you because of some

---

[1]From *Combined Standards Glossary,* Project Management Institute, Inc. (Third Edition, 2007). Copyright and all rights reserved. Material from this publication has been reproduced with the permission of PMI.

type of problem where data quality was a contributing factor. For example, the inability to ship products correctly may influence the customer to work with another company. The inability to pay invoices in a timely manner may influence the vendor to refuse to provide parts, materials, or supplies to your company.

Unnecessary or excessive costs—where the company incurs costs due to wasted time and materials from rework, data correction, cost to recover lost business, impact to processes, and so forth. For example, manufacturing stops because materials were not ordered and available in a timely fashion due to incorrect inventory data.

Catastrophe—where poor data quality contributed to disastrous results such as legal repercussions, loss of property, or loss of life.

Increased risk—where data quality issues increase risk to your company. Examples are compliance and security failures due to poor-quality data or exposure to credit risks when purchases by one customer are associated with duplicate customer master records, causing the credit limit for that customer to be exceeded.

Shared processes and shared data—where several business processes share the same information, and quality problems in the data impact all of them; or one key business process central to the organization is affected by the lack of good data quality. For example, supplier (or vendor) master records impact the ability to quickly place an order with your supplier and also impact the timely payment of that supplier's invoices. If your company only interfaces with its customer via the website, then the quality of information presented on the website is of critical importance.

2. Indicate the basis of each issue.

Based on what you know now, indicate if the basis of each issue is data, processes, people/organizations, and/or technology. Brainstorm and capture your ideas about importance and precedence. Use the Issue Capture Worksheet (Template 3.1) in the Sample Output and Templates section at the end of this step.

3. Discuss and prioritize the issues.

Choose the issues in which you suspect data quality to be a large component and contributing factor. Use your favorite technique for prioritizing, or you may want to use *Step 4.4— Benefit versus Cost Matrix* to determine which issue should be the focus of your project. Invite data and process stakeholders to contribute their concerns and perspectives.

4. Identify the associated data, processes, people/organizations, and technology associated with the issue(s) chosen.

Answer the following questions:

- Which business processes are impacted?
- Who are the people or organizations involved?
- Which data subject areas are impacted?
- Where do the data reside (i.e., applications, systems, databases involved)?
- Are there other tools associated with the issue?

Sample Output and Templates

There are many ways to capture and prioritize issues. The Issue Capture Worksheet (Template 3.1) is one simple example of capturing and categorizing business issues at this early stage of the project.

Template 3.1 • Issue Capture Worksheet

No.	Issues	Data	Process	People/Organization	Tools/Technology	Comments
				Basis of the Issue		
1						
2						
3						
4						
5						

Step 1.2   Plan the Project

Business Benefit and Context

Using good project management techniques is essential to the success of any project. The intent of this step is not to teach project management in detail, but to show how to use project management skills as they relate to data quality. If you are new to project management, there are many books, articles, conferences, and websites devoted to this topic. Effective planning is essential to the successful execution of an information improvement project, and defining the business need and approach will provide the necessary focus for the improvement activities.

Approach

1. Identify the steps from The Ten Steps process needed to meet the business need.

Does the sponsor need a high-level assessment to seek further funding/support? Study your environment and business context. Are there specific items that need to be assessed?

2. Create a project charter.

Create a project charter that is "right-sized" for your project. See the Project Charter template (Template 3.2) in the Sample Output and Templates section of this step.

3. Create a high-level context diagram.

Visually describe the high-level data, processes, people/organizations, and technology involved. A picture is really worth a thousand words at this point. A good context diagram is very useful for communicating the scope of the project.

4. Develop a project plan and timeline.

Use The Ten Steps process to plan your project and work breakdown structure. Choose the appropriate steps and techniques for your individual work or for a data quality project. Choose the appropriate steps and techniques if incorporating into another methodology or project, and ensure that the activities are integrated into it.

5. Use other good project management practices.

For example, create a template and process for tracking action items and issues. See the Tracking Issues/Action Items template (Template 3.3) in the Sample Output and Templates section of this step.

6. Create your initial communication plan.

See *Step 10—Communicate Actions and Results.*

7. Document all information gathered in *Step 1—Define Business Need and Approach.*

8. Confirm and ensure
- Management support
- Approval for the project
- Resources committed to the project

9. Kickoff!

Sample Output and Templates

Project Charter

If your company does not have a required template for project charters, use Template 3.2 as a starting point. Discard those sections that do not apply and add sections relevant to your situation. Try to keep the charter to one to two pages. You may need a more detailed project

Template 3.2 • Project Charter

PROJECT NAME	[Insert project name here.]*
Date	[At a minimum, include last update date. Include creation and subsequent revision dates if you need to track revision history.]
Prepared by	
PROJECT RESOURCES	[Include pertinent information such as name, title, department/team.]
Executive Sponsor Project Sponsors Stakeholders Project Manager Project Team Members Extended Team	
PROJECT OVERVIEW	
Project Summary and Background	[Include • Brief description of project goals and purpose • Triggering problem statement or description of situation leading to the project • Business justification or rationale for the project Make this information a brief paragraph (executive summary) that anyone can read and easily understand.]
Benefits	[Include expected benefits from the project.]
PROJECT SCOPE	
Goals and Objectives	1. 2. 3.
Major Deliverables	1. 2. 3.
The Project IS:	[Include (at a high level) • Data: • Processes: • People/Organizations: • Technology:]
The Project IS NOT:	[Include (at a high level) • Data: • Processes: • People/Organizations: • Technology:]
PROJECT CONDITIONS	
Critical Success Factors	[Those things that must be in place for the project to be successful.]
Assumptions, Issues, Dependencies, and Constraints	[Items that can impact the project scope, schedule, timeline, or quality of deliverables.]
Risks	[Items with a chance of negatively impacting the project. For each risk, the likelihood of it occurring and what action will be taken if it does.]
Metrics/Performance Measures and Targets	[What you will track to measure success. These may be developed as the project progresses.]
Timeline	[Summary of the timeline and major milestones.]
Costs	[Estimated costs.]

*The words within the brackets are descriptions of what kind of information should go into your own template.

Template 3.3 • Tracking Issues/Action Items

No.	Description	Owner	Status	Open Date	Due Date	Close Date	Comments/Resolution
1							
2							
3							
4							

charter than the one shown in Template 3.2. If you do, maintain a one- to two-page summary version and update it throughout the project to provide an at-a-glance view that anyone involved with the project should see. Refer to the summary for content when summarizing your project in various communications. Even if you are an individual, spend 30–60 minutes considering these categories for yourself—it will provide a basis for discussion with your manager to ensure that you are both in agreement as to your activities and goals.

Action Items

Use your preferred method for tracking action items throughout the project. The Tracking Issues/Action Items template (Template 3.3) shows one option. This template also works well in a spreadsheet format. Keep one sheet for open action items. As the items are closed, move to a different sheet. That way you can easily see all open items and all closed items in their respective sheets.

Step 1 Summary

Determining your business need and approach sets the foundation for all future data quality activities. All projects require some level of prioritization and planning—whether as a focused data quality project, as an individual contributor implementing ideas yourself to support your own job responsibilities, or if integrating data quality into another project or methodology.

Completing this step at the right level of detail and focusing on what is relevant and appropriate are critical. If you ignore this step or do it poorly, you have already guaranteed failure, no more than partial success, or lots of time and effort focusing on the wrong thing. But if you do it well, you have a springboard for a successful project and the real opportunity to bring value to your organization.

Communicate

Here are a few ideas for communicating at this point in the project:

- If working with a project team, communicate with and get support from IT and business management, sponsors, stakeholders, and team members.
- If integrating data quality activities into another project or methodology, communicate closely with the project manager and ensure that the tasks are integrated into the project plan and known by team members.
- If working on a specific data quality issue yourself, clarify with your manager that you both agree on the focus of your project.
- Use your one- to two-page project charter as input to your communications.
- Create a draft of your communication plan.

Checkpoint

Step 1—Define Business Need and Approach

How can I tell whether I'm ready to move to the next step? Following are guidelines to determine completeness of the step:

✓ Are the business issues and project objectives clearly defined, understood, and supported by management, sponsors, stakeholders, and the project team?

✓ Are the high-level processes, data, people/organizations, and technology associated with the issue understood and documented?

✓ Has an appropriate project plan been created, along with applicable documents such as a project charter, context diagram, timeline, and work breakdown structure (i.e., task list, assigned resources, dependencies)?

✓ Is the sponsor supportive of the project and have the appropriate resources been committed?

✓ If working with a project team, has the project been properly initiated (e.g., a project kickoff)?

✓ Has an initial communication plan been created?

✓ Has other communication needed at this time been completed?

Step 2   Analyze Information Environment

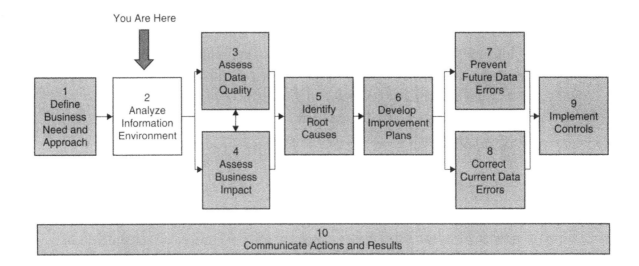

You Are Here

Introduction

This is the step at which you first put on your investigator hat (see figure above and Table 3.3 on page 78). Whether you relate to Sherlock Holmes or *CSI* (Crime Scene Investigation), the common theme is using techniques to solve a mystery. Solving the "Case of Poor Data Quality" requires interpreting clues that can only be uncovered by investigating the information environment.

Read Chapter 2 before starting this step. The concepts combined with the process (Steps 2.1–2.7) will help you understand what can often be a complex environment. When you understand the environment you will do better analysis and make better decisions on where to focus as you continue throughout your project.

The natural inclination is to skip this step and jump right into data quality assessment. However, completing *Step 2—Analyze*

Key Concept

Step 2—Analyze Information Environment provides a foundation of understanding that will be used throughout the project:

- Ensures that you are assessing the relevant data associated with the business issue.
- Provides an understanding of requirements—the specifications against which data quality is compared.
- Provides a context for understanding the results of the data assessments and helps in root causes analysis. The more you understand the context and the environment that affect the data, the better you will understand what you see when you assess the data.
- Provides an understanding of the processes, people/organizations, and technology that affect the quality and/or value of the data.
- Allows you to develop a realistic data capture and assessment plan.

Information Environment ensures that the data extracted and assessed are the data associated with the business issue. Otherwise, it is not unusual to find that data have to be extracted multiple times before getting the data you really need. Analyzing the information environment will usually be more in-depth for a data quality assessment than for a business impact assessment.

For business impact assessments, focus on the Apply phase of the Information Life Cycle POSMAD. Spend enough time on this step to link the business issues so there is confidence that a detailed impact assessment will focus in the right areas.

No matter what type of assessment is next in your project, everything learned in this step will help you interpret your results after completing your assessments, find root causes, and identify people with the knowledge that should be included in the project.

> ⚠️ **Warning**
>
> If you are going to assess data quality in any depth, avoid wasting time and money by resisting the temptation to immediately start extracting and analyzing data. Immediately extracting without understanding the information environment often results in multiple extracts and rework before you get to the actual data relevant to the business issue.
>
> Spend just enough time in Step 2 to understand your information environment so you can ensure that the data being assessed for data quality and the information being assessed for business impact are actually related to the business issue to be resolved.

There are seven substeps within Step 2. The flow of this step is shown in Figure 3.2 on page 80. Use *Step 2—Analyze Information Environment* to

- *Understand relevant requirements*—Not understanding requirements is often a factor in data quality problems.
- *Understand relevant data, processes, people/organizations, and technology*—the four key components in the Framework for Information Quality.
- *Document the Information Life Cycle*—in which you combine the data, processes, people/organizations, and technology to define and understand the life cycle through the POSMAD phases.
- *Develop a realistic data capture and assessment plan*—based on your background investigation.

IMPORTANT!!! Each of the substeps in Step 2 are interrelated. Start with the area in which you have the most information or with which you are most familiar (requirements, data, process, people/organizations, or technology) and work out from there in any order until you have obtained the relevant information at the appropriate level of detail. Define the Information Life Cycle and Design Data Capture and Assessment Plan will most likely be the last steps, as they require understanding from the previous steps.

You will make many choices along the way about what is relevant to the business issues. Table 3.4 (see page 80) discusses three extremely important questions you need to consider throughout the life of your project: What is relevant? What is appropriate? What is the right level of detail? The answers to these questions will impact where you focus your efforts, how much time is spent, and the nature of your results. Make rapid decisions

Table 3.3 • Step 2—Analyze Information Environment

OBJECTIVES	• Gather, compile, and analyze information about current information environment—appropriate level of detail for requirements, data and specifications, processes, people/organizations, and technology associated with the business issue. • Document the life cycle of the information associated with the business issue. • Develop the initial plan for capturing and assessing the data.
PURPOSES	• Ensure that the data to be assessed are the data associated with the business issue. • Provide a foundation for all other steps and activities throughout The Ten Steps process.

INPUTS	Output from *Step 1—Define Business Need and Approach:*
	• Clear agreement and documentation of the business issue to be addressed and the relationship to data quality
	• Description of the high-level data, processes, people, and technology related to the issue
	• Appropriate project plan:
	  – New project plan, including project charter, context diagram, work breakdown structure, timeline, resource estimates (with a team or as an individual), OR
	  – Existing project plan with applicable data quality tasks integrated
	• Initial communication plan
	
	Additional input: existing documentation relevant to business issue and information environment:
	• Known requirements and constraints: business, technology, legal, contractual, industry, internal policies, privacy, security, compliance, regulatory
	• Data specifications
	• Business process documentation
	• Data acquisition/purchase contracts
	• Organization charts
	• Job roles and responsibilities
	• Technology architecture and data models

TOOLS AND TECHNIQUES	• The Framework for Information Quality (Chapter 2) • The Information Life Cycle (Chapter 2) • Information Life Cycle Approaches (Chapter 5) • Capture Data (Chapter 5) • Analyze and Document Results (Chapter 5) • Data Quality Tools (Chapter 5)
OUTPUTS	(*Note:* All output is at the level of detail and applicable to business issues!) Step 2 deliverables: • Information Life Cycle (from *Step 2.6—Define the Information Life Cycle*) • Data capture and assessment plan (from *Step 2.7—Design Data Capture and Assessment Plan*)

- Results of analyzing the information environment—documentation with lessons learned such as potential impact to data quality and/or the business, possible root causes, and initial recommendations at this point

Step 2 example intermediate deliverables:
- Finalized requirements (from *Step 2.1—Understand Relevant Requirements*)
- Detailed data list and data specifications; data mapping if assessing more than one data source; initial source-to-target mappings if migrating data (from *Step 2.2—Understand Relevant Data and Specifications*)
- Data model—with detail needed to understand the structure and relationships of the data so the data can be captured and analyzed correctly (from *Step 2.2—Understand Relevant Data and Specifications*)
- Background on technology (from *Step 2.3—Understand Relevant Technology*)
- Process detail (from *Step 2.4—Understand Relevant Processes*)
- Organizational structures, roles, and responsibilities (from *Step 2.5—Understand Relevant People/Organizations*)
- Applicable interaction matrices (e.g., data-to-process, data-to-job role)

CHECKPOINT
- Has the information environment (the relevant data, processes, people/organizations, and technology) been analyzed at the appropriate level of detail to support project goals?
- Has the Information Life Cycle been documented at the appropriate level of detail?
- Have resources needed for assessments been identified and committed?
- If conducting a data quality assessment:
  - Have requirements, detailed data lists and mappings, and data specifications been finalized?
  - Have any problems with permissions and access to data been identified?
  - Is there a need to purchase any tools?
  - Have training needs been identified?
  - Has the data capture and assessment plan been completed and documented (including the definition of the data population to be captured and the selection criteria)?
- If conducting a business impact assessment:
  - Have the data quality and business issues been understood and linked sufficiently that there is confidence a detailed business impact assessment will focus In the right areas?
  - Are the business processes, people/organizations, and technology related to the Apply phase of the Information Life Cycle clearly understood and documented?
- Have analysis results, lessons learned, and initial root causes been documented?
- Has the communication plan been updated?
- Has communication needed to this point been completed?

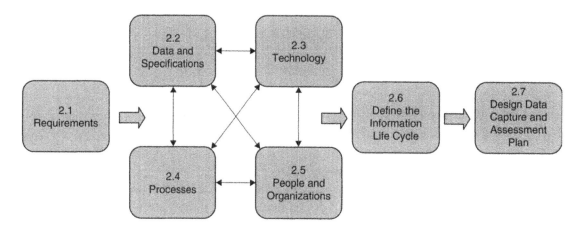

Figure 3.2 • Process flow for *Step 2—Analyze Information Environment.*

Table 3.4 • Learning to Scope

What is relevant? What is appropriate? What is the right level of detail?

Determining what is relevant, what is appropriate, and what is the right level of detail needed to meet your objectives is important throughout The Ten Steps process. Using good judgment regarding these three ideas starts in *Step 2—Analyze the Information Environment.* Use the following information to help:

Relevant—in this context means that what you are looking at is associated with the business issue to be resolved. Focus on that issue.

Human Element—As you explore the business issue, you may find that the problem is broader than you imagined. This can feel overwhelming. Thinking about what is relevant helps you to narrow your focus to the business issue at hand.

Manageable—If the scope is too broad, can you focus on specific parts of an issue and build upon results?

Appropriate—Choosing the applicable steps from The Ten Steps process and understanding

the key components and other factors affecting information quality and the Information Life Cycle at the suitable level of detail.

Level of Detail—The level of detail required for each step will vary depending on the business needs and your project scope. Start at a high level and work to lower levels of detail only if useful.

Questions to Ask:
- Will the detail have a significant and demonstrable bearing on the business issue?
- Will the detail provide evidence to prove or disprove a hypothesis about the quality of the data?

Use your best judgment and move on:

As you proceed throughout the step and the rest of the methodology, if you find that more information is needed, gather more detail at that time. You will be most successful if you implement this step as an iterative process.

based on what you know at the time and move on. If circumstances change or new knowledge comes to light, you can make adjustments from there.

You will uncover many items of interest. On one project team we gave each other permission at any time to ask, "Are we going down a rat hole?" This was the signal to stop and ask ourselves if the level of detail or item of interest was relevant to the business issue.

If yes, we agreed to spend more time. If no, we refocused our efforts on the activities and analysis that kept our eyes on the business issue. This method helped us stay on track and use our time well.

Spend enough time to get the foundational information needed to proceed effectively. Don't skip this step, but don't get too far into detail that may be unnecessary. You can always come back later and get additional detail if needed.

Step 2.1 Understand Relevant Requirements

Business Benefit and Context

Requirements indicate those things necessary for the business to succeed, such as processes, security, or technology. Some requirements may be external—those with which the business is obligated to comply, such as privacy, legal, governmental, regulatory, and industry. Because the data should support compliance with all these requirements, it is important to understand them as soon as possible in the project.

 Key Concept

As Olson notes in *Data Profiling: The Accuracy Dimension:* "You cannot tell if something is wrong unless you can define what being right is."

– Jack E. Olson

Approach

1. Gather requirements.

Ensure that the requirements are relevant to the business issues, associated data, and data specifications necessary for compliance with them. Consider requirements in the following areas: business, technology, legal, contractual, industry, internal policies, privacy, security, compliance, and regulatory. You may need to contact your company's finance, legal, or other departments for help.

Use the Requirements Gathering template (Template 3.4) as a starting point to capture requirements and pertinent information.

Following is a sampling of regulatory and legal requirements that impact data or require

high levels of data quality in order to achieve compliance[2]:

- The National Data Privacy Law
- Federal credit laws
- Federal privacy and information security laws (e.g., HIPAA)
- State laws
- Data laws affecting the Indian Business Process Outsourcing (BPO) industry
- The California Security Breach Notification Law
- The Sarbanes-Oxley Act of 2002
- The Data Quality Act
- The U.S.A. Patriot Act
- The Corporate Information Security Accountability Act of 2003

2. Identify constraints.

Identify any constraints such as security, permissions, or access to data that may impact your project.

3. Analyze the requirements gathered.

Look at the various requirements for the same information, for the same organizations, and so on. These requirements will eventually need to turn into detailed data specifications to ensure that the data support adherence to them.

You will eventually need to detail how to comply with requirements from a data quality point of view. This can take place in *Step 2.2—Understand Relevant Data and Specifications* or in *Step 3—Assess Data Quality*. Also see the section Projects and The Ten Steps in Chapter 4 for suggestions on including data quality requirements gathering as part of the project life cycle.

4. Document results.

In your project documentation, list the requirements and constraints that will affect your project, and make action items to address them. Start tracking analysis results. See the Analyze and Document Results section in Chapter 5 for a template to help you track results.

Sample Output and Templates

Following are explanations of the information to insert into the Requirements Gathering template (Template 3.4):

Requirement—Title and brief description.

Source of Requirement—The person who provided the information along with the specific source such as a particular law or internal policy.

Type of Requirement—Business, technology, legal, contractual, industry, internal policies, privacy, security, compliance, or regulatory. (Other categories may apply to your situation; discuss a meaningful way to categorize them.)

Associated Information—Information that must be in place in order to comply with the requirement OR the information itself that must comply with the requirement (if the requirement specifies the information).

Associated Processes—Processes in place when the information is collected or used. (You may decide to expand to processes that impact the information throughout the POSMAD life cycle at some point.)

Associated Organizations—Organizations, teams, departments, and the like, impacted by the requirement.

Impact If Requirement Not Met—The result if the requirement is not met: legal action, risk of fines, and the like. (Be as specific as possible with what is known at this time. This will drive decisions if trade-offs need to be made based on resources and time, or if there are conflicting requirements.)

Template 3.4 • Requirements Gathering

Requirement	Source of Requirement	Type of Requirement	Associated Information	Associated Processes	Associated Organizations	Impact If Requirement Not Met
Information captured to ship products must be specified formally and changes must be under formal change control.	GMP Regulations*	Compliance	• Customer • Product • Shipment	• Order entry • Returns management • Recall management	• Customer sales • Shipping and logistics	• Patient health • Company reputation • Financial penalties

*Good Manufacturing Practice Regulations are "promulgated by the U.S. Food and Drug Administration under the authority of the Federal Food, Drug, and Cosmetic Act. These regulations, which have the force of law, require that manufacturers, processors, and packagers of drugs, medical devices, some food, and blood take proactive steps to ensure that their products are safe, pure, and effective. This quality approach to manufacturing protects the consumer from purchasing a product which is not effective or even dangerous. Failure of firms to comply with GMP regulations can result in very serious consequences including recall, seizure, fines and jail time." *Source:* GMP Institute. "What Is GMP?" (*http://www.gmp1st.com/gmp.htm*), January 24, 2008.

Step 2.2 Understand Relevant Data and Specifications

Business Benefit and Context

In this step you will identify in detail the data and the related data specifications relevant to the business issue. (See the Data Specifications section in Chapter 2 for more information.) The step will help you ensure that the data you assess for quality or business impact are the same information the business is concerned with. Data and information can be described at a high level by common business terms or by data subject areas or groupings. These subject areas or groupings can be further broken down to the detail of field names.[3]

Figure 3.3 illustrates different levels of data detail. The business terms are usually related to how the business sees and thinks about the information. The most detailed are the actual tables and fields where the data are stored. In between are the data subject areas or groupings. It is critical that the information terms used by the business are linked to the actual data to be assessed.

Best Practice

Use Information Already Available: You may expect that 80 percent of what is asked for in *Step 2—Analyze Information Environment* already exists. The value of this step is in bringing together existing knowledge in such a way that you can understand it better now than you did before.

You may start with the business terms or data subject areas relevant to the business issue. Then move to the detail of where the data are *stored*. Conversely, if you are more familiar with the fields where the data are stored, start with those terms. Trace fields in the database back to the business terms if you start with the database elements. This step is closely related to *Step 2.3—Understand Relevant Technology*; you may want to complete these two steps in parallel.

Approach

1. **Identify the business terms and data subject areas or groupings relevant to the business issue and associated requirements.**
   - Capture the language used by the business through interviews, evaluation of documents, and examination of current system screens.
   - Understand and document the data model, entities, and relationships, with a focus on what is relevant to the business issue and at the appropriate level of detail. A good data modeler is a valuable resource. Find one, get him or her on your project, and make use of his or her expertise!

The data model should be captured at one or both of the first two levels of abstraction as described in Table 2.5 in Chapter 2. Figure 3.4 shows an example of a context model that is useful for providing an overview of the scope of your assessment. In addition, a detailed conceptual model can be useful to show system scope, processes that can and cannot

---

[3] I use the word *field* to indicate an individual attribute, fact, column, or data element.

High Level	Detail	More Detail
Business Term	**Data Subject Area or Groupings**	**Fact, Attribute, Data Element, Column, Field***
Supplier Information	Supplier Company Name	Company Name Division
	Supplier Contact Name	Prefix First Name Middle Name Last Name Suffix
	Mailing Address	Site Name Division Street Address City State/Province Postal Code Country

*Additional distinctions for More Detail may be needed. You may want to give the business term for the fact or attribute along with the actual data element, column, or field name in the physical application.

Figure 3.3 • Levels of detail—data.

be supported because data do or do not exist, and related business rules. At a minimum, you need to know relationships at a very high level. This is yet another case when you will have to use your judgment as to the level of detail needed at this time. If there is no data model, developing one should be one of the first items on your recommendations list.

2. **Identify the systems/applications/ databases where the data are used and the corresponding databases where the data are stored.**

This activity is closely related to *Step 2.3— Understand Relevant Technology.*

3. **Correlate the business terms or data subject areas with the specific fields that store the data in the database.**

See the example in Figure 3.3. The business terms will most likely be associated with how the information is applied; the more detailed terms, with where the data are stored. This is

a key activity to ensure that the data you will be assessing are actually the data the business cares about.

4. **Create a detailed data list for the data of interest.**

See the Detailed Data List template (Template 3.5) in the Sample Output and Templates section of this step. Include all data that you may assess. Even if you actually assess only a subset of the data, it is easier to collect them all at this time. If you already have this information documented in another format, use that. Remember, the goal is to have a clear understanding of the data you plan to assess—not to put it in the exact format shown as an example.

5. **Collect relevant data specifications for each of the fields of interest.**

See the section Data Specifications in Chapter 2 for more detail. Describe the data standards, data models, business rules, metadata and reference data, and other pertinent information

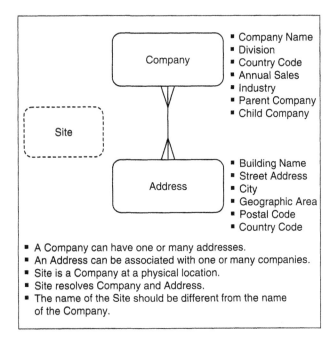

- A Company can have one or many addresses.
- An Address can be associated with one or many companies.
- Site is a Company at a physical location.
- Site resolves Company and Address.
- The name of the Site should be different from the name of the Company.

Figure 3.4 • Context model.

known at this time. See Table 3.5 in the Sample Output and Templates section for examples.

Data specifications can be obtained from the following:

- Relevant requirements gathered in *Step 2.1— Understand Relevant Requirements.* (You may need to create specifications, such as detailed business rules and associated data quality checks, to support those requirements.)
- People knowledgeable about the data: business analysts, data analysts, data modelers, developers, database administrators (DBAs), and the like. Remember subject matter experts and knowledge workers applying the information in the course of their work, especially for business rules.
- Descriptions of the data available in existing data dictionaries, metadata repositories, or other documentation forms
- A relational database directory or catalog for data in a relational system for metadata on the column-level layout of the data
- Other sources that give you the layout that best represents the data according to the most likely extraction method

- A COBOL copybook or a PL/1 INCLUDE file that lays out the data if accessing an IMS or VSAM data source
- Interface definitions to application programs that feed data to the data source
- Structural information within the database management system (For example, in relational systems you can extract primary key, foreign key, and other referential constraint information.)
- Any TRIGGER or STORED PROCEDURE logic embedded within the relational system to find data-filtering and validation rules being enforced
- The program specification block (PSB) in IMS, which gives insight into the hierarchical structure being enforced by IMS

6. Understand and document the relevant data model, entities, and relationships.

Understand the data model, focusing on what is relevant to the business issue at the appropriate level of detail. Use and understand a detailed data model if available. As suggested previously, make a good data modeler a member of your project team.

The data model can show the system's scope, processes that can and cannot be supported because data do or do not exist, and business rules supported by it. You may need to simplify a detailed model when speaking with those in the business. At a minimum, you need to know data relationships at a very high level.

7. If more than one data store is being assessed and compared, create a detailed data list for each one.

Once you have a detailed data list for each of the data stores, map the fields in each data store to the corresponding fields in the others. See the Data Mapping template (Template 3.6, page 89) in the Sample Output and Templates section of this step.

Best Practice

Source-to-Target Mappings: You may be including source-to-target mapping activities in another project (such as a data migration). If so, document what you know about the mappings at this point. You will increase their quality and the speed at which they can be completed if you profile your data. See *Step 3.2—Data Integrity Fundamentals* for techniques to help you assess data for the purpose of mapping. You will confirm or change anything that you suspect about the mappings after you have completed your profiling.

8. Document additional information needed for the assessment.

See the Capture Data section in Chapter 5 for more information. Include what you know at this point for each of the data populations:

- Population to be assessed and associated selection criteria
- Output format needed for the assessment
- Anything you know about the sampling method
- Timing for extracts
- Anything else applicable and known now

All of these will be refined as needed in *Step 2.7—Design Data Capture and Assessment Plan* and finalized just before the data are extracted for the various quality and value assessments in Step 3 and Step 4.

9. Document any potential effects on data quality or business impacts recognized at this time.

For example, do you anticipate any problems with permissions and access to the data you want to assess?

If you haven't already started systematically tracking results, do so now. See the Analyze and Document Results section in Chapter 5 for a template to help you do this. Remember, anything learned in Step 2 is valuable input to your data quality or business impact assessments.

Sample Output and Templates

Use the Detailed Data List template (Template 3.5), to document the data of interest. Use the suggestions in Table 3.5 when collecting relevant data specifications for the data to be assessed.

Template 3.5 • Detailed Data List

Application/system/database:									
Business Term or Data Category	Table	Field Name	Data Type	Field Size/ Length	Description	Mandatory or Optional	Data Domain	Format	Other

Table 3.5 • Collecting Data Specifications

DATA SPECIFICATION	CONSIDERATIONS
DATA STANDARDS	• Naming conventions for table and field names • Data entry guidelines—rules to follow when entering the data (can include accepted abbreviations, casing (upper, lower, mixed), punctuation, etc.) • Standards the company uses or with which they are required to comply (e.g., SIC codes, NAICS codes)
DATA MODELS	• Data models applicable to the data that will be assessed, including identifying primary keys and foreign keys • Cardinality—how many instances of one entity class can be related to an instance of another entity class (zero, one, or many) • Optionality—if an instance of one entity class exists, if it is necessary for there to be an instance of a related entity class • Whether the field is mandatory, optional, or conditional (with conditions documented) as required by the *technology* • Higher-level information architecture plans related to the scope of your project
BUSINESS RULES	• Whether the field is mandatory, optional, or conditional (with conditions documented) as required by the *business* (which may or may not be enforced by the technology). (Data quality issues are often found when the business requires data but the technology does not enforce them.) • Explicit or implicit statements about how and when an instance (a record) or a particular data field should be treated throughout the POSMAD life cycle • Documented business rules and dependencies—conditions that govern business actions and establish data integrity guidelines (e.g., where major state changes can occur and the corresponding data behavior rules that state when a record is obtained/created, maintained/updated, or deleted)
METADATA	• Database/data store • Table names and descriptions • Field names and descriptions • Date type • Field size/length • Description • Indicators of validity (e.g., formats—a specified form, style, or pattern) • If the field is validated by the system and any associated reference tables • If the field is generated by the system
REFERENCE DATA	• Data domain—the set of allowed values • Names of reference tables containing valid values and descriptions • Domain and format guidelines for lists of values

DATA SPECIFICATION	CONSIDERATIONS
REAL-WORLD USAGE	• Data quality issues often found when the technology requires data but the business does not have the information available when the record needs to be created or updated • Common business usage or "real-world" usage of which you are aware. (For example, the system requires a physical address. If the physical address is not known when the record is created, a period is often put in the field. This technically fulfills the system requirement of a value in the field and allows the knowledge worker to complete the record. However, it creates data quality issues for downstream systems needing the address.)
OTHER LEARNINGS	• If it is clear that a particular field should or should not be included in an assessment, document this and the reasons.

Template 3.6 • Data Mapping

	APPLICATION/DATABASE 1			APPLICATION/DATABASE 2			NOTES
BUSINESS TERM	TABLE	FIELD NAME	DESCRIPTION	TABLE	FIELD NAME	DESCRIPTION	(DIFFERENCES, INITIAL TRANSFORMATION RULES, ETC.)

Use the Data Mapping template (Template 3.6) as a starting point if you will be assessing data in more than one application or database or if you are creating source-to-target mappings as part of another project.

Step 2.3 | Understand Relevant Technology

Business Benefit and Context

Much of the information about technology will be discovered in the course of understanding the relevant data and specifications. This step is included to ensure that other technology is considered besides the obvious technology of the database where the data are stored. You may want to consider technology involved throughout the POSMAD life cycle—for example, any networks or messaging technology involved with sharing the data.

📖 **Definition**

Technology can be both high tech, such as databases, and low tech, such as paper copies. Examples are forms, applications, databases, files, programs, code, or media that store, share, or manipulate the data, are involved with the processes, or are used by people and organizations.

There are different levels of detail for technology (see Figure 3.5). If preparing for a data quality assessment, understanding technology related to the data at a table and field level will usually be required. If preparing for a business impact assessment, knowing an application and database may provide enough information to proceed.

This step is closely related to *Step 2.2— Understand Relevant Data and Specifications*. You may want to complete both steps in parallel.

Approach

1. Understand and document the technical environment.

Understand the applications and associated data stores. A data store is a repository for data, such as a relational database, an XML document, a file, or file repository, or a hierarchical database (LDAP, IMS).

For each type of technology understand the name of the software (the common name used by the business and the "legal name" used by the vendor if a third-party package), the version in use, the teams responsible for supporting the technology, the platform, and so forth.

You may need to understand the technology associated with *sharing* the data, such as networks or an enterprise service bus. Look at supporting technology throughout the POSMAD life cycle.

2. Make use of already-existing documentation and knowledge from Information Technology (IT) resources.

Those with a background in IT may be familiar with four data operations known as CRUD (Create, Read, Update, and Delete). CRUD indicates the four basic data operations—that is, how the data are processed in the technology. Many IT resources will relate to the CRUD point of view and you can learn

Figure 3.5 • Levels of detail—technology.

valuable information about the POSMAD life cycle by discussing it in terms with which they are familiar. (It's also a good idea to make them aware of the life cycle.)

If you are focusing on a business impact assessment, see how many programs relate to the Read phase of CRUD. This can also give you an idea of how the information is being applied.

Table 3.6 maps the six phases of the POSMAD life cycle to the four data operations (CRUD). It also illustrates how technology is just one aspect to be considered when understanding the Information Life Cycle.

Understanding how the POSMAD phases map to the data operations will help in tracing potential causes of data quality problems within the application—for example, if an issue is found during the Maintain phase when a knowledge worker is changing a record, a starting point for investigating possible technical causes would be the application's update programs.

Table 3.6 • Mapping the POSMAD Life Cycle to CRUD Data Operations

POSMAD PHASE		CRUD DATA OPERATION
Plan	Prepare for the information resource. Identify objectives, plan information architecture, model data and processes, develop standards, design processes, organizations, etc.	
Obtain	Acquire the data or information. Purchase data, create records.	Create: Produce a record or attribute.
Store and Share	Store data and make it available for use. Hold information about the resource electronically or in hardcopy and make available for use through a distribution method.	
Maintain	Ensure that the resource continues to work properly. Update, change, manipulate, standardize, cleanse, or transform data; match and merge records, etc.	Update: Modify or change existing data.
Apply	Use information and data to accomplish goals. Retrieve data; use information. (Includes all information usage such as completing a transaction, writing a report, making a management decision, running automated processes, etc.)	Read: Access the data.
Dispose	Discard the resource when it is no longer of use. Archive information; delete data or records.	Delete: Remove existing data.

3. Capture any impact to data quality that can be seen through understanding the technology.

For example, data may be moved between data stores using some kind of messaging technology. Mapping or transformation of the data takes place to put the data in alignment with the format required for messaging. Any time you have these changes you increase your chances of negatively impacting data quality.

You may also be looking ahead at the types of data quality assessments you will be conducting. Do you anticipate the need to purchase any tools to help in the assessments? What is the cost and lead time for purchase? What training will be needed? (See the Data Quality Tools section in Chapter 5 for a summary of data quality tools.)

4. Document results.

Capture any insights, observations, potential impacts to the business or to data quality, and initial recommendations as a result of this step. If you haven't already created a form for tracking results, see the section Analyze and Document Results in Chapter 5 for a template to help you get started.

Step 2.4 Understand Relevant Processes

Business Benefit and Context

Focus on the processes that affect the quality of data and information throughout the six phases of the POSMAD life cycle—Plan, Obtain, Store and Share, Apply, and Dispose. (See the Information Life Cycle section in Chapter 2 for more detail.)

A quality assessment may look at some or all phases of the Information Life Cycle since the quality of the data is affected by activity within any of the six phases. A value assessment focuses on the Apply phase—those processes that apply and use the information. Applying the data means *any* use to accomplish business objectives.

For example, the data may be used to complete a transaction or it may be in the form of a report to support decision making. The data may also be used by an automated program such as electronic funds transfer where money is pulled from a customer's account on the date a payment is due. Some may consider this IT use (and it is), but it is also a process on which the business depends.

As with data, technology, and people and organizations, there are different levels of detail for processes. See Figure 3.6 for an example of an account management process. Only go to the level of detail necessary to explore the business need you are addressing.

Approach

1. List and identify processes at the appropriate level of detail.

Refer to the high-level business functions and processes described in *Step 1—Define Business Need and Approach*. Use these as your starting point.

Functions—Major high-level areas of the business organization (Sales, Marketing, Finance, Manufacturing, etc.) or high-level areas of responsibility (lead generation, vendor management, etc.).

Processes—Activities or procedures executed to accomplish business functions (e.g., "External sales rep enters customer data into handheld and synchronizes with central database" is one activity relating to the account management function). Processes can also be activities that trigger a response by the business (e.g., "Customer sends request for more information via company website").

Function versus process is a relative relationship, with function being higher level and process being more detailed. What could be called a function in one project may be a process in another. Determine which level of process detail is most helpful at this time for your project.

Best Practice

To determine relevance ask

- Which processes are affected by the business issue?
- Which processes impact the data relevant to the issue?

Business Function Using Customer Information	Processes	Activities
Account Management	• Data exchange between external sales representative and internal customer support representative (CSR)	• External sales representative enters data into handheld and synchronizes with central database • CSR receives daily report noting required follow-up action • CSR completes follow-up and closes action in central database • External sales representative sees status of action during next synchronization with central database
	• Data exchange between external sales representative and online sales representative	
	• Customer record update via the Internet	
Territory Management		
Quota Assignment		
Customer Interaction Management		
Business Intelligence, Market Analysis, Decision Support		
Data Management		

Figure 3.6 • Levels of detail—processes.

2. Determine the business functions and processes within scope.

List and describe those functions and processes associated with the business issue, the data, the technology, and the people/organizations within the scope of your project. Account for the activities throughout the Information Life Cycle at the level of detail to meet your needs. Research and use existing documentation related to the processes of interest.

3. Relate the relevant data to the relevant business processes and indicate the life cycle phase or data operation taking place.

This can be done by creating a Business Process/Data Interaction Matrix. There are examples of two levels of detail in the Sample Output and Templates section at the end of this step. Table 3.7 shows the interaction between business functions and data groupings. An X indicates where data are applied or used, but no further detail is provided.

Table 3.8 on page 97 uses one of the business functions, account management, from Table 3.7 and indicates which account management processes obtain, maintain, and apply the specific data. (Note that they chose to include only three of the six POSMAD life cycle phases.) You may need both or only one level of detail to understand your data. Using a matrix is just one approach.

4. Analyze and document results.

Look for patterns of **similarities** and **differences** across the rows and down the columns.

For instance, in Table 3.8 there are four processes that obtain the data but only three that maintain them. Since data from sales events only result in adding records, there is a possibility that duplicates could be created. All processes that obtain and maintain data should be similar and training should be instituted to encourage consistency in data entry.

Capture lessons learned, impact to the business, potential impact to data quality and/or value, and initial recommendations learned from analyzing processes.

Key Concept

Be aware that the actual output of the substeps in *Step 2—Analyze Information Environment* may take a different form than in the examples shown. For instance, for *Step 2.4—Understand Relevant Processes,* the output shown is in the form of a matrix. However, the output is not really a matrix; *the output is knowledge* about the processes and related data, how they interact, and how that interaction can impact data quality. Your output may physically take the form of a matrix, a diagram, or a textual explanation. *The format used should enhance understanding.* It is the learning that comes out of completing a step that is important. This applies to all steps.

Sample Output and Templates

In Table 3.7 an X indicates where data are applied or used during the associated business function. The function account management is further described in Table 3.8.

Table 3.7 • High-Level Function/Data Interaction Matrix: Business Functions That Use Customer Information

Data Categories / Business Function	Sales Representative	Name and Address				Customer Profile			
	SR Code	Contact Name	Division	Street Address	Zip Code	Industry Code	Position Level Code	Department/ Function Code	Product Class
Account Management*	X	X	X	X	X	X	X	X	X
Territory Management	X	X	X	X	X				
Quota Assignment	X	X	X	X	X	X			
Market Analysis/ Decision Support	X	X			X	X	X	X	X
Lead Generation	X	X	X		X	X	X	X	X
Deal Management	X	X	X		X	X	X	X	X
Data Management	X	X	X	X	X	X	X	X	X

Note: Account management is described in more detail in Table 3.8.

Table 3.8 • Detailed Process/Data Interaction Matrix: Account Management Processes That Obtain, Maintain, or Apply Customer Information

FUNCTION: ACCOUNT MANAGEMENT   DATA: CUSTOMER DATA

Data Categories / Processes	Sales Rep — SR Code	Name and Address — Contact Name	Division	Street	City	Etc.	Customer Profile — Industry Code	Position Level Code	Department/Function Code	Etc.	System Codes — Change Reason Code	Delete. Reason Code	Etc.
Customer Adds/Updates by Sales Rep	OM	OM	OM	OM	OM	OM	OM	OM	OM		OM	OM	
Changes from Call Center	OM	OM	OM	OM	OM		OM	OM	OM		OM	OM	
Data from Sales Events		O	O	O	O			O	O				
District Territory Assignment	OMA	OMA	OMA	OMA									

O = Obtain or Create; M = Maintain or Update; A = Apply or Use

Note: If there is a need, you may decide to further detail the activities in the interaction matrix. For example, Obtain may be designated as C = manually created through application interface and L = load from external source.

Step 2.5   Understand Relevant People/Organizations

Business Benefit and Context

The purpose of this task is to understand people and organizations as they affect information quality and value. Choose the appropriate level of detail needed to meet your business needs (see Figure 3.7). Understanding organizations at a group/team/department level may be sufficient; knowing roles, titles, and job responsibilities may be necessary. At some point, knowing the individuals who fulfill roles of interest, along with pertinent contact information, may be needed as well. Remember, you can look at a higher level the first time through and go back for more detail later.

Connect Information Quality to Roles

Information roles fit into the POSMAD life cycle, and understanding the connection will lead you to people who can provide input to the project and impact to the data. Table 3.9 describes concepts about information roles that affect information quality. Understanding the concepts can help you look for people within your company who fit the descriptions.

Approach

1. Identify appropriate people and organizations.

Look at organizations, teams, roles, responsibilities, or individuals throughout the Information Life Cycle. Identify the various groups utilizing information relevant to your business issue. Gather and use existing documentation such as organization charts and job descriptions.

2. Relate the data to be assessed to the people and organizations.

An interaction matrix can be used to show how the various roles impact each of the data

High Level	Detail		More Detail	
Organization	Group/Team	Role (may include responsibilities)	Individual	Contact Information
Sales and Marketing, North and South America	Marketing: • Customer Information Management (CIM) • Marketing Communication • Business Intelligence	In CIM: • Data analyst • Database administrator (DBA) • Order coordinator	Data analysts: • Maria Jones • Sanjay Patel	Maria Jones 888-555-1111 mjones@company.com San Francisco, CA Sanjay Patel 888-555-2222 spatel@company.com Austin, TX
	Call center	• Customer service representatives • Service supervisors		
	Field sales	Sales representatives		

Figure 3.7 • Levels of detail for people and organizations.

Table 3.9 • Information Quality Roles and POSMAD

Planner: *Gathers requirements and designs* the processes, applications, databases, and other technology that impact the information throughout its life cycle. ***Titles:*** • Data analyst • Business analyst • Subject matter expert • Data architect • Developer • DBA	**Information Life Cycle Phase: PLAN** Building quality processes into information database designs and information process plans is the best way to prevent data errors. Teach those with planning roles the value of quality data and information and best practices for including quality improvement in design and architecture.
Producer: *Captures, creates, or maintains* data as a part of his/her job function or as part of the process he/she performs. ***Types:*** • *Internal:* originates the facts within the company • *Internal intermediary:* responsible for entering the data into a database or application • *External:* external to the company ***Titles:*** • Customer • Data entry clerk • Almost any individual contributor within the organization has the potential of being a data producer	**Information Life Cycle Phase: OBTAIN and MAINTAIN** ***Source:*** The original source of the information. ***Types:*** • *External to the company* (e.g., a customer is the origin of customer information and order information) • *Internal to the company* (e.g., a product developer is the origin of information about a specific product) • *Nonperson* (e.g., a physical product may be the source of the information about the physical dimensions of the product)
Developer/Technical Support ***Titles:*** • DBA • IT support • Developers • Operations	**Information Life Cycle Phase: STORE and SHARE** ***Technology (IT):*** • Hardware, software, networks, etc. that store and share the data. Affects data by determining how they will be available to knowledge workers—security, synchronization, etc. • The code and queries used for accessing data and maintaining the required data sets to conform to regulations. • Can be low tech such as hardcopy forms and applications in a file cabinet. (In this case there will be other roles to consider in the Store and Share phase.)

(Continued)

Table 3.9 • Information Quality Roles and POSMAD (Continued)

Knowledge Worker: *Requires or uses* data as part of the job function or in performing a process. ***Types:*** • *Internal:* Those within the company applying the data and information. • *External:* A knowledge worker external to the company. ***Titles:*** • Information customer • Information consumer • Employee	**Information Life Cycle Phase: APPLY** ***Multiple Roles:*** Knowledge workers can both obtain and maintain the data. • Buyer procures supplies and materials for the company and creates a vendor master record (role: internal data producer). • Buyer uses that master record to create a purchase order (role: knowledge worker—using the master information to purchase a product—and data producer—creating the purchase order). ***Quality Gap:*** Those who obtain the data can be different from those who use them and may not be aware of the knowledge workers' requirements, which often results in data quality problems.
Records Manager ***Titles:*** • Archivist • Change management specialist • Records management specialist • DBA	**Information Life Cycle Phase: DISPOSE** ***Managing Records:*** Deleting data or records is usually a natural part of the maintenance process. The Dispose phase of the life cycle also includes archiving data. The archiving, storing, and later retrieval of the information can impact the quality of the data.

subject areas or fields. (See the example in Table 3.10 of this step.) The goal is to understand how the people and organizations impact the data or information. Use your best judgment as to the level of detail for both the people/organization axis and the data axis.

3. Analyze and document results.

In Table 3.10, look at the rows across and the columns going down for similarities and differences. For example, one project team knew that many departments could apply or use the data, but they thought that only one could create or update them. Through this exercise the team found that people in other departments actually had the ability to create and update data as well. They could immediately see the impact to data quality: There were no consistent standards for entering data across the departments. Initial recommendations included looking at the organization to determine if it was appropri-

ate to have create and update ability distributed across departments or if it should be centralized in one. At a minimum, all teams creating and updating data should have training.

 Best Practice

Identify Allies and Advocates: If you can identify people who may be suffering from data quality problems, they can be good advocates and sources of information to support many of your project activities.

Document lessons learned, potential impact to data quality and to the business, potential root causes, and initial recommendations in your results tracking sheet.

Table 3.10 • Role/Data Interaction Matrix

Business Role	Contact Name	Site Name	Division	Department	Address	Phone	Title	Profile
Sales Rep	O, M, A	O, M, A	O, M, A	O, M, A	O, M, A	O, M, A	O, M, A	O, M, A
District Manager	O, M, A	O, M, A	O, M, A	O, M, A	O, M, A	A	O, M, A	O, M, A
Customer Service Rep	O, M, A	O, M, A	O, M, A	O, M, A	O, M, A	O, M, A	O, M	
Order Coordinator	O, M, A	O, M, A	O, M, A	O, M, A	O, M, A	O, M, A		
Quote Coordinator	O, M, A	O, M, A	O, M, A	O, M, A	O, M, A	O, M, A	O, M	
Collection Coordinator	A	A	A		A			
Business Center Mailroom		A	A		A			
Online Tech Support	O, M, A	O, M, A	O, M, A	O, M, A	O, M, A	O, M, A	O, M, A	O, M, A
Sales Finance		A	A		A	A		
Data Management Team	O, M, A	O, M, A	O, M, A	O, M, A	O, M, A	O, M, A	O, M, A	O, M, A

O = Obtain or Create; M = Maintain or Update; A = Apply or Use

Step 2.6 Define the Information Life Cycle

Business Benefit and Context

In this activity, you will describe the flow of the Information Life Cycle POSMAD from planning or creation to disposal. The goal is to represent and summarize the life cycle by bringing together what you have learned about the data, processes, people/organizations, and technology. Focus on the POSMAD phases that apply to your business issue—Plan, Obtain, Store and Share, Maintain, Apply, and Dispose.

Understanding the Information Life Cycle is important to

- **A quality assessment**—All of the POSMAD phases affect the quality of the data. Your quality assessment will focus on those phases relevant to your business issues; therefore, you may choose to focus on only a few of the phases during your quality assessment.

- **A business impact assessment**—You will focus on the Apply phase—value is only received when the information is retrieved, applied, and used.

- **An understanding of how the data currently flows**—so you can better determine what to look at for each type of assessment.

The Information Life Cycle can be used to

- Develop new processes. Use the steps, techniques, and concepts to help you create a new life cycle that produces quality data, prevents quality problems, and increases the value of the information by promoting its use.

- Review current processes for improvement. This will show gaps, unexpected complexity, problem areas, redundant activities, and unnecessary loops.

- Further identify and improve key control activities needed. This will show where simplification and standardization may be possible and where to minimize complexity and redundancy (therefore minimizing cost) and maximize the use of the information (therefore maximizing value).

- Determine if associated people/organizations, technology, and data have been accounted for.

See Framework for Information Quality and Information Life Cycle sections in Chapter 2 for more background on the Information Life Cycle.

 Key Concept

The business receives value from information only during the POSMAD life cycle Apply phase—when information is retrieved, applied, and used.

Approach

1. Determine the scope of the Information Life Cycle.

If your project is for an initial assessment, depict the Information Life Cycle *as it is currently*, not as it should be. The life cycle will help show gaps, duplicate work, and inefficiencies that could be affecting the quality of information. You can use the "as is" view of the life cycle at a later time to change or improve it. If you are improving processes or creating new ones, create an Information Life Cycle that will fulfill your data quality and business needs.

Focus on the business issue affected by the information. You may be interested in the Information Life Cycle for a specific data subject area or for information used in a particular business process.

If a process/data matrix was created earlier (see *Step 2.4—Understand Relevant Processes*) look for pieces of information that have similar entries for the various data operations as one life cycle. Each type of information—for example, customer name and address or inquiries—could have a separate life cycle of its own.

2. Determine the appropriate level of detail for the life cycle.

Determine the level of detail needed to understand the process and identify problem areas. Your life cycle may be a simple high-level flowchart showing only sufficient information to understand the general process flow. Or it might be very detailed to show every action and decision point. If you are unsure which level is appropriate, start out at a high level and add detail later or only where it is needed.

3. Determine the approach for illustrating and documenting the life cycle.

Various methods for depicting the life cycle have been used successfully. For example, some process flows use a swim lane approach; others use a table approach. The approach you use will be influenced by the level of detail and the scope of your life cycle. (See the Information Life Cycle Approaches section in Chapter 5 for details, templates, and examples.)

4. Determine the steps in the life cycle and sequence them.

One technique is to write the life cycle steps on sticky notes or large index cards so they can be moved as the life cycle is developed. Place notes on a whiteboard and move them around until you are satisfied with the

sequence and dependencies. This allows you to easily make changes as you go along. (Refer to the outputs from the previous substeps in *Step 2—Analyze Information Environment.*)

5. Document the life cycle.

Record the life cycle in a tool such as Visio or PowerPoint. Your company may have other tools available that will allow reuse. Remember to label and identify your work. Include the title of your process, the date the life cycle was created, any needed definitions or explanation, and so forth.

6. Analyze the life cycle.

The Information Life Cycle will show gaps, unexpected complexity, problem areas, redundancy, and unnecessary loops. It will also show where simplification and standardization may be possible. Note the hand-offs between operations. These are areas where there is potential for error, thus affecting the quality of the data. For example, the life cycle may show that more than one team is maintaining the same data. This is important to know so the business can determine if this is still the best organizational model. If so, the business will want to ensure that both groups receive the same training in data entry, updating, and the like. If the organizational model, roles, or responsibilities should be changed, the life cycle can help the business understand possible alternatives and serve as a high-level checklist to make sure various processes are being covered in the reorganization or realignment of duties.

If reviewed on a periodic basis, the Information Life Cycle will provide a systematic way to detect change. The life cycle can be used to answer the following questions:

- Has the process changed?
- Did any of the tasks change?
- Did the timing change?
- Did the roles change?
- Did any of the people filling the roles change?
- Did the technology change?

- Did the data requirements change?
- What impact do the changes have on the quality of information?

7. **Document the results, lessons learned, possible impact to data quality and the business, and preliminary recommendations.**

Capture what you have learned to this point. (See the Analyze and Document Results section in Chapter 5.) After the quality and/or value assessments have been completed, one of the recommendations may be to return to this step to create and implement a more effective life cycle.

Sample Output and Templates

See the Information Life Cycle Approaches section in Chapter 5 for ways to represent your life cycle.

Step 2.7 Design Data Capture and Assessment Plan

Business Benefit and Context

Based on what you have learned so far in this step, you are now ready to design how you will capture and assess the data. Capturing the data refers to either extracting them (such as to a flat file) or accessing them in some manner (such as via a direct connect to a database).

Approach

1. **If needed, further prioritize the data to be assessed to fit within your project scope, schedule, and resources.**

2. **Finalize the population to be assessed and describe the selection criteria.**

3. **Develop the plan for data capture. Include:**
   - Data access method and tools required (For example, is there a front-end application currently in use that can provide the needed access or files?)
   - Output format (For example, extract to a flat file, copy tables to a test server.)
   - Sampling method
   - Timing (Coordinate extracts across multiple platforms.)
   - People who will be involved with the data extraction and assessment activities

Be sure to refer to the Capture Data section and Table 5.2 in Chapter 5 for additional information to help complete this step.

4. **Develop the sequence for your data assessment.**

5. **Document the plan and ensure that those involved are aware of and agree to their responsibilities.**

Step 2 Summary

Before starting on Step 2, you already knew something about your data, something about your processes, something about your technology, and something about your people and organizations. This step gave you the chance to bring together existing knowledge in such a way that you now better understand all these components and their impact on information quality. You delved into more detail when necessary and uncovered gaps where additional information needed to be gathered. This step gave you the opportunity to see all of this knowledge in new ways, and you have made (and will continue to make) better decisions about information quality because of it.

The main deliverables from *Step 2—Analyze Information Environment* include:

- Data capture and data quality assessment plan
- Results of analyzing the information environment
- Documentation with lessons learned (such as impact to the business, potential impact to data quality, suspected root causes, and initial recommendations discovered to this point)

Additional outputs that will be used during your assessments include

- Detailed data list
- Data specifications (enough detail to understand the structure and relationships of the data so data can be extracted correctly and assessment results can be interpreted)
- Detailed data mapping (if assessing more than one application/database or if source-to-target mappings for migrating data are needed)
- Requirements
- Information roles and their descriptions
- Information Life Cycle (at the level of detail appropriate to your needs)
- Updates to your communication plan

Tracking of results was mentioned at the end of every substep within Step 2. Take the time now to organize your thoughts and document your results if you have not yet done so. (If I mention it enough times you might actually do it!) Documentation gives you the ability to easily recall results. It provides a reminder of things to look out for when conducting your assessments—you will prove or disprove the opinions about the data you have acquired as part of analyzing your information environment. Documenting your observations and theories as they are discovered will save you time when uncovering root causes and developing specific improvement recommendations and actions.

 Communicate

- Have management, business, and stakeholders been appropriately apprised of project progress?
- Are periodic status reports being sent?
- Are all members of the project team aware of progress and of the reasons for the project?

Checkpoint

Step 2—Analyze Information Environment

How can I tell whether I'm ready to move to the next step? Following are guidelines to determine completeness of the step:

✓ Has the information environment (the relevant data, processes, people/organizations, and technology) been analyzed at the appropriate level of detail to support the project goals?
✓ Has the Information Life Cycle been documented at the appropriate level of detail?
✓ Have resources needed for assessments been identified and committed?
✓ If conducting a data quality assessment:
  • Have requirements, detailed data lists and mappings, and data specifications been finalized?
  • Have any problems with permissions and access to data been identified?
  • Is there a need to purchase any tools?
  • Have training needs been identified?
  • Has the data capture and assessment plan been completed and documented (including the definition of the data population to be captured and the selection criteria)?
✓ If conducting a business impact assessment:
  • Have the data quality and business issues been understood and linked sufficiently that there is confidence a detailed business impact assessment will focus in the right areas?
  • Are the business processes, people/organizations, and technology related to the Apply phase of the Information Life Cycle clearly understood and documented?
✓ Have analysis results, lessons learned, and initial root causes been documented?
✓ Has the communication plan been updated?
✓ Has communication needed at this point been completed?

Step 3 Assess Data Quality

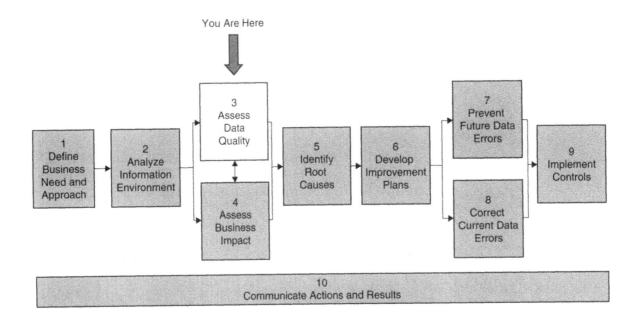

Introduction

You have been introduced to data quality dimensions—aspects or features of information and a way to classify information and data quality needs. Dimensions are used to define, measure, and manage the quality of the data and information. (See the Data Quality Dimensions section in Chapter 2 if you need a reminder.) As noted in Table 3.11, *Step 3—Assess Data Quality* provides one substep with detailed instructions for each of the 12 dimensions of quality listed in Table 3.12 (see page 111). The assessments provide a picture of the actual quality of your data and information.

The most rewarding benefit of the data quality dimension assessment will be concrete evidence of the problems that underlie the business issue you identified in *Step 1—Define Business Need and Approach*. The assessment results

also provide background information needed to investigate root causes, correct data errors, and prevent future data errors.

If by chance you decided to skip Step 2, please reconsider! Every successful project has needed to analyze the information environment in some form or another. Feedback from project teams confirms that analyzing the information environment is essential before quality assessments and is needed to ensure meaningful results. Start at a high level of detail and work down only if needed. It is much more efficient to get at least some background prior to your quality assessment.

Approach to Step 3

The overall approach to Step 3 is straightforward: First, make a conscious decision about which dimensions to assess; second, complete the assessments for the dimensions chosen; and third, synthesize the results from your assessments (if more than one data quality assessment is performed).

Choose the Data Quality Dimensions to Assess
Familiarize yourself with the various data quality dimensions and what is required to complete an assessment for each one. Revisit your project goals and the output from *Step 1—Define Business Need and Approach*. Ensure that the business situation and needs have not changed. If the needs have changed, make a deliberate decision to modify your data quality approach to meet the new needs and ensure that everyone involved is informed and supportive of the modifications.

Prioritize and finalize the appropriate quality tests to be performed. If you are considering several dimensions and need to minimize the scope to meet your timeline, prioritize the tests that will return the most value. Any investment in assessing data quality will yield valuable results, the long-term benefit will only be realized when the root causes of the issues found during the assessment have been addressed.

Assess Quality for the Dimensions Chosen
Become familiar with the details of each quality dimension chosen. Review and finalize the data capture and assessment plan from *Step 2.7— Design Data Capture and Assessment Plan*. You may need to modify the plan based on your current scope, timeline, and resources. You will need a data capture and assessment plan for each of the quality dimensions chosen. Use the detailed instructions for each dimension to help you complete its quality assessment.

Document the lessons learned, possible impact to the business, root causes, and preliminary recommendations from each quality

assessment. (See the Analyze and Document Results section in Chapter 5.) Capture these results throughout the project, not just at the end. Almost everyone has had the experience where the team has a very productive working session, results are analyzed, and good ideas about root causes or impact to the business are discovered—but no one documents what was learned. Two weeks later everyone remembers the good meeting, but can't remember the details. In the worst case that knowledge is lost and at a minimum time has to be spent to recover what was already learned. Capture those flashes of insight when they appear!

 Best Practice

Document results throughout the project, not just at the end. Use the template in the Analyze and Document Results section in Chapter 5 to get started. This will ensure that the knowledge and insight learned during each step are retained. It will save you time when specific recommendations and action plans are prepared.

Synthesize Results from Completed Quality Assessments
Combine and analyze the results from all of the quality assessments. Look for correlations among them. For example, if you conducted a survey of the knowledge workers' perceptions of data quality, do those perceptions match the actual quality results from other dimensions assessed? Interpret the combined results and tie them into the original business issues. (See the Analyze and Document Results section in Chapter 5 for suggestions.) Document the lessons learned, possible impact to the business, root causes, and preliminary recommendations from all quality assessments performed.

Table 3.11 • Step 3—Assess Data Quality

OBJECTIVE	Assess and evaluate data quality for dimensions applicable to the issues.
PURPOSE	Assessment results: • Identify the type and extent of the data quality problems. • Provide a basis for root cause analysis, needed data corrections, and appropriate improvements to prevent future errors.
INPUTS	Output from *Step 1—Define Business Need and Approach* to keep your project focused: • Business issues and opportunities where quality of data/information is suspected to be a component • Known or suspected data quality problems • Business goals and objectives Output from *Step 2—Analyze Information Environment*. Important! Your input from Step 2 will vary from project to project based on what is relevant and appropriate, and at the level of detail for your business needs. The input should include, at a minimum, the items listed below: • Information Life Cycle (from *Step 2.6—Define the Information Life Cycle*) • Data capture and assessment plan (from *Step 2.7—Design Data Capture and Assessment Plan*) • Results of analyzing the information environment—documentation with lessons learned such as potential impact to data quality and/or the business, and initial recommendations at this point The input may also include applicable intermediate deliverables from Step 2: • Finalized requirements (from *Step 2.1—Understand Relevant Requirements*) • Detailed data list and data specifications; data mapping if assessing more than one data source; initial source-to-target mappings if migrating data (from *Step 2.2—Understand Relevant Data and Specifications*) • Data model—with detail needed to understand the structure and relationships of the data so data can be captured and analyzed correctly (from *Step 2.2—Understand Relevant Data and Specifications*) • Background on technology (from *Step 2.3—Understand Relevant Technology*) • Process detail (from *Step 2.4—Understand Relevant Processes*) • Organizational structures, roles, and responsibilities (from *Step 2.5—Understand Relevant People/Organizations*) Applicable interaction matrices (e.g., data-to-process, data-to-job role)
TOOLS AND TECHNIQUES	• Techniques applicable to the dimension (see substeps for details for each dimension) • Additional tools appropriate to the assessment being conducted (see Data Quality Tools section in Chapter 5)—for example, data profiling tools, reporting tools or SQL, data-cleansing tools, and other data quality–related tools • The Capture Data section in Chapter 5

OUTPUTS	• Data quality assessment results
	• Documentation, including potential impact to the business and possible root causes
	• Initial recommendations for action based on data quality assessment results
	• Necessary communication, along with updated communication plan
CHECKPOINT	• Have the applicable data quality assessments been completed?
	• Has necessary follow-up to the analysis been completed?
	• For each quality assessment, have the results been analyzed and documented?
	• For each quality assessment, have preliminary impacts to the business, suspected root causes, and initial recommendations been included in the documentation?
	• If conducting multiple assessments, have results from all assessments been brought together and synthesized?
	• Has the communication plan been updated?
	• Has communication needed to this point been completed?

Table 3.12 • Data Quality Dimensions

No.	DIMENSION	DEFINITION
1	Data Specifications	A measure of the existence, completeness, quality, and documentation of data standards, data models, business rules, metadata, and reference data
2	Data Integrity Fundamentals	A measure of the existence, validity, structure, content, and other basic characteristics of the data
3	Duplication	A measure of unwanted duplication existing within or across systems for a particular field, record, or data set
4	Accuracy	A measure of the correctness of the content of the data (which requires an authoritative source of reference to be identified and accessible)
5	Consistency and Synchronization	A measure of the equivalence of information stored or used in various data stores, applications, and systems, and the processes for making data equivalent
6	Timeliness and Availability	A measure of the degree to which data are current and available for use as specified and in the time frame in which they are expected
7	Ease of Use and Maintainability	A measure of the degree to which data can be accessed and used and the degree to which data can be updated, maintained, and managed
8	Data Coverage	A measure of the availability and comprehensiveness of data compared to the total data universe or population of interest
9	Presentation Quality	A measure of how information is presented to and collected from those who utilize it. Format and appearance support appropriate use of information.
10	Perception, Relevance, and Trust	A measure of the perception of and confidence in the quality of the data; the importance, value, and relevance of the data to business needs
11	Data Decay	A measure of the rate of negative change to the data
12	Transactability	A measure of the degree to which data will produce the desired business transaction or outcome

Determine how the results of the quality assessment(s) will impact the rest of the project. Estimating the full project timeline before the assessment is difficult. The reason is that until you actually assess the data, you don't know how large a problem you may have. What you find in *Step 3—Assess Data Quality* will impact the time needed for the remaining steps. Once completed you have actual results to determine your next steps and how they will affect the project scope, timeline, and resources needed.

Frequently Asked Questions about Data Quality Dimensions

Do Multiple Data Quality Dimensions Make Assessments more Complicated?

Having multiple dimensions actually makes the assessments less complex because you can

- Match actions against a business priority—choose only those dimensions that support the priority
- Perform tasks in the most effective order—assess dimensions in the most useful sequence

with the result of

- A better defined and managed sequence of activities within time and resource constraints
- An understanding of what you will and will not get from the various quality assessments

How Do I Choose Which Dimensions of Quality to Assess?

When choosing dimensions of quality to assess, ask yourself these questions:

- *Should* I assess the data? Only spend time testing when you expect the results to give you actionable information related to your business needs.

- *Can* I assess the data? Is it possible or practical to look at this quality dimension? Sometimes you cannot assess/test the data, or the cost to do so is prohibitive.

Only assess those dimensions when you can answer yes to both questions! If you need help prioritizing, a useful technique can be found in *Step 4.4—Benefit versus Cost Matrix*. Table 3.25 (page 180) in the Sample Output and Templates section of that step lists decisions resulting from the use of the matrix to prioritize the data quality dimensions to be assessed. Don't make this too difficult. Simply list each quality dimension, quickly determine the possible benefit to the business (high to low) and estimated/perceived effort (high to low), and map to the matrix. Don't do in-depth research—make your best judgment based on what you know now.

The costs associated with assessing data quality dimensions can vary widely, depending on the dimension you choose to assess and whether you will use third-party data profiling or data cleansing tools. The best way to decide which dimensions to assess is to balance your business need against the resources available. Document the dimensions chosen, the rationale behind the decision, and the assumptions on which the decision was made.

Any Suggestions Regarding Which Dimensions to Assess First?

You will have already collected requirements in *Step 2—Analyze Information Environment* (see *Step 2.1—Understand Relevant Requirements*). Those requirements form the basis of *Step 3.1—Data Specifications*. You will need to take higher-level requirements and turn them into the more detailed data specifications (or match them to already existing specifications) to ensure that you will be able to interpret the results of your data quality assessments. If you have concerns that the data specifications are missing or incomplete, you may want to start with Step 3.1.

In practice, at this point most people are ready to look at the actual data and do not want to spend time on more specifications and requirements. If you really can't convince the team otherwise, at least have a minimum level of specifications and add to that as you go through your other assessments. If you begin data quality assessments with no requirements, just realize that the analysis will take longer as you gather the specifications needed to interpret your results.

It will not be unusual to find that poor-quality data specifications and business rules end up being one of the root causes of the data quality problems you find when assessing the other dimensions. Once you have proven the need for good data specifications, you can come back to this dimension. However, if you are fortunate enough to have support to start with data specifications, by all means do so!

Once you have your data specifications (at whatever level of detail), it is strongly recommended that you start with *Step 3.2—Data Integrity Fundamentals*. These are fundamental measures of validity, structure, and content, and data profiling is a technique often employed here. If you don't know anything else about your data, you need to know what this dimension provides. Often people will say they are really interested in accuracy or in understanding levels of duplication. Even if that is your end goal, you should still profile your data first.

For example, to determine duplication you have to understand which data field or combination of data fields indicates uniqueness. If you do not know the basic completeness (or fill rate) and content of each of the data elements, you can develop an algorithm for determining duplication based on fields that are missing the data expected or that contain data you didn't know were there. These situations lead to incorrect duplication assessment results.

Another valid approach is to conduct a survey of the knowledge workers first (*Step 3.10— Perception, Relevance, and Trust*) and use its results to prioritize other data quality dimensions. Still, once you start looking at the actual data, you should begin with the data integrity fundamentals and build from there.

 Best Practice

Save yourself rework! Most data quality dimensions require information found in the Data Integrity Fundamentals dimension (Step 3.2). Therefore, you will save yourself time if you start there. Once Step 3.2 is completed, move on to any other quality dimensions that address your business concerns.

One accurate measurement is worth a thousand expert opinions.
– Grace Hopper (1906–1992)
Admiral, U.S. Navy

Step 3.1 Data Specifications

Business Benefit and Context

An assessment of the Data Specifications dimension refers to a focused effort to collect and evaluate specifications and rules. You want to know if they exist, if and where they are documented, and their quality. (See the Data Specifications section in Chapter 2 for an introduction to this topic.) Data specifications provide the context for interpreting the results of your data quality assessments and provide instructions for manually entering data, designing data load programs, updating information, and developing applications.

 Definition

Data specifications measure the existence, completeness, quality, and documentation of data standards, data models, business rules, metadata, and reference data.

There are various ways you can apply this step:

- **Gather data specifications for use in the other data quality dimensions**—to provide input to data quality tests that should be conducted and to provide a standard against which to compare other data quality assessment results.

- **Assess the quality of the data specifications themselves**—data standards, data models, business rules, metadata, and reference data. Nonexistent or poor-quality data specifications themselves are often a cause of data quality problems.

- **Assess the quality of the** *documentation* **of the data specifications**—if that documentation is available, accessible, and easy to understand. Documentation quality can also be a cause of data quality problems.

When preparing for *any* quality assessments, you will collect at least a minimum amount of information about data specifications. This could have been completed in *Step 2.1—Understand Relevant Requirements* and *Step 2.2—Understand Relevant Data and Specifications*. Use the work done in those steps as a starting point here.

This step may be as simple as ensuring that the associated reference data are identified and will be extracted as part of your data integrity fundamentals assessment. Or it may be an in-depth articulation of business rules with which to test data being migrated as part of an ERP implementation.

Approach

1. Determine the scope of your data specifications assessment.

Decide if you will gather specifications for use in other assessments, assess the quality of the specifications themselves, or assess the quality of the specification documentation. (See Template 3.7, Data Specifications Scope, in the Sample Output and Templates section for guidance.) Apply the remaining process steps depending on your scope.

2. Develop and execute a process for gathering or creating data specifications.

If the specifications exist, which ones will be gathered? Who will collect them and by when?

If the specifications do not exist, which ones specifically need to be written or created? Who will write them and by when? This is the place where you can take higher-level requirements and turn them into more detailed instructions as they apply to your data.

In either case, in what format do the specifications need to be documented? Who will be using them for other data quality dimensions and how will they be used?

3. Develop and execute a process for evaluating the quality of the data specifications.

Determine your source of reference for comparison—Will you be comparing your data specifications within the database itself, to organizational-unit or enterprise-wide specifications, or to other sources of reference external to your company? For example, you may use ISO (International Standards Organization) codes as the source of reference for some of your domain values.

If a definitive enterprise-wide standard does not exist, look for common databases used in your particular part of the business—for example, a standard for Sales and Marketing databases. Is there a regional or worldwide data warehouse or data store that is used by several business groups that could be considered a source of reference for data specifications, such as naming standards?

Determine who will do the evaluation—Appropriate reviewers are internal auditors, data management, or data quality professionals from within the business unit whose data are being assessed. Reviewers could also come from outside the business unit. A reviewer must not have a vested interest in the specifications being reviewed—for example, he or she should not be the creator of the data definition.

Complete the data specification assessment—Use Table 3.13 in the Sample Output and Templates section for things to consider when evaluating the quality of data specifications.

4. Develop and execute a process for evaluating the quality of the documentation.

Determine who will do the evaluation of the documentation and when. Gather or gain access to the various documentation items. Complete the evaluation. (See Table 3.14 in the Sample Output and Templates section for considerations when assessing documentation quality.)

5. Analyze results of the data specifications and documentation quality assessments.

Most results will be qualitative, such as an opinion of the quality of the documentation and how that impacts the quality of the data. For example, you can expect the data to be entered inconsistently if data entry standards have not been updated in five years or if the documentation is not easily available to those doing the data entry, or if you find conflicts in data entry standards from team to team. That expected inconsistency is something to look for when assessing the quality of the data itself.

Quantify the results, if possible, such as by reporting percentage of specifications that conform to standards or percentage of existing versus expected specifications.

Does what was learned in this step impact your project timeline, resources needed, or deliverables? If so, how? Has that been communicated?

6. Track the progress of gathering or creating data specifications.

Ensure that the work is progressing according to schedule and that the documented specifications meet expectations. (Refer to Table 3.13 to help you create high-quality data specifications.)

7. Document results and recommended actions.

Highlight specifications that you will want to test in other data quality dimensions to prove or disprove assumptions. Include what was learned, potential impacts to data quality and the business, initial root causes, and preliminary recommendations.

Sample Output and Templates

This is the starting point for determining the scope of your data specifications efforts (refer to Template 3.7, Data Specifications Scope).

Table 3.13 contains a list of examples to consider when evaluating the quality of existing data specifications or when creating new ones. Table 3.14 lists things to consider when assessing the quality of current data specification documentation or when creating new documentation.

Table 3.13 • Data Specification Quality

SPECIFICATION TO BE REVIEWED	CONSIDERATIONS
Data Standards	*Table and Field Names:* • Compare actual physical structure names to naming conventions (physical structure can mean tables, views, fields, etc.). • Ensure that any abbreviations used in names are accepted standard abbreviations. • If there are no stated naming conventions, look for any consistency within the names themselves. *Data Entry Guidelines:* • Rules to follow when entering the data can include accepted abbreviations, casing (upper, lower, mixed), punctuation, etc.
Data Models	• Look for names and definitions that are clear and understandable. • Review data models to ensure that entities and data relationships are consistent. • Identify how the data model is being communicated and used. • Ensure that the naming structure (including casing and punctuation) is consistent with naming conventions.
Business Rules	• Review business rules for accurate and complete definitions. • Look for explicit or implicit statements about how and when an instance (a record) or a particular data field should be treated throughout the POSMAD life cycle. • Determine where major state changes can occur and the corresponding data behavior (e.g., prospects become customers when they purchase a product). The corresponding rule would be "When a prospect becomes a customer, change the customer-indicator flag to A (for active customer)."
Metadata	*Data Definitions:* • Ensure that each field and table has a definition. • Ensure that each definition is complete, accurate, and understandable. • Ensure that fields are identified as mandatory, optional, or conditional (with conditions documented).
Reference Data	*Domain and format guidelines for lists of values:* • Check if lists of values contain only valid values. • Check if values include a quality definition (see Metadata). • Determine if the list of values is complete (i.e., includes all values needed). • Determine if the values are mutually exclusive (i.e., there will be no confusion when choosing the value; the meanings of the values do not overlap).

Template 3.7 • Data Specifications Scope

Specification	Does Specification Exist? (Yes or No)	Gather or Create for Other Data Quality Assessments? (Yes or No)	Evaluate Quality of Specification? (Yes or No)	Evaluate Quality of Documentation? (Yes or No)	Notes
Data Standards					
Data Models					
Business Rules					
Metadata					
Reference Data					

Table 3.14 • Documentation Quality

	Considerations
Background	• Name of documentation • Description of documentation • Location of documentation • Type of documentation (hardcopy manual at each desk, online help feature in the application, data modeling software, etc.) • Purpose of documentation
Assessment	• Who has ownership and responsibility for updating the documentation? • Who currently uses the documentation and is it for the stated purpose or another purpose? • Who should use the documentation and is it for the stated purpose or another purpose? • Do those who need to reference the documentation know it is available? • Is the documentation easily accessible? • Is the documentation easy to understand? • How often is the documentation supposed to be updated? • When was the documentation last updated? • Is there a consistent version history with the supported application versions?

Step 3.2 Data Integrity Fundamentals

Business Benefit and Context

The Data Integrity Fundamentals dimension of quality is a measure of the existence, validity, structure, content, and other basic characteristics of data. It includes essential measures such as completeness/fill rate, validity, lists of values and frequency distributions, patterns, ranges, maximum and minimum values, and referential integrity. Michael Scofield, manager of Data Asset Development at ESRI in Redlands, California, puts it this way:

> When it comes to data if you buy it, sell it, move it, transform it, integrate it, or report from it you must know what the data really means and how it behaves.

Data integrity fundamentals provide that knowledge. If you don't know anything else about your data, you need to know what you will learn from this data quality dimension.

 Definition

Data integrity fundamentals: a measure of the existence, validity, structure, content, and other basic characteristics of the data.

You will need to use some type of analytical technique to discover the data's structure, content, and quality. Tools for understanding fundamental data integrity, often referred to as data profiling or analysis tools,[4] look at but do not change the data. Jack Olson defines data profiling as "the use of analytical techniques to discover the structure, content, and quality of data." The term "profiling" is used in this step to indicate the assessment of the Data Integrity Fundamentals dimension.

It is recommended that Data Integrity Fundamentals be one of the first dimensions assessed because most of the other dimensions build on what is learned through profiling. For example, even if your top priority is to determine duplicate records, in order to get valid results from a matching algorithm, the quality and fill rate at the field, column, or data element level must be high. Any issues at the field level will be made visible through data profiling.

Profiling can be accomplished with one of the data profiling tools on the market or by other means such as SQL to write queries or some type of report writer to create ad hoc reports. Even if you are not using a purchased data profiling tool, look at the functionality of and output from such tools to help guide the queries or reports to write so you can understand the Data Integrity Fundamentals dimension.

If you are trying to establish the business case for data quality, you may write a few queries to bring visibility to data quality issues and prove the point that they exist. If you are planning on establishing a data quality baseline, are part of a large-scale integration project, or are serious

---

[4] I refer to profiling or analysis tools as profiling tools since that has become a fairly well-known and accepted term.

about an ongoing data quality program, I highly recommend purchasing a data profiling tool.

At times, data profiling tools are looked at with disdain or suspicion by developers or others who enjoy writing queries. ("I can write a profiling application this weekend.") However, for large-scale or ongoing quality efforts you cannot write a profiling application that will run the multitude of queries needed, present the results, and store the results for future use the way already existing profiling tools can within any reasonable period of time. Let the profiling tools do the basics (which they are very good at).

Put your developers' skills to work supplementing what cannot be automatically done by the profiling tools, such as in-depth checking of business rules or relationships. Some of the advanced work can be done *within* the profiling tools, but requires human intervention; sometimes it requires work outside the tools. This is a much more effective use of your deep knowledge of your data and your business. I would much rather see people spend their time analyzing and taking action on the profiling results instead of writing queries to obtain them.

Uses of Data Profiling

Profiling can be used to assess an existing data source for suspected quality problems, in a solution development project such as building a data warehouse or a transactional application, when migrating data to an ERP, or when moving or integrating data. As outlined in the following list, profiling can be used to assess any data source and to provide input, information, and insight.

Uses of Data Profiling

Create or validate a data model—Profiling allows the creation of new models that support data to be moved into a new application, and it exposes structural differences between an existing target data model and the source data to be moved.

Inventory data assets—Profiling provides visibility to create an inventory of your company's data assets—that is, the ability to identify or validate the existence and availability of information. It provides rapid assessment of which fields are consistently populated compared to expectations and can provide input to determining whether your company already has the needed data or if external data need to be purchased.

Check data coming from external data sources—Profiling provides input to determine whether to purchase data from sources external to your company. Once data are purchased, profiling can be used to check the data source each time prior to loading to the company's databases.

Improve source-to-target mappings—Profiling shows the data content of fields and the inconsistencies between column headings and content. Use of data profiling results for source-to-target mappings yields better mappings in a shorter time than a traditional mapping method in which only column headings are looked at. Without visibility of the data content, incorrect mappings are often not discovered until testing.

Uncover specific data quality problems—Profiling provides visibility of the actual location and magnitude of data quality errors. This provides input for root cause analysis and allows the business to prioritize actions for preventing future problems and correcting current ones.

Confirm selection criteria—Profiling uncovers data that may be unknown to the subject matter expert. It provides the visibility to make good decisions on data (both fields and records) that should or should not be migrated.

Determine system of record—Profiling provides input to decisions about the best system to use.

Compare, analyze, and understand source, target, and transitional data stores (e.g., files, staging areas)—Profiling source, target, and transitional data stores shows the state of the data in any system, highlighting differences and their magnitude and pointing out where to focus cleansing, correction, transformation, or synchronization. A special case of looking at source and target systems is when integrating data from two companies because of mergers and acquisitions.

Identify transformation rules—Profiling highlights the differences between source data and target system data requirements. It leads to more accurate and comprehensive transformation rules so that data will load properly.

Control test data—When application functionality testing fails, time is spent investigating root causes because it is not known if the source is related to data or software functionality. Data profiling helps in the first step of testing to catch data errors prior to the testing cycle. By using good-quality data for testing, less time is spent searching for errors and there is more focus on the application's functionality needs.

Initial step to finding root causes—Profiling is the first step to identifying root causes of data quality issues because the actual data content is made visible.

Support ongoing data quality monitoring—Profiling results provide the basis for continuous improvement. After the initial baseline profiling, project teams typically choose the data quality issues with the most impact for regular monitoring.

Benefits from Data Profiling

Data profiling will

- Improve predictability of project timelines. Data quality issues often delay timelines and take the project team by surprise. Uncovering issues early helps prevent costly surprises and lowers the risk of design changes late in the project.

- Focus resources and efforts where they are really needed. Expensive, large-scale data clean-up is often begun based on opinions. By profiling and seeing the actual quality of the data, investments in data quality can be focused where they will provide the most benefit.

- Determine whether your company already has needed data or if external data need to be purchased.

- Support data integration and migration testing.

- Support compliance and audit requirements.

- Improve visibility of the quality of the data that support business decision making, providing input to determine where to assess business impact and where to focus root cause analysis for data deemed to be of high impact.

Typical Profiling Functionality

Typical profiling functionality lets you look at your data from different viewpoints.[5] (See Figure 3.8.)

1. **Column Profiling**—Analyzes each column[6] in a record, surveying all records in the data set. Column profiling will provide results such as completeness/fill rates, data type, size/length, list of unique values and frequency distribution, patterns, and maximum and minimum ranges. This may also be referred to as domain analysis or content analysis. It enables you to discover true metadata and content quality problems, validate if the data conform to expectations, and compare actual data to target requirements.

2. **Profiling within a Table or File**—Discovers relationships between columns within a table or file, which enables you to discover actual data structures, functional dependencies, primary keys, and data structure quality problems. You can also test user-expected dependencies against the data. This is also referred to as dependency profiling.

3. **Profiling across Tables or Files**—Compares data between tables or files, determines overlapping or identical sets of values, identifies duplicate values, or indicates foreign keys. Profiling results can help a data modeler build a third normal form data model, in which unwanted redundancies are eliminated. The model can be used for designing a staging area that will facilitate the movement and transformation of data from one source to a target database such as an operational data store or data warehouse.

---

[5] Specific data-profiling capability, terms, and results vary depending on the particular profiling tool used.
[6] A column refers to a field, data element, or attribute.

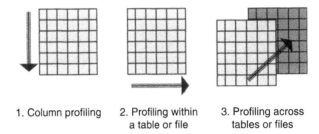

1. Column profiling   2. Profiling within   3. Profiling across
a table or file   tables or files

Figure 3.8 • Typical profiling functionality.

Approach

1. Finalize your data capture and assessment plan.

See *Step 2.7—Design Data Capture and Assessment Plan* and the Capture Data section in Chapter 5 for additional information. Update and finalize your plan if you started it earlier. Create and finalize it if not yet begun.

2. Access or extract the data.

3. Profile the data.

Use the tools that best meet your needs. As mentioned earlier, data can be profiled using a commercial data profiling tool, a query program such as SQL, a report-writing program, or a statistical analysis tool. However, if your company is serious about data quality and you are rigorously establishing a baseline for continuous improvement, strongly consider purchasing a data profiling tool. Get appropriate training and use any best practices available from your tool vendor.

When beginning the profiling and analysis of a data file, consider how much risk the data entail. Data considered to be critical that are extracted from an unreliable source require more focused analysis than less critical data extracted from a reliable source. Considering risk will help in determining the depth of the analysis to be performed or whether additional profiling is necessary.

4. Analyze the results.

No matter which tools you use, refer to Table 3.15, which describes various characteristics of data to be tested, their definitions, and examples of analysis and potential action. You will get into in-depth root cause analysis later (see *Step 5—Identify Root Causes*), but at this point start asking yourself why the data look the way they do.

Include subject matter experts, data experts, and technical experts to interpret what you are seeing in the profiling results. Be prepared to conduct additional profiling tests based on your initial analysis.

5. Document results and recommended actions.

Capture your profiling assessment results and lessons learned (including confirmation of opinions and surprises). Include possible impact to the business revealed through your analysis, potential root causes, and preliminary recommendations for addressing the issues found.

Table 3.15 • Data Integrity Fundamentals—Tests, Analysis, and Action

TESTS	EXAMPLE ANALYSIS AND ACTION
Number of records: Total count of records in the data set being assessed	Check whether the total number of records matches what is expected. If not, investigate the causes of missing records and profile the data set again.
Completeness or fill rate: A measure of the count (#) and percentage (%) of the fields that contain a value	Completeness or fill rate is based only on the *existence* of a value. Additional analysis is needed to determine if the values are *valid*. To interpret results, you need to know which fields are required (mandatory), optional, or conditional. If the field is required (by the application or by the business, or if it is a primary key), fill rate should be 100 percent. If the fill rate is less than 100 percent for a required field, investigate causes: • If it is a field required by the business, see if the application requires an entry. • If the application does not require an entry, see if it can be modified to require the data. • If the application cannot be modified, document and train those who enter data. In this case, the data should be monitored closely. • Check the feasibility of enforcing not null in the database. **Check the completeness/fill rate at two different levels:** • *For a single column or field:* Determine if any data exist in the field—e.g., "80 percent of the customer records have a code in the department field." • *For a grouping of data:* Determine the fill rate for a set of fields required to complete a specific essential process. For instance, mailings in the United States require a name, address, city, state, and zip code. To assess the fill rate for these fields, determine the number of records where all the required fields have a value—e.g., "75 percent of the customer records have the required data to create a mailing label."
Nulls: A measure of the count (#) and percentage (%) of fields that are empty (i.e., it is null because the field contains nothing)	Nulls are the opposite of completeness or fill rate. The same analysis under completeness or fill rate applies here; you are just looking at it from the opposite point of view.
List of unique values: A list of distinct or unique values within a field	• Make sure the values are allowed or valid. The set of valid values will vary from field to field. The set of valid values may also be referred to as a data domain or a set of domain values. • Check the *number* of distinct values against the number of valid values for that field. • Compare the list of *actual* distinct values to a list of expected valid values, if available. The expected valid values may come from a list of values such as a reference table or a code list, from a subject matter expert, or from an external standard to which your company adheres.

(Continued)

Table 3.15 • Data Integrity Fundamentals—Tests, Analysis, and Action (Continued)

TESTS	EXAMPLE ANALYSIS AND ACTION
List of unique values (cont'd)	• If the business does not have a list of valid values, use the list from your profiling as a starting point to develop one. • Look for *default* values—e.g., the application automatically inserts a value into a blank field such as "999-999-9999" if no telephone number is entered. You may decide to consider any field with the default value as not filled because it does not supply any meaningful information. Document the default values. • Look for values that *duplicate* meanings—e.g., varying abbreviations for the same company name. • If changes are made to the list of values, document any mappings of the values and update records with the values that need to be changed.
Validity: Test of whether values in the field are within a set of allowed or valid values	• Define and document what "valid" means for each field; what constitutes validity will vary from field to field. • Validity tests may include format or pattern, domain, valid codes, type (alpha/numeric), dependency, business rules, data entry standards, maximum and minimum ranges, etc. • For instance, are all codes in the records valid codes as defined by the business in code tables in the system? If the field is numeric, are there characters in the field? Does the date in a date field fall within the required range? • Validity test results may be reported as a percentage of the completeness/fill rate—e.g., U.S. zip code field has a 95 percent fill rate; of those records with a value, 90 percent conform to a pattern indicating a valid U.S. zip code.
Frequency distribution: Distribution of unique values within a field by count (#) and percentage (%)	• Frequency distribution gives an idea of usage—look at the values with the highest and lowest counts. • For those values with a low frequency, consider dropping them and changing to another comparable value that is frequently used. • Research any constants found. A constant is any column that has the same value for every record. This may be an indication of a data element that was never used or is no longer used. • Determine if the distribution of values is what you would expect—e.g., if you have a distribution of sales records across countries, does the frequency distribution of the country code align with your expectations of percentage of sales for each country? • If changes are made to the list of values, document any mapping of the values and update records with the values that need to be changed. • Look for occurrences of unusual values that may have been uncovered when analyzing your information environment and that is being used generally by the business. For instance, if those creating the records tell you they are putting a period (.) in a system-required field if the value is unknown, determine the number of periods (.) in that field. • Look at the frequency distribution of default values or false values such as "999-999-9999" in a phone number field or "Mickey Mouse" in a name field.

Tests	Example Analysis and Action
Frequency distribution (Cont'd)	• Use frequency distribution to determine candidates for primary keys. "100 percent unique" or "near 100 percent" may be candidates—but have dirty data. • If there is a low percent of distinct values, fields with equal value may be related. Many nulls or zeroes (0) can be a problem. • A mid-range percent of distinct generally identifies pure business data that will be determined by other columns. • Fields that have # of distinct = 1 (i.e., all records always have the same value in the field) are potentially unused or constant attributes. Determine if space should be taken in the database for this. Consider putting in a constant table.
Range of values, maximum and minimum: The range of values shown by maximum and minimum values	• Any values at the top or bottom of the value range may quickly show data quality problems—e.g., "999-99-9999" for a social security number or ID field; "ZZZZZ" for a name field. • Look at maximum and minimum values for key date fields—e.g., look for dates on open invoices or purchase orders to determine if they fall within business guidelines, such as there should be no open purchase orders older than six months from today's date. • Look for values outside the expected or documented range.
Recency: Frequency distribution of critical date fields and/or date ranges	• A type of frequency distribution related to date fields and/or data ranges—e.g., "20 percent of the records were updated in the last 0–12 months; 25 percent updated in the last 13–24 months," etc., or "Based on the create date, 50 percent of the records were created in the last year." • May also be used to simulate or provide input to two other data quality dimensions: Timeliness (the degree to which data are current) and Data Decay (the rate of negative change to the data).
Content: Match of data content and column or field names	• Compare column or field names with data content. • Does the field contain the data expected—e.g., does the phone number field really contain phone numbers or are they Social Security numbers?
Duplication: Determines if unwanted duplication exists	• Get a high-level view of duplicate data by looking at the list of values for duplicate meanings. • Some tools provide a comparison between different columns' data values and overlap percentages that are usually based on exact string matches of the distinct values. • Some data profiling tools highlight duplicate data based only on extract string matches, but others use what is often referred to as "fuzzy matching." Soundex and NYSIIS (New York State Identification and Intelligence System) are phonetic coding systems that are widely used to help identify duplicate data.

(Continued)

Table 3.15 • Data Integrity Fundamentals—Tests, Analysis, and Action (Continued)

TESTS	EXAMPLE ANALYSIS AND ACTION
Data type	• Look for differences between the expected data type and the actual data type inferred by the profiling tool. • The tool may show the documented data type (or expected data type per the metadata) and compare to the data type inferred from the actual data content. It may also flag incompatibilities between a source data type and a target data type that need to be addressed when migrating data. • For data modeling, the tool may show the data type and examples of alternate data types that could be used in the model.

Size or length: Length of data in the field	• Look for differences between actual data size and expected data size.
	• Look for a large number of records with exactly the same size. This could indicate that the data in that field were truncated.
	• If there are differences in size between a source and a target system, determine the number and percentage of source records that exceed the target size:
	   a) If a small number, you may need to update the records manually.
	   b) If a large number, you need to understand the impact to the business if the data are truncated when migrated.

Patterns: Count (#) and percent (%) of unique patterns found in the data	• Look for unexpected patterns—e.g., there are only a few valid patterns for U.S. zip codes: #####, #####-####, ##### ####, and #########. If a pattern in the field is any other than these, there is a data quality problem. • Expected or valid patterns will vary depending on the field. • Look for identical patterns for ID fields.
Precision	• For numeric data, determine whether the number of places to the right of the decimal point are at the level of precision needed.
Consistency: Reasonability tests for related fields in the same record. Referential integrity	• Look at consistency of data within a record. • Look at consistency of data across records. • Look at high-level business rules to understand relationships and look for compliance (e.g., order date must always be before ship date; if the ship date is before the order date, you know you have a data quality problem). • Look for other dependencies. The value in one field is in the correct format relative to the value in another field (e.g., addresses in the United States have postal codes within the valid formats). • Look for calculations: A stored calculated value is correct as per the source elements (e.g., Sales Item Total Amount is equal to Sales Item Price multiplied by Sales Item Quantity).

TESTS	EXAMPLE ANALYSIS AND ACTION
Concurrency and timeliness: Synchronization of data and timing of data flow between various databases, applications, processes, etc.	• Profile multiple databases and compare results for differences.
Business rules	• Determine if the business/data rules not embedded in the data structure are being enforced by the application program logic. This is usually done against a subset of the data that has its own rules. For example, you may have different party types (organization, contact, etc.) with specific rules that require some columns to be null and others to be populated.

 Best Practice

Profiling
- Document anomalies and decisions.
- Have a subject matter expert available at all stages of the process to ensure rapid answers to questions and resolution of open issues.
- Because the actual data show what is really happening, always refer to them if there are differences of opinion about what exists. Let the data tell "the rest of the story."

Step 3.3 Duplication

Business Benefit and Context

There are many hidden costs associated with duplicate data. Following are a few reasons why it is important to avoid duplicates:

- As companies' credit limits change, they are updated on one account and usually remain static on any duplicate accounts. The customer may be told the credit limit based on one record and later find the credit constrained by the amount on a different record.

- Multiple records for the same customer can, in effect, multiply the extended credit limit two or more times depending on the number of duplicate records, exposing the company to unnecessary credit risks.

- Customer service representatives have difficulty locating a transaction placed on a duplicate account. This can result in delayed shipments or confusing messages to customers.

- Web integration for accounts and sites becomes difficult if multiple records exist for the same customer. Customers and the company can become confused.

- Multiple records for the same customer make it hard to determine the value of that customer to the business.

  Definition

Duplication is a measure of unwanted duplication existing within or across systems for a particular field, record, or data set.

Checking for duplicates is the process of determining uniqueness. Some third-party tools are available to help reveal whether there are duplicate records or fields, within or across databases. These tools are usually referred to as data cleansing tools, and they serve several functions—identifying duplicates is one of the more popular. (See the Data Quality Tools section in Chapter 5 for more information on tools and terms used.)

  Definition

Uniqueness means that the record, entity, or transaction is the one and only version of itself that exists—it has no duplicates.

"Matching" is a term sometimes used to mean de-duplication and sometimes used to mean linking. In either case, de-duplication identifies two or more records that represent the same real-world object, such as multiple records representing the same customer, employee, supplier, or product.

Linking associates records through a user-defined or common algorithm. For example, householding is a linking concept often used by banks to understand the relationships among various customers. All records associated with a particular household are linked, such as that of a young adult with a new checking account linked to that of his or her parents, who may have a number of accounts with the bank. Linking is also used to identify households with multiple investment accounts with the same company so only one privacy notice is sent to each household, therefore saving printing and mailing costs (and helping our environment also).

Both linking and de-duplication require an algorithm for matching, which is some combination of fields that identify unique records. Weights can be set for the individuals fields, if needed, to indicate which are more important and should have more bearing in the algorithm. The better the quality of the data in these fields, the better the tool will identify matches. Standardizing and/or parsing the data prior to running the matching algorithms (also referred to as match routines) results in better matching, linking, and identification of duplicates.

Once the potential duplicates are identified, someone has to decide which of them are real duplicates, which record should survive, and which pieces of the records should be carried into a new combined record. This is also referred to as "survivorship" or "match-merge."

The process of identifying duplicates will take many rounds of testing and manual intervention before you can be satisfied with the results of the algorithms. It takes additional testing to be satisfied with the automated merge or survivorship process. Finding duplicates can never be 100 percent automated, but over time, with testing and adjusting match algorithms and threshold levels, trust in the match-merge results should increase.

Matching Definitions

Real World

- *Match*—Two or more records represent the same real-world thing.
- *Nonmatch*—A unique record; no other record in the population represents the same real-world thing.

Representation of the Real World through Business Rules and Tool Usage

- *True Match*—Business rules as implemented within the tool have identified a match that is confirmed by business review.
- *Nonmatch*—Business rules as implemented within the tool have identified a unique record that is confirmed by business review.
- *False Negative*—Cases have been classified as unmatched, but should have been matched—that is, missed matches. The results are impacted by the business rules and use of the tool.
- *False Positive*—Cases have been incorrectly classified as matches. They are actually nonmatches—that is, mismatches. The results are impacted by the business rules and use of the tool.

When you use an automated tool, results will show those records that are not matches and those records that are. There is always a "gray" area where the matches and nonmatches overlap, which means that it is not clear if the particular item is a match or a nonmatch. The further you move away from the gray area (in either direction), the more confident you are that the matches are true matches and the nonmatches are really nonmatches (as illustrated in Figure 3.9).

Look closely at the gray area in Figure 3.10. When you look at the detail there you can see the difference between the false negatives (the matches that have been missed) and the false positives (nonmatches incorrectly classified as matches). The threshold is the point at which two objects are sufficiently alike to be considered potential duplicates; it can be adjusted.

Balancing Act

Setting the threshold is as much an art as a science. The list that follows on the next page contains a few ways to think about the trade-offs.

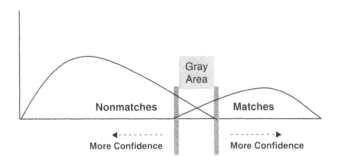

Figure 3.9 • Matching results: Matches, nonmatches, and the gray area.

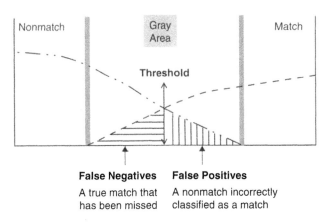

Figure 3.10 • Matching: False negatives and false positives.

- Moving the threshold to the left maximizes matches, but increases incorrect matches (false positives) while decreasing missed matches (false negatives).

- Moving the threshold to the right increases the number of missed matches (false negatives) while minimizing the number of incorrect matches (false positives).

- If the business does not want to miss the true matches, it must see more incorrect matches (false positives).

Approach

1. State the expected goals of the de-duplication activity.

In the planning of a de-duping project, there needs to be a clear idea of the expected outcome and the people or processes that will be impacted by it. For example, in one company a high-level duplicate assessment was conducted in order to provide input for a decision on which application should be considered the source of reference for customer data. This required only an initial assessment.

In another project, a new Customer Master was being created from several sources. The records from this Customer Master were to be migrated into a new ERP application. This required months of work and intensive use of a data cleansing tool.

If the end result is to reduce data duplicates within source systems:

- All impacted systems will need to be identified and appropriate changes to those systems incorporated into the project plan. How will you handle transactional records (such as invoices or sales orders) that are still open and linked to master records that have been identified as duplicates? You may have to flag the duplicate master record so that it will no longer be used, and then delete it after all the associated transactional records have been closed.

- A complete cross-reference of old to new identifiers should be maintained throughout the project and retained for future reference. (One ERP project used the cross-references for months after the project was over.)
- The analysis step will need to include survivorship processing (more detail on survivorship shortly).
- However, if the objective is to provide metrics from which decisions can be made relative to an actual data cleansing effort, there may be no need to examine duplicate sets for survivorship.

2. Determine how the business looks at uniqueness and list the rules.

How does the business determine if a record is a duplicate of another record? What combination of data elements constitutes a unique record?

For example, does a unique combination of sold-to, ship-to, and bill-to addresses constitute one unique record? Should there be only one occurrence of a particular customer name in the database? (Refer to your review of the data model in *Step 2.2—Understand Relevant Data and Specifications* for input.)

Decide at which level to test for uniqueness:

Record level—For instance, there should only be one occurrence of a particular customer in the database. Do you care about sites and/or contacts? For uniqueness of sites, you may want to look at combinations of address fields. For uniqueness of persons, you may want to look at combinations of name and address fields.

Field level—For instance, phone numbers should generally be unique unless you are assessing site phone numbers where there is

one central number for all contacts at that site. ID numbers should be unique. Simple field level uniqueness based on exact string matches can be accomplished using a data profiling tool. If you need a more sophisticated algorithm, use a data cleansing tool.

3. Determine the tool(s) to use for finding duplicates and testing for uniqueness.

This is where you will most likely use a third-party tool—the process of finding duplicates is best automated. A data profiling tool can provide some high-level checks for uniqueness (usually based on an exact string match). It can easily show if all records in an ID field are unique. Anything more rigorous than that requires a specialized tool.

As previously mentioned, specialized tools are often called data cleansing tools and sometimes called data quality tools. With cleansing tools you have the option of looking at and also changing the data.

If you have no tool, this step can be quite time consuming as you will need to go through whatever process your company requires for software acquisition (research options, determine tool selection criteria, schedule demos, make a purchase decision, negotiate and finalize the contract, obtain and install the software). If a tool is currently available, check your licensing agreement and ensure that the contract is up to date.

In either case, you will need training in order to use the particular tool. All explanations in this step are for a general understanding of the concepts behind duplication; features and a particular approach to de-duplication may vary depending on the tool you use.

4. Analyze the data to be de-duplicated.

The more you know about your data, the better you will be able to customize the standardization and matching routines required by your tool. Profiling is a great way to understand the data. Everything learned from profiling will provide input to customizing your standardization and matching routines.

(See *Step 3.2—Data Integrity Fundamentals* for more on understanding your data.)

Most tools come with out-of-the-box algorithms, but they need to be tuned to your specific data. You will need to translate business needs to the rules and algorithms the tool requires:

- Determine fields to be compared and match criteria.
- Determine standardization rules, de-duplication algorithms, weights, and thresholds.
- Expect several rounds of testing to get your standardization and matching routines to an acceptable level.

Expect difficulty in preparing the data and matching across languages. In countries like Switzerland, where multiple languages are spoken, it is difficult to programmatically see what language is being used in order to standardize the data, so you will have to use different algorithms and thresholds for different languages and address formats.

You will also have to deal with differences in how the data were entered and the point of reference and knowledge of the person who performed the data entry. For example, a person in France entering a French address and a person in Germany entering the same address often do so in very different ways.

Allow plenty of time for analysis activities. This is critical to obtaining successful results when you are ready to perform the matching.

5. Design the duplicate assessment process.

Include the following:

- What is your population of interest and associated selection criteria (both business and technical)?
- Who will extract the data and when; what output format is needed?
- Who will run the data through the de-duplication tool and when?
- Who will review the results of de-duplication and when?

- Who will report the results of testing and analysis and when?
- What metrics will be gathered and what reporting is required?

6. Extract the data.

Refer to the Capture Data section in Chapter 5 to ensure that you are extracting the correct set of data.

7. Test the data for duplicates.

Use the tools that best meet your needs. For your initial assessments, you will probably only look at the matching results. Do not automate data changes until you have thoroughly tested and refined those results. Be appropriately trained and use any best practices available from your tool vendor.

Manage and adjust standardization routines, threshold levels, and matching algorithms as needed. Do not be surprised if you have to go through the cycle of reviewing results/adjusting algorithms several times before you are satisfied. Flag those records that show as duplicates but are acceptable to leave as is. Report your metrics and discuss the impact.

Plan more time into your schedule if you want to automate the survivorship process. Even if survivorship will be done manually by people reviewing results and choosing the surviving records, you must have some guidelines for what records or fields take precedence. Document the rules and provide training in order to get more consistent results from survivorship.

In hindsight, one project recommended keeping the standardized data in a separate field from the original data field. The standardized data were used to help with the matching. If the team made adjustments to the standardization routines, the data could be restandardized using the updated algorithms. If you don't have the original data, it will not be possible to do this.

Another recommendation is to keep the cross-reference data you will receive after matching. In one data migration, new source systems that were found needed to be updated with the new identifiers that had been assigned by previous matching. The project team could match the additional source data to the cross-reference file and then assign a new customer number.

Many of these are things you learn from experience, but a few are presented here to give an idea of the complexity of de-duplication. Even so, the cost of de-duping is still less than the cost of the impact of duplicates.

8. Analyze the results and determine next steps.

Keep the goals of your de-duplication effort in mind. Following are questions to consider:

- What is the level of duplication found? Does duplication vary by country, geographic region, or some other category that is meaningful to your company?
- Is the level of duplication found significant? What is the impact of the duplicates to the business? Has anything learned during the assessment provided enough information about impact to determine if it is worthwhile to continue addressing duplicates?
- Do you expect this to be a one-time assessment only? Have you learned anything about duplicates that will change that plan?
- How will you handle the clean-up of duplicate records? How will you handle transactional records (such as invoices or sales orders) that are still open and are linked to master records that have been

identified as duplicates? You may have to coordinate across systems such as by flagging the duplicate master record so it can no longer be used, and then delete it after all the associated transactional records have been closed.

- How can you prevent the creation of duplicate records?
- How will de-duplication be handled in the future? On an ad-hoc basis? As a scheduled batch job on a regular basis? Integrated into another application and used in real time?
- How much of the process will be automated? If instituting de-duplication as part of an ongoing process, you may decide to eventually automate the identification piece and use manual review for only some match categories. You can then decide whether to fully or partially automate the merge process.

9. Document results and recommended actions.

Include lessons learned such as potential impact to the business from the duplicates, possible root causes, and preliminary recommendations.

Determine whether you want to continue using the data cleansing tool. Initial assessment is only one of its uses. Tools can be built into production processes to prevent future data errors (*Step 7—Prevent Future Data Errors*) or used to correct current data errors (*Step 8—Correct Current Data Errors*). They may also be used when implementing ongoing controls (*Step 9—Implement Controls*).

Step 3.4   Accuracy

Business Benefit and Context

It's easy to associate data quality with data accuracy. It seems obvious that the goal of data quality should be to produce correct data. However, for the purpose of assessing and managing data quality it is important to make a distinction between the dimension of Accuracy and other data quality dimensions.

Accuracy differs from data integrity fundamentals in that the latter refer to the basic measures of data validity, structure, and content. Data accuracy requires comparing the data to what they represent (the authoritative source of reference). *Conducting this assessment is usually a manual process.*

 Definition

Accuracy is a measure of the correctness of the content of the data (which requires an authoritative source of reference to be identified and accessible).

For example, assume you are looking at the quality of item master records. The data profile assessment reveals the following:

- The percentage of records that contain a value in the item number field
- The percentage of records in which the item number conforms to an acceptable pattern
- That all records contain a value of M (for make) or B (for buy) in the item type field
- That the business confirmed that M and B are the only two valid values for item type

These are all fundamental aspects of data quality and are important to know. However, only someone who is familiar with a specific item can say if it is really a make part or a buy part—that is, if it accurately reflects what it represents.

Accuracy requires an authoritative source of reference and a comparison of the data to it. That comparison can take the form of a survey (such as a phone call to a customer or an emailed questionnaire) or an inspection (such as a comparison of the inventory count in the database to the actual inventory on the shelf).

Now assume you are checking the quality of customer records. You use profiling tools or run queries to determine if a zip code is in the zip code field and if it conforms to the acceptable pattern indicating a valid U.S. zip code. Using the right tools you can also check if each city, state, and zip code group creates a valid combination. But only the customer can tell you if that particular zip code is his or hers—once again, this is accuracy. The authoritative source of reference is the customer.

When deciding where to assess accuracy, ask yourself these questions:

What is the authoritative source of reference?—For inventory levels, accuracy can only be verified through physical counts of the product inventory. For accuracy of business names and company hierarchies you may decide to verify through an industry source such as Dun and Bradstreet.

Is the source of reference available and accessible?—There is often no way to corroborate data gathered some time in the past. Another issue may be regulations that constrain direct contact of customers to verify their information in your database.

Do you know the number of records that the business can afford to check for accuracy?—Because of the expense of determining accuracy, accuracy checks are usually done against a sampling of records, while with profiling tools you can often check all records. If a problem with accuracy is found in the sample, at that point the business can determine if accuracy updates on all the data are worth their cost.

Approach

Start an accuracy assessment by preparing for the inspection or survey, completing the inspection, and scoring and analyzing the results. Do not perform updates to the database while inspecting. You may lose important context and information needed when you research root causes. Make corrections at a later date.

Prepare

Complete the following items prior to executing your accuracy survey/assessment/inspection.

1. Decide which data elements can be assessed for accuracy.

Is there an authoritative source of reference? Discover what or who is the authoritative source of reference for the data. *Important!* More examples:

- A customer may be the authoritative source of reference for customer information.
- A scanned application and resume may contain the authoritative data for personnel-recruiting information.

- An administrative contact may be able to verify site information.
- Product itself may be the source for a product description.
- An upstream order system may contain authoritative data about orders that are passed onto a warehouse.
- A generally accepted "Golden Copy" (controlled and validated version) might serve as an authoritative source of reference.
- A recognized industry-wide standard, such as Dun and Bradstreet for company names and hierarchies.

Is that source of reference accessible? Are there any constraints (such as privacy or security) that would prevent you from accessing the source for an accuracy comparison?

2. Decide which method of assessment to use.

You will use tools to capture the *results* of the assessment, but the assessment itself usually cannot be performed by an automated tool. Examples of survey and inspection methods include:

- *Telephone survey*—expensive, but a greater chance for confirmation
- *Mailed survey*—less expensive, but less chance for confirmation (Some contacts may not respond or may not be reached because of address errors. Telephone follow-up, if allowed, can offset a lack of response.)
- *Physical inspection* of objects
- *Manual comparison* of data in the database against a printed source of reference

Consider the following factors when finalizing the method of assessment:

- *Cultural*—What is acceptable in your environment?
- *Response*—What is the best way to obtain input from the authoritative source?
- *Schedule*—How quickly do you need a response? For example, mailed surveys

have a much slower turnaround time than phone surveys.

- *Constraints*—Are there any legal requirements that restrict you from using a particular source of reference?
- *Cost*—What are the costs for the various approaches?

3. Determine who will be involved in conducting the accuracy assessment.

Involve those familiar with, but not responsible for, the data being assessed. For example, an inspection of inventory may be done by an objective third party who understands inventory systems.

4. Determine the sampling method.

Sampling is a technique in which representative members of a population are selected for testing. The results are then inferred to be representative of the population as a whole. The sample has to be representative so that the accuracy of the sampled records will approximate the accuracy of all those in the population.

There are two characteristics of a sample that determine how well it represents the population:

- *Size relative to population*—What is the minimum required number of records that need to be checked and completed in order to provide statistically valid results for the population?
- *Stability*—If a sample size produces a result and if it is increased and produces the same results, the sample has stability.

There are different *sampling methods*, but random sampling is very common. *Random* means that every member of the population has an equal chance of being chosen to be part of the sample.

Important: Involve someone experienced in statistics to ensure that your sampling methods are valid! For example, your software quality assurance group may already have best practices for sampling.

5. Develop the survey instrument, survey scenarios, record dispositions, and update reasons.

The *survey instrument* is the set of questions used for assessing accuracy, whether by questioning a respondent or by manually checking against a source of reference.

- For a telephone survey, develop the set of questions and the script for obtaining input from respondents.
- For a hardcopy, mailed, emailed, or website survey, develop the questionnaire to be completed and returned by respondents.
- For manual comparisons, decide what forms will be used to capture results and how the data from the database will be presented to facilitate easy comparison to the source.
- Determine if questions should have predefined answer choices. For instance, product questions may correspond to a product table in the database. If so, ensure that your list of choices matches the valid reference in the database.

Survey scenarios are possible situations the surveyor might encounter throughout the survey period. An example for a survey of customers includes the following: "Unable to contact customer"; "Contacted customer but customer declines to participate"; "Customer starts survey but does not complete it"; and "Customer completes survey." Assign a code that corresponds to the status of each record at a particular state. These codes are referred to as *record dispositions*. For example, if the surveyor is able to verify the status of each data element within the record, the disposition for that record is "fully checked." Other record dispositions include "partially checked" or "not checked," "contact not located," "declined," and so forth. Only those records with the disposition "fully checked" are later scored for accuracy. However, tracking ALL record disposition types can yield an additional important quality measure.

Update reasons explain the results of the comparison between the information in the database and the information supplied by the source of reference. You may want to track an update reason for each field that is compared for accuracy. For example, the update reasons could be

- *Correct*—No updates are needed; the information provided by the source of reference is the same as that contained in the database.
- *Incomplete*—The information in the database is blank; the source of reference provided the missing information.
- *Wrong*—The information provided by the source is different from the information in the database.
- *Format*—The content of the information is correct, but the formatting is incorrect.
- *Not applicable*—The information was not validated with the source.

Update reasons are noted while the inspection is being performed or the survey is being conducted.

6. Develop the survey or inspection process.

The survey or inspection process is the standard process that will be used for comparing the data with the source of reference and capturing the results. Determine

- Overall process flow—If the survey is to be sent, determine where and how it is to be distributed, returned, and processed. If the accuracy assessment involves inspection, determine when and how the inspection will take place.
- Overall timing—any key dependencies (For example, the data in the database should be extracted at a time as close as possible to the time the assessment starts.)
- That the update reasons, scoring guidelines, survey scenarios, and record dispositions have been finalized and documented.
- That any list of choices and corresponding codes are correct.

7. Develop reports and the process for reporting results.

Reporting needs must be clarified up-front to ensure that the correct information is collected and readily available on the back end. Reports should include how the data from the database will be extracted and formatted, and in what form the information will be available for those conducting the inspection or survey.

- At a minimum, include output for every record showing a before and after picture of each data element (Output should include information about every record assessment, whether fully checked or not.)
- The number and percentage of records for each of the record dispositions
- Mock-ups of the reports to ensure agreement on the content and format of the information to be reported
- Finalization of the reports

8. Prepare the process for scoring accuracy.

Scoring quantifies the results of the accuracy assessment. *Scoring guidelines* are the rules that determine whether the update reasons will be scored as correct or incorrect. Each field compared for accuracy will be scored as correct or incorrect. The scoring guidelines are applied to the survey or inspection results after the survey or inspection has been completed.

In order to score the accuracy results, follow these steps:

Prioritize and weight the data—Decide which data are the most important and assign a ranking of value relative to other data elements (e.g., low, medium, high, or 1, 2, 3).

Create scoring guidelines—The scoring guidelines are the rules that determine the score to be assigned to each update reason. For example, a field with an update reason code of "correct," "blank," or "format" may be assigned a score of 1, while a field with an update reason code of "wrong" may be assigned a score of 0. Whether the record is a 1 or a 0 is determined when the scoring is completed. The scores are put into the scoring mechanism (such as a spreadsheet) to calculate accuracy statistics.

Create a scoring mechanism—This may be a spreadsheet that calculates the data element, record level, and overall accuracy statistics based on the assessment.

9. Extract the appropriate records and fields for assessment.

Verify that the extracted data meet your selection criteria and that the sample is random and representative of the population. Refer to the Capture Data section in Chapter 5 to ensure that you are correctly extracting the data needed for the accuracy assessment.

10. Train those who are conducting assessments.

Assessments carried out by multiple people must be conducted consistently to ensure correct results.

11. Run and test the inspection or survey process from beginning to end.

Make changes to the process, survey instrument, survey scenarios, record dispositions, scoring methods, and reports as needed.

Execute

Complete the following while the assessment is being conducted.

1. Collect results.

If too much time has passed between initially extracting the data and finalizing your assessment plan, you may need to extract the data again to ensure that the most recent data are being assessed. Capture assessment results throughout the survey period.

2. Monitor the progress of the assessment throughout the survey period.

This will allow you to confirm if the work is on schedule and is being done correctly and consistently. It is important to find problem areas early on. If needed, stop and make adjustments to the survey instrument, provide additional training to surveyors, and so forth.

3. Stop the assessment when the desired number of completed (fully checked) records has been reached.

Analyze

Finish the following items after the survey has been completed.

1. Obtain final reports.

2. Score the survey according to your scoring guidelines.

Scoring refers to evaluating the differences between what was originally in the database with what was found during the assessment, assigning a score, and calculating the accuracy levels.

- Choose an objective third party to do the scoring.
- Prepare materials and document the process for scoring so it can be done consistently.
- Only score records that have been "fully checked."
- Compare what is in the database against the assessment or survey results and apply a score for each data element.

3. Analyze results of the survey.

Look at accuracy at the data element and record level. Also look at overall sample accuracy. Analyze the record disposition statistics—the number and percentage of records for each disposition. Other considerations:

- What is the accuracy level? If you have targets for accuracy, compare the actual results to them.
- How do results compare with your expectations? Any surprises?
- Do accuracy results vary by country, geographic region, or some other category that is meaningful to your company?

- Has anything been learned during the assessment that provides enough information about impact to determine if it is worthwhile to continue addressing accuracy?
- Did you expect this to be a one-time assessment only? Have you learned anything about accuracy that will change that plan?
- How will you handle the correction of records found to be inaccurate? Who will do this and when?

- How can you prevent the creation of inaccurate records? Any ideas on root cause?

See the Analyze and Document Results section in Chapter 5 for additional suggestions.

4. Document results and recommended actions.

Include lessons learned such as potential impact to the business from the accuracy results, possible root causes, and preliminary recommendations.

Step 3.5 Consistency and Synchronization

Business Benefit and Context

Consistency refers to the fact that the same data stored and used in various places in the company should be equivalent—that is, the same data should represent the same fact.

Equivalence is the degree to which data stored in multiple places is conceptually equal. It indicates that the data have equal values and meanings or are in essence the same. *Synchronization* is "the process of making the data equivalent" (Larry English).

Definition

Consistency and synchronization are measures of the equivalence of information stored or used in various data stores, applications, and systems, and the processes for making data equivalent.

For example, your company makes (manufactures) some parts for building products and buys other parts. A make part is indicated in the first database as M. In another database a make part is coded as 44. Any make part record moved from the first database with a value of M should be stored in the second database with a value of 44. If not, there is a data quality problem with consistency (how the data are stored) and synchronization.

An example of being consistent, but not directly equivalent, may be in a hierarchy where one system shows medical specialty as breast cancer and another shows medical specialty as oncology. They are not equivalent but consistent.

This type of assessment looks at equivalent information throughout its life cycle as stored or used in various data stores, applications, processes, and the like, and determines if it is consistent.

Consistency and synchronization are important because the same data are often stored in many different places in the company. *Any* use of the data should be based on those data having the same meaning. It is not uncommon for management reports on the same topic to have different results. This leaves management in the uncomfortable position of not really knowing the "truth" of what is happening in the company and makes effective decisions difficult.

Approach

1. Identify the databases where data are stored redundantly.

Refer to the results from *Step 2.6—Define the Information Life Cycle* to determine the various locations where the data are stored. (*Note:* Whether the redundancy is necessary or not is not determined at this point.)

2. For each field of interest identify the detail about it for each database where it resides.

This is a detailed mapping of the same data as they are stored in each database. Refer to

Step 2.2—Understand Relevant Data and Specifications.

3. Extract the data from the first database and select the corresponding records from each redundant database.

Use the Capture Data section in Chapter 5 to ensure that the right data are being extracted.

4. Compare the data from each redundant database with the data in the original database.

Determine if one database is considered the authoritative source of reference.

5. Analyze and report the consistency results.

Note where *unwanted* redundancy exists.

6. Document results and recommended actions.

Include lessons learned such as potential impact to the business from the accuracy results, possible root causes, and preliminary recommendations.

Sample Output and Templates

The Situation

Background—Sales reps in your company are one of the main vehicles for obtaining customer information. That information eventually makes its way through various processes and ends up in the Customer Master Database, where it is further moved and used in transactional and reporting systems. The project team looked at the high-level Information Life Cycle that was an output of *Step 2—Analyze Information Environment* to determine all systems where the data were stored. Because of resource constraints they could not look at every system at this time.

Focus—The team decided to focus on the front end of the Information Life Cycle and

test data for consistency between the Customer Master Database and one of the transactional systems that uses the customer data—the Service and Repair Application (SRA).

Inquiry, the "override" flag—The project team paid particular attention to what is called the "override" flag. The SRA allowed the phone reps to override the data pulled in from the Customer Master Database when creating service orders. The team wanted to understand the magnitude of the differences for those records with the override flag set to yes (Y) and the nature of the differences in the data.

Extract records—The project team extracted records from the SRA where the override flag was set to Y. They then extracted the associated records from the Customer Master Database. When performing the comparisons, the Customer Master Database was considered the system of record. The project team used a data profiling tool to run column profiling (content profiling) against both sets of data and then compared the data for equivalence.

Method—random sample and manual comparison—For some data elements (such as Company Name and Address) the comparison was done manually. In addition, the team wanted to further segment the results to see if there were significant differences between countries in the SRA. A random sample of the population from profiling for each country was selected for the manual comparison.

(See *Step 3.6—Timeliness and Availability* for a continuation of this example that includes the timeliness dimension.)

The Results

Table 3.16 shows the results of the manual comparisons for consistency.

Table 3.16 • Consistency Results

SUMMARY: CONSISTENCY FOR COUNTRY 1*	COUNT (#)	PERCENTAGE (%)
Total closed orders from Service and Repair Application		
Orders with override flag = Y		

ANALYSIS OF ORDERS WITH CHANGES	% TYPE OF OVERRIDES	NUMBER OF OVERRIDES	% OF TOTAL RECORDS
MAJOR—Company name and address completely changed			
MAJOR—Address attributes changed; indicates different physical location or different site			
Minor or no changes			

Impact: 35 percent of orders have major changes to company name and/or address.

These data are lost when the repair order is closed. The assumption is that these data are more up to date than the data in the Customer Master Database.

SUMMARY: CONSISTENCY OF REPAIR ADDRESSES	COUNTRY 1	COUNTRY 2	COUNTRY 3
Total number of service orders in Quarter 1			
Total number of service orders with override flag			
Sample size			
Company name and address completely changed			
Address attributes changed			
Override flag on, but no changes to name or address			
SRA number not in Customer Master Database			

*There was one consistency report for each country examined.

<table>
<tr><td>**Step 3.6**</td></tr>
</table>

Step 3.6 Timeliness and Availability

Business Benefit and Context

Data values change over time and there will always be a gap between when the real-world object changes and when the data that represent it are updated in a database and made available for use. This gap is referred to as *information float*. There can be manual float (the delay from when a fact becomes known to when it is first captured electronically) and electronic float (time from when a fact is first captured electronically to when it is moved or copied to various databases that make it available to those interested in accessing it).

The phrase "use as specified" in the definition of this dimension refers to having the data available when the business requires them. Another way to describe timeliness is as

> [A] measure of the degree to which an information chain or process is completed within a pre-specified date or time. Timeliness is related to currency—data are current if they are up-to-date and are the usual result of a timely information chain.
>
> —Tom Redman[7]

 Definition

Timeliness and availability are measures of the degree to which data are current and available for use as specified and in the time frame in which they are expected.

Approach

1. Confirm the Information Life Cycle.
Review the Information Life Cycle developed in *Step 2.6—Define the Information Life Cycle* and update if necessary. (See the example in the Sample Output and Templates section at the end of this step.)

2. Determine which phases of the Information Life Cycle to assess for timeliness and availability.
You may want to focus on only a portion of the life cycle.

3. Determine the process for measuring information float throughout the process.
Work with your information technology group to understand database updates and load schedules. If necessary, have data producers keep a log of date and time when specific occurrences of data become known during the assessment period.

4. Select a random sample of records to trace through the Information Life Cycle.
You may be moving either forward or backward through the life cycle.

5. Determine the time elapsed between the steps in the process for each of the records.
Document the start time, stop time, and elapsed time for each step in the process. Be sure to take geographic locations and time zones into account.

6. Compile and analyze results of the timeliness test.
Consider the following:
- What are the timeliness requirements? When does the information need to be available at each step of the process?

[7] From *Data Quality: The Field Guide* (Digital Press, 2001), p. 227.

- Are processes and responsibilities completed in a timely manner? If not, why?
- Is there anything that can be changed to help?

7. Document results and recommended actions.

Include assessment results, lessons learned, possible impact on the business, suggested root causes, and preliminary recommendations.

Sample Output and Templates

The situation: This example continues the example from *Step 3.5—Consistency and Synchronization*. Assume an assessment for consistency was completed. Now the business wants to understand the timing of events in the process as the data move through the life cycle. A subset of the life cycle for one country was examined in detail for timeliness and availability.

The requirement: Changes to customer information must be reflected in the Customer Master Database and made available for transactional use within 24 hours of knowledge of the change. All sales reps should synchronize their personal handheld databases with the central database every evening (Monday through Friday) by 6 p.m. U.S. Pacific Time.

Table 3.17 shows the results of tracking one record through the process. Table 3.18 shows results after compiling and analyzing output from all records tracked for timeliness.

Table 3.17 • Tracking and Recording Timeliness

Information Life Cycle Process	Date	Time	Elapsed Time	Notes
Customer changes location.	Unknown	Unknown	–	
Company notifies sales rep via email of change.	Monday, March 5	8:00 a.m.	–	
Sales rep reads email.	Monday, March 5	11:30 a.m.	3.5 hours	
Sales rep updates personal database.	Monday, March 5	6:00 p.m.	6.5 hours	
Sales rep synchronizes data with central Customer Master Database.	Friday, March 9	8:00 p.m.	98 hours (4 days and 2 hours)	
Customer Master Database batch processing starts.	Monday, March 12	8:00 p.m.	72 hours (3 days)	Synchronization missed Friday processing* Records not processed until Monday evening
Updates available for transactional systems (when batch processing completes).	Monday, March 12	11:00 p.m.	3 hours	
Used by Service and Repair Application(SRA)**	–	–	–	
			183 hours	Monday, March 5, 8 a.m. to Monday, March 12, 11 p.m.

Note: All times U.S. Pacific Standard Time.

*Customer Master Database starts additional batch processing daily (Monday–Friday) at 8:00 p.m. When processing is complete (approximatey 3 hours), the changes are available for transactional systems.

**Time tracking from the Customer Master Database forward to various transactional and reporting uses (e.g., sales reps taking calls from customers and creating service orders) was determined to be out of scope at this time.

Table 3.18 • Timeliness Results and Initial Recommendations

Number of records tracked _____
Number of associated sales reps _____
Timeliness assessment period _____

	AVERAGE	HIGH	LOW
Length of time between customer changes known by sales rep to changes available to be used by transactional and reporting systems			
Sales rep's time to complete synchronization	35 min.	90 min.	15 min.
Number of times a month sales reps synchronize personal databases with Customer Master Database	2	4	0

FINDINGS	SUSPECTED ROOT CAUSES	INITIAL RECOMMENDATIONS
Longer than expected delays occur between when sales reps learn about changes and when data can be used by rest of company.	See below.	Determine the impact to the business use of transactional data when changes are delayed to determine if recommendations should be pursued.
Most sales reps rarely synchronize databases more than two times a month.	Sales reps generally update personal databases at end of day—usually after 6:30 p.m. Technical problems often prevent reps from completing synchronization. IT help desk is not open after 7:00 p.m. No technical help is available when needed.	Investigate and correct causes of technical problems preventing synchronization. Is there a way to simplify the synchronization process?
Updates from Friday evening's synchronization often miss Friday's batch processing, thus delaying updates' availablility until Monday evening.	Daily batch processing starts at 8:00 p.m. Most sales reps don't synchronize their databases until after that time.	Check into update schedules for the Customer Master Database. Are there any changes to the processing schedule that better fit into sales rep timing for synchronization?
New sales reps synchronize databases less than once a month.	New sales reps do not know how to complete the synchronization.	Train sales reps in synchronization.
Some sales reps do not synchronize their databases at all.	Sales reps don't know what happens to their data once they leave personal databases. There is distrust of the central system.	Document and educate sales reps on use of their customer data. Work with sales managers to devise incentives for synchronizing databases.

Step 3.7 Ease of Use and Maintainability

Business Benefit and Context

Having the data available in the database so they can be used is not the same as how easy it is to use them. For example, sales information may be available in various databases, but the ability to pull the information together for a report may not be a simple matter.

Executives may request information on their top ten accounts, knowing that the information exists in the company databases. What is not known is that it takes a small team of people five working days each month to pull together what appears to be a simple report. In many cases if managers knew how long it took to get the information, they would either decide it was not worth the time spent or give their people time to determine how to make it easier to generate.

As with the example of use, it may also be important to understand how easy (or difficult) it is to maintain data. Knowing the degree of maintainability coupled with how important the data are to the business will help businesses make better decisions on investments in managing those data.

Ease of use and maintainability are closely related to timeliness and availability, and you may do much of the work for these dimensions together. They are separated here to make it easier for you to determine which aspects are most important to assess at any given time. If you have completed *Step 4.5—Ranking and Prioritization* AND have included the ability to collect and maintain the data as one of the criteria for ranking and prioritization, use those results for this assessment.

Ease of use and maintainability are impacted by the data model. Proper data architecture allows data reuse and availability.

Approach

1. Determine which data or information you want to assess for ease of use and why.

For example, you may have completed an assessment on duplication. You found that the knowledge workers create duplicates because it is easier to create a new record than it is to find an existing one. This would be a reason to focus on ease of use and maintainability for that process.

2. Evaluate the data for ease of use.

- Reference your information life cycle for any clues that are relevant to ease of use.
- You will most likely need to interview knowledge workers and have them show you their processes.

Definition

Ease of use and maintainability are measures of the degree to which data can be accessed and used, and the degree to which data can be updated, maintained, and managed.

- Ensure that both knowledge workers and managers agree on the time being spent in interviews.
- Document and time the process steps.

3. Evaluate the data for maintainability.

See the suggestions for evaluating ease of use just given; they also apply when evaluating for maintainability.

4. Document results and recommended actions.

Include lessons learned, possible impact to the business, suggested root causes, and preliminary recommendations.

Step 3.8 Data Coverage

Business Benefit and Context

Coverage is concerned with how comprehensive the data available to the company are in accounting for the total population of interest. In other words, how well does the database capture the total population of interest and reflect it to the business? The idea of coverage can also be used when determining what population should or should not be included in any particular assessment, process, or project. (See the Capture Data section in Chapter 5.)

Approach

1. **Define coverage in the context of your project, total population, and goals as it relates to business needs.**

The following are examples of specific project definitions for coverage and total population:

Coverage—an estimate of the percentage of active installed equipment collected in the customer database.
- *Total population:* This is the installed base market (either customers or installed products) that exists in Asia Pacific.
- *Goal:* Determine how well the database being measured captures and reflects the

total installed base market within the region.

Coverage—an estimate of the percentage of all sites collected in the customer database.
- *Total population:* This is all U.S. sites for a specified strategic account that purchases your company's products.
- *Goal:* Determine how well the database being measured captures and reflects the sites for the specified strategic account.

2. **Estimate the total size of the population or data universe.**

For example, assume you want to determine the installed market (either customers or installed products) that exists in a country for each product line. This will give you an idea of how large your database should be if all customers and /or installed products are to be captured in it. You may look at orders and shipments over the past few years to determine the number of customers. Work with your Sales and Marketing department and utilize the figures they already have.

3. **Measure the size of the database population.**

Perform record counts for records that reflect the population of interest.

4. **Calculate coverage.**

Divide the number of records obtained from doing step 3 by the estimated total population. This provides the percentage coverage in your database.

5. **Analyze the results.**

Determine if the coverage is enough to meet business needs. It is possible that the coverage will be greater than 100 percent. This indicates as much of a problem as a very low figure, such as 25 percent. Specifically,

 Definition

Data coverage is a measure of the availability and comprehensiveness of data compared to the total data universe or population of interest.

coverage numbers greater than 100 percent indicate other data quality problems such as duplicate records.

Consider if there is a connection between coverage and ease of use and maintainability. Does difficulty in use affect coverage? For example, assume that a sales rep is the source of customer information and the only way those data get into the database is by syncing the database and the rep's handheld. How difficult is that process? Does the synchronization complete smoothly and in a timely manner? Is the sales rep reluctant to share information?

In one company, the sales reps did not want to share their customer information because from their point of view those data went into a "black box." Once moved into the central database, the reps knew the data were being updated and transformed, but they had no visibility to what was happening and did not trust the data that came back to them through the synchronization process.

6. Document results and recommended actions.

Document assessment results, lessons learned, possible impact on the business, suggested root causes, and preliminary recommendations.

Step 3.9 Presentation Quality

Business Benefit and Context

Presentation quality refers to the manner in which information is presented. Presentation quality affects information when it is collected *and* when it is reported.

Reporting can mean presenting results of a quality assessment using graphs and charts, a file of data records with columns that are clearly labeled, a report showing sales results for the last month, and so on.

Assessing presentation quality involves two perspectives: the assessor's perspective and the perspective of those using the information—the knowledge workers. For the assessor to understand the knowledge workers' perspective, he or she must become familiar with how the information is being applied (its purpose) and the context of that usage (what happens when and where it is used). If there are inconsistencies, mistakes, or a design that facilitates misunderstanding, the assessor can then recommend that presentation quality be improved.

Important: Presenting information (for both collecting and reporting) in a way that is easy and effective from the knowledge workers' perspective increases overall information quality.

Approach

1. **Define the information and associated presentation media.**

   * *Decide* which information will be checked for presentation quality.
   * *Discover* when and where it is presented, and the media associated with its presentation.
   * *Find out* who applies the information.

   Refer to your Information Life Cycle:

   * What are the various ways those data are obtained? For example, check user interface screens.
   * What are the the original sources?
   * When is information presented?
   * Who are the people who use the information and for what reason?

   You may be looking only at one medium, or you may be looking at multiple media that collect or store the same information. For example, you may want to compare all the ways that customers provide information about themselves, and the media may be an email campaign, an online Web survey, and a hardcopy response form completed

---

 Definition

Presentation quality is a measure of how information is presented to and collected from those who utilize it. (Format and appearance support the appropriate use of the information.)

 Definition

Media are the various means of communication, including (but not limited to) user guides, Web surveys, hardcopy forms, and database-entry interfaces.

during an in-person customer seminar. (See Example 1 in the Sample Output and Templates section.)

2. Outline the assessment process.

Plan a consistent process for the assessment. Decide who will perform it. Ensure that all those performing the assessment are trained and that they and their managers understand and support the activity.

3. Analyze the information and format for quality.

- Interview users to find out if they have trouble using the medium correctly.
- Compare information gathered through several media to determine whether any of the media are affecting information collection.

Use the following questions to evaluate presentation quality:

- Is the form design easy to follow?
- Are the data being requested clearly defined?
- Are the questions clear? Does the respondent understand what is being asked?
- Where appropriate, are there lists of possible answers (e.g., these may be shown as a dropdown list on a screen or as a list with checkboxes on a hardcopy)?
- Are there redundant questions?
- Are the possible answers complete—do they cover all potential responses?
- Are the possible answers mutually exclusive—is there only one correct response for one answer?
- Does the presentation require interpretation that could introduce errors?
- Are there complete process instructions?

If looking at presentation quality of reports, consider the following:

- Are report titles concise and representative of the report content?
- If using tables, are column and row headings concise and representative of the content?

4. Document results and recommended actions.

Include lessons learned, possible impact to the business, suggested root causes, and preliminary recommendations. For example, you may want to meet with the contacts responsible for each of the media, discuss the differences, determine what needs to be changed, and ensure that the database can support what is needed.

Sample Output and Templates

Example 1

One company conducted a data profiling assessment and found some quality issues. Through root cause analysis, they determined that some of their data quality problems were due to the many different methods of collecting customer information, particularly company revenue, number of employees, department, position level, and so on. Each of the various media presented the questions and offered possible responses in a different way. There was no process for standardizing responses and developing the questions. Table 3.19 gives an example.

Because there was no consistency in how the data were gathered, there were issues with how the data were entered and issues with being able to use the data later.

 Best Practice

Always consider who will be using the information, their purposes, and what makes sense for them when thinking about presentation.

Table 3.19 • Presentation Quality Comparison

DATA ELEMENT	NUMBER OF EMPLOYEES		
Type of Media	Email campaign (name and date)	Online Web survey (name and date)	Response form from in-person customer seminar (date)
Team Responsible for Media	Marketing	Marketing	Sales
Specific Question	How large is your company?	How many employees are there in your company?	Number of employees
Possible Responses	1 2–10 11–50 51–100 101–500 501–1000	1–100 101–1000 1001–10,000 10,001–100,000 Over 100,000	1–10 11–100 101–1000 Over 1000
Analysis	• Ranges vary greatly: email campaign has much more detailed ranges for number of employees. Is this level of precision really required by the business? Web survey goes up to 100,000. • Question in email campaign not as clear as could be. • Does the database allow for entry of the various responses? • Ask the business about the need for the various ranges. Does it make sense to standardize the responses for this type of question across all media?		
DATA ELEMENT	**POSITION LEVEL**		
Specific Question			
Possible Responses			
Analysis			

Example 2

Collecting credit card information is common when ordering via a website. There are many ways to request credit card expiration dates, as shown in Table 3.20. How could these different ways of presenting and capturing dates affect the quality of the customer credit card information?

Table 3.20 • Presentation Quality—Collecting Credit Card Information

OPTIONS FOR ENTERING CREDIT CARD EXPIRATION MONTH	EXAMPLE	ANALYSIS
Customer types in month	01, 02	Opportunities for mistyping. Better to have a set list of values.
Dropdown list with month written as month name	January, February, March	Poor presentation. On the card, the month is usually specified as a number. This option requires the customer to translate the number on the card to the month name. This is an opportunity for introducing error.
Dropdown list with month as two digits	01, 02, 03	Good presentation because the values match the original source (the customer's credit card).
Dropdown list with month as two digits along with month name	01–January 02–February 03–March	Good presentation because the values match the original source and includes the month name, which is helpful for some customers.

Step 3.10   Perception, Relevance, and Trust

Business Benefit and Context

It is often said that perception is reality. If users believe that data quality is poor, they will not use the data. This assessment looks at the quality of data from the knowledge workers' point of view. It can be used to

- Understand which data are of most value to the business and therefore which data should have first priority in management and maintenance.

- Understand the data quality issues affecting the knowledge workers in order to prioritize them in a focused data quality project.

- Understand, from the knowledge workers' point of view, the impact of poor-quality data on job responsibilities. Use the information to help build a business case for data quality efforts.

- Understand how knowledge workers feel about the data and then compare their perception to actual data quality assessment results.

- Address any gaps between perception and reality through communication.

This assessment takes the form of a knowledge worker survey. An effective means of conducting

this type of survey is usually person to person, in the form of an interview using consistent questions and encouraging additional dialogue.

Approach

Prepare

Complete the following items prior to conducting your survey.

1. Define the goal of the survey.
Determine what decisions will be supported and what answers need to be obtained. What do you need to know and at what level of detail? Decide if answers need to be on a general business level or on a more detailed data subject level. (A field-by-field survey is often not effective; you will find resistance to answering the survey and will not get more useful results than you would if you asked questions from a broader perspective.)

2. Determine survey participants.
Select representative knowledge workers to participate in the survey. Determine whether you want only those who apply the information or those who also create and maintain the data. Document and include job title/function, name of participant, and total number of similar knowledge workers within the group.

3. Decide which survey method to use.
Examples include telephone, mailing, Web, email, and focus group.

4. Develop the survey instrument.
The survey instrument is the standard list of questions and possible answers with which you capture the survey responses. The format can be hardcopy or softcopy.

 Definition

Perception, relevance, and trust are measures of the perception of and confidence in the quality of the data; the importance, value, and relevance of the data to the business needs.

Your survey may be a few open-ended questions, where you want to encourage dialogue, rather than a structured set of questions. See the Sample Output and Templates section for an example of how such an approach was successfully used.

Keep in mind the people being surveyed and how they are using the data. Some will not have a tolerance for detail. You may have different surveys for different knowledge workers. For instance, a survey for someone doing data entry or using the data at the field level may be more detailed than a survey of a sales rep using the information for customer contacts. Even for those creating data, it may be more helpful to understand perceptions at a high level than at a detailed level.

If you are asking more questions in a more ordered fashion, consider the following suggestions to ensure that the information is presented clearly and that the survey respondents have enough background to complete the survey. Include

Introduction—This should have a customer service focus, call attention to the confidentiality of the survey (if that is true), and describe the benefit to the respondent, or the organization represented by the respondent. Include a deadline for returning the survey, who to call with questions, and so forth.

Body—This is the question-and-response section. It should be designed to be comprehensive but concise. Responses should be in a format easy for the respondent to complete and easy for those collecting the data to store and document. Questions should draw out the information you need to support your goals.

Conclusion—This should give the respondent the ability to provide additional information, insights, or feedback. End with a genuine thank you.

Determine the scale to be used for answering the questions. (See example at bottom of this page.)

General question statements for scaling could include:

- This information is important to me in performing my job. (Indicates relevance or value.)
- In my opinion, this information is reliable. (Indicates perception of quality.)

If needed, solicit the help of someone experienced in creating and administering surveys.

5. Develop the process for conducting the survey and capturing results.

Recruit those who will conduct the survey. Ensure that they have background on the survey and on why it is being conducted. Gain their support and enthusiastic participation. Provide training as needed to those conducting the survey so they can encourage participation and provide consistent results. Develop the method for capturing results and the process for reporting results.

6. Test the survey process.

Test for clarity to ensure that respondents understand and can answer appropriately. Revise as needed to create a participant-friendly questionnaire. Test entering the results into a survey tool, if one is being used. Test for ease of data entry and for the ability to analyze the survey results properly. Revise the survey as needed to create an effective data-gathering device.

Strongly Agree	Agree	Neither Agree Nor Disagree	Disagree	Strongly Disagree	Not Applicable
1	2	3	4	5	0

7. Create or extract the list of those to survey.

One project decided to survey knowledge workers who used a particular application. The results were going to be used to prioritize the data quality issues to address. The project team pulled a list of those with logins, only to find that the list was outdated. People had left the job, changed responsibilities, or shared logins and passwords with coworkers. A clean-up effort on the logins and the list of users had to be completed before the survey could be started!

Execute

While the survey is being conducted, remember these points.

1. Collect results.
2. Monitor the responses throughout the survey period to confirm that the survey is on track.
3. Stop the survey when the desired number of knowledge workers has been surveyed or the time period has ended.

Analyze

After the survey has been completed, do the following.

1. Confirm that all responses have been entered and documented.

2. Analyze results.
Compare perceptions of quality with the actual quality results from other data quality assessments. If asking the two general questions

Best Practice

Encourage candid responses: When performing a person-to-person survey, it is less intrusive to capture results by taking notes and then enter them into the survey tool later.

about importance/value and reliability/quality, you may want to plot results to an importance/ reliability matrix and look for trends.

3. Document results and recommended actions.

Include a copy of the survey, those surveyed, those conducting the survey, the process used, and the number of respondents. Include specific survey results, lessons learned, impact to the business, suggested root causes of data quality problems, and preliminary recommendations.

4. Communicate.
Provide feedback to the survey participants. You may choose to hold a focus group meeting with respondents to discuss responses and perceptions. Use the survey results to achieve project goals.

Sample Output and Templates

To document the impact of data quality from a knowledge worker's point of view, C. Lwanga Yonke, Information Quality Process Manager at Aera Energy LLC, conducted a survey of stakeholders. The survey was sent to more than 60 knowledge workers (engineers, geoscientists, technicians, etc.) and consisted of two requests: (1) "Describe an example where *bad* things happened because of poor quality information. If possible describe the impact in operational terms, then quantify it in terms of production loss and in terms of dollars"; and (2) "Repeat, but provide examples of *good* things that happened because you had quality information available."

The anecdotes and examples received were compiled into one document, which was then widely distributed throughout the company. The power of the document came from the fact that it captured the voice of the information customers, not that of IT or the information quality team. All the anecdotes were from knowledge workers—the people best placed to describe the impact of information quality on their ability to execute the company's work processes.

The document served several purposes:

- It helped build the case for action for various data quality improvement projects.
- It helped solidify wide support for Aera's data quality process in general.
- It was used as a training manual to show others how to quantify the cost of poor quality information and the return on investment of information quality–improvement projects. Lwanga fondly recalls, for example, how the leader of one Enterprise Architecture Implementation project drew on several stories to rally support for incorporating specific data quality process improvements and data remediation work into his project plan.

Also see *Step 4.1—Anecdotes* for another example of how results from a similar survey were used to secure approval and funding for Aera's Enterprise Architecture Implementation program.

Step 3.11 Data Decay

Business Benefit and Context

Data decay is also known as *data erosion*. It is a useful measure for high-priority data that are subject to change as a result of events outside a system's control. Knowing data decay rates helps determine whether mechanisms should be installed to maintain the data and the frequency of updates. Volatile data requiring high reliability would require more frequent updates than less important data with lower decay rates.

Arcady Maydanchik, in his book *Data Quality Assessment,* presents 13 categories of processes that cause data problems (2007, p. 7). Five are processes causing data decay: Changes Not Captured, System Upgrades, New Data Uses, Loss of Expertise, and Process Automation. If you see these processes in your environment, you can be sure your data are decaying. If the business is dependent on data known to change quickly, do not spend time determining the decay rate—spend time on ways to keep the data up to date.

This step is less about the actual measure of data decay than it is about situations that may cause that decay and generally which data may decay most quickly. Combine that with your understanding of which data are most important and you can focus data quality prevention,

Definition

Data decay is a measure of the rate of negative change to the data.

improvement, correction, and management on them.

Approach

1. Quickly examine your environment for processes that cause data to decay and for data already known to decay quickly.

Some data are widely known to change quickly—for instance, in the United States, phone numbers and email addresses. If your business is dependent on phone numbers or email addresses, immediately put processes into place to keep the data up to date. Also, use what you learned from prior work on your Information Life Cycle.

2. Use results from prior assessments to determine data decay.

Reference statistics that include changes over time from previous data assessments, such as data integrity fundamentals, accuracy, and concurrency and timeliness. If you have profiled your data, you may have visibility to last update dates. Categorize by useful date ranges. If you have conducted an accuracy survey, use the data samples and assessment results for accuracy. (See Figure 3.11 in the Sample Output and Templates section.)

Look for information about rates of change from external sources. For example, does the postal service in your country publish rates about how quickly addresses change?

While data decay focuses on the rate of negative change to the data, also consider the rate of change from a data creation point of view. How quickly are records being created? If you are analyzing last update dates, you may want to analyze create dates at the same time.

3. Use processes already in place to determine data decay.

For example, one marketing group surveys their resellers every four months to update reseller profiles, contact name and job title information, and product sold. The vendor that administers the survey determines during data entry if the contact name has been added, deleted, or modified, or if it is unchanged. This information is used to see percent changes to reseller data.

4. Analyze results.

If you are also looking at create dates, look at the rate of new records being created. Is it more than you expected? Are you staffed to handle the rate of creation? Are new records being created because existing records are not being found? If so, are duplicate records increasing?

5. Document assessment results and recommended actions.

Include lessons learned, possible impact on the business, suggested root causes, and preliminary recommendations.

Sample Output and Templates

Figure 3.11 compares the results of updates in two countries for the same application. The application had a field called Customer Contact Validation Date that was supposed to be updated whenever the customer information manager contacted the customer. By looking at that field, some assumptions could be made about the rate of customer data decay.

In Country 1, 88 percent of the records had not been updated for more than 60 months

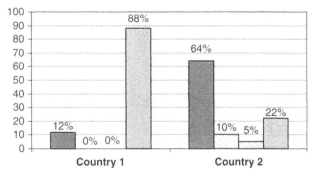

Number of months since updated: ■ 0–18 ▢ 19–36 ▢ 37–60 ▢ >60

Figure 3.11 • Use of Customer Contact Validation Date field to analyze data decay.

(that is, 5 years) and only 12 percent had been updated in the last 18 months. Contrast that with Country 2, where 22 percent of the records had not been updated for more than 5 years, and 64 percent had been updated in the last 18 months.

It would appear that Country 1 had had contact activity more than 5 years ago, yet the efforts had languished until 18 months prior to the analysis, when it appeared that renewed efforts were taking place. Another factor that came into play (which the numbers do not show) is that the customer contact validation date had to be manually updated.

The field for updating was not easily available and it was known that customers had in fact sometimes been contacted but the date had not been updated. This led to one recommendation that user screens be changed (presentation quality) to make the Customer Contact Validation Date field readily available to those contacting customers.

Step 3.12 Transactability

Business Benefit and Context

Even if the right people have defined the business requirements and prepared the data to meet them, it is important that the data produce the expected outcome: Can the invoice be correctly generated? Can a sales order be completed?

This type of assessment would usually be included in a standard project life cycle as part of testing. It is mentioned here to point out that those developing requirements, creating transform rules, and cleaning source data need to be involved in testing the data they helped clean or create. None of the standards or requirements are any good if the business processes cannot be completed satisfactorily.

Approach

1. Enlist the support of your project testing team.
This step cannot be done in isolation. Work closely with the testing team.

2. Ensure that the data you are testing are data that meet requirements.
This is a good use of data profiling to quickly look at the data prior to running them through the process.

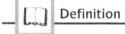

Definition

Transactability is a measure of the degree to which data will produce the desired business transaction or outcome.

3. Ensure that there is a feedback loop from the testers to those responsible for the data.
It is not unusual to find that data are changed in the course of testing to complete the transaction successfully. However, this fact does not always make it to those responsible for creating the data so they can learn from the changes and thus update data requirements.

4. Update data requirements based on the results and retest.

5. Document assessment results and actions.
Quick action should be taken in this step, as it should be in any standard testing cycle. Ensure that any needed changes are made to transformation rules or source data clean-up activities that may be part of the project.

Step 3 Summary

Congratulations! You have completed your data quality assessments (or have learned about them in preparation for an assessment). This is an important milestone in your project. Remember to communicate and document results and preliminary recommendations. Use the data dimensions when conducting an initial data quality assessment, setting a baseline for improvement, and implementing controls such as ongoing data quality monitoring and metrics.

You can also use the *concepts* of the data quality dimensions (not the step-by-step implementation). For instance, use the data quality dimension concepts when capturing high-level requirements from business analysts. See

Projects and The Ten Steps in Chapter 4 for a good example of how to use these concepts in requirements gathering.

Review the questions in the checkpoint box to help you determine if you are finished and ready to move to the next step.

 Communicate

- Have stakeholders been apprised of quality assessment results, preliminary impact to the business, suspected root causes, and initial recommendations? What are the stakeholders' reactions to what has been learned and your current plan of action?
- Are all members of the project team aware of the same information? What are the team members' reactions?
- Have you communicated possible impact or changes to project scope, timeline, and resources based on what was learned during the data quality assessment?

 Checkpoint

Step 3—Assess Data Quality

How can I tell whether I'm ready to move to the next step? Following are guidelines to determine completeness of the step:

✓ Have the applicable data quality assessments been completed?

✓ Has necessary follow-up to the analysis been completed?

✓ For each quality assessment, have the results been analyzed and documented?

✓ For each quality assessment, have preliminary impact to the business, suspected root causes, and initial recommendations been included in the documentation?

✓ If conducting multiple assessments, have results from all assessments been brought together and synthesized?

✓ Has the communication plan been updated?

✓ Has communication needed to this point been completed?

Step 4 | Assess Business Impact

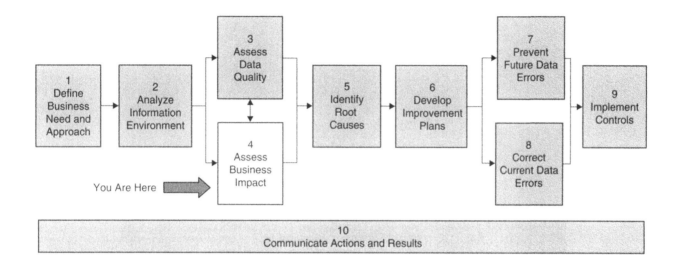

Introduction

Anything known about data quality issues immediately leads to the "So what" and "So why" questions—"What impact does this have on the business?" and "Why does this matter?" Add the question "What's the return on my investment?" and you can see why assessing business impact is so important. *Step 4—Assess Business Impact* (see Table 3.21) provides a variety of techniques for answering those questions by determining the impact of poor-quality data on your company (see Table 3.22, page 165).

The techniques are presented in terms of relative effort from less complicated (1) to more complex (8). In this step, you assess the business impact of data quality problems using the techniques that are the most appropriate to your situation and time and resources available. There is one substep with detailed instructions for each of the eight business impact techniques (Steps 4.1–4.8).

As discussed in Chapter 2, business impact techniques are both quantitative and qualitative. Business impact is primarily based on how the information is used since that is when its value is realized. Remember the Apply phase of the Information Life Cycle? Impact can also be shown in other phases of the Information Life Cycle (e.g., impact due to increased maintenance costs—the Maintain phase).

If you have completed any data quality assessments, you should have documented potential impacts to the business as they were discovered. The synthesis from those assessments compiles all initial thoughts about impacts. Sometimes the thoughts differ—that is not unexpected and it is important to capture all points of view.

If you know specific results and the magnitude of the data quality issues, use that knowledge in this step assessment. You may want to assess data where there are a high number of errors or where the subject matter expert has

Table 3.21 • Step 4—Assess Business Impact

OBJECTIVE	Establish the impact on the business of data quality issues. Both qualitative and quantitative measures can be used.
PURPOSE	Provide input to • Establish the business case for data quality improvement • Gain support from management for information quality investments • Determine appropriate investments in your information resources such as needed data corrections and improvements to prevent future errors
INPUTS	Output from *Step 1—Define Business Need and Approach* • Business issues and opportunities where quality of data/information is suspected to be a component • Known or suspected data quality problems • Business goals and objectives Output from *Step 2—Analyze Information Environment* • Understanding of people/organizations, processes, and technology in the Apply phase of the Information Life Cycle POSMAD and related to the data quality issue • Results of analyzing the information environment where the data quality and business issues have been understood and linked sufficiently so there is confidence a detailed business impact assessment will focus in the right areas • Documentation with lessons learned such as potential impact to data quality and/or the business and initial recommendations at this point Output from *Step 3—Assess Data Quality* • Detailed assessment results, if applicable to your business impact assessment • Necessary communication completed, along with updated communication plan
TOOLS AND TECHNIQUES	• Methods applicable to the particular business impact technique, such as surveys and templates for gathering information anecdotes. See detail for each business impact technique.
OUTPUTS	• Business impact assessment results (quantitative and/or qualitative measures) • Recommendations for action based on impact results (e.g., where investments in information quality should be made, project next steps) • Necessary communication complete, along with updated communication plan
CHECKPOINT	• Have impacts to the business been assessed? • For each business impact assessment, have the results been analyzed and documented? • Has necessary follow-up to the analysis been completed? • For each impact assessment, have initial recommendations and anything learned that could effect possible root causes been documented? • If conducting multiple assessments, have results from all assessments been brought together and synthesized? • Has the communication plan been updated? • Has necessary communication been completed?

Table 3.22 • Business Impact Techniques

No.	BUSINESS IMPACT TECHNIQUE	DEFINITION
1	Anecdotes	Collect examples or stories about the impact of poor data quality.
2	Usage	Inventory the current and/or future uses of the data.
3	Five "Whys" for Business Impact	Ask "Why" five times to get to the real business impact.
4	Benefit versus Cost Matrix	Analyze and rate the relationship between benefits and costs of issues, recommendations, or improvements.
5	Ranking and Prioritization	Rank the impact of missing and incorrect data on specific business processes.
6	Process Impact	Illustrate the effects of poor-quality data to business processes.
7	Cost of Low-Quality Data	Quantify the costs and revenue impact of poor-quality data.
8	Cost–Benefit Analysis	Compare potential benefits of investing in data quality with anticipated costs, through an in-depth evaluation. Includes return on investment (ROI)*—profit from an investment as a percentage of the amount invested.

*The phrases ROI or return on investment are often used in a general sense to indicate any means of showing some type of return on an investment. ROI in technique 8 refers to the formula for calculating return on investment.

already assigned a high priority. Use *all* of these results as input—now is the time to look at business impact specifically.

If a data quality assessment has not been conducted, but there are specific data quality issues of which the business is aware, you can still apply the techniques in this step to determine their impact. You may need to determine whether it is worthwhile to correct those issues, determine root causes, and prevent the issues in the future. In another case, your focus may be on building a business case for *starting* data quality activities.

With few exceptions, data quality should not be viewed in terms of obtaining a state of "zero defect" or perfect data. This very high level of quality entails cost and can take considerable time. More cost efficient is a balanced, risk-based approach that defines data quality needs and investments in improvements based on business impacts and risks.

Understanding the impact to the business of any data quality issues will help you establish the business case for information quality, gain support for investing in information quality, and make informed investment decisions.

Table 3.22 lists eight techniques for assessing business impact. (See also the Business Impact Techniques section in Chapter 2.)

Figure 3.12 shows a continuum of the relative time and effort for each technique, from generally less complex and taking less time (technique 1) to more complex and taking more time (technique 8).

Figure 3.12 • Business impact techniques relative to time and effort.

The overall approach to this step is straightforward. First determine the techniques to use; second, assess the business impact using the techniques you have chosen; and third, synthesize results from the completed assessments if more than one has been done.

Choose Business Impact Techniques to Use

Become familiar with the various techniques and what is required for each. Determine which data issues you need to assess for business impact. Make an informed and conscious decision about which techniques to use and choose the ones that support your situation and data issues.

Think about relative time and effort. Note that the continuum shows relative effort—not relative results. You can understand business impact even without completing a full cost–benefit analysis. Less complicated does not necessarily mean less useful results; more complex does not necessarily mean more useful results (and vice versa).

The best results come from using the techniques most appropriate to your situation, time, and resources available. Many of them can be used alone or provide input to other techniques. Briefly document the techniques chosen, the rationale behind the decision, and the assumptions upon which the decision was made. See the Business Impact Techniques section in Chapter 2 for more considerations.

Assess Business Impact Using the Techniques Chosen

Complete the business impact assessment for each technique chosen using the detailed

Best Practice

Be aware of what business impact means to different people and organizations. Do they want to see results in terms of

- Increased revenue (data quality will help us make more sales)
- Money saved (data quality will save us x dollars in costs)
- Operational efficiency (data quality will decrease production time by two days)
- Headcount (data quality will save us x number people)
- Risk (data quality will lower the risk of xyz)
- Other?

Try to translate and express your business impact results in the ways most meaningful to those from whom you need support.

instructions provided in the substeps (Steps 4.1–4.8). Always document lessons learned, anything discovered about possible root causes, and preliminary recommendations.

Synthesize Results from All Business Impact Assessments Completed

Combine and analyze results from the assessments you have completed. Determine how the results will influence your recommendations, communication, and the rest of the project. You may find that data quality issues have more impact than thought. Develop and document recommendations, possible root causes, and other lessons learned from synthesizing results. Use these results to determine your next steps (e.g., communication needed, business action required, adjustments to project scope, timeline, and resources needed).

Step 4.1 Anecdotes

Business Benefit and Context

Collecting stories is the easiest and most low-cost way of assessing business impact. However, it can still produce good results. Stories are a way to provoke interest in a topic in a way that listeners can relate to their own experiences. The right story can engage leadership quickly—especially when it provides context for facts and figures. Even without quantitative data, a story can still be useful.

> **Definition**
>
> **Anecdotes** are examples or stories of the impact of poor data quality.

Approach

1. Collect anecdotes.
Anecdotes are useful for immediate issues where the business is trying to get a first understanding of data quality impact. You can also document and save anecdotes as you collect them. When you hear about problems at your company caused by data quality, investigate and find out the specifics—who, what, when, where, and why. The anecdotes will be useful for future communication.

Collect examples or stories from news sources, websites, and industry that relate to your company, and specific company examples about actual business events.

See the Information Anecdote template (Template 3.8) in the Sample Output and Templates section for an easy way to collect anecdote specifics. *Caution:* Use the template for *collecting* results, not for *presenting* them. You will tell the story based on your audience and the point you need to make.

2. Get specific.
Use the following questions to get more specific as to the impacts learned through a particular incident:

Critical business decisions—What information is required to make those decisions? What happens if the information is wrong? How does that impact the business?

Key processes or key business flows—What information is required to carry out those processes? What happens if the information is wrong—to the immediate transaction, to other processes, to reporting, to decisions made from those reports, and so forth?

Business impact—What is the impact if the data are wrong (e.g., poor decisions, impact to customers, lost sales, increased rework, data correction)?

Master data (e.g., customer, vendor, item master, bills of material)—What processes or other transactions are dependent on the integrity of the master data? What will happen to the transactions if the master data are wrong? Are the data used to support transactions consistent with the system of record? Are other categories of data also impacted?

Transactional data—What will happen if the transactional records are wrong (e.g., the purchase order or the invoice is wrong)?

Required fields—How does the knowledge worker get those data? What happens if they are not available at the time the record is created? What will happen if incorrect data are entered just to satisfy a system requirement for an entry in a field?

3. Quantify the impact, if possible.

Quickly quantify parts of the anecdote, if possible. This is all about what you can learn with the least amount of time and effort, but you may be able to quantify the impact by asking questions such as "How often does this happen?" and "How many people were affected?" You can further analyze the impact of what you have found by using other techniques in this step.

4. Generalize the impact.

Take the isolated anecdote and determine the impact if the same experience were to be applied across the organization.

5. Determine how to tell the story.

Be creative. See the Sample Output and Templates section for an example of how one company used anecdotes to obtain funding for an Enterprise Architecture Plan supported by a comprehensive data quality program.

Use the anecdotes to support your communication needs. For example, do you have

30 seconds, or 3 minutes to tell the story? What does the audience need to hear? What point are you emphasizing?[8] (See *Step 10—Communicate Actions and Results*.)

I had one manager tell me that many important business decisions are based on stories. Collecting and using anecdotes is a low-cost way of showing business impact.

6. Document your results.

Document the anecdotes along with source and supporting information. Include tangible and intangible impact quantified in numbers and dollars, if possible.

Sample Output and Templates

Template 3.8, along with Tables 3.23 and 3.24, illustrate how to document anecdotes on business impact.

Warning

DO NOT use the Information Anecdote template in presentations! Use it to collect content, but don't present it. Tell the story in your presentation in a way that will engage your audience.

Key Concept

Not long ago a manager was explaining how often management and investment decisions are based on real anecdotes and said: "Never underestimate the power of a good story!"

The narrative that follows describes one company's experience with using anecdotes to assess business impact (see pages 171–172).

---

[8]If you want to explore the subject of storytelling further, Lori Silverman, in her book, *Wake Me Up When the Data Is Over: How Organizations Use Storytelling to Drive Results* (Jossey-Bass, 2006), shows how to increase the visibility and influence of stories and their practical application to a number of business disciplines. Resources listed in that book, along with her book *Stories Trainers Tell* (ASTD, Jossey-Bass/Pfeiffer, 2003), also include how to craft a story.

Template 3.8 • Information Anecdote

Title:	
Data:	People:
Processes:	Technology:
Scenario:	
Impact (quantify if possible): Initial recommendations or next steps:	
Submitted by:	
Contact information:	Date:

Table 3.23 • Information Anecdote—Example 1

TITLE: Duplicate Customer Master Records

DATA: Customer Master Records and Associated Transactional Records   **PEOPLE:** Customer Service Representatives

PROCESSES: Order Management   **TECHNOLOGY:** System A

SCENARIO:
- There are a large number of duplicate customer master records. Business transactions for one customer are associated with multiple master records.
- The company does not have one view of the customer and cannot make effective decisions to help the customer.

IMPACT (quantify if possible):
- When purchases by one company are associated with duplicate customer master records, the credit limit for that company can be unknowingly exceeded. This exposes our company to unnecessary credit risks.
- Customer service reps have difficulty locating a transaction placed on a duplicate account. This delays shipments or sends confusing messages to the customer.
- Duplicate records for one customer will contain differing information—it is not known which is correct.
- Duplicates increase costs of managing unnecessary records.

Submitted by: _____

Contact information: _____   Date: _____

Table 3.24 • Information Anecdote—Example 2

TITLE: Legal Requirement to Prove Pricing

DATA: Pricing for Government Contracts

PEOPLE: Purchasing Agents

PROCESSES: Procurement

TECHNOLOGY: System A

SCENARIO:

- For government contracts, the company has a legal requirement to prove pricing for the last ten years from the expiration of a contract. The only way to prove compliance is through pricing history.

- In the system, the pricing history is not created automatically—the audit trail is a single layer meaning that it only tracks one previous change. Therefore, in the system the only way to create the required history is to create a new price list line instead of changing the data for the existing line.

- Knowledge workers figure out quickly that an existing price list line can easily be updated—probably faster than adding a new one. Unless they know the reasons for adding the new line they will take the quickest route, with the result that pricing history is missing or incomplete—and the company is legally required to have this information.

IMPACT (quantify if possible):

- Compliance to legal requirements is at risk if this manual process is not followed. Check with legal about the penalty for noncompliance.

INITIAL RECOMMENDATIONS OR NEXT STEPS:

- Investigate technical solutions (modifications to system) to support this requirement.

- If possible, address the issue through complete audit trails at the database level so that complete histories are generated, regardless of training or access method.

- Address the issue through training. When teaching how to create and update price list lines, also include this process of creating new price list lines instead of changing the data for the existing line. Emphasize why the process needs to be done this way (compliance to legal requirements).

Submitted by: _____

Contact information: _____ Date: _____

Information Anecdote—Example 3

A popular story used at Aera Energy LLC, an oil company based in Bakersfield, California, revolved around the Winchester Mystery House in San Jose. As the story goes, Sarah Winchester, widow of the inventor of the Winchester rifle, believed her family was cursed and was told by a medium that she was being haunted by the ghosts of individuals killed by the Winchester rifle. The medium further advised her to move, build a new house, and keep that house under perpetual construction as a way to appease said ghosts. And so she did, spearheading a 38-year construction project with no apparent master plan; it only stopped when she died.

The result was a jumbled floor plan and strange features such as stairs that lead directly to ceilings, doors that opened to walls, and so on. In his book, *Enterprise Architecture Planning*,[9] Steven Spewak draws an analogy between that house and information systems in most organizations, asserting that those systems are built like the Winchester Mystery House: a bunch of components poorly connected, poorly integrated, redundant, and disparate because there was no plan, no architecture, just a commitment to build.

Members of Aera's Enterprise Architecture Plan (EAP) team used the story and Spewak's analogy to build a case for enterprise architecture. The story became well known and popular in the company because it illustrated in simple terms that everyone could understand the importance of building an information systems architecture. Aera also used internally

generated data to assess the financial impact of poor information quality.

As part of the process, the EAP team conducted an assessment of the time enterprise knowledge workers spent finding, cleaning, and formatting data before they could analyze them and make decisions that create value. The average time quoted was 40 percent. This statistic convinced Aera management of the need to implement the Enterprise Architecture Plan. The salary cost alone for everyone in the enterprise spending that much non-value-added time would pay for the project. However, the real opportunity was the increased time available for knowledge workers to spend on analysis and decision making.

The assessment consisted of a survey of well-respected engineers, geoscientists, and other knowledge workers in the company, chosen because of their credibility with their peers and with company leaders—the executives who had final authority over whether Aera was going to invest in enterprise architecture implementation and data quality.

Each of those interviewed was asked: (1) their opinion about the data quality at Aera and (2) specifically what percent of their time they spent looking for, reconciling, and correcting data before they could use it for analysis and decision making. Survey participants were also individually photographed in their work environments.

The stories and pictures were compiled and presented in a very creative way. Imagine a series of slides, each one containing the

[9]Steven H. Spewak, *Enterprise Architecture Planning: Developing a Blueprint for Data, Applications and Technology*. Copyright © 1993 Steven H. Spewak, Ph.D. (pp. xix–xx). Reprinted with permission of John Wiley & Sons, Inc.

picture of one knowledge worker, the person's name and pithy quote about data quality at Aera, and the percentage of time that person spent dealing with bad data. In the various presentations where the slides were used, their cumulative impact was the same: For most managers, knowing that their valuable engineers and geoscientists were spending 40 percent of their time dealing with bad data instead of making value-adding decisions provided a convincing argument for a radical change.

With the Winchester Mystery House anecdote and the internal pictures and interview results, Aera built compelling business impact stories, which resulted in the approval of a five-year, multimillion dollar project. The core of the subsequent Enterprise Architecture Implementation (EAI) program was an ambitious system development schedule, supported by a comprehensive data quality process. Since 2000, Aera has successfully replaced hundreds of disparate legacy systems with robust applications, as defined in their Application Architecture. Each project included specific plans to standardize work processes, prevent future data quality errors, and correct the existing data errors. Time spent finding, cleaning, and formatting data was reduced significantly.

Also see the story in *Step 3.10—Perception, Relevance, and Trust* about a survey of knowledge workers.

Step 4.2 Usage

Business Benefit and Context

Another easy way to show business impact is to list how the information is *currently* being used and its *planned future* uses.

- *Current uses* come from the Apply stage phase of the POSMAD life cycle. The Apply phase refers to any retrieval and use of the information, such as completing transactions, creating reports, making decisions, running automated processes, or providing an ongoing source of data for another downstream application.

- *Future uses* come from business strategic plans or road maps.

Documenting these uses is a low-cost way to show that the data have an impact on the business simply because of the number of ways they are used.

 Definition

Usage: Inventory of the current and/or future uses of the data.

Approach

1. List current uses.

Reference the Apply phase of the life cycle. Include actual uses of the information, the people and/or organizations using it, and the technical applications where it is accessed.

2. List future uses.

Look at business plans and road maps. Talk to the managers of the business process areas or the technical applications.

3. Quantify uses as much as possible.

Try to quantify current uses as much as possible. For example, determine the number of people using the information or the technical application, or the number of times it is being used. If those who apply the information have to access it through someone else, such as via a request to a reporting team, quantify the number of requests, how often, for how many records, and so forth. If the use is through a particular report, determine how many people receive the report and how often.

4. Document the results.

Capture the uses along with the sources and supporting data, tangible and intangible impact, any aspects that can be quantified, what was learned (any surprises?), and initial recommendations.

Even though most people know, at some level, that the information supports what they are doing, often even a simple list can startle the business into paying attention. One company, just by seeing a list of how the customer data were being utilized (account management, sales rep assignments, inquiry/interaction history, Customer Relationship Management (CRM),

 Best Practice

Be creative. Illustrate usage in an interesting way or craft a story that can be quickly told that demonstrates the business impact based on usage.

literature requests, direct mail projects, and event registration), needed very little additional motivation to support a project that would address known data quality issues.

Sample Output and Templates

One company kept hearing that no one was using their Customer Master data. Upon investigation, however, it was found that those data were being used in the following ways:

- Market planning
- Web marketing
- Targeting
- Product launch teams
- Brand teams
- Data acquisition
- Customer finance and compliance
- As the base universe for other projects

After further questioning, it was also found that managers were already aware of how the information was currently being utilized, but the real value of the Customer Master data was as a foundational building block of the business strategy for the upcoming year. As a result, both current and future uses were included in any communication about business impact.

Step 4.3 Five "Whys" for Business Impact

Business Benefit and Context

The Five "Whys" are an easy technique that can be used by an individual, group, or team. It is often used in manufacturing to get to root causes (used in *Step 5.1—Five "Whys" for Root Cause*). In this step the same technique will be used by starting with the known data quality issue and asking "Why" five times to determine business impact.

Definition

The Five Whys ask "Why" five times to get to the real business impact.

Best Practice

Combine this technique with gathering information anecdotes. Once you get to the final "Why," collect details about a specific situation, so you can better tell the story.

Approach

1. State the issue associated with poor data quality.
This can be an issue uncovered during a data quality assessment (*Step 3—Assess Data*

Quality) or some other known data quality problem where the specific data have not yet been assessed.

2. Ask "Why" five times.
Ask "Why" five times until you get to business impact. (See the examples in the Sample Output and Templates section.) You may do this exercise yourself or involve a few others. If working with others, explain what you are trying to accomplish. Make it an easy conversation. You don't have to use the word "why" each time if another phrase will accomplish the same result. (Otherwise, you may start sounding like a two-year-old who constantly peppers his parents with "Why?" "Why?" "Why?")

3. Document the results.
Capture what you have learned along with the source and supporting data, tangible and intangible impact, any aspects that could be quantified, what was learned (any surprises?), and initial recommendations.

Sample Output and Templates

Example 1

Issue
There are complaints about the quality of information in reports coming out of the data warehouse.

Ask: **Why** does the data quality matter?
- *Answer:* The data are used in reports.

Ask: **What** reports?
- *Answer:* The weekly sales reports.

Ask: **Why** do the weekly sales reports matter?

- *Answer:* Compensation for sales reps is based on these reports.

Ask: **Why** does that matter?

- *Answer:* If the data are wrong a highly effective sales rep may be undercompensated or another may be overcompensated.

Ask: **Why** does that matter?

- *Answer:* If the sales reps do not trust their compensation, they will spend time checking and rechecking the compensation figures—time better spent selling.

Being able to discuss poor information quality in terms of impact to sales reps is much more meaningful than saying, "The report is wrong."

Example 2

Issue

Inventory data are incorrect.

Ask: **Why** does the inventory data matter?

- *Answer:* Inventory data are used in inventory reports.

Ask: **Why** do the inventory reports matter?

- *Answer:* Procurement uses the inventory reports.

Ask: **Why** (or how) does procurement use the inventory reports?

- *Answer:* Procurement makes decisions about purchases based on the inventory reports. Procurement orders (or does not order) parts and materials for manufacturing.

Ask: **Why** do procurement decisions matter?

- *Answer:* If the inventory data are wrong, then procurement may not purchase at the right time. Lack of parts and materials can impact the manufacturing schedule and delay products being sent to customers. This affects company revenue and cash flow.

Once again, being able to discuss poor information quality in terms of the impact of bad data on inventory levels, manufacturing schedules, and product time to customer is much more meaningful than saying, "The report is wrong."

Step 4.4 Benefit versus Cost Matrix

Business Benefit and Context

This technique looks at relationships between benefits and costs. (See Figure 3.13 in the Sample Output and Templates section.) As it relates to data quality improvement, use it anytime you need to quickly review and prioritize solutions by comparing cost and benefits—for example, to determine which issues to address in your project in *Step 1—Understand Business Need and Approach*, to determine quality dimensions to assess in *Step 3—Assess Data Quality*, or to prioritize which recommendations to implement in *Step 6—Develop Improvement Plans*.

While this technique can be used on the basis of a thorough cost–benefit analysis, it is most useful with a first-pass "gut feeling" approach, in the form of a priority-ranking exercise. Ranking shows the relative business impact of the various options.

Definition

Benefit versus Cost Matrix: Analyze and rate the relationship between benefits and costs of issues, recommendations, or improvements.

Approach

1. Determine who will be involved in the priority-ranking exercise.

Prepare those attending so that they have the background needed, support what you are trying to accomplish, and come prepared to participate. Determine the method for discussing and capturing rankings. Be creative. Use a whiteboard or large sheets of paper with sticky notes or dots, or use a presentation program such as PowerPoint.

Any method that allows a quick change to rankings if needed and that will enhance, not hinder, the flow of the prioritization, is suitable.

2. List and clarify each item, action, or recommendation to be prioritized.

Be clear on what is being prioritized. Bring a documented list of items to be prioritized for each of the attendees.

3. Define and name each axis on the matrix—what benefit and cost mean.

Use the terms that are most meaningful to those doing the prioritizing. Give examples so everyone is clear on meanings. Come to the meeting with your recommendation, but be prepared to make adjustments if needed. (See Figure 3.13 in the Sample Output and Templates section.)

Benefit may mean

- Impact—positive impact to the business if the recommendation is implemented
- Payoff—performance and features
- Any other definition of benefit that is meaningful to your company

Cost may mean

- Effort—the relative effort to implement a recommendation
- Cost—the relative outlay in dollars
- Any other definition of cost that is meaningful to your company

4. Determine criteria for assessing the benefit and cost for each item to be prioritized.

Criteria can be qualitative (e.g., customer perspective) or quantitative (e.g., effects on cycle time). Discuss what is important to your particular organization or processes.

Use the following examples of criteria to get you thinking:

- Support of the business issue (keep it visible)
- Improved customer satisfaction
- Report availability—decreased time from receiving data to having them available in reports
- Simplified business or data management processes
- Time to implement the recommendation
- Cost versus expected profits or savings
- Skills and resources required to implement the solution

For example, if customer satisfaction is an important criterion for benefit, you would ask when ranking: "What is the impact of recommendation number one on customer satisfaction (low to high)?"

If time to implement is an important criterion for cost, ask: "What is the time to implement for recommendation one (from low to high)?" You can have multiple criteria to balance when ranking, but make it a manageable number.

5. Rank and place each recommendation.
Use the criteria previously identified. Ranking can be done by the team as a whole or individually. One approach is to let each individual quickly write down his or her ranking and then discuss the rankings as a group. Another is to place the various options on the matrix so the varying opinions can be seen and discussed and then agreement reached on final placement. The goal is to reach agreement for each of the placements fairly rapidly. Ensure that the final ranking is visually placed on the matrix.

6. Evaluate results.
Discuss the results of the placement. Evaluate each item according to the definitions within

each quadrant. (See Figure 3.14 in the Sample Output and Templates section.) Agree on final placement on the matrix.

7. Document results.
Include any important assumptions or considerations used to determine the rankings and final priority.

Sample Output and Templates

Example 1

Figure 3.15 shows how the Benefit versus Cost Matrix in Figure 3.13 is used to prioritize 34 specific recommendations that came out of a data quality assessment project. The recommendations were placed on the chart. The team then analyzed and prioritized them.

The result was nine top "Must-Do" recommendations to implement and four "Very Important" recommendations. All recommendations were documented. The remaining 21 recommendations were listed by the impact/cost priority.

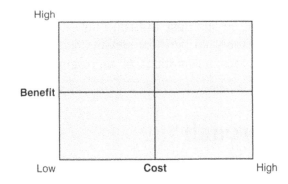

Figure 3.13 • Benefit versus Cost Matrix.

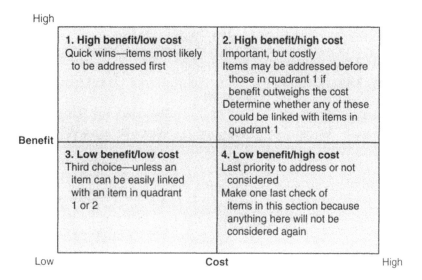

Figure 3.14 • Benefit versus Cost Matrix—evaluating the results.

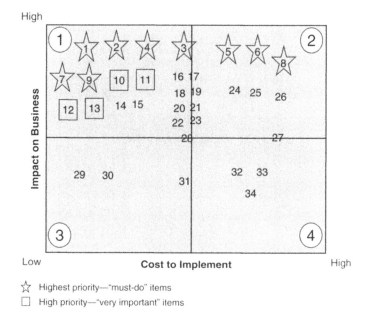

Figure 3.15 • Example 1—project recommendation results.

Example 2

Table 3.25 shows the documentation of results from using the Benefit versus Cost Matrix to prioritize which dimensions of quality should be assessed. Note that the terms "Possible Payback" and "Perceived Effort" were the definitions used for *Benefit* and *Cost*, respectively, and the matrix was called a "Payoff" matrix. Each of the data quality dimensions was discussed and ranked.

Table 3.25 • Example 2—Prioritized Data Quality Tests

| Quality Dimension/Test | From Payoff Matrix (Low, Medium, or High) | | Decision* (Yes or No) | Rationale for Decision/Assumptions on Which Decision Was Made |
	Possible Payback	Perceived Effort		
Data Specifications	High	Medium	Yes	• Consensus on high payback but effort level not clearly perceived. • Will evaluate only those standards documented and readily available. • Will evaluate data domains, business rules, and data entry guidelines. • Will not evaluate detailed data model or naming conventions for tables and data elements.
Data Integrity Fundamentals	High	High	Yes	• Can use profiling tool to help automate the effort. • Profile data for two countries.
Accuracy	High	High	Yes	• Authoritative source of reference (by direct contact through telemarketing or other means) still to be decided.
Timeliness and Availability	High	Medium	No	• Not enough resources or time available. • Consider for next project.
Consistency and Synchronization	High	Medium	No	• Not enough time to look at two countries' data in two systems. • Consider for next project.

*Note: This is where you decide whether to perform the quality test as part of the project—Yes or No?

Step 4.5 Ranking and Prioritization

Business Benefit and Context

Prioritization indicates relative importance or value. Thus, anything that has a higher priority than any other thing implicitly has a higher impact on the business. This step ranks the impact on business processes when the data are missing or incorrect. You can use it to help determine which data are worth assessing for data quality.

Definition

Ranking and prioritization is the ranking of the impact of missing and incorrect data on specific business processes.

Key elements in determining the importance of data are usage and the business risks and opportunities associated with it. The importance of data quality will vary for different data and for different uses of the same data. Ranking and determining business impact are best performed by those who actually use the data or those who are designing new business processes and practices that will reshape data usage.

The task is to rank the impact of missing and incorrect data on specific business processes using the approach described here, once again a priority-ranking exercise.

Approach

1. Determine the business processes and the uses of the information that will be prioritized.

Focus on the business processes that use and retrieve the information. Refer to the Apply phase in the Information Life Cycle POSMAD. A facilitated session is the most effective method for conducting the ranking. Preparation is required to determine business focus and the specific processes and data to rank.

The ranking can be applied to specific information or data groupings consisting of several related elements.

Examples

- To complete a mailing to a customer, one must have complete name and address information.
- To make a sale of a high-priced product, one must know the technical buyer name, the decision maker, the sales cycle state, and so forth.
- To establish a CRM program, in addition to customer name and address, one must know the customer profile with attributes about a customer's behavior.
- To pay a vendor, one must have complete and current invoice information.

2. Determine who will be involved in the prioritization exercise.

Based on the business processes and on information usage, decide who to invite to the session.

It helps to involve people representing various interests, including senior managers. Then the very process of considering these questions becomes a way to facilitate understanding of the various uses and importance of data, build data quality awareness, and support data quality improvement.

Prepare those attending so they have the background needed, support what you are trying to accomplish, and come prepared to participate. Determine the method for discussing and capturing the rankings. Use one where you can quickly change the rankings if needed. The method should enhance, not hinder, the flow of the prioritization.

3. In the ranking session, agree on the final processes and information to be ranked.

Ensure that there is understanding and agreement among the participants on what is to be ranked and why. Explain the process of ranking, and give examples from your business of each ranking on the scale to be used (see Table 3.26). For instance, an incorrect prefix in a name would not cause complete failure of the mailing process (i.e., the ability to deliver the mail) and so it may be ranked a C or a D. However, an incorrect zip code would cause complete failure (i.e., mail could not be delivered) and so it would be ranked an A.

4. Rank the data for each business process.

The facilitator will lead the attendees through the ranking. For each process, discuss the impact of poor-quality data by **asking**: "If this information were missing or incorrect,[10] what would the impact be on the process?"

For example, if "Contact Name" were missing or incorrect, what would be the impact to the Mailings process? What would be the impact to the Territory Assignments process?"

As each of these questions is answered, a value judgment is made by the individual attendees. Go through each piece of information and each process. The leader should encourage discussion as the ranking continues.

The questions can apply to the organization as a whole, to a specific division, or to business processes. You may choose an alternate scale such as high, medium, low, or 1, 2, 3.

Consider the following additional questions:

- What decisions do we make that rely significantly on these data?
- What are the impacts of these decisions in terms of
  - Lost revenue?
  - Increased costs?
  - Delays in responding to changing business conditions?
  - Regulatory and legal exposure and risk?
  - Relations with customers, suppliers, and other external parties?
  - Public embarrassment and corporate standing?
  - Business process halts or unacceptable delays?
  - Substantial misapplication of resources?

Table 3.26 • Scale for Ranking Data

A	=	Complete failure of the process or unacceptable financial, compliance, legal, or other risk is likely.
B	=	Process will be hampered and significant economic consequences will result.
C	=	Minor economic consequences will result.
D	=	Nuisance, but minimal economic consequences, will result.
N/A	=	Not applicable.

[10]Missing information refers to fields with blanks or nulls. Then, if the data exist, are they correct? Use the same ranking for both missing and incorrect data. Rank them separately only if they seem to differ significantly.

This is a subjective process, but it has proven to be very effective. There is no "correct" ranking; it depends on the use of the data and personal opinion. The process does not call for in-depth analyses. The initial "gut feel" ranking is usually correct and should be the one used.

Participants in the exercise will not always rank data the same way. If you are ranking for different uses or processes, let each participant rank the data individually. For instance, the customer's job title for reporting may be given a high ranking by a sales rep who personally contacts that customer. Or a marketing group may rank job title low if they are not using it in their mailing process. Realize that the given data should be managed to the highest level of business impact indicated. A ranking of C by one business process and a ranking of A by a different process indicates that the data should be treated as an A.

Warning

Avoid "analysis paralysis" in this technique by moving quickly through the rankings and relying on your initial reactions.

5. Complete an additional level of ranking, if needed.

Rank each data element based upon the ability to *collect* and *maintain* it:

1 = easy; 2 = medium; 3 = difficult.

Rank the ability to collect and maintain separately only if they seem to differ significantly.

6. Assign a final overall ranking.

There will be differences in the individual rankings. The final overall ranking is the highest one given by any of the processes. (See Table 3.27, Example—Ranking Results, in the Sample Output and Templates section.)

7. Analyze the rankings.

The analysis shows the impact to the business and can be used to prioritize what information is important enough to improve. (See Table 3.28.)

8. Document the results.

Capture what was learned (including both surprises and confirmations of opinion) and initial recommendations based on the results. In one session, the area sales manager found that his sales reps were responsible for collecting information that they didn't use, but which they passed through to Marketing. The information was essential to the marketing processes. This knowledge resulted in a promise by the area sales manager to convey and motivate his sales reps to spend the time required to ensure the accuracy of the information.

Key Concept

While the rankings themselves are very useful, one of the biggest benefits from this technique is the conversation between those who utilize or affect the quality of the same information, yet may not usually interact with each other. A successful session will result in increased understanding and cooperation between those who are responsible for the quality of the information and those who depend on the information.

Sample Output and Templates

Situation: The business wanted to understand the impact of poor-quality customer data to its processes. One representative from each team (Sales, Marketing, and Data Management) participated in a focused session. Prior to this facilitated session, each of the representatives had been educated about the reasons for the session and had agreed that the time spent would be worthwhile; they came prepared to participate.

One critical business process from each of the areas was chosen for ranking:

- Marketing chose mailings (for special events, promotions, subscriptions, etc.).
- Sales chose territory management (for maintaining sales rep geographic assignments within each district).
- Data management chose reports (for making business decisions, such as account lists and territory assignments).

Each piece of information was discussed, using the approach outlined in this step. Table 3.27 summarizes the outcome. The column Final Overall Ranking uses the highest-ranked impact from any of the processes. For example, if one process ranked the impact of missing or incorrect data as A and another ranked it as C, the final overall ranking was A, *not* the average (B).

Note that you may choose to rank impact alone. Rank the ability to collect/maintain the information only if you think the knowledge gained will help you make decisions and take action in some way. Table 3.28 will help you interpret the ranking results and provide input to possible actions.

Table 3.27 • Example—Ranking Results

	IMPACT OF NON-QUALITY DATA ON THE BUSINESS PROCESSES INDIVIDUAL PROCESS RANKINGS			ABILITY TO COLLECT/ MAINTAIN THE INFORMATION	FINAL OVERALL RANKING
	MAILINGS	REPORTS	TERRITORY MANAGEMENT		
Sales Representative's Code	C	A	A	1	A1
Prefix	D	D	N/A	2	D2
Contact Name	B	A	B	2	A2
Site Name	C	A	A	2	A2
Division	D	B	B	3	B3
Department	B	B	B	3	B3
Address	A	A	B	2	A2
City, State, Zip	A	A	A	2	A2

Table 3.28 • Ranking Analysis

IMPACT OF NON-QUALITY DATA ON THE BUSINESS PROCESSES	ABILITY TO COLLECT/ MAINTAIN THE DATA	CONSIDERATIONS
A—Complete failure of the process	Easy	The data are very important to the business process and are easy to collect. This implies the business is actually using, collecting, and maintaining the data on a regular basis. Is this being done?
	Medium	The data are very important, but are not easy to collect and maintain. This implies there will be some possibility of data quality problems and a potential need to improve the processes for managing the data.
	Difficult	The data are very important, but are hard to collect and maintain. There is a high probability of poor data quality and a high possibility of and need for process improvement.
B—Process hampered, significant economic consequences	Easy	The data are somewhat important to the business and are easy to collect and maintain. This implies the business is using the data and that the data are actually being collected and maintained. Is this being done?
	Medium	Determine if the consequences of not having the correct data are great enough to warrant the extra effort to collect and maintain them.
	Difficult	Determine if the consequences of not having the correct data are great enough to warrant the extra effort to collect and maintain them.
C—Minor economic consequences	Easy	May want to continue collecting/maintaining this data as long as it is easy to do so.
	Medium	May not want to spend resources to collect/maintain data.
	Difficult	May not want to spend resources to collect/maintain data.
D—Nuisance, minimal economic consequences	Easy	Appears data provide no value to the business. Continue to collect/ maintain data only if easy to do so as part of processes that already collect/maintain critical data.
	Medium	Appears data provide no value to the business. However, double-check yourself by asking, "If you could get data more easily, would they be more important?" If yes, should the business find better ways to collect and maintain data? If not, why spend any resources collecting them in the first place?
	Difficult	Appears data provide no value to the business. If true and the data are difficult to collect/maintain, why spend any resources collecting them in the first place? Should any resources be spent storing and maintaining the data? If not, can the data be removed or a warning set for knowledge workers so it is clear they are not reliable?

Step 4.6 Process Impact

Business Benefit and Context

Workarounds hide poor-quality data. They become a normal part of business processes, and people don't realize that change is possible—that poor-quality data cause costly problems and distractions that are not necessary. By showing the effect on the processes and the resulting costs, the business can make informed decisions about improving issues that were previously unclear.

This technique will most likely be done by a single person working with other individuals or by a small team with knowledge of the business processes.

 Definition

Process impact illustrates the effects of poor-quality data on business processes.

Approach

1. Outline the business process when good data are used.
Use the Information Life Cycle from *Step 2—Analyze Information Environment* as a starting point to detail the business process first with high-quality data. (See Figure 3.16 in the Sample Output and Templates section.)

2. Outline the Information Life Cycle with poor-quality data.
Include additional support roles and activities needed to deal with the bad data. (See Figure 3.17 in the Sample Output and Templates section.)

3. Analyze the differences to the process with good data and compromised data.
Often just by illustrating the differences, it becomes clear that action needs to be taken. It does not always require that costs be quantified. Capture any recommendations for improving the business processes.

4. Quantify the impact, if needed and if possible.
Look at steps in the process that lend themselves to quantifying. Using the example in the Sample Output and Templates section, how much time is spent investigating and resolving rejection issues? Who is responsible and how much is that person's time worth? Look at *Step 4.7—Cost of Low-Quality Data* for additional ideas for quantifying impact.

5. Document the results.
Ensure that your documentation includes supporting data needed to understand the results, any tangible and intangible impact, and quantified impact in dollars, if possible. Include initial recommendations for improving the business processes.

Sample Output and Templates

Example

In this example a supplier master record is required in the ERP (Enterprise Resource

Planning) system to place supplier orders, pay invoices, and reimburse employee expenses.

- Company buyers or employees submit a request for a supplier master record setup through an application outside the ERP.
- A central data administration team uses the requests to create the supplier master record in the ERP.
- If the setup request is complete, the central data administration team creates the supplier master record in the ERP so that orders, invoice payments, and reimbursements can be processed.

Figure 3.16 shows an Information Life Cycle process with good data. Analysis demonstrated that setup requests could be rejected for a number of reasons:

- Incomplete or wrong information
- Duplicate request
- Not approved
- No document
- Incorrect employee request
- Other

The majority of setup request rejections were the result of incomplete or wrong information.

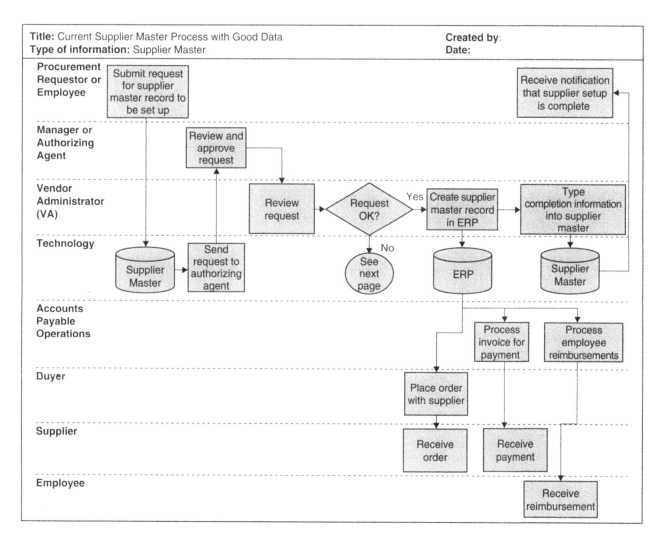

Figure 3.16 • Information Life Cycle with high-quality data.

Figure 3.17 shows the same process with poor data. What is the impact of rejected setup requests?

- *Time delay* in placing orders with suppliers, paying supplier invoices, and reimbursing employees for expenses
- *Rework* by the central data administration team (rejecting the request, ensuring investigation and resolution, re-reviewing the updated request)

- *Rework* by the requestor who submitted the original request (to investigate and resubmit)
- *Rework* by the support employee (to investigate and resolve)
- *Frustrated employees*
- *Frustrated suppliers*, many of whom are also customers of the company
- *Loss of service* to the company because payment has not been made

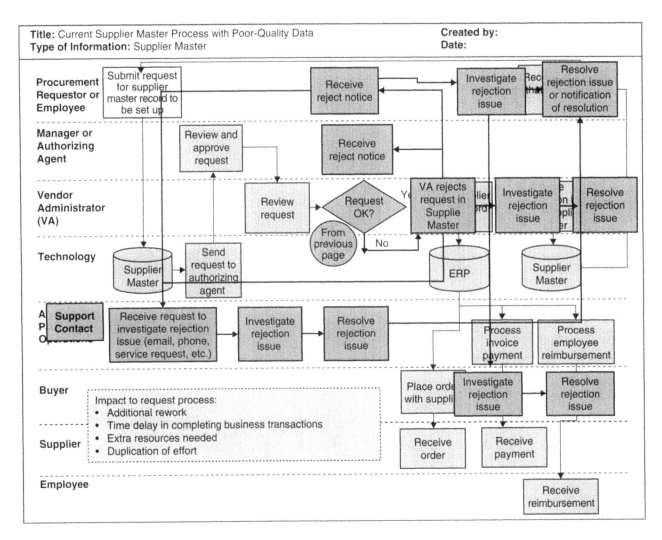

Figure 3.17 • Information Life Cycle with poor-quality data.

Step 4.7 Cost of Low-Quality Data

Business Benefit and Context

Poor-quality data cost the business in many ways: waste and rework; missed revenue opportunities; lost business, and so forth. This step quantifies the costs that may have only been understood by stories or observation. Quantifying costs shows impact with a measure best understood by the business—money.

 **Definition**

Cost of low-quality data: Quantify the costs and revenue impact of poor-quality data.

Approach

1. Identify the key indicator of poor data quality.

The key indicator provides the basis for your research and calculations. One example is the mailing process, which could be mailing catalogs or other promotional material to customers. Marketing groups track the specific mailing events, the nature of the mailing (catalog, letter, brochure, etc.), the total pieces mailed, the number of returns (undeliverable), and positive responses, if applicable.

The number of returns or undeliverables could be used as an indicator of poor-quality data, since mail is returned if the address is incorrect. If there are issues with undeliverable mail for other processes (such as a high number of returns when mailing invoices or

mailing responses to insurance claims), those can also be included in an assessment.

The following can provide input for selecting your key indicators:

- Issues identified during your data quality assessment in *Step 3—Assess Data Quality*
- Other data quality issues known to impact the business but for which no formal data quality assessment has been conducted
- Processes known to be suboptimal and data are likely contributors
- Other business performance measures based on business vision, mission, strategy, and goals and objectives—where the poor quality of information appears to have a significant impact
- Results from other business impact assessments, if applicable

For example, if you have completed *Step 4.5—Ranking and Prioritization*, you may decide to concentrate on information ranked as having a high impact on the business processes.

Find where the business is feeling the pain and connect your key indicator to that. Start with one business process or one area to determine if the impact is significant. You may then want to add in other business processes or areas to show a broader impact across the enterprise.

2. Define/verify the Information Life Cycle of the key indicator.

Reference any work done in *Step 2—Analyze Information Environment* that will help you understand other processes or uses of the information that are associated with the key indicator.

3. Determine the types of costs to include in the calculations.

Of course it is the goal of every for-profit organization to maximize revenues and minimize costs. But we need to get more specific in order to quantify costs. Nonprofits or other organizations may have different goals, but the suggestions that follow from two data quality experts can help you identify the kinds of costs most important to your organization and therefore where you should concentrate your business impact assessment. I recommend going to the sources and reading their explanations in depth to help you further understand the items listed.

David Loshin discusses (1) hard impacts —those that can be measured, and (2) soft impacts—those evident to the observer but difficult to measure. He further explains impacts to operational, tactical, and strategic domains. Table 3.29 outlines costs due to poor-quality data for each of these categories.

Loshin also characterizes the impacts of poor-quality data in four categories, those that (3) decrease revenue, (4) increase costs, (5) increase risk, and (6) lower confidence. Table 3.30 outlines costs due to poor-quality data for each of these categories.

Larry English presents three categories of costs: (1) process failure costs—a process does not perform properly as a result of poor-quality information; (2) information scrap and rework costs—where scrap means rejecting or marking data in error and rework means the cleansing of defective data; and (3) lost and missed-opportunity costs— revenue and profit not realized because of poor information quality. Table 3.31 summarizes costs due to poor-quality data within each of these categories.

Table 3.29 • Loshin's Poor-Quality Data Types of Costs—Categories 1 and 2

(1) Hard impact—effects that can be measured	• Customer attrition • Costs attributed to error detection • Costs attributed to error rework • Costs attributed to prevention of errors • Costs associated with customer service • Costs associated with fixing customer problems • Time delays in operation • Costs attributed to delays in processing
(2) Soft impact—effects evident to the observer, but difficult to measure	• Difficulty in decision making • Costs associated with enterprise-wide data inconsistency • Organizational mistrust • Lowered ability to effectively compete • Data ownership conflicts • Lowered employee satisfaction
Impacts by Domain	• Operational • Tactical • Strategic

Source: David Loshin, *Enterprise Knowledge Management: The Data Quality Approach* (Morgan Kaufmann, 2001), pp. 83–93. Used by permission.

Table 3.30 • Loshin's Poor-Quality Data Types of Costs—Categories 3 to 6

(3) Decreased Revenue	• Delayed/lost collections • Customer attrition • Lost opportunities • Increased cost/volume
(4) Increased Costs	• Detection and correction • Prevention • Spin control • Scrap and rework • Penalties • Overpayments • Increased resource costs • System delays • Increased workloads • Increased process times
(5) Increased Risk	• Regulatory or legislative risk • System development risk • Information integration risk • Investment risk • Health risk • Privacy risk • Competitive risk • Fraud detection
(6) Lowered Confidence	• Organizational trust issues • Impaired decision making • Lowered predictability • Impaired forecasting • Inconsistent management reporting

Source: David Loshin, "The Data Quality Business Case, Projecting Return on Investment." Informatica White Paper, June 2006. Used by permission.

4. Calculate the costs you have chosen.

Use the Direct Cost template (Template 3.9) in the Sample Output and Templates section.

5. Calculate the impact to revenue.

Use the Missed Revenue template (Template 3.10) in the Sample Output and Templates section.

6. Document the costs and assumptions.

Document all assumptions and formulas upon which the calculations were made. If there is disagreement later, the assumptions can be changed and the numbers recalculated.

Table 3.31 • English's Poor-Quality Data Types of Costs

Process Failure Costs	• Irrecoverable costs • Liability and exposure costs • Recovery costs of unhappy customers
Information Scrap and Rework Costs	• Redundant data handling and support costs • Costs of hunting or chasing missing information • Business rework costs • Workaround costs and decreased productivity • Data verification costs • Software rewrite costs • Data cleansing and correction costs • Data cleansing software costs
Lost and Missed-Opportunity Costs	• Lost-opportunity costs (e.g., alienate and lose a customer—customer chooses to take business elsewhere) • Missed-opportunity costs (e.g., customer did not get the chance or choice of doing business with your company; missed prospects that an unhappy customer could have influenced) • Lost shareholder value (e.g., accounting data errors)

Source: Larry P. English, *Improving Data Warehouse and Information Quality* (Wiley, 1999), pp. 209–213. Used by permission.

Sample Output and Templates

Costs

Template 3.9 provides a starting point for gathering and calculating the costs of poor-quality data. Create a spreadsheet file. You may have more than one worksheet depending on how many types of costs you will be calculating.

Using the previous example of mailings, let's assume that ten mailings were completed in a one-month time period and that Marketing kept statistics about each mailing event. One spreadsheet will be used for each mailing event (M1–M10). If your time period is one month, and the activity in that one month represents an average month, you can further estimate costs on an annual basis by multiplying your results by 12.

Look at each of the mailings. What was the cost to print the piece (a catalog, a brochure, etc.). What were the postage costs? What was the cost for the return postage? Are there any labor costs that need to be included? What was the purpose of the mailing and is there a way to determine a positive response? For example, if the mailing was an invitation to a sales seminar, how many recipients responded? How many actually showed up to the event? How many of those purchased? What was each purchase worth?

Be sure to have a summary sheet that pulls together the final sums for all events of costs and impact to revenue if both are completed.

Missed Revenue

Template 3.10, Missed Revenue, is an example of calculating missed revenue based on

Template 3.9 • Direct Costs

Key Indicator: _____

Event: _____

Date: _____

Prepared by: _____

Include background or notes about the key indicator, performance measure, processes involved, time period in which the statistics were generated, and other information that puts the results into context.

Note the time period being used (1 month, 1 quarter, 1 year).

This template can also be used to calculate the cost of unusual cases such as the missed revenue due to an event where the company received bad publicity and the resulting costs.

1	2	3	4	5
TYPE OF COST	DESCRIPTION	COST PER INSTANCE	NUMBER OF INSTANCES PER TIME PERIOD	3*4 TOTAL COSTS PER TIME PERIOD
State applicable categories. For each category determine:				
– Time				
– Materials				
– Other				
TOTALS				

Source: Adapted from Larry P. English, *Improving Data Warehouse and Information Quality* (Wiley, 1999). Used by permission. For a detailed process for calculating nonquality information costs, see Chapter 7 in Mr. English's book.

our mailings example. A key assumption is that customers who would have received the mailing but did not (because of bad addresses) would have had the same positive response as those who did receive the mailing.

The first row indicates the column number. The second row indicates the source of the data or the formula for the calculation. Column 11 brought in costs calculated in separate worksheets using the Direct Cost template. The last line, Total Missed Revenue from All Mailings, also includes totals for other columns where it makes sense, for example, Total Number of Returns and Total Number of Missed Opportunities.

Template 3.10 • Missed Revenue

1	2	3	4	5	6	7	8	9	10	11	12
	From marketing statistics	From marketing statistics	From marketing statistics	4/3	From marketing statistics	6/3	6 x 5	From sales and marketing	8 x 9	From cost worksheets	10 + 11
Mailing event	Drop date	Total mailed	Number of positive responses	Percent positive responses	Number of returned mail pieces	Percent returns	Number of missed opportunities	Average revenue per response	Total missed revenue	Total direct costs	Total missed revenue and direct costs
M1	10/30/07	100,000	10,000	10%	3000	3%	300	$250	$75,000		
M2											
M3											
…											
M10											
Total missed revenue from all mailings					Total number returns (sum column 6)		Total number missed opportunities (sum column 8)		Total all missed revenue (sum column 10)	Total all direct costs (sum column 11)	Total all missed revenue and direct costs (sum column 12)

Step 4.8 Cost–Benefit Analysis

Business Benefit and Context

Cost–benefit analysis and return on investment (ROI) are standard management approaches to making financial decisions. Your company may require this type of information before considering or proceeding with any significant financial outlay—and investments in information quality improvement are often significant. Management has the responsibility to determine how money is spent and will need to weigh its investment options.

It is unlikely that a technique this involved will be necessary for most business impact assessments. It may be needed for very large investments, but I have seen large investments approved for data quality based on results from less time-consuming techniques.

 **Definition**

A cost–benefit analysis compares potential benefits of investing in data quality with anticipated costs, through an in-depth evaluation. It includes return on investment, that is, the profit calculated as a percentage of the amount invested.

Approach

Cost–Benefit Analysis

A cost–benefit analysis evaluates if the benefits of a new investment or business opportunity over a given time frame outweigh its associated costs.

1. **Look for and use any standard template or form employed by your company for this purpose.**

This form probably already exists somewhere. Check with your manager or someone involved in finance or the budgeting process. The form will contain sections for both costs and benefits.

2. **Identify the costs associated with the new investment or business opportunity.**

Include human resources, training, hardware, software, and support costs.

3. **Identify the potential additional revenues and other benefits that will result.**

Being able to identify the benefits of high-quality data has been a perennial challenge. The value of data improvements and the cost of poor-quality data are opposite sides of the same coin. Use output from other business impact techniques to present the benefits.

4. **Identify the cost savings.**

Cost savings are the difference between benefits and costs.

5. **Estimate a timeline for the anticipated revenues and expected costs.**

6. **Evaluate the benefits and costs that cannot be quantified.**

Though the form may not ask for these, include them in a comment area or cover letter. Benefits and costs that cannot be quantified should still be made visible.

Return on Investment

ROI compares the benefit (or return) on an investment compared to the cost or amount

Definition

Return on investment is the profit calculated as a percentage of the amount invested.

of money invested. It is the profit calculated as a percentage of the invested amount.

1. Calculate the ROI.

What is included in the gains and costs can be modified to suit your situation. You may look at cost savings, incremental profit, or value appreciation. Use input from the cost–benefit analysis. The formula for calculating ROI is

$$ROI = \frac{(Gain\ from\ investment - Cost\ of\ investment)}{Cost\ of\ investment}$$

2. Evaluate the ROI.

The investment should have a positive return.

3. Compare your ROI to the ROI of other opportunities.

Having a positive ROI is not enough. The investment will also be compared to the ROI of other opportunities before being undertaken. Be aware of the competition for money and resources within the company.

Step 4 Summary

Congratulations! Assessing business impact is yet another important milestone in your project. Remember to communicate and document results and recommendations. Use the results to make good decisions about your next steps—communication needed, business action and effect on project goals, scope, timeline, and resources needed. Review the questions in the checkpoint box to help you determine if you are finished or ready to move to the next step.

Communicate

■ Have management, business, and stakeholders been apprised of quality assessment results, impact to the business, root causes, and initial recommendations?

■ Do all members of the project team have the same information?

■ Have you communicated the impact of the quality results to the rest of the project team, along with impact on project scope, timeline, and resources?

Checkpoint

Step 4—Assess Business Impact

How can I tell whether I'm ready to move to the next step? Following are guidelines to determine completeness of the step:

✓ Have impacts to the business been assessed?

✓ For each business impact assessment, have the results been analyzed and documented?

✓ Has necessary follow-up to the analysis been completed?

✓ For each impact assessment, have initial recommendations and anything learned that could effect possible root causes been documented?

✓ If conducting multiple assessments, have results from all assessments been brought together and synthesized?

✓ Has the communication plan been updated?

✓ Has necessary communication been completed?

Step 5 | Identify Root Causes

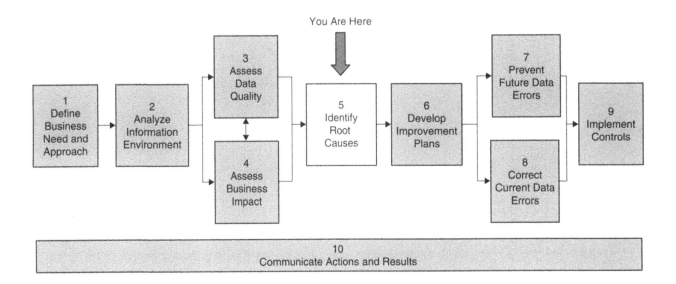

Introduction

There are usually multiple ways of dealing with problems that arise from data quality—all of which require different levels of time, money, and human resources. There is a tendency to jump to a solution that appears to be the most expedient in order to deal quickly with a situation. The result is that the symptoms are often treated rather than the fundamental underlying problem that caused them.

Root cause analysis looks at all possible causes of a problem, issue, or condition to determine its actual cause (see Table 3.32). Often time and effort are spent treating symptoms of a problem without determining its actual causes, which would prevent the problem from recurring. The primary goals in this step are to find out why a problem happened and what can be done to prevent it from happening again.

It is not unusual to find that when a data quality issue is uncovered the company only corrects the data—sometimes at great cost for large clean-up efforts. Then it is back to business as usual until a few years later, when those same issues cause the business to once again invest in data clean-up. This costly and unproductive cycle misses root cause analysis—which is essential for prevention.

Common Situations Needing Root Cause Analysis

Following are two common situations where root cause analysis is important.

In the Course of a Data Quality Assessment Project

Assessments of one or more data quality dimensions have been completed, either by you alone or as part of a team, and specific incorrect data have been identified and located. For the data supporting a genuine business need, you now want to identify root causes before correcting the data errors. In this case you should already

Table 3.32 • Step 5—Identify Root Causes

OBJECTIVE	• Identify and prioritize the true causes of data quality problems. • Develop recommendations for addressing the root causes.
PURPOSE	Ensure that recommendations and future improvement plans focus on the true causes of data quality issues.
INPUTS	Possible root causes, lessons learned, and preliminary recommendations from all previous steps completed, such as Output from *Step 2—Analyze Information Environment* • Information Life Cycle • Results of analyzing the information environment • Documentation with lessons learned such as potential impact to data quality and/or the business, possible root causes, and initial recommendations at this point Output from *Step 3—Assess Data Quality* • Data quality assessment results • Documentation including potential impact to the business and possible root causes • Initial recommendations for action based on the data quality assessment results Output from *Step 4—Assess Business Impact* (if applicable) • Business impact assessment results if they provide help in identifying root causes Necessary communication completed, along with updated communication plan
TOOLS AND TECHNIQUES	• Techniques applicable to the particular root cause technique: For example, the Cause-and-Effect/Fishbone diagram (See each root cause substep.) • Payoff Matrix (See *Step 4.4—Benefit versus Cost Matrix.*)
OUTPUTS	• Specific recommendations for addressing root causes of data quality issues (with supporting documentation) • Specific recommendations and next steps based on business impact results (with supporting documentation) • Updated communication plan
CHECKPOINT	• Have the root causes of the data quality issues been identified and documented? • Have specific recommendations for addressing those root causes been determined and documented? • Has any additional learning about impact to the business been documented? • If applicable, have specific recommendations and next steps based on business impact results been determined and documented? • Has the communication plan been updated? • Has necessary communication been completed?

have an Information Life Cycle, so use what you know at this point. You may have to go to an additional level of detail in your life cycle to get to root cause.

To Address a Specific Issue Impacting the Business

Root cause analysis is necessary to address a specific data quality issue that has been identified. This issue is most often related to an urgent problem that has recently caused major impacts to the business—services cannot be provided, a production line is down, products are not shipped, orders cannot be taken—and it is suspected that data quality is a significant factor. Once the issue itself has been addressed, management wants to ensure that it will not happen again.

It may be that the specific issue did not cause an emergency but is something that everyone knows about and has accepted as a cost of doing business. You may decide to spend time on root cause analysis to address the issue with the hope of stopping the constant waste of time and money it creates. In this case, you probably don't have an Information Life Cycle, so you will need to define one, at least at a high level.

Approaches to Root Cause Analysis

Three of the approaches to root cause analysis (Table 3.33) are detailed in this step. Depending on the urgency of the business issue and the complexity of the root causes you discover, you may want to use just one approach; combinations of the three; or the fastest approach, the Five "Whys," to get started.

Note that the instructions for the root cause techniques include less detail than in other steps. This is not because root causes are not important but because you should have already been collecting potential root causes as you went through your project and should have some ideas about what to do at this point. This applies whether you have gone through Steps 1 to 4 at a high level or at a more detailed level. Suggestions regarding potential root causes can be found in the previous steps and examples.

You may have a number of data quality issues and need to prioritize which are most important to look at first for root cause. After that, what is needed is a commitment to gather the right people and work through the root cause process.

Once you get to the root causes, you will want to evaluate the best way to fix them so that the problem won't happen again and your current condition will be improved. For this reason, specific recommendations should be the output of this step.

Table 3.33 ● Root Cause Techniques

1	Five "Whys" for Root Cause	Ask "*Why*" five times to get to root cause.
2	Track and Trace	Identify location of the problem by tracking data through the Information Life Cycle and determining root causes where the problem first appears.
3	Cause-and-Effect/ Fishbone Diagram	Identify, explore, and graphically display all possible causes of an issue by using a standard quality technique.

Step 5.1 Five "Whys" for Root Cause

Business Benefit and Context

The five "Whys" is a technique often used to get to root causes in manufacturing. It can also be applied to information quality and can be used by an individual, group, or team. This technique is also used in *Step 4.3—Five "Whys" for Business Impact*.

Definition

The **Five "Whys" for Root Cause** ask "Why" five times to get to root cause.

Approach

1. State the issue associated with poor data quality.
Gather any pertinent background information. The more clearly you state the issue, the more easily you can find the root causes.

2. Ask "Why" five times.
Start with the stated issue and ask, "Why did we get this result?" or "Why did this situation occur?" From that answer repeat the question again five times. (See the example in the Sample Output and Templates section.)

3. Analyze the results.
Are there multiple root causes? Are there common features found among the root causes?

4. Make specific recommendations to address the root causes.
Develop specific actions to address the root causes found. If you need to prioritize a number

of recommendations, use the prioritization technique in *Step 4.4—Benefit versus Cost Matrix*.

5. Document the results.
Include the root causes, the recommendations for addressing them, and how conclusions were reached. Also include any additional impacts to the business, tangible and intangible, that were uncovered or verified while going through this process.

Sample Output and Templates

Example 1

The issue—There is a concern about duplicate customer master records. (*Note*: You may or may not have done an assessment to determine the actual percentage of duplicates.)

Ask: **Why** are there duplicate records?
- *Answer:* Customer service reps create new master records instead of using existing ones.

Ask: **Why** do they create new records instead of using existing records?
- *Answer:* The reps don't want to search for existing records.

Ask: **Why** don't the reps want to search for existing records?
- *Answer:* It takes too long to enter the search request and get results back.

Ask: **Why** is the search time too long?
- *Answer:* The reps have not been trained in the proper search techniques and system performance is poor.

Ask: **Why** is the long search time a problem?
- *Answer:* The reps are measured by how quickly they create the records and complete the transaction. Data quality is not

rewarded, and the reps have no visibility or understanding of why duplicate records are a problem to other parts of the business.

You may find more than one root cause and need to continue questioning along each of the branches. Decide which ones can be addressed, considering the results of the five whys, and which require further investigation before a solution can be implemented. In this example, you may have enough information to put together a short training course on search techniques for the reps. However, further investigation is needed to understand any system performance problems.

If needed, use the techniques in Steps 5.2 and 5.3 to explore more detail on root cause analysis.

Step 5.2 Track and Trace

Business Benefit and Context

This technique identifies the specific location of a problem by tracking the data through the Information Life Cycle and identifying where it first appears. Once you have identified the location you can use the other techniques to get to the root causes.

 **Definition**

Track and trace is a way to identify the location of the problem by tracking data through the Information Life Cycle and determining root causes where the problem first appears.

Approach

1. State the issue associated with poor data quality.

Gather any pertinent background information. The more clearly you state the issue, the more easily you can find the root causes.

2. Agree on the Information Life Cycle and the route for tracing the information.

Remember to use the work already done with the life cycle as a starting point. You will probably go to an additional level of detail in order to trace information for your root cause analysis.

3. Compare the data at the entry and exit points for each step through the process.

Do a careful job of capturing and comparing the data. (See the Data Capture section in Chapter 5.) One technique is profiling the data at the entry and exit points and comparing the results. You will eventually find the place where the data are correct when entering a process step but incorrect when exiting it.

4. Determine what needs to be changed to ensure that the data will be correct.

Analyze activities at the problem location. Identify the activities impacting the data between the point of entry (where correct) and the point of exit (where incorrect). Apply the other root cause techniques as needed.

You may decide to use the Five "Whys" for Root Cause or the Cause-and-Effect/Fishbone diagram here.

5. Make specific recommendations to address the root causes.

Develop specific actions to address the root causes found. If you need to prioritize a number of recommendations, use the prioritization technique in *Step 4.4—Benefit versus Cost Matrix*.

6. Document the results.

Include the root causes, the recommendations for addressing them, and how conclusions were reached. Also include any additional impacts to the business, tangible and intangible, that were uncovered or verified while going through this process.

Step 5.3 Cause-and-Effect/Fishbone Diagram

Business Benefit and Context

The Cause-and-Effect diagram comes from Kaoru Ishikawa, a Japanese quality control statistician and highly regarded quality management expert. Also known as the Ishikawa diagram, or Fishbone diagram,[11] the technique is used to identify, explore, and arrange the causes of an event, problem, condition, or outcome in which the relationships between causes are illustrated according to their level of importance or detail. The approach is well known and effective and has been used in manufacturing. It can be applied to information as well.

You may want to use it once you have isolated the specific location of the problem through Track and Trace. The Cause-and-Effect diagram considers more than the most obvious causes and takes advantage of the knowledge of the group.

 Definition

A **Cause-and-Effect/Fishbone Diagram** identifies, explores, and graphically displays all possible causes of an issue by using a standard quality technique.

Approach

1. Create your team and prepare for the meeting.

Gather any information pertinent to the issue (most of it output from previous steps). Provide any needed background prior to the meeting so the team comes to it supporting the goals and are prepared to participate. Ensure that the physical setup of the meeting space is conducive to discussion and encourages collaboration.

2. State the issue associated with the poor data quality.

Explain the purpose of the meeting. The more clearly you state the issue, the more easily you can find the root causes. Allow time for discussion so everyone agrees on the issue to be analyzed. State the defect/issue/problem. This is indicated as the "effect," which appears as the head of the fishbone.

Start drawing the diagram by writing the effect in a box on the right side of the diagram. Use a whiteboard or a large sheet of paper that everyone can see.

3. List categories of the problem.

You may start with categories of common causes and place them on the diagram. Table 3.34 lists categories you can use (see page 206). You can also include possible causes found throughout your project.

Alternatively, you may take a brainstorming approach and have attendees list all possible causes on sticky notes. Include the possible causes you have documented throughout the project and then categorize the causes and place them together on the diagram.

Draw a horizontal line to the left of the stated effect (the head). (See Figure 3.18 on page 206.) Then draw bones off the line and label them with the major categories. Use the categories that fit the problem—there is no perfect set or number. You may have to prioritize with which of the major categories to continue your questioning.

---

[11]The term "fishbone" comes from the graphical nature of the output, with the stated problem being the head and the causes the bones of a fish.

4. Continue questioning until you get to the root causes.

For each of the categories ask, "What is affecting or causing the problem? Why does this happen?" For example, "What people/organizational issues are causing the problem and why do the problems happen?" List these as smaller bones off the major bones. Reference the root causes you collected throughout your assessment.

5. State the root causes found.

Document and agree on the root causes found.

6. Make specific recommendations to address the root causes.

Develop specific actions to address the root causes found. If you need to prioritize a number of recommendations, use the prioritization technique in *Step 4.4—Benefit versus Cost Matrix.*

When analyzing causes, also consider the distinction between chronic and acute problems. Chronic problems have been around for a long time and have been ignored. Acute problems have come up recently and are putting new pressures on the system or the business.[12]

7. Document the results.

Include the root causes, the recommendations for addressing them, and how conclusions were reached. Also include any additional impacts to the business, tangible and intangible, that were uncovered or verified while going through this process.

Sample Output and Templates

Table 3.34 lists common categories of root causes. There is no perfect set or number of categories—use the categories that fit the issue.

Step 5 Summary

Discovering root causes is one of the most important milestones in your project—a main goal for all of your previous work. Now you can make informed decisions about your next steps—business action and communication needed—and see how discovery of root causes affects project goals, scope, timeline, and resources needed.

After your root cause analysis, you may need to spend more time conducting tests to verify potential root causes, or you may be confident enough that you can institute changes based on what you discovered. In either case, your recommendations should flow naturally to developing improvement plans. In some cases you may go directly to implementing controls. You decide.

Of course, remember to document results and recommendations. Review the questions in the checkpoint box to help you determine if you are finished or ready to move to the next step.

 Best Practice

When determining the cause of the problem, David Loshin suggests looking for

- *Chronic problems*—those that have been around for a long time and ignored
- *Acute problems*—those that have cropped up recently and are putting new pressures on the system

---

[12]For additional questions to ask when tracking the source of chronic and acute problems, see David Loshin's book *Enterprise Knowledge Management: The Data Quality Approach* (Morgan Kaufmann, 2001), pp. 389–391.

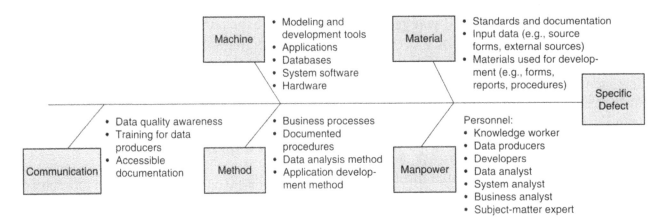

Figure 3.18 • Example Cause-and-Effect diagram.

Table 3.34 • Common Categories of Root Causes

The 4 M's—often used in production processes*	• Machines (tools and equipments) • Methods (how work is done) • Material (components or raw materials) • Manpower or people (the human element)
The 4 P's—often used in service processes*	• Policies (higher-level decision rules) • Procedures (steps in a task) • People (the human element) • Plant (equipment and space)
Production and service processes often also use*	• Environment (buildings, logistics, space) • Measurement (metrics, data collection)
From the Framework for Information Quality (discussed in Chapter 2) (These may be used as categories in your root cause analysis.)	• The POSMAD interaction matrix • Location (where) and Timing (how long) • Requirements and Constraints (business, technology, legal, contractual, industry, internal policies, privacy, security, compliance, regulatory) • Responsibility (accountability, authority, governance, stewardship, ownership, motivation, reward) • Improvement and Prevention (root cause, continuous improvement, monitor, metrics, targets) • Structure and Meaning (definition, context, relationships, standards, rules, architecture, models, metadata, semantics, taxonomies, ontologies, hierarchies) • Communication (awareness, outreach, education, training, documentation) • Change (management of change and associated impact, organizational change management, change control)

*Reprinted with permission of GOAL/QPC, Salem NH 03079; *www.memoryjogger.com*.

Best Practice

An often overlooked root cause—architecture and constraints. A good data model combined with constraints at every level of the execution of it—database design, application interaction, and accessibility—will help produce quality, reusable data, and prevent many postproduction data quality problems (e.g., redundancy, conflicting data definitions, and difficulty in sharing data across applications). An optimum architecture and constraint design puts the appropriate constraints at the correct levels of the data and application architecture. Rules about validation and constraints should be considered and implemented across the enterprise, whether for applications developed in house or for those purchased from vendors.

- Constraints at the database level must be general enough for all uses of the data by all applications, but only the DBA should be able to override them.
- At the application layer, nuances of usage may be enforced.
- Some accessibility rules may be enforced in the middle layer(s).

 Communicate

- Have you communicated the root causes and preliminary recommendations from this step?
- Are you including project sponsors and stakeholders with appropriate updates throughout the project?
- Are you starting to include management of other teams who could be called upon in the future to help implement recommendations? Don't wait too long to let them know what is happening.

 Checkpoint

Step 5—Identify Root Causes

How can I tell whether I'm ready to move to the next step? Following are guidelines to determine completeness of the step:

- ✓ Have the root causes of the data quality issues been identified and documented?
- ✓ Have specific recommendations for addressing those root causes been determined and documented?
- ✓ Has any additional learning about impact to the business been documented?
- ✓ If applicable, have specific recommendations and next steps based on business impact results been determined and documented?
- ✓ Has the communication plan been updated?
- ✓ Has necessary communication been completed?

Step 6 | Develop Improvement Plans

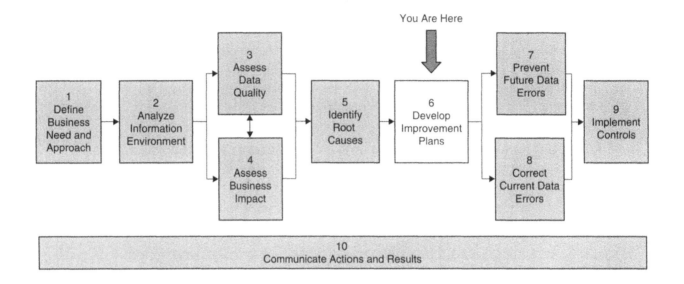

Business Benefit and Context

Specific recommendations for improvement may have already been determined during *Step 5—Identify Root Causes*. Or you may be developing both specific recommendations and improvement plans in this step. (See Table 3.35.)

This is a critical point in the project where communication is key to ensuring that final recommendations are implemented. Because ownership of implementation often lies with groups outside the project team who completed the assessments this step may entail (1) developing improvement plans that can be implemented by the existing project team, (2) developing specific recommendations or high-level improvement plans that can only be implemented by others, and (3) increased communication activity. Plans and recommendations may be both short-term and one-time

activities, or may require a new project for implementation.

Communication is an important part of this step to share results of the assessments and to obtain buy-in from those who can see that the recommendations are implemented. Do not underestimate the effort to prepare and communicate project results.

Approach

1. Gather results from each of the assessments and root cause activities.

If you have been documenting results and lessons learned throughout the project, then gathering results will be quite easy. If you have not been documenting results along the way, then you may want to look at the Analyze and Document Results section in Chapter 5 for suggestions. Go back to any documentation from each of the prior steps and compile it.

Table 3.35 • Step 6—Develop Improvement Plans

OBJECTIVE	Develop an action plan based on the recommendations from the data quality and/or business impact assessment results and from root cause analysis.
PURPOSE	Ensure that the data quality assessment and business impact results and recommendations are turned into action plans.
INPUTS	For data quality assessments: • List of high-priority issues, root causes, and specific recommendations for addressing root causes (output from *Step 5—Identify Root Causes*) • Output of data quality assessment results as reference For business impact assessments: • Business impact assessment results and specific recommendations for action based on results—e.g., where investments in information quality should be made, project next steps (output from *Step 4—Assess Business Impact*) • Any learning related to business impact that may come out of a root cause analysis (output from *Step 5—Identify Root Causes*)
TOOLS AND TECHNIQUES	• Prioritization: Benefit versus Cost Matrix (See *Step 4.4—Benefit versus Cost Matrix*) • Template 3.11 (Recommendations for Action) in the Sample Output and Templates of this step. • Any planning approaches with which you are familiar • Communication plan (see *Step 10—Communicate Actions and Results*)

OUTPUTS	• Specific action plan and recommendations for addressing root causes, preventing data quality issues, and correcting data errors (along with supporting documentation):
	  – Improvement activities that do not require a project
	  – Plans for additional projects or small-scale pilots to implement changes
	• Personnel and organizations impacted by the plans and improvements
	• Communication for raising awareness and "selling" the changes
	• Any additional needed communication completed, along with updated communication plan

CHECKPOINT	• Have the improvement plans been developed and documented? • Have results of the project and recommendations been communicated? • Has support for the improvement plans and recommended action been obtained? • Has other necessary communication been completed? • Has the communication plan been updated?

2. Develop and prioritize specific recommendations to address the issues found.
You may have done this as part of a root cause analysis. If not, do it now by synthesizing results from it and from each assessment; expect several recommendations. Every improvement doesn't need to be a full project to be implemented. Look for quick wins and short-term activities that will provide benefits.

Look for similarities across the recommendations. (For example, are they related to the same business processes?) You may want to group them before prioritization. Prioritize the recommendations using an approach such as a cost–benefit matrix. See *Step 4.4—Benefit versus Cost Matrix* for more detail about this technique.

Ensure that improvement plans include prevention, correction, and communication. A conscious effort to raise awareness and "sell" the plans will need to be made to turn recommendations into action.

 Key Concept

Expect to see both improvement activities that do not require a project and plans for additional projects or small-scale pilots to implement changes.

3. Identify accountability and develop plans.

Identify the personnel and organizations most likely to be accountable for implementing the recommendations. For recommendations that can be implemented

By the existing project team—With the team, develop improvement plans using the project management skills you have learned working as a group.

By those outside the project team—Develop communication to share results of the project and your recommendations. Ideally those you suspect will be impacted will have been kept informed throughout the project and the fact that they are being asked to help implement recommendations will come as no surprise. The more involved people are throughout the project, the less likely they will be to reject efforts to include them in solving the problems found.

What I call a "magic moment" occurred during one of the final team meetings to prioritize specific recommendations from a data quality project. As responsibility for the recommendations were being assigned, the data management team leader agreed that Data Management should institute some of them. But she lamented that there was no money to spare for recommendation implementation.

The marketing manager was also in attendance. Because she had been appropriately involved and informed throughout the project, she was aware of the recommendations' value to company (and her) marketing goals. She asked, "How much will it cost for your team to institute these recommendations?" The data manager replied with an estimate. The marketing manager laughed, "I waste more money than that in one marketing campaign. I'll pay for those changes!"

As you can see from this true story, it is well worth the effort required to communicate and ensure that the right people are involved throughout the project.

Don't try to fix everything at once, but be sure the plans you put in place will address the root cause. Don't let the solutions miss the root cause because of preconceived notions about them.

4. Document and communicate results.

See suggestions in the Communicate box in this step's summary.

 Best Practice

Sustaining information and data quality requires management support. Make sure your plans include the appropriate communication to ensure that support.

Sample Output and Templates

Template 3.11, Recommendations for Action, can be used to capture specific recommendations for action that you have developed from compiling and synthesizing all project results to this point. The recommendations and resulting improvement plans will vary. In the list that

Template 3.11 • Recommendations for Action

No.	RECOMMENDATION	PRIORITY	NOTES
1			
2			
3			
4			
5			
6			
7			

follows are a few examples of the range you may expect to find.

Root cause analysis activities—One data quality accuracy project team was surprised to learn that 36 percent of their contacts could not be located (via telemarketing). A high-priority recommendation was to investigate the causes of this situation. Ideally, that investigation would have taken place earlier; but now was the time to obtain agreement to actually get to root causes using the techniques in *Step 5— Identify Root Causes*.

Small project team—In one project, the root cause of many data quality issues in the Customer Master Database was suspected to lie in data entry. The real root cause was found to be a variety of methods through which customer information was collected. Analysis showed that the same question was often asked in different ways with different answer choices. Or questions were unclear

or presentation quality prevented customers from providing accurate information. In this case, the proposal was for a specific project that would (1) improve the clarity, content, and phrasing of questions so customers could understand how to answer each question; (2) standardize questions for consistency and effectiveness of data collection and use; and (3) obtain buy-in to change the various forms, websites, and so forth. This recommendation was ranked as having a high impact but being fairly low cost to implement. It could not be done in just a few days, but could probably be accomplished over several weeks with a small project team.

Data correction—While other prevention measures were under way, a clean-up campaign to address widespread data errors was needed. Since a clean-up would entail the purchase of data-cleansing tools for identifying duplicates, this improvement, while considered high impact, was also high cost.

Step 6 Summary

 Communicate

- Are you getting buy-in for improvement plans?
- Are you raising awareness among those who will be impacted by the improvements identified?
- Have you updated your communication plan?

 Checkpoint

Step 6—Develop Improvement Plans

How can I tell whether I'm ready to move to the next step? Following are guidelines to determine completeness of the step:

- ✓ Have the improvement plans been developed and documented?
- ✓ Have results of the project and recommendations been communicated?
- ✓ Has support for the improvement plans and recommended action been obtained?
- ✓ Has other necessary communication been completed?
- ✓ Has the communication plan been updated?

Step 7 | Prevent Future Data Errors

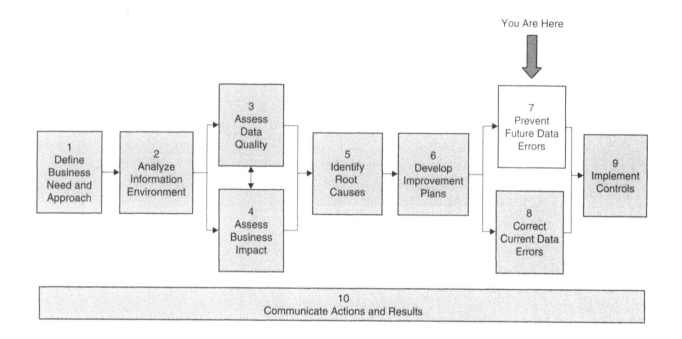

Business Benefit and Context

This is the step where you will start to see the fruits of your assessment labors. Preventing future data errors means that a business can install processes that produce quality data, instead of facing future data-cleansing activities (see Table 3.36). Improving information quality is an iterative endeavor, but preventing *known* errors can help build a foundation of quality from which to further improve information processes.

The natural tendency is to skip prevention and start immediately on correcting current errors—that is why prevention is Step 7 and correction is Step 8. Prevention reaps long-term benefits and increases trust in information quality. If a company is going to ignore prevention, it should do so consciously only after it has been able to justify cleansing the data without any effort to prevent those problems from recurring.

The Human Element

Improvement project participants will also be encouraged by success—and preventing future data errors is ongoing success. While not every error can be prevented, vastly improved information will raise morale throughout the business and raise expectations for the success of subsequent improvement projects.

Approach

1. Ensure that improvement activities or projects focus on root causes.

Review the causes discovered in *Step 5—Identify Root Causes*. This is particularly important if some time has passed between implementation

Table 3.36 • Step 7—Prevent Future Data Errors

OBJECTIVE	• Implement appropriate solutions that address root causes of the data quality problems.
PURPOSE	• Prevent future data errors from occurring by dealing with the causes of those errors. • Implement appropriate improvement plans. • Ensure that that investment in clean-up or correction of current errors is not wasted.
INPUTS	Output from *Step 6—Develop Improvement Plan:* • Improvement plans • Small-scale pilots or additional projects to implement changes, if needed • Communication for raising awareness and "selling" the changes • Personnel impacted by the improvements • Updated communication plan
TOOLS AND TECHNIQUES	• Tools and techniques chosen to fix the data errors specific to each problem • Building the use of data profiling and/or data cleansing tools functionality into the standard processes
OUTPUTS	• Solutions for addressing root causes and preventing future data errors • Documented changes to the current business that result from the improvements implemented • Personnel affected by changes trained and with a consistent understanding of changes, expectations, new roles/responsibilities, new processes, etc. • Changes and their results documented for future users, and successes communicated • Necessary communication completed, along with updated communication plan
CHECKPOINT	• Have the solutions for addressing root causes and preventing future data errors been implemented? • Have changes to the current business from the new processes been documented? • Have participants in the new processes received training? • Do all participants have a consistent understanding of changes, expectations, roles/responsibilities, and the like? • Have results from the changes been documented and communicated? • Has other necessary communication been completed? • Has the communication plan been updated?

and the original assessments and root cause analysis. Ensure that the improvement activities still apply to the current environment.

2. Refer to the Framework for Information Quality (FIQ) for factors that impact information quality.

Table 3.37 provides additional ideas for preventing information quality problems based on the RRISCC section of the FIQ.

3. Identify which improvements need to be implemented.

Ask if there are urgent and important changes that need to be pursued and if there are projects that would yield long-term benefit. Expect many of the improvements to be related to processes. After all, data are products of business processes. Some improvements will take the form of "quick-win" activities that can easily be implemented; others will require more resource-intensive effort.

If the number of prevention improvements needed is overwhelming, quickly prioritize your options. Use the Benefit versus Cost Matrix (in *Step 4.4—Benefit versus Cost Matrix*) to determine where to focus your efforts first.

Following are examples of prevention activities and projects:

- Train customer service reps in data entry standards.[13] Include awareness of the dependency that other parts of the business have on the quality of the data they collect, and awareness of the impact to the company if the quality is poor.

Table 3.37 • RRISCC Questions for Prevention

REQUIREMENTS	Do requirements need to be understood and documented?
RESPONSIBILITY	Does clear accountability, with appropriate motivation and rewards for ensuring information quality, need to be insititued?
IMPROVEMENT AND **P**REVENTION	Do processes for monitoring data quality along with key metrics need to be implemented?
STRUCTURE AND **M**EANING	Do clear definitions, standards, business rules, and models need to be documented and made easily available? Do processes for keeping them updated need to be put into place? Does a data model need to be documented?
COMMUNICATION	Does training need to be updated or developed and delivered? Does an effective communication plan need to be developed and carried out?
CHANGE	Are there any organizational changes that need to be made to ensure data quality? Do any roles and responsibilities need to be updated or put into place? Is a standard change control process in effect?

[13]I'm a big believer in the value of training in preventing data problems. I once worked with an individual who was responsible for a database that contained information about product sales collected from resellers. The information was used to give refunds based on certain incentives. Five years earlier she had been responsible for entering data into the database. Her comment: "If I had known then what I know now about how the data are used, I would have been a lot more careful!"

- Institute a governance process for developing and enforcing data standards. Include business impact to help sell the changes that will be required.
- Implement metrics for data quality that complement the business metrics for quick customer call turnaround—often the only metric that currently exists for customer service reps. Ensure that managers of the Support Center are aligned with the new metrics to be implemented.
- Ensure that data quality–related activities are included in the customer service reps' job responsibilities and are part of their annual performance review.
- Work to increase trust in and thus usage of the Customer Master database by developing communication with its users. Include results of the initial baseline assessment, prevention activities currently under way, correction activities already completed, and business impact results that created the motivation for improvement. Engage executive management in the communication sessions with individual contributors.

4. Finalize an implementation plan for each of the prevention improvements.

You can use the table approach to the Information Life Cycle (Chapter 5) to carefully plan and implement your improvements to ensure that harmful side effects do not result from the correction work. Reference the Framework for Information Quality to ensure that you have accounted for components that will affect your plan.

For example, make sure that you have accounted for the people/organizations that will be responsible for improvements. Look at the POSMAD Interaction Matrix Detail—Sample Questions in the Appendix or Figure 2.3 in Chapter 2 to help you plan effective improvements.

5. Ensure that improvements are assigned and implemented.

All the same principles for good project management addressed in *Step 1—Determine Business Need and Approach* apply here. You don't need a project charter for each improvement activity, but you may need one for large-scale improvements.

6. Communicate results.

The same suggestions for communication outlined in *Step 10—Communicate Actions and Results* apply here.

Step 7 Summary

 Communicate

- Have you obtained final buy-in for prevention plans to be implemented?
- Have personnel affected by the changes been trained?
- Do all those impacted (executives, management, project managers, individual contributors) have a consistent understanding of changes, expectations, new roles and responsibilities, new processes, and the like?
- Do they have an understanding of why these changes are being implemented?
- Are you addressing any resistance to the implementations?

 Checkpoint

Step 7—Prevent Future Data Errors

How can I tell whether I'm ready to move to the next step? Following are guidelines to determine completeness of the step:

- ✓ Have the solutions for addressing root causes and preventing future data errors been implemented?
- ✓ Have changes to the current business from the new processes been documented?
- ✓ Have participants in the new processes received training?
- ✓ Do all participants have a consistent understanding of changes, expectations, roles/responsibilities, and the like?
- ✓ Have results from the changes been documented and communicated?
- ✓ Has other necessary communication been completed?
- ✓ Has the communication plan been updated?

Step 8   Correct Current Data Errors

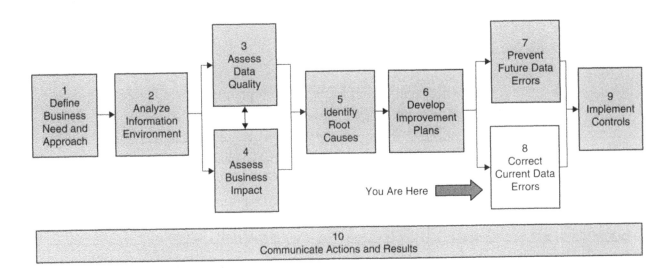

Business Benefit and Context

The correction of current data errors is an exciting milestone in the information and data quality improvement process (see Table 3.38). However, for continuous improvement it is important not only to correct current data errors, but also to prevent future ones. Larry English strongly recommends that data correction activity should be a "one-time event only, coupled with process improvement to prevent occurrence of those defects."

What if data errors are stopping business processes? In this case they should immediately be corrected (as in the example in *Step 5—Identify Root Causes* where incorrect master data records were halting product shipments). Once the critical records are changed, add prevention to the improvement activities.

Approach

1. Identify the records to be changed and the specific changes needed.

Document instructions for identifying the records to be changed and the modifications expected. Train team members involved in identifying and changing the records.

2. Decide how to make the changes.

What is the best way to make the changes? Who will be involved? How long will it take? Are there other timing constraints that will affect the data correction efforts (for example, software updates to the application or needed resources that are unavailable)?

Some solutions for updating:

Manual—Individuals use the standard application interfaces, screens, and keyboard.

Screen emulator—This automates the use of the standard application interfaces by replicating the keystrokes as if done manually; it is sometimes referred to as *screen scraping*. Data updated through this method should

Table 3.38 • Step 8—Correct Current Data Errors

OBJECTIVE	• Implement solutions that correct the existing data errors.
PURPOSE	• Correct existing data errors that are causing problems for the business.
INPUTS	• Data quality assessment results from *Step 3—Assess Data Quality* • Improvement plans from *Step 6—Develop Improvement Plans* • Small-scale pilots or additional projects to implement changes, if needed • Communication for raising awareness and "selling" the changes • Personnel impacted by the improvements
TOOLS AND TECHNIQUES	• Data cleansing tools • An application capable of updating data on a large scale • Standard interface with existing applications
OUTPUTS	• Data corrected according to specifications • Necessary communication complete, along with updated communication plan
CHECKPOINT	• Have the current data errors been corrected? • Have the results been documented and communicated? • Has other necessary communication been completed? • Has the communication plan been updated?

conform to all the internal data integrity rules of the application. Tools such as these still require human monitoring and may have poor error handling/correction.

Mass update directly to the database—The caution regarding direct updates to the database is that they bypass any edits, validations, and triggers that are part of the application interface. This in itself can cause additional data quality problems and issues with the database's referential integrity.

Data cleansing tool—Several data cleansing tools are available on the market that standardize and parse data and identify and merge duplicate records.

Custom interface programs—Sometimes the complexity and volume of changes require a custom interface program. Be wary of spending too much time on the correction piece and ensure that it will not come at the expense of preventing problems over the long term.

Following are criteria to help determine the appropriate update solution:

Volume—Lower volumes (less than 200 records) may be updated manually. Mid-level volumes (200–600) may use a screen emulator. Large volumes (more than 600) may require mass updates directly to the database or development of customized interface programs.

Complexity of changes—Consider the number of data elements being changed.

Time to make changes—The time needed to make changes manually will not be feasible.

Impact on system performance—Some changes will have more impact on system performance and should be scheduled during times of lower usage.

Dependencies—For example, changes to some supplier attributes could impact the product master.

Life of the solution—Balance the investment in the particular solution with how long you anticipate being able to use it.

3. Determine who will make the changes and when.

The method you choose to make the changes will drive the choice of who implements them. Take into account any dependencies from a time point of view—for example, avoid making data changes during the last few days of the quarter when you don't want any potential impact on system performance to delay sales orders. Ensure downstream processes are prepared to accept the new data as corrected.

4. Make the changes.

Use the documentation to ensure consistency of changes—particularly if more than one person is making them. Use an analysis of data dependencies to make sure that the changes themselves don't produce data quality problems, and stay alert—the changes may

 Best Practice

Correcting data is another phase of the Information Life Cycle. Use the table approach to the life cycle (see Chapter 5) to carefully plan and implement your changes so that harmful side effects are not created as a result of the correction work.

have affects on downstream processes that you did not predict.

Consider changes to master data versus transactional data. For example, merging duplicate master records may not be possible until all associated open transactional records are closed. You may have to flag a duplicate record as not to be used before it can be merged or deleted—pending all associated transactional record closings. Take into consideration any other system dependencies or timing constraints.

5. Document the changes.

Describe the changes in structured documents so that future improvement teams can follow the data correction process. Structured documents mean an organized method of collecting, storing, and sharing the information such as through an enterprise knowledge management system or website. It does not mean storing documents on your hard drive, making them accessible only to you.

6. Communicate results.

The structured documents that describe the changes should be used to inform future technical teams; however, the results of data correction should be communicated to the data and information stakeholders as well. This kind of communication will emphasize the success of the data correction and describe how it will benefit the business in the future. Furthermore, all of the knowledge workers need to know how the changes will affect the data they receive.

Step 8 Summary

 Communicate

- Is management aware of the resources needed to correct data errors?
- Has management agreed to provide those resources?
- Are those making the changes aware of how and why these activities are happening?

 Checkpoint

Step 8—Correct Current Data Errors

How can I tell whether I'm ready to move to the next step? Following are guidelines to determine completeness of the step:

✓ Have the current data errors been corrected?

✓ Have the results been documented and communicated?

✓ Has other necessary communication been completed?

✓ Has the communication plan been updated?

Step 9   Implement Controls

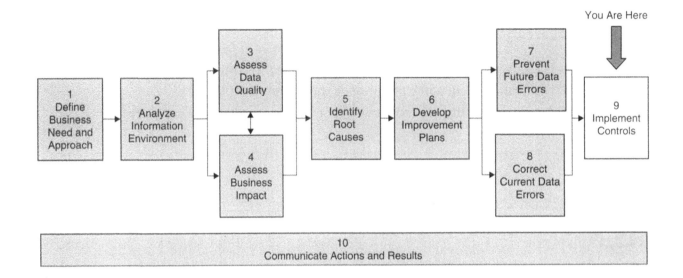

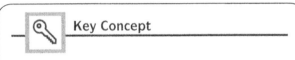

Business Benefit and Context

As Juran notes: "The control process is a feedback loop through which we measure actual performance, compare it with a standard, and act on the difference."[14] While this step is focused on implementing controls, understand that quality does not come from inspection and it is not a monitoring process. Rather, quality should be built into the information processes—hence the emphasis on earlier steps to identify root causes and implement improvements to prevent errors. The best prevention is to build in data quality controls (see Table 3.39) as new solutions are identified and deployed.

There will always be some type of assessment, inspection, and review. Businesses need visibility to what needs to be managed and therefore

measured. Any controls should point to understanding the processes and determining if improvements made have led to the intended results.

> **Key Concept**
>
> The best control is to prevent data quality problems in the first place.

Approach

1. Plan and implement controls.

Appropriate controls will vary widely depending on your issues, the scope of the project, and previous work done. Look at your specific improvement recommendations and the root causes discovered, and determine which data quality dimensions need to be assessed regularly.

---

[14]From Joseph Juran, *Juran's Quality Control Handbook*, Fourth Edition (McGraw-Hill, 1988) p. 24.2.

Table 3.39 ● Step 9—Implement Controls

OBJECTIVE	• Implement ongoing monitoring and metrics. • Monitor and verify the improvements that were implemented. • Make sure new solutions have appropriate data quality controls.
PURPOSE	• Determine if the improvement actions achieved the desired effect. Maintain improvements by standardizing, documenting, and continuously monitoring them. • Encourage continuous improvement and avoid returning to old processes and behaviors.
INPUTS	• Results from *Step 6—Develop Improvement Plans* • Results from *Step 7—Prevent Future Data Errors* • Results from *Step 8—Correct Current Data Errors* • Updated communication plan
TOOLS AND TECHNIQUES	• Dependent on controls implemented
OUTPUTS	• Controls implemented • Necessary communication complete, along with updated communication plan
CHECKPOINT	• Have the controls been implemented? • Have improvements been monitored and verified? • Have all results (both positive and negative) been documented? • Have the successful improvements been standardized? • Has necessary communication been completed? • Has the communication plan been updated?

There are many methods for evaluating improvements to your data quality. Data are the output (artifacts) of your processes, and your controls should assess the dimension of quality that will reflect the improvements you put into place.

Use the data quality dimensions—Metrics should be indicators of process improvements and of the fact that other root causes have been addressed. (See the Metrics section in Chapter 5.) How you actually measure data quality will be the same as how you measure the applicable data quality dimensions—it is just done on a recurring basis. The processes and techniques for ongoing monitoring are contained in *Step 3—Assess Data Quality*.

If you have conducted an initial assessment, all the work done at that time can be evaluated when developing an ongoing process. Review your previous data quality assessments. Look at what worked in them. What did not work? What needs to change so that you can assess quality on an ongoing basis (versus a one-time–only basis)?

If you have not yet performed a quality assessment, go to *Step 3—Assess Data Quality*. Choose your dimensions, conduct your initial assessment to set the baseline data quality, and create a monitoring process. See the Metrics and RACI template (Template 3.12 on page 226). You can also use the table approach from the Information Life Cycle section in Chapter 5.

Statistical quality control—Statistical quality control (SQC), also referred to as statistical process control, was invented by Walter Shewhart in the 1920s and is an established practice in manufacturing. The purpose of SQC is to predict future process performance and to judge process stability by examining current and past performance.[15]

Survey knowledge workers—You may decide that periodic surveys are a good way to determine how knowledge workers and others feel about the quality and importance of the information. (See *Step 3.10—Perception, Relevance, and Trust.*)

Business impact—You may employ some of the business impact techniques in Step 4 to validate the value of the metrics to the business.

Include controls for reference data—Once domains of allowed values are specified and translated into edits where possible, monitor usage of the various values (to spot trends or misuse) and correct those records that fail.

Important: Use everything you have learned and the processes you have developed from your initial quality assessments to modify and implement processes for ongoing monitoring.

2. Obtain buy-in for what you are implementing.

Develop incentives for supporting the controls and for ensuring data quality. If your data quality is dependent on action from knowledge workers (such as taking the extra time to check that contact information is updated when support reps talk to customers on the phone), be sure that that responsibility is supported by their management and is a recognized part of their job description and performance evaluation.

3. Evaluate the improvements that have been implemented.

See if the expected results have occurred and determine next steps. If you (and, more important, those in the business and other stakeholders) are satisfied, and there are no negative side effects, then standardize the improvements. Ensure that the processes and controls become part of the standard operating procedure, including training, documentation, and job responsibilities. Document any final changes.

If there are any issues, such as satisfactory improvements with harmful side effects or unsatisfactory improvements (because of poor implementation or because the control itself was not a good idea), return to *Step 6—Develop Improvement Plans, Step 7—Prevent Future Data Errors,* or *Step 9—Implement Controls* to reassess your implementation plan or the improvement itself.

4. Communicate, communicate, and communicate some more!

Market the benefits through education and feedback. Celebrate and advertise success. Promote the value provided to the business and the team's success with the project.

5. Identify the next potential area for data and information quality improvements.

Start again using The Ten Steps process and make use of work done in previous projects.

You may want to go back to the list of recommendations from *Step 5—Identify Root Causes* and *Step 6—Develop Improvement Plans.* Determine whether the recommendations still apply to the current environment, reprioritize, and implement more improvements.

[15]Tom Redman, *Data Quality for the Information Age* (Artech House, 1996), pp. 155–183. Tom has written about applying SQC to information quality and has applied it in his own work.

Sample Output and Templates

The Metrics and RACI template (Template 3.12) combines the RACI technique (See *Step 10—Communicate Actions and Results*) with specific actions related to ongoing reporting and follow-up. This is a useful template for planning your metrics process.

In the template, "Accountable" indicates the overall owner of the specified activity. That person could also be answerable for all aspects of the metrics process. Names should be entered into the Accountable, Responsible, Consult, and Inform columns. It is possible that N/A (for Not Applicable) will appear in some places. Examples of timing are monthly or weekly—by Thursday 4 p.m. PST.

Step 9 Summary

 Communicate

- Have you obtained buy-in at all levels for implementing controls?
- Have personnel affected by the changes been trained? Do you continue to have regular checkpoint meetings or status communication meetings with interested parties and supporters?
- Are you addressing any resistance to the continuous improvement you are encouraging?
- Are you marketing benefits and celebrating successes?

 Checkpoint

Step 9—Implement Controls

How can I tell whether I'm ready to move to the next step? Following are guidelines to determine completeness of the step:

- ✓ Have the controls been implemented?
- ✓ Have improvements been monitored and verified?
- ✓ Have all results (both positive and negative) been documented?
- ✓ Have the successful improvements been standardized?
- ✓ Has necessary communication been completed?
- ✓ Has the communication plan been updated?

Template 3.12 • Metrics and RACI

	ACTION	TIMING	ACCOUNTABLE	RESPONSIBLE	CONSULT	INFORM
Reporting and Communication	Produce and distribute detailed report.					
	Receive detailed reports.					
	Summarize and create metric.					
	Send metric for posting to dashboard.					
	Post metric on business dashboard.					
	Send communications.					
Data Improvement	Analyze root cause of data errors and make recommendations for action.					
	Correct data errors.					

Step 10 Communicate Actions and Results

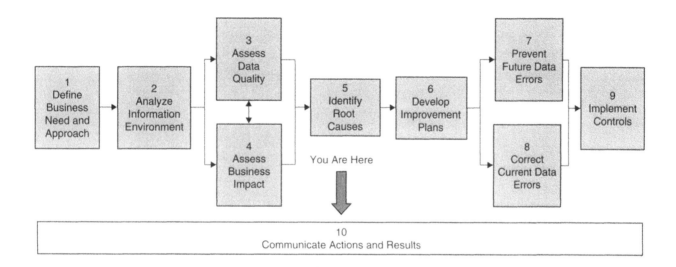

Business Benefit and Context

Communication is essential to the success of any information and data quality improvement project (see Table 3.40). For example, communicate with

- Sponsors of your data quality project, to keep them apprised of progress

- Stakeholders, to demonstrate the value of information and data quality improvement

- Process owners, to gain cooperation in data correction and data error prevention

- Knowledge workers (those dependent on the information to perform their jobs), to let them know how continuous improvement will affect how they use the data.

Refer to the Communicate boxes throughout The Ten Steps process for advice about communicating during each step.

Approach

1. Determine who needs to be included in your communication.

RACI is a management technique, originally used to identify roles and responsibilities in a change process, that can be applied to your communication efforts. (See Table 3.41.) It

---

☎ Communicate

If you don't communicate, your project will fall somewhere between failing miserably and receiving only limited reception to your results and recommendations. While communicating takes time and effort, failing to do so will ensure wasted time and effort. Ignoring communication won't get you anywhere near success.

Table 3.40 • Step 10—Communicate Actions and Results

OBJECTIVE	• Communicate results and progress as appropriate throughout the project.
PURPOSE	• Educate about and raise awareness of the importance and impact of data quality to the business. • Obtain and sustain management support throughout the project. • Provide visibility to and maintain support from all those impacted by the project. • Obtain and maintain support for resulting action plans and improvements. • Show successes.
INPUTS	• Results from any of the steps
TOOLS AND TECHNIQUES	• Communication Plan template (Template 3.13) • RACI (Table 3.41) • 30-3-30-3 of Selling Data Quality (Table 3.42) • Any communication or presentation techniques that are helpful in your environment
OUTPUTS	• Communication plan and schedule • Presentation and training materials • Communications completed based on timeline and communication plan
CHECKPOINT	• For *each step* in your project, were the project progress, results, and standardized improvements documented and appropriately communicated to the needed audiences? • At the *end* of your project, were the project results documented and appropriately communicated to the needed audiences? • If additional activities and/or projects resulting from your project have been identified, have support and resources been committed? • Are you receiving the necessary support? If not, what additional communication is needed to obtain what is required?

can be used at the beginning of your project to determine who needs to be involved and can also be used to determine who needs to receive communications.

Communication must be modified to fit various audiences and timing needs (i.e., when the communication should be received). For example, those who are in the Inform role (see Table 3.41) receive communication after work is completed and less frequently than those in the Responsible, Accountable, and Consult roles.

2. Create a communication plan.

Create your plan early in the project. (See Communication Plan, Template 3.13, in the Sample Output and Templates section on page 231.) Use it, refer to it, and update it throughout the project because it is helpful as a reference tool to remind you to communicate and to document completed communication efforts. Communication is two way so be sure to include venues and vehicles for obtaining feedback from your audiences, creating the opportunity for

Table 3.41 • RACI

RESPONSIBLE	Person who completes or implements the work.
ACCOUNTABLE	Person who must answer that the work was accomplished and has ultimate responsibility. May delegate some of the work (to someone who is "responsible"), but cannot delegate accountability.
CONSULT	Person who provides input to the work or decision.
INFORM	Person who is notified of the work or decision. Does not need to be consulted.

Note: A variation on RACI adds an S (RASCI) for Supportive. This person provides resources or plays some other supporting role. If you use Supportive, be sure to describe what that means for your project.

dialogue, and dealing with questions and concerns.

You may want to create the overall communication plan in a spreadsheet. Additional worksheets in the same file can be used to document the details of each communication needed.

3. Develop your communication material.

When creating your communication and determining the types needed, consider the time available. Table 3.42 offers suggestions. The columns show different times allowed for a communication, from 30 seconds to 3 hours. Shown for each are suggested purpose, focus, and so forth.

4. Continue appropriate communication throughout the project.

Continue to update and modify your communication plan throughout the project to ensure that communication is accomplished. Not much more can be said here except—do it!

5. Increase your skills related to communication.

Think of communication as the starting point for the various soft skills that come into play with any information or data quality project. After all, companies are "just a collection of people"[16] so the human factor cannot be ignored if you expect to be successful. Resources abound to help you increase your skills in communication and related areas.

Coaches, mentors, books, classes, professional organizations, and websites can provide assistance in such areas as presentation skills, negotiating, facilitating, listening, writing, project management, internal consulting, change management, and networking. Even consider sales and marketing since you are selling information quality and marketing your project or program.

 Key Concept

Presentations do require audience analysis, and digging. But what you are really doing is applying your knowledge strategically, so that every bit of it relates directly to the self-interest of your audience.

– Ron Hoff[17]

[16]From Chip Conley, *PEAK: How Great Companies Get Their Mojo from Maslow* (Jossey-Bass, 2007).
[17]Reprinted from Ron Hoff, *"I Can See You Naked": A Fearless Guide to Making Great Presentations* (Andrews and McMeel, 1992), p. 149. Copyright © 1992, 1988 by Ron Hoff. All rights reserved. Reproduced by permission of Browne & Miller Literary Associates, Chicago.

Table 3.42 • 30-3-30-3 of Selling Data Quality

	30 SECONDS	**3 MINUTES**	**30 MINUTES**	**3 HOURS**
Purpose of session	Generate curiosity (e.g., "elevator speech")	Describe status (e.g., status report)	Educate on value (e.g., review session)	Collaboration (e.g., conference or workshop)
Focus of session	Future oriented and focus on the positive	Current status and value provided to business and technology users	Issues, concerns, success stories	Whole picture: cover all aspects of data quality; leave no stone unturned . . .
What you want audience to think	Your enthusiasm and passion for data quality	How much you have achieved with funding and resources available	Data quality is valuable but not easy	For example, data quality is integrated into all aspects of the project life cycle
Message	Simple and high level; establish connections or relationships	Segmented into layers; simple and straightforward	Points of integration; how data quality impacts the business; ROI	Detailed definitions, examples of value, and stress on the importance of growth
Audience action desired	Request for additional information regarding data quality and your initiative	Support for data quality	Understand the value as well as the utility of data quality	Agreement and consensus

Are you prepared???

Source: Adapted from R. Todd Stephens, Ph.D. Used by permission.

Sample Output and Templates

Use the Communication Plan template (Template 3.13) as a starting point for your communication plan.

Audience—Who needs to hear? Who will be affected? Consider organizations, teams, and individuals. Is there anyone specifically who should NOT receive the communication? Expect to have several audiences identified.

Message and desired action—What does the audience need to know? What is changing? How will the audience be impacted? What action do they need to take?

Trigger—What initiates the communication? Is it timing, an event (e.g., the first week in the quarter, a monthly management meeting, when a phase of a project is completed)?

Communication vehicle—What is the method of communication (e.g., in-person presentation, one-on-one meeting, Web seminar, email with attached files, website, newsletter article)?

Development—Who is responsible for *developing* and *creating* the communication? Who provides content and input?

Delivery—Who will present the communication (and when)?

Preparation action—What action needs to be taken to prepare for and complete the communication?

Target date—What is the planned date for the communication?

Complete date—What is the date when the communication will be completed?

Status—What is the status of the communication?

Template 3.13 • Communication Plan

Audience	Message and Desired Action	Trigger	Communica- tion Vehicle	Develop- ment	Delivery	Preparation Action	Target Date	Complete Date	Status

Step 10 Summary

 Communicate

- Have you communicated project progress?
- Are you continuing contact with those who support the project?
- Are you addressing resistance to the project?
- Are you sharing project successes and improvements implemented?

Checkpoint

Step 10—Communicate Actions and Results

How can I tell whether I'm ready to move to the next step? Following are guidelines to determine completeness of the step:

✓ For *each step* in your project, were the project progress, results, and standardized improvements documented and appropriately communicated to the needed audiences?

✓ At the *end* of your project, were the project results documented and appropriately communicated to the needed audiences?

✓ If additional activities and/or projects resulting from your project have been identified, have support and resources been committed?

✓ Are you receiving the necessary support? If no, what additional communication is needed to obtain what is required?

The Ten Steps Process Summary

The Ten Steps process provides the activities, instructions, and techniques for putting the concepts of information quality into action. You have seen that you have to make good choices as to what is relevant, what is appropriate, and what is the most useful level of detail.

Go back and read the best practices and guidelines for applying the methodology that were presented at the end of Chapter 2. They will be more meaningful now that you are familiar with The Ten Steps process.

You have been given suggestions throughout The Ten Steps as to how the processes can be applied to different projects. This discussion continues in Chapter 4.

Concepts and Action—Making the Connection

Now that you know The Ten Steps process, let's tie it into the Framework for Information Quality (FIQ). Tables 3.43 and 3.44 provide two ways of referencing and linking the concepts and the instructions, with one mapping the framework to The Ten Steps process and the other mapping The Ten Steps process to the framework.

In actuality any of the concepts may show up in any of The Ten Steps and vice versa, but the tables highlight specific connections between the two.

Use Table 3.43 if you are working in one of The Ten Steps and want to see the concepts used there. You can then use this to gather more information on those concepts. Use Table 3.44 if you are looking at the concepts and want to see how they are put into action.

Table 3.43 • Mapping The Ten Steps Process to the Framework

THE TEN STEPS PROCESS	FRAMEWORK FOR INFORMATION QUALITY
Step 1—Define Business Need and Approach	• Business Goals, Strategies, Issues, Opportunities (Why) • Requirements and Constraints • Communication • Change • Culture and Environment
Step 2—Analyze Information Environment	• Business Goals, Strategies, Issues, Opportunities (Why) • POSMAD Life Cycle • Key Components of Data, Process, People/Organizations, and Technology • Interaction Matrix • Location (Where) and Time (When and How Long)

Table 3.43 • Mapping The Ten Steps Process to the Framework (Continued)

THE TEN STEPS PROCESS	FRAMEWORK FOR INFORMATION QUALITY
Step 2 (Cont'd)	• Requirements and Constraints • Structure and Meaning • Communication • Change • Culture and Environment
Step 3—Assess Data Quality	• Business Goals, Strategies, Issues, Opportunities (Why) • POSMAD Life Cycle • Key Components of Data, Process, People/Organizations, and Technology • Interaction Matrix • Location (Where) and Time (When and How Long) • Requirements and Constraints • Structure and Meaning • Communication • Change • Culture and Environment
Step 4—Assess Business Impact	• Business Goals, Strategies, Issues, Opportunities (Why) • POSMAD Life Cycle (focus on Apply phase) • Key Components of Data, Process, People/Organizations, and Technology • Interaction Matrix • Location (Where) and Time (When and How Long) • Communication • Change • Culture and Environment
Step 5—Identify Root Causes	Use all components of the FIQ as a checklist. Anything that is missing is a potential root cause of data quality problems.
Step 6—Develop Improvement Plans	• Business Goals, Strategies, Issues, Opportunities (Why) • POSMAD Life Cycle • Key Components of Data, Process, People/Organizations, and Technology • Interaction Matrix • Location (Where) and Time (When and How Long) • Responsibility • Improvement and Prevention • Communication • Change • Culture and Environment

THE TEN STEPS PROCESS	FRAMEWORK FOR INFORMATION QUALITY
Step 7—Prevent Future Data Errors	• Business Goals, Strategies, Issues, Opportunities (Why) • POSMAD Life Cycle • Key Components of Data, Process, People/Organizations, and Technology • Interaction Matrix • Location (Where) and Time (When and How Long) • Requirements and Constraints • Responsibility • Improvement and Prevention • Structure and Meaning • Communication • Change • Culture and Environment
Step 8—Correct Current Data Errors	• Business Goals, Strategies, Issues, Opportunities (Why) • POSMAD Life Cycle • Key Components of Data, Process, People/Organizations, and Technology • Interaction Matrix • Location (Where) and Time (When and How Long) • Responsibility • Communication • Change • Culture and Environment
Step 9—Implement Controls	• Business Goals, Strategies, Issues, Opportunities (Why) • POSMAD Life Cycle • Key Components of Data, Process, People/Organizations, and Technology • Interaction Matrix • Location (Where) and Time (When and How Long) • Responsibility • Improvement and Prevention • Communication • Change • Culture and Environment
Step 10—Communicate Actions and Results	• Business Goals, Strategies, Issues, Opportunities (Why) • Responsibility • Communication • Change • Culture and Environment

Table 3.44 • Mapping the Framework to The Ten Steps Process

FRAMEWORK FOR INFORMATION QUALITY	THE TEN STEPS PROCESS
Business Goals, Strategies, Issues, Opportunities (Why)	• These are specifically addressed in *Step 1—Define Business Need and Approach* • Keep them visible at each step, throughout each step, to keep activities focused • *Step 4—Assess Business Impact* helps answer why
POSMAD Life Cycle • Key Components of Data, Process, People/Organizations, and Technology • Interaction Matrix • Location (Where) and Time (When and How Long)	• *Step 2—Analyze Information Environment* • *Step 3—Assess Data Quality* • *Step 4—Assess Business Impact* • *Step 5—Identify Root Causes* • *Step 6—Develop Improvement Plans* • *Step 7—Prevent Future Data Errors* • *Step 8—Correct Current Data Errors* • *Step 9—Implement Controls*
All FIQ Components Used as a Checklist for Root Cause Categories	• *Step 5—Root Cause Analysis*
Requirements and Constraints	• *Step 1—Define Business Need and Approach* • *Step 2—Analyze Information Environment* • *Step 3—Assess Data Quality* • *Step 6—Develop Improvement Plans* • *Step 7—Prevent Future Data Errors* • *Step 8—Correct Current Data Errors* • *Step 9—Implement Controls*
Responsibility	• *Step 6—Develop Improvement Plans* • *Step 7—Prevent Future Data Errors* • *Step 8—Correct Current Data Errors* • *Step 9—Implement Controls*
Improvement and Prevention	• *Step 5—Identify Root Causes* • *Step 6—Develop Improvement Plans* • *Step 7—Prevent Future Data Errors* • *Step 8—Correct Current Data Errors* • *Step 9—Implement Controls*
Structure and Meaning	• *Step 2—Analyze Information Environment* • *Step 3—Assess Data Quality* • *Step 7—Prevent Future Data Errors* • *Step 9—Implement Controls*
Communicate	• *Step 10—Communicate Actions and Results* • Communication applies to all steps throughout your project
Change	• Address aspects of change throughout your project
Culture and Environment	• Understand and work with culture and environment throughout your project

Chapter 4

Structuring Your Project

*You don't have the luxury of choosing
between building infrastructure and
producing results. You need both.*

– John Zachman, originator of the Framework
for Enterprise Architecture

In This Chapter

Projects and The Ten Steps   240

Data Quality Project Roles   252

Project Timing   253

Projects and The Ten Steps

The first questions asked for any project are, "What do you need to do, how long will it take, and who is going to do it?" From this can be estimated the most important question: "How much is this going to cost me?" This chapter provides guidance to help you answer those questions. Most people want something very prescriptive ("If you have xyz problem, then you should do exactly these steps, at this level of detail, using this many resources, and it will take you this long"). That is impossible to provide since there are so many ways to apply The Ten Steps methodology. However, I can give you additional information to help you make better choices as to how to address data quality in projects.

You already know that a project (as referred to in this book) is any significant effort that makes use of the methodology. A project team can consist of a single person or a group of people. A project can be (1) focused on data quality improvement, (2) the conscious application of specific steps or techniques in the methodology by an individual to solve an issue within his or her area of responsibility, or (3) data quality tasks integrated into another project or methodology, such as new application development, or a data migration or integration, such as in a data warehouse or Enterprise Resource Planning (ERP) implementation.

You also already know you don't have to use all of the steps in the same project and that you can use them to structure a project that fits your situation.

Now that you are more familiar with the Ten Steps, let's explore how they can be applied to the seven project approaches introduced in the section Approaches to Data Quality in Projects in Chapter 1. Those approaches are

1. Establish Business Case
2. Establish Data Quality Baseline
3. Determine Root Causes
4. Implement Improvements
5. Implement Ongoing Monitoring and Metrics
6. Address Data Quality as an Individual
7. Integrate Data Quality Activities into Other Projects and Methodologies

These are not the only approaches to data quality in projects, but are the ones commonly seen.

Remember, no matter what the project (e.g., whether you are working on a system implementation project, focused only on data quality such as testing the quality of purchased data from an outside supplier, or integrating data from two companies), look at where you are in it and use the project approaches to help you decide which of the Ten Steps to use.

You may be joining a data warehouse project and therefore have the opportunity to integrate data quality activities into that project plan (approach 7). You can make an impact on data quality whether you are joining in the early planning stage or in a later project stage.

You may decide to do an initial assessment of an external vendor's data before signing a purchase agreement. In that case, Establish Data Quality Baseline (approach 2) may be the best approach. You may be invited to join a team that was quickly created to find the root cause of a business issue and that now suspects data quality to be a component. Determine Root Causes (approach 3) will be helpful here.

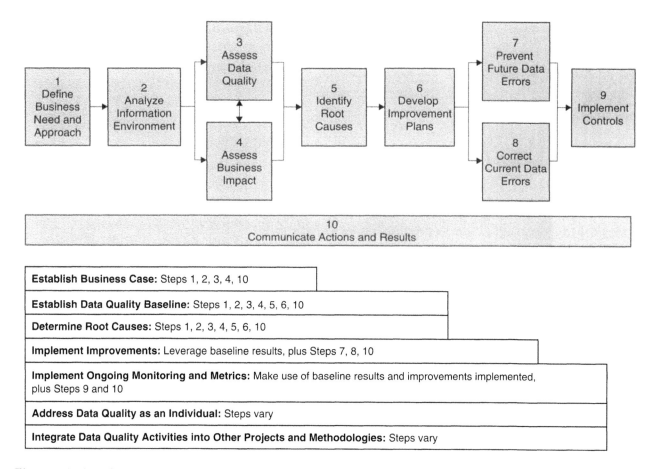

Figure 4.1 • Approaches to data quality in projects and The Ten Steps process.

While you may choose to complete the steps in The Ten Steps process in different combinations, some of them should[1] precede others. For instance, it is essential to define the business need before completing any of the other steps, so *Step 1—Define Business Need and Approach* should come first. (Remember, you might spend one hour or one month on this step depending on your scope, the project approach, where you are in the project, and what is already known about the business need.)

Furthermore, you should identify the root causes of data errors in order to prevent them, not just treat the symptoms. *Step 5—Identify Root Causes* should precede *Step 7—Prevent Future Data Errors*. Finally, you must[2] use *Step 10—Communicate Actions and Results* in every improvement project, regardless of how you use the other steps.

Figure 4.1 shows which of the Ten Steps would most likely be used in each of the approaches. A discussion of the approaches follows with suggestions on the steps, on

---

[1]While I am tempted to say "must," I'm realistic enough to know that no one *has* to do anything. All I can do is point my readers in a useful direction.

[2]Okay, this is one place where I will say "must." If you don't communicate, you will fall somewhere between failing miserably and receiving only limited reception of your results, actions, and recommendations. Ignoring communication won't get you anywhere near success.

communication and documentation, and on notes about timing. The figure does *not* indicate level of detail for each of the steps—that is another choice. Let's start with which steps apply to each approach.

Establish Business Case

An Establish Business Case approach may be an exploratory assessment or a quick proof of concept assessing data quality on a very limited set of data. As an individual, you can implement a brief project that will help you make a business case for further data quality improvements. If you already have a specific data quality problem, you may just want to assess its business impact without further quality assessment. As a member of a project team, you may have already assessed your data quality and have specific improvements you want to implement, but you need to establish a business case before getting permission to do so.

Suggested Ten Steps Activities
Include the following process steps:

Step 1—Define Business Need and Approach

Step 2—Analyze Information Environment

Step 3—Assess Data Quality

Step 4—Assess Business Impact

Step 10—Communicate Actions and Results

Use the methodology to think through the problem, understand the information environment at a very high level, and write a few queries against the data. Use some of the less complicated or less time-consuming business impact techniques such as the Benefit versus Cost Matrix to quickly demonstrate the business impact of the data quality problems you discover. Decide if there is a need for in-depth efforts to deal with data quality.

Documentation and Communication— Document what you have learned and put together communication for the audiences whose support you will need. Your results and impact will help you build the business case for additional data quality activities and resources.

Timing—An Establish Business Case project may extend over a few days or weeks with one person doing the bulk of the work while enlisting help from colleagues (e.g., to gain access to data or help determine business impact).

Establish Data Quality Baseline

An Establish Data Quality Baseline approach is used when the business has committed to improving data quality and there is support for a project team and resources. The project may include purchasing and/or using some data quality tools for profiling or cleansing.

Suggested Ten Steps Activities
Include the following process steps:

Step 1—Define Business Need and Approach

Step 2—Analyze Information Environment

Step 3—Assess Data Quality

Step 4—Assess Business Impact

Step 5—Identify Root Causes

Step 6—Develop Improvement Plans

Step 10—Communicate Actions and Results

Structure Activities—The project follows Steps 1 to 4 in the methodology but will go into more detail. The project team will be looking at a large set of data within a database or comparing data across databases. The data quality assessment will take longer than in Establish Business Case, with Steps 1 to 4 going into more detail. The goal of this project is not just to uncover problems but to determine which ones are worth addressing, to identify the root causes for the high-priority issues, and to develop realistic action plans to improve the data. Often those who can correct the data errors found or implement the recommended improvements are not those on the project team. Sometimes implementing the improvement plan takes the form of another project.

Documentation and Communication— Communicate, from *beginning to end*, with the stakeholders who are sponsoring and supporting the project. Regular status reports will ensure that sponsors have a good idea that their investment is producing a return. Include others who may be affected by the results of the project. Remember, communication goes two ways and you need to keep in touch with stakeholders to understand how they perceive the project and if changes to the business could impact and change a project's goals.

Important: You want those who can take action to be appropriately informed throughout the project and be willing to take action based on your project results.

Timing—Estimating the timeline for this approach is difficult. The reason is that until you assess the data, you don't know how large a problem you may have. What you find in *Step 3—Assess Data Quality* will determine the time for the remaining steps. However, there are some guidelines if you are trying this kind of project for the first time.

Timing Guidelines—Scope the project for no longer than 3 to 4 months. Companies tend to lose interest when initial results take too long to deliver. For a 4-month project, allow about 2 weeks for *Step 2—Analyze Information Environment.* You should be able to learn enough to put together a solid assessment plan within 2 weeks. Allow 3 to 4 weeks for *Step 3—Assess Data Quality*. The magnitude of the data quality issues uncovered in the assessment will drive the remainder of the project, but 2 to 4 weeks for *Step 4—Assess Business Impact* and at least 2 weeks each for *Step 5—Identify Root Causes* and *Step 6—Develop Improvement Plans* are good guidelines.

Step 2—Analyze Information Environment seems to be somewhat problematic for projects specifically focused on data quality assessment, such as when establishing the data quality baseline. The activities in this step are less familiar to some team members and project managers, and the level of detail can vary widely. Obviously the amount of time spent on Step 2 depends on your scope. Table 4.1 provides guidelines to help you estimate the time to spend on this step for data quality projects.

Determine Root Causes

A Determine Root Causes approach is used when you already know the specific data quality issues and have decided that further

Table 4.1 • Estimated Time to Spend on Step 2

ESTIMATED LENGTH OF PROJECT TO ESTABLISH DATA QUALITY BASELINE	TIME TO SPEND ANALYZING YOUR INFORMATION ENVIRONMENT
4 weeks	Approximately 3–5 days
3–4 months	Approximately 2 weeks
9 months	Approximately 1 month

investigation into the root causes is needed. If a number of organizations or processes are impacted by the issues, this project may take the form of a workshop or series of workshops to bring together people who have the knowledge to get to the root causes. Once the root cause or causes are uncovered, this project could include developing specific recommendations for addressing them. The end result of this project approach could be to find owners and gain commitment to implement the improvements.

Suggested Ten Steps Activities
Include the following process steps:

Step 1—Define Business Need and Approach

Step 2—Analyze Information Environment

Step 3—Assess Data Quality

Step 4—Assess Business Impact

Step 5—Identify Root Causes

Step 6—Develop Improvement Plans

Step 10—Communicate Actions and Results

The steps just listed are the same as for Establish Data Quality Baseline. The difference is in the level of detail for Steps 1 to 4. They are noted here because you need some kind of background before jumping into root cause analysis. Get enough information from those steps to provide the context for analyzing root causes and choosing the techniques to employ.

Documentation and Communication—
Communicating the root causes found and the resulting recommendations are two of your most important tasks. You will need support (funding, headcount, etc.) to actually implement improvements, and this is where the efforts to prevent data quality issues will really pay off. But don't be surprised if you have to establish a business case (again) to continue.

Timing—Plan on 3 to 6 weeks for determining root causes. Time can slip by quickly when trying to coordinate schedules for those who need to meet to analyze root causes. In some emergency situations, you may have only a few days. In any case, try to get this done as quickly as possible so you can keep the interest of management and move into implementing your recommendations.

Implement Improvements

An Implement Improvements project approach executes the recommendations developed when the data quality assessment and business impact analysis have generated a plan for data quality improvement. Implementing improvement will take the form of both correction of current errors and steps to prevent future errors.

Suggested Ten Steps Activities
Make use of the results from Establish Data Quality Baseline (see the steps listed for that approach) plus the following three steps:

Step 7—Prevent Future Data Errors

Step 8—Correct Current Data Errors

Step 10—Communicate Actions and Results

Many companies have resources dedicated to correcting data errors. Correcting data errors is important, particularly if they are causing critical business problems. (For example, a product cannot be shipped and the problem has been traced back to faulty master data.) However, spending the majority of resource time on correction with little or no time on prevention is a common pitfall and will only lead to more time wasted in fixing future problems.

As important as it is to correct data errors, it is more important to ensure that data errors are prevented. Some of the prevention activities will warrant a new project while others may focus on, for example, instituting training. Some recommendations will require the business to improve its processes; others may involve updating technology or fixing bugs found.

Documentation and Communication—
Assign ownership and document the improvements—goals and processes. Update those who will be involved with the implementation as to the reasons for the improvements (results of data quality dimension assessments and associated business impact techniques).

Timing—No timing estimates are given since the nature of the improvements will vary greatly.

Implement Ongoing Monitoring and Metrics

An Implement Ongoing Monitoring and Metrics project approach focuses on instituting operational processes for monitoring, evaluating, and reporting results. When designing and implementing your control processes, remember to include actions for addressing issues found—both to correct current errors and prevent future ones. It is less expensive and more efficient to incorporate monitoring and metrics during the initial system implementation. This may continue what was started in Implement Improvements by standardizing some of the improvement activities as a regular control.

Suggested Ten Steps Activities
Make use of the results from the project approach Establish Data Quality Baseline as part of a new project or system or as improvements implemented (see the steps listed for that approach) plus the following two steps:

Step 9—Implement Controls

Step 10—Communicate Actions and Results

The data quality assessment will show many data quality issues—some big, some small, some important, some not. For data assessed to be of high business value you may want to institute monitoring and metrics to track their quality on a regular basis. Monitoring may also verify if prevention improvements put into place are achieving the desired results.

Documentation and Communication—
Because there is a cost to monitoring and reporting metrics, be sure to monitor processes that are essential to the business. Determine the appropriate audiences to receive the metrics results and teach them how to interpret the metrics—what is being measured and why it is important.

Timing—No timing estimates are given since the nature of the monitoring and metrics will vary greatly.

Address Data Quality as an Individual

In the Address Data Quality as an Individual approach, any approach that has been previously described can apply—with the project scaled to fit what one person can accomplish. A one-person project requires good project management practices, such as managing scope, obtaining management support, and communicating effectively. You may find specific techniques applicable to particular situations that are a normal part of your responsibilities.

Suggested Ten Steps Activities
Any of the Ten Steps may apply. You may find some techniques that will become a standard part of your individual processes. For example, if you are responsible for loading data from external sources and have had issues with changing formats and content from the supplier, you may want to institute quick

profiling of the data prior to the load. This prevents the rework created when problems are found only when the load program fails. An even better prevention approach would be to institute regular communication with the data provider and improve the process.

You may also institute your own short-term project—say a 4-week focused one—based on any of the approaches already described, if you carefully manage its scope.

Documentation and Communication—
Communication is not just for project teams. Ensure that your manager is aware of and supports your work. Institute regular status reports and obtain feedback. Inform team members in your regular department meetings of your activities.

Timing—No timing estimates are given since the nature of how you as an individual apply the Ten Steps will vary greatly.

Integrate Data Quality Activities into Other Projects and Methodologies

Most projects, such as system implementations, ERP migrations, data warehousing, and any data integration project, can benefit from having appropriate data quality activities incorporated into their plans. Details follow, with discussions on project life cycles and data quality activities in the phases of a project life cycle, and an example of using the data quality dimensions during requirements gathering.

Suggested Ten Steps Activities
Any of the steps can be used. See the more detailed discussion that follows.

Documentation and Communication—
Ensure that the data quality activities show up on the project plan, just as any other tasks do. You might hear "Oh yes, we think data quality is important. Why don't you go work on it (over there) and we'll continue our project. Be sure and talk to us when you're done." That is missing the essential piece—*integrating* the data quality work. Be sure those doing the data quality activities are acknowledged as core or extended team members or resources. Data quality work has to be visible, just as the other project tasks have to be visible.

Timing—The timing will vary greatly. A more detailed discussion follows.

Project Life Cycles
As you integrate The Ten Steps into existing project methodologies, use common sense in combining their concepts and techniques with your company's favored project management style and your specific project plan.

There are many different approaches to running a project. A project life cycle defines the approach for developing solutions and the phases within the project. Examples of solutions include building a new application, migrating data from existing to new applications, or process improvement. The project life cycle provides the basis for the project plan and the tasks to be undertaken by the project team.

The project life cycle may also be referred to as the Solution (or Software or Systems) Development Life Cycle (SDLC), although some may argue that a project life cycle and an SDLC are not the same. The point as it applies to data quality is that there are opportunities to address data quality during almost any project that will increase the chances of project success and prevent data quality problems once in production. For example, in almost every project there is some type of activity related to gathering requirements. You may call that phase by a different name; however, if you are gathering requirements, some data quality activities should be considered during that phase of your project plan.

There are different ways of structuring a project life cycle, and many companies and vendors have their own approaches to this. Figure 4.2 shows the phases in a typical project life cycle along with the phases used in five other project life cycle variants.

No matter which approach you use, data quality tasks from this methodology can be integrated into any project plan. Careful planning at the beginning of a project will guarantee that appropriate data quality activities are integrated into the entire project.

Data Quality Activities in the Project Life Cycle

Data quality issues discovered early in the project life cycle are much less expensive to correct than if they are addressed during final testing or just before going live with a new system. Including data quality–related tasks during the normal course of projects will prevent many problems from occurring once in production. The quality of data can make the difference between a smooth transition and the ability of business to continue as usual and a rocky conversion and the inability to conduct even basic business activities (e.g., completing a timely financial close versus a late financial close; meeting manufacturing and shipping commitments versus needing expensive workarounds while issues are resolved).

Table 4.2 provides a brief list of data quality activities that should be considered in each of the phases of the typical project life cycle.

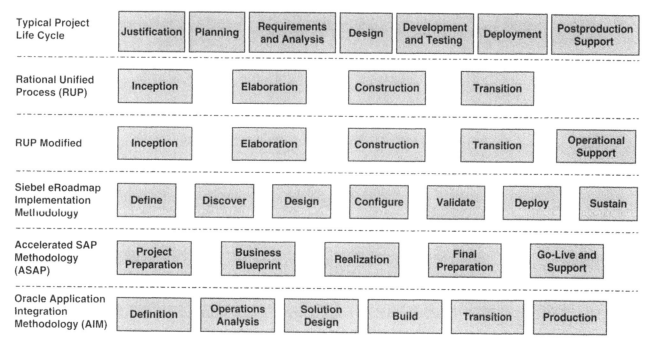

Figure 4.2 • Project life cycle comparison.

Table 4.2 • Data Quality Activities in the Project Life Cycle

JUSTIFICATION	Include the impact of data quality issues when presenting the business problem (or opportunity), the proposed solution, and the rationale for the project.
PLANNING	Consider data quality activities when setting the project scope, schedule, and deliverables. Include data quality deliverables in the project charter. Ensure that the project plan takes time and resources for the data quality activities into account. Plan for data quality control throughout the project for (1) data to be created, (2) master and transactional data to be moved from existing databases and applications, and (3) associated reference data and metadata. Institute data governance to ensure appropriate representation from the business, technology, and those with background on the data when decisions are made.
REQUIREMENTS AND ANALYSIS	Understand the data categories involved in the project. (See the Data Categories section in Chapter 2.) Define data specifications (data standards, data model, business rules, metadata, and reference data) for data to be created and data to be moved from existing databases and applications. Begin by capturing the *semantics* of an organization's data. Creating a semantic data model (described in Table 2.5 in Chapter 2) is a good place to start. What are the definitions of the terms used, and how is the same term used differently in different parts of the organization? Analyze existing data via, for example, data profiling. This will expedite source-to-target mappings, making it possible to map current databases to the new one, and confirm selection criteria for data to be migrated.
DESIGN	Use the semantic data model from the previous activity to update or create a new database design. Define data specifications for data to be created and data to be moved from existing data stores. Data profiling tools can be used to analyze existing data and provide input into the creation of new models that support data to be moved into a new application. Profiling also exposes structural differences between an existing target model and the source data to be moved. Ensure that database designers have access to data specifications that define quality. Ensure a solid feedback process between those analyzing the data, those doing the design, those writing the transformation rules, and those cleansing data. Institute data clean-up (preferably at the sources) as early in the project as possible. If clean-up is not possible or practical at the source, determine where in the migration path (e.g., in a staging area) appropriate clean-up activities or transformations will take place.
DEVELOPMENT AND TESTING	Be sure that those doing programming and creating physical databases understand the importance of their work to the data quality effort. Continue the iterative process of assessing data and providing results to those cleansing data and those writing transformation rules. Check the quality of data being created, in addition to that of existing data to be migrated. Check and ensure quality of reference data and metadata. Profile and check data prior to and after test loads. Update transformation rules, business rules, and other data specifications as necessary.

DEVELOPMENT AND TESTING (Cont'd)	When first testing for software quality assurance, profile the test data and ensure that their content is known. Much time can be spent chasing suspected software problems when the problem is actually in the test data. Controlling the test data well allows the team to focus their efforts on software functionality if issues are found. Ensure that the data can create the expected business transaction; for example, they may conform to known requirements, but can the invoice be generated? Can the sales order be completed? Can the claim be processed? If the data have to be changed by the testing team to complete the transaction, it can indicate that the data specifications were incorrect. Ensure that those changes are communicated to those managing the design specs, those cleansing the data, and those writing transformation rules.
DEPLOYMENT	Use quick data quality assessments to confirm that data extracts are correct prior to the final data loads at go-live. Conduct quick data quality assessments after data loads, before the system is released to the users.
POSTPRODUCTION SUPPORT	Institute appropriate ongoing monitoring and metrics to check data quality and provide the ability to take quick action if needed. Make sure that data governance is applied in the production environment to ensure sustained data quality after go-live.

Use the suggestions in Table 4.2 to stimulate your thinking about data quality and to determine how you can integrate data quality activities into your project. The end goal is that the resulting applications and processes produce high-quality data, which will reduce the negative impact of poor quality on the business and increase trust in the data by those dependent on them.

Data Quality and Requirements Gathering

Regardless of methodology, every system implementation project has a requirements-gathering effort. This effort typically focuses on what users need to see in terms of screens or high-level data flows, but frequently does not get into the quality of the information itself.

By gathering key data quality requirements at the beginning of the project, you can both assess if current data quality levels are acceptable and ensure that data quality can be maintained once the system is successfully implemented. If through assessing current levels data quality is found to be *unacceptable*, you can plan up front

the necessary data cleansing and improvement needs as part of the project or, depending on the business impact, make plans for improving quality over a period of time through focused data quality project initiatives.

The same data quality dimensions, explained in detail in *Step 3—Assess Data Quality*, can be used at a high level to gather the data quality requirements. To follow shortly is a set of guidelines provided by Mehmet Orun, who is the principal data architect and leads Data Services at a large life sciences company. As part of his work with business and IT groups, he advises his colleagues on how to capture data quality requirements to develop innovative solutions while seeking to improve delivery quality, efficiency, and effectiveness.

Note that the order in which the dimensions were discussed does not follow the order in which they are presented in The Ten Steps methodology. This is a good example of how to use the dimensions to fit a particular situation.

You can also use data quality requirements in planning other aspects of a project, such as data migration or even application integration. In the following scenario, Mehmet shares an experience where a project team needed to make integration technology decisions. The business representatives knew what they needed from the ERP system and there were a number of technology options. Instead of focusing on the technology Mehmet facilitated the session using Information Life Cycle concepts and data quality requirements. He was then able to make a recommendation about interfaces (batch, real time, etc.) based on the specific business use.

Mehmet's meeting was with people who were representing the business on the project—the knowledge workers who applied the information in their jobs. Providing background for those he was questioning sounded something like this:

> With today's technologies, we have many different data exchange options. We can exchange information in real time or on established schedules. Even for real-time exchange, we have the option to receive information as soon as it's available (publish-and-subscribe) or we can choose when to retrieve it, with an immediate turnaround time (request–response).
>
> To implement the right interfaces and maintain data quality across systems, we need to understand how business users will use the information, including indirect users of the application such as management.

(*Note*: Technical terminology, such as *publish-and-subscribe*, was not a part of the dialogue but is included for readers in a technology role.)

Mehmet started by using the Information Life Cycle concepts to understand how the information is used by discussing with the following three points:

- Do you need to change this information in your application? Why?
- Does this change need to be sent back to the ERP? Why/Why not?
- "Let's talk about your information needs ..."

He then used the data quality dimensions shown in Table 4.3 in order find out how the knowledge workers perceived data quality needs and the likely impact of poor data quality. The table outlines a way to handle that discussion.

Mehmet suggests the following best practices for capturing data quality requirements:

- Always provide a brief description of what you are trying to achieve and be ready to give examples. This will help your interview or workshop go more smoothly.

- Capture requirements at the business entity level (e.g., purchase order) using business terminology. Conceptual data models would support this effort effectively and allow you to see dependencies as well, to ensure that your requirements are complete.

- Use the terms consistently within and across projects, including the data quality dimensions.

- Compare the results of requirements gathering, per business entity and data quality dimension, to ensure that there are no conflicts. With regard to timeliness, for example, one person may want the entity to be updated within one business day, but not to be changed more than every 4 hours. Another person may want it updated in real time. You have a requirements conflict that needs to be resolved. If you did not capture requirements at the business entity level with consistent terminology, you will rely on luck or work much harder to detect conflict.

- Capture requirements as distinctly as possible. The more specific you are in the

Table 4.3 • Data Quality Dimensions and Requirements Gathering

DIALOGUE	DATA QUALITY DIMENSION	EXAMPLE
How up to date does the information have to be? How long after a piece of information is available do you need access to it? Is a particular delay desired?	Timeliness	We need to know when new employees are hired the same business day in order to create all appropriate accounts for them.
Which data elements *must* be correct in order to make the decision/ perform the transaction?	Accuracy	Vendor tax ID and billing address must be accurate to place a transaction. If the accuracy of a vendor's minority status is not required to complete a transaction, but must be up to date each quarter for financial reporting, track this as a separate Timeliness/ Accuracy requirement.
Are there other systems or data sources the data must match? How often must they be synchronized to other financial systems? Is there an external trigger to this?	Consistency	Finance and Sales organizations may be using different systems to track their capital spending. There may be a forecast schedule that drives the need for consistency.
How much of the total data universe must be available/accessible? What are the criteria to subset the population?	Coverage	How many of all practicing prescribing doctors must be stored in the Sales Force Automation system? All oncologists, immunologists, etc.?
Is duplicate data acceptable? If not, but duplication is likely, what is the timeframe in which duplicates must be resolved?	Duplication	Duplicate data is not acceptable. Can existing records be identified in real time to avoid creating duplicates?
How formally must data specifications be captured and maintained? What are the policies or regulations that require this?	Specification	FDA GMPs (U.S. Food and Drug Administration Good Manufacturing Practices) require preimplementation documentation and formal change control of all design documents.

requirements phase, the easier it will be to design and test solutions.

• Use business impact to prioritize the testing of your requirements. Remember that some of these requirements cannot be automatically tested and require specific coordination. For example, many projects test whether interfaces work properly but do not test their timing (the Timeliness data quality dimension).

Data Quality Project Roles

The specific skills and knowledge needed for any data quality project will vary depending on the project goals, scope, and timeline. But having the necessary expertise in the data, processes, and technology associated with the information is important to project success. Figure 4.3 illustrates this idea.

Many people have experience that crosses one or more of the areas shown in the figure—use them if possible on your team. It will be rare to find one person who has the level of knowledge needed in all three areas of data, business processes, and technology. In some cases, it may be necessary to have more than one person represent each area.

Table 4.4 lists roles along with corresponding skills and knowledge commonly needed in data quality projects. Unfortunately, there are no standards for job roles and titles and corresponding responsibilities, skills, and knowledge. The roles listed here may (and probably will) differ in title from those used by your company.

For each role, pay particular attention to its skills and knowledge and then find the people within your company who have them. Realize that there may be more than one person needed to represent all the skills and knowledge in each role.

If you are working on a data quality-focused project, Table 4.4 can help you choose your project team and extended team members. (Extended team members are not part of the core team but are necessary resources familiar with the project who have a lesser time commitment than the core members.) If you are

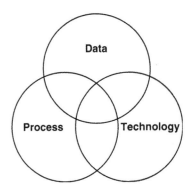

Figure 4.3 • Areas of knowledge a project team needs.

integrating data quality activities into another project, it is important for you to understand those fulfilling the various team roles. You will need to work with them to complete your data quality activities.

If your project is just yourself as an individual contributor, consider the roles and know that many roles can apply in a scaled-down way. Your manager may informally fulfill the role of project sponsor, and you may not have an official team. Think through who would be interested in the work you are doing (potential stakeholders) and others with expertise with whom you may need to consult.

Consider each of the roles as you plan your project and ask:

- Do you need this role for your project?
- What do you call the role in your company or organization?
- Who will fulfill the role for your project?
- Who manages the person you need on your project?
- Can you get the potential team member's (and his or her manager's) agreement and support to participate?

Note how the role applies to your project in the third column of Table 4.4 (see pages 254–255).

Project Timing

We have discussed timing as it applies to each of the approaches to data quality in projects. Now, let's talk about timing from a more general point of view.

Projects that assess data quality or business impact are like other projects, and good project management principles are needed for them to be successful. Information and data quality improvement projects may be difficult to estimate. The *assessment* aspect is what brings uncertainty into a project's plan. Only assessments show the magnitude of any problems. What is learned from analyzing the information environment and the data quality and business impact assessment results will affect the rest of the project timeline.

Assessments often reveal more problems than the one you set out to solve, and root causes may involve more processes than you have the time or resources to improve. Incorporating regular checkpoints throughout the project (to see results and then estimate next steps) will help you prioritize, make adjustments to the project based on what you learn, and keep your project on track.

Improvement also involves *change*, and change is not easy for the people who are involved in instituting new processes or who are receiving information that looks different, even if it is better. Therefore, every time you institute a change during improvement, you should also provide an education plan. Documentation, marketing, and training form the triad of good change management education. A project timeline should account for these activities.

Your company probably has processes in place for project management and change management. Recruit knowledgeable people in these fields to advise you about your project's scope and timing, and to obtain input about the most effective channels for communicating change. The following are strategies for time management[3]:

Focus—Keep a tight focus on the business issue during meetings and activities. Appoint a meeting moderator who is known for his or her ability to keep the group on topic and can deflect tangential conversations with respect.

Early Victories—As your first task, choose activities that have a good chance of success so that a team can report successes during the project's first few weeks.

Prepare the Path—Discuss your team members' responsibilities with their individual managers. Give managers estimates of how much time you think members will spend on your project, and ask them to provide support when your team members need resources.

Spread the Word—Make sure other working teams know about your project, its goals, and its status. Enable sharing of information across projects in order to foster collegiality as well as to prevent confusion and duplicated effort.

Divide and Conquer—When you are facing a tight deadline, divide the project into several subtasks and assign them to small groups to accomplish simultaneously. Use your best judgment on dividing up the tasks—not every task in a project can be completed at the same time.

Celebrate—When your team has successfully completed a difficult set of tasks, give them a break and congratulate them. While this may not seem like a time-management strategy, it will increase morale as well as help team members to perceive the project as manageable.

---

[3]Thanks again to Rachel Haverstick for her assistance in describing these ideas.

Table 4.4 • Project Roles and Skills and Knowledge

ROLES	SKILLS AND KNOWLEDGE	HOW DOES THIS APPLY TO YOUR PROJECT?
Project Sponsor	The person or group who provides the financial resources, in cash or in kind, for the project.	
Project Stakeholders	A person or group with a direct interest, involvement, or investment in the information quality work. Stakeholders are those "actively involved in the project, or whose interests may be positively or negatively affected by execution or completion of the project. [They] may also exert influence over the project and its deliverables."* For example, the person responsible for manufacturing processes would be a stakeholder for any data quality improvements that impact the supply chain. Examples of stakeholders include customers, project sponsors, the public, or organizations whose personnel are most directly involved in doing the work of the project. The list of stakeholders may be long or short depending on the expected scope of the project.	
Project Manager	The person responsible for accomplishing the project objectives. He or she leads the project by applying and integrating the project management processes of initiating, planning, executing, monitoring and controlling, and closing.	
Data Analyst	• Has knowledge of technology (systems/applications/ databases) where data are used and stored. • Understands data structures, relationships, data/ information models, and data requirements. • Understands data standards and metadata. • Understands industry standard languages (SQL, XML) and best practices for data store design (abstraction, normalization, etc.). • Has knowledge of data profiling. • Produces source-to-target mappings. • Understands or researches meaning.	
Subject Matter Expert (SME) (for processes)	• Understands business processes in-depth. • Has knowledge of the information that supports the processes. • Understands the business use and meaning of the data. • Understands the applications that work with the data being assessed.	

(Continued)

Roles	Skills and Knowledge	How Does This Apply to Your Project?
Subject Matter Expert (Cont'd)	• Familiar with organizations, teams, roles, and responsibilities that impact the information throughout its life cycle. • Understands how data relates to processes. • Understands data definitions, including valid values and business rules.	
Data Expert	• Has knowledge of the data content and related metadata.	
Data Modeler	• Responsible for data models and data dictionary. • Has knowledge of related metadata.	
Database Administrator (DBA)	• Specifies, acquires, and maintains data management software. • Designs, validates, and ensures security of files or databases. • Performs day-to-day monitoring and care of the databases. • Works with the physical database design.	
Developers (e.g., application, ETL, Web services)	• Develops programs and writes code. • Unit-tests programs and code. • Understands and develops ETL data processes to and from source systems, databases, and data warehouses. • Has knowledge of languages and technology related to your environment (e.g., XML, canonical models, integration programming, enterprise service bus).	
Enterprise Architect	• Ensures that an organization's strategic goals are optimized through enterprise data standards and technologies. • Understands architecture for the company, business area, and/or applications within the scope of the project. • Ensures that quality and governance processes align with overall architecture for the company.	
Data Architect	• Understands architecture for the company, business area, and/or applications within the scope of the project. • Understands the nature of information management and how to effectively structure and apply data within his or her environment.	
IT Support	• Responsible for IT infrastructure, systems, software, network, system capacity, etc.	

*Project Management Institute, *Combined Standards Glossary, Third Edition* (2007), p. 92.

Chapter 5

Other Techniques
and Tools

*Great things are not done by impulse, but by a
series of small things brought together.*

– Vincent van Gogh

In This Chapter

Introduction   258
Information Life Cycle Approaches   258
Capture Data   263
Analyze and Document Results   263
Metrics   269
Data Quality Tools   271
The Ten Steps and Six Sigma   277

Introduction

Information quality work uses many of the standard tools and techniques employed for years in product quality improvement. This chapter provides additional detail and examples related to data quality for a few of them. These techniques and tools are included in a separate chapter (not in just one of the Ten Steps) because they can be applied throughout The Ten Steps process.

The techniques can be used to understand and improve a current life cycle or to create a new one. Consider the various approaches to documenting your Information Life Cycle described in the following section, Information Life Cycle Approaches, and apply the ones most useful for your project. The ideas presented in this chapter's Capture Data section can be used any time you need to extract or access data. Because it is strongly recommended that you document results from the project's very beginning, the ideas in the Analyze and Document Results section and particularly Template 5.2, Assessment Results, provide an easy way to track key lessons learned, issues, and initial recommendations.

The Data Quality Tools section is an introduction to the various tools on the market to support data quality efforts. Finally, the The Ten Steps and Six Sigma section presents a high-level mapping of The Ten Steps to Six Sigma's DMAIC (Define–Measure–Analyze–Improve–Control).

Information Life Cycle Approaches

This section outlines various approaches for representing an Information Life Cycle. See *Step 2.6—Define the Information Life Cycle* for specific steps. Also see the sections Framework for Information Quality and Information Life Cycle in Chapter 2 for more background.

The Swim Lane Approach

The swim lane approach is one method for visually representing the Information Life Cycle. A swim lane is a type of process flow diagram made popular in Geary Rummler and Alan Brache's book.[1] It can be used to indicate the key components (data, processes, people and organizations, and technology) that impact information throughout the life cycle phases. You decide the level of detail needed for your project.

1. Create the swim lanes.
A useful application of this technique is to show the people aspect (organizations, teams, or roles) as the individual swim lanes. Technology can be presented in its own swim lane or as part of the process flow. The lanes can be horizontal or vertical. Figure 5.1 is a swim lane template with a horizontal orientation as a starting point.

2. Add the process flow using standard flowchart symbols.
Figure 5.2 contains a list of easy reference symbols to use as you get started with your swim lanes. Figure 5.3 shows the high-level life cycle for a supplier master record from initial request to use of the master record data for ordering supplies, paying vendors, and reimbursing employees for expenses.

---

[1]Rummler and Brache, *Improving Performance: How to Manage the White Space on the Organization Chart* (Jossey-Bass, 1990).

Title: Type of information:		Created by: Date:
Role A		
Role B		
Technology		
Role C		
Role D		
Role E		

Figure 5.1 • Swim lane template.

Symbol	Description
Activity	Indicates an activity or a task in the process. This symbol can also be used when no other symbol is suitable. A brief title or short description of the activity is included in the rectangle.
Process Flow	Indicates the flow or direction of the process.
Decision Point	Indicates a point in the process where a decision is necessary. The outputs from the diamond are usually marked with options (e.g., Yes or No, True or False, or another required decision). The flow from the diamond proceeds in the direction of the option chosen with the resulting activities varying based on the decision.
Electronic File	Indicates an electronic file.
Database	Indicates where the information is retrieved from or placed in a database (as a result of obtaining, storing, sharing, maintaining, applying, or disposing of the information).
Paper Document	Indicates information is captured on paper-based documentation (e.g., hardcopy forms, written reports, computer printouts).
Connector	Indicates the beginning and end points of a flowchart. It can also be used when there is a break in the flowchart by placing a letter or a number inside the circle to show where it is continued on the same page or a different page.
Inspection	Indicates an inspection activity where the process flow has stopped and the quality of the output is evaluated. The person who performed the previous activity does not normally perform the inspection. It can also designate when an approval signature is required.
Annotation	Used to note additional information about the symbol to which it is connected. A dotted line connects the open rectangle to the flowchart symbol so that it will not be confused with a solid line arrow that indicates the process flow.

Figure 5.2 • Common flowchart symbols.

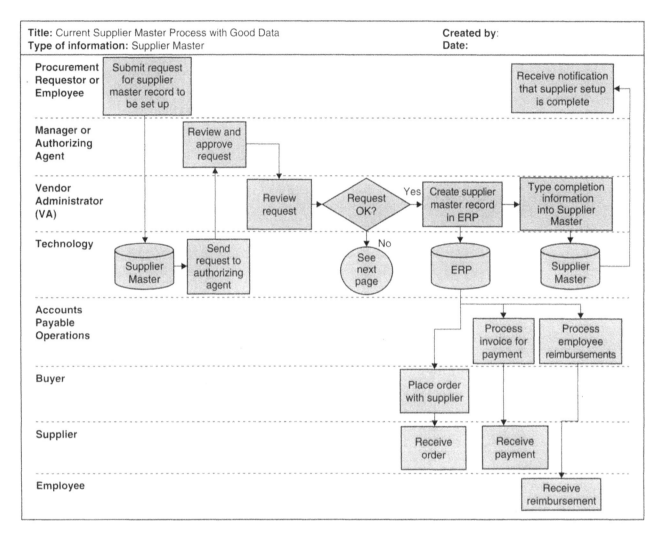

Figure 5.3 • Example of the swim lane approach.

The Table Approach

The table approach is particularly useful if you need *detailed* documentation of your Information Life Cycle, because it easily shows gaps or conflicts in tasks, roles, timing, and dependencies. You can also use this approach to develop new processes for your life cycle.

1. Create the table.

Use Template 5.1 as a starting point. The following list explains the template columns:

Activity—Describe the task or activity in a verb–noun format.

Manual or automatic—Whether the task is completed by a person or automatically by a program.

Timing—When the activity takes place (e.g., daily, monthly, quarterly). If important, be more specific and list time of day, when in the month, and any high-level dependencies on other processes (e.g., daily—8:00 a.m. PST; monthly—tenth working day or workday 10; quarterly—at

Template 5.1 • Table Approach

No.	Activity	Manual or Automatic	Timing	Role	Employee/Contractor/ Third-Party Vendor	Notes/ Deliverables
Title:				Created by:		
Type of Information:				Date:		

completion of quarter-end financial close).

Role—Title of the person who performs the task.

Employee/contractor/third party—Is the person performing the task a company employee, a contractor, or a third-party vendor? This information is useful in case of escalation and for communication—different methods may be used depending on the answer to the question.

Note/deliverables—Any additional information such as the output of this step, reference documents, and the like.

Associated technology—The associated technology might apply to all of the tasks and is therefore listed as a template column heading. If the activities in the Information Life Cycle use various technologies, you may want to add a column for technology.

2. Document the processes at the level of detail most useful for your needs.

Table 5.1 illustrates the Dispose phase of the life cycle for financial information,

including tracking the security of the information to be disposed of and verification of proper disposal.

3. Look for gaps in the process and in the information.

Note the many blank spaces in Table 5.1, which indicate gaps in the understanding of the life cycle. The associated technology (tape backup and servers in Computer Center XYZ) is indicated at the header level, which may or may not be enough detail to meet your needs. Use the gaps as an opportunity to ask questions and fill in the missing pieces.

Other Approaches

You may be familiar with or actually be using other approaches that capture information pertinent to the Information Life Cycle, such as data flow diagrams, business process flows, an IP Map, or SIPOC.

SIPOC, a technique from manufacturing, stands for Supplier–Input–Process–Output–Customer. As it applies to information, the

Table 5.1 • Example of the Table Approach

TITLE: Disposition of Financial Data
TYPE OF INFORMATION: Any financial information
ASSOCIATED TECHNOLOGY: Tape backups and servers in Computer Center XYZ

CREATED BY: John Doe
DATE:

No.	TASK	MANUAL OR AUTOMATIC	TIMING	ROLE	EMPLOYEE/ CONTRACTOR/ THIRD-PARTY VENDOR	NOTES/DELIVERABLES
1	Identify records that need to be archived.	Manual	?	Legal? Finance?	Employee	Who determines when records should be archived? What are the criteria?
2	Tag associated media for archiving.	Manual				
3	Store tagged media in secure data center separate from all other media.					
4	Transfer tagged media to the vaulting vendor.					How are tagged media transferred to the vaulting vendor?
5	Store archived media until final disposition.					
6	Tag archived media for final destruction.					Who determines when records should be destroyed? What are the criteria?
7	Destroy unusable media by shredding.			Offsite vaulting vendor	Third party?	
8	Create certificate of destruction.			Disposal vendor		Where is this certificate kept?
9	Record destruction date, tape ID, who, location, etc.					Are destruction date, tape ID, who, location, etc. indicated in any information application?

Supplier is Input to a Process; the Process has an Output, which goes to the Customer, who applies it. And so the chain continues.

An Information Product Map (IP Map), according to a book coedited by Elizabeth Pierce (2005), is

> [A] graphical model designed to help people to comprehend, evaluate, and describe how an information product such as an invoice, customer order, or prescription is assembled. The IP Map is aimed at creating a systematic representation for capturing the details associated with the manufacture of an information product that is routinely produced within an organization.[2]

No matter which approach you use, your goal is to understand the interaction between data, process, people, and technology throughout the life cycle of your information. Use available documentation and knowledge as you define the life cycle. Supplement what is already on hand with additional research and documentation as needed.

Capture Data

Data capture (see Table 5.2) refers to extracting or accessing data—a key activity for any data assessment. It often turns out to be more problematic than expected. Therefore, adequate preparation will save time, prevent errors, and ensure that the data extracted/accessed are the data you need. *Do not underestimate the effort required to extract the right data for your assessments.*

Develop your initial plan for data capture during *Step 2.7—Design Data Capture and Assessment Plan*. Further refine and finalize it prior to each data quality assessment in *Step 3—Assess Data Quality*.

Use Table 5.2 as a template when developing your data capture plan. In summary, prepare and document your plan so that you will extract or access

- The right data (records and fields).
- Within the right timeframe.
- For the right process steps.
- From the right systems.
- In the right output.

Verify that the extract specifications were met after the extract and before conducting assessments.

Analyze and Document Results

The objective of this technique is to better analyze and track what is learned throughout your project using the Approach steps (pages 265–267). Scrutinize and interpret results and make initial recommendations. Start tracking results at the beginning of the project and continue with each step. Add to your results documentation as important observations are made and assessments are completed. If multiple assessments are conducted, be sure to synthesize results by evaluating and interpreting them together.

---

[2]Richard Y. Wang, Elizabeth M. Pierce, Stuart E. Madnick, and Craig W. Fisher (Eds.), "Introduction," *Information Quality* (M. E. Sharpe, 2005), p. 10.

Table 5.2 • Data to Be Captured

POPULATION DESCRIPTION	Describe the type of records to be extracted. Defining the population provides a basis for the selection criteria when extracting the data to be assessed. For instance, assume the population to be assessed is "Active Customers." Include any time considerations—when the record was created or last updated.
SELECTION CRITERIA	Describe how to select the population described: List exact table and field names (may include SQL statements). For example, determine how "Active Customers" are identified in the system. If the application has a flag designating that population, then the extract is relatively simple. Often the criteria are not so straightforward. The selection criteria for "Active Customers" may be "All customer records where the central delete flag in ABC table = blank AND the reference server flag in SUB table = blank." Consider the age of the records of interest by looking at an insert or update date. You might also want to consider history/journal/audit tables. Consider the data model. How do the relationships affect the data to be extracted? For example, do you want site data and associated contacts or contacts with associated sites?
TYPE OF ACCESS OR EXTRACT	Examples: • Extract to a flat file (e.g., pipe-delimited with carriage return to indicate end of record). • Extract to tables (and put into Oracle tables in staging area). • Extract from production database (and put into Access database). • Direct-connect to the reporting database (where data are 12 hours behind the production database). • Direct-connect to a production database. (I don't recommend this because of possible impacts on production, but I have been told there are companies who use this approach successfully.) • Copy data into the application test environment.
ADDITIONAL DATA ELEMENTS OR TABLES	Identify additional data elements or tables to be captured that will not be tested for quality themselves but may be needed for • Reference—code descriptions, associated reference tables • Identification—unique record identifiers, cross-reference identifiers • Analysis—last update date, grouped by certain codes • Reporting—by certain categories such as sales reps or geographic territories • Root cause analysis—who created, updated, or deleted the record
RESPONSIBILITIES	• Who is responsible for finalizing and documenting the data capture specifications? • Who is responsible for completing the data capture?

SAMPLE METHOD	Often every record for the desired population can be extracted and tested (e.g., if you have an automated profiling tool). Some tests are too expensive to carry out on the total population (e.g., manual comparison to source for accuracy). In this case you need to ensure that the sample is valid.
	Sampling is a technique in which representative members (in our case records) of a population are selected for testing. The results are then inferred to be representative of the population as a whole, and thus the quality assessment results of the sampled records approximate the quality of the entire record population. There are two characteristics of a sample that determine how well it represents the population:
	• *Size*—The minimum required number of records that need to be checked and completed in order to provide statistically valid results for the population.
	• *Stability*—If a sample size produces a result and if it is increased and it produces the same results, the sample has stability.
	Sampling method: Among sampling methods, random sampling is very common—every member of the population has an equal chance of being picked as a member of the sample.
	Important: *Involve someone experienced in statistics to ensure that your sampling methods are valid!*
TIMING	When files will be extracted. Take into consideration any update schedules and production calendars. You will be taking a snapshot in time when you extract the data. Plan to conduct your assessment as soon after the extract as possible.
	If connecting directly to a database to run assessments, time the access when you will have the least impact on the production system.
ESTIMATED NUMBER OF TABLES AND RECORDS	Understanding the number of tables and records can help provide an estimate for the amount of work and time to assess the data and the space required to store the data during the assessment.

Approach

1. Prepare for the analysis.

Be able to answer the following questions. This places the results to be analyzed in the appropriate context.

- What did we measure?
- How did we measure it? (Include who measured it and when.)
- Why did we measure it?
- What assumptions were used?

2. Format your results in a way that enhances understanding and is conducive to analysis.

Books that focus on the most effective way to visually communicate data are readily available. Edward R. Tufte and Stephen Few are two authors whose work is worth investigating.

- It is often easier to analyze results visually and graphically in charts rather than numerically in a large table spreadsheet.

- Be clear about what you are graphing—is it a fact (e.g., a city field has a fill rate of 99 percent) or an observation (e.g., by glancing through the records, you see what seems to be a high number of universities in the customer file).

- Keep visible any assumptions made while conducting the tests.

> At their best, graphics are instruments for reasoning about quantitative information. Often the most effective way to describe, explore, and summarize a set of numbers—even a very large set—is to look at pictures of those numbers. Furthermore, of all methods for analyzing and communicating statistical information, well-designed data graphics are usually the simplest and at the same time the most powerful.
>
> — Edward R. Tufte (1983)

3. Conduct the analysis.

Carefully review and discuss the assessment results. You may be analyzing broadly across many data or deep within a focused data set. Consider the following ideas[3]:

Identify patterns or trends—This is one of the most basic forms of analysis.

Check for misinformation—This is information that is incorrect because of factors such as misinterpretation, improper recording, purposeful misrepresentation, and errors. Look for the following clues:

- Does the information deviate significantly from what was expected or from other data that should be comparable?
- Are there conflicting data from multiple sources (e.g., information collected on the same subject by different members of the team)? Major discrepancies should be investigated.

Identify omissions or displacement—What is not present can often be as significant as what is. Omissions are missing data that should be available. Displacement involves significant changes in data trends without an explanation.

Check out-of-place information—Some information won't seem to "fit" with respect to other information, or it may deviate noticeably from the information you thought you would find.

Compare actual results to targets or requirements:
- Are there differences (either higher or lower)?
- Is there an explanation for the differences (e.g., targets were off due to unknowns at the time targets were set)?
- Are the differences in key or less critical data?

Ask questions—Such as the following:
- Are there any immediately visible red flags or issues?
- Are there any possible causes and effects?
- What impact could these findings have on the business? It is always important to answer this question in as much detail as possible—even if the answers are qualitative, not quantitative.
- Is there a need for more information on business impact? If yes, see *Step 4— Assess Business Impact.*
- Does additional information need to be gathered or do additional tests need to be conducted?
- Is this step considered complete for now?

---

[3]Adapted from and used with permission of AMACOM Books, from Michael J. Spendolini, *The Benchmarking Book* (AMACOM, 1992), pp. 172–174; permission conveyed through Copyright Clearance Center, Inc.

Capture reactions—To the results:

- What is the team's reaction to the results?
- What results were expected?
- What results were surprises?

4. Complete any follow-up, if needed.

5. Draw conclusions and make recommendations.

Consider the following:

- Recommendations resulting from the individual data quality and business impact assessments should be considered preliminary. Once all tests have been completed, they will be finalized.

- It can be a challenge to make logical comparisons and draw reasonable conclusions.

- Give yourself time to rest from the detail and then review again before finalizing the recommendations.

6. Document the results of the analysis.

Use Template 5.2, Tracking Results, for documenting results—starting with *Step 2— Analyze Information Environment* and

continuing throughout the project. Much will be learned during the assessments. Conscientious tracking will prevent extra work when the time comes to look for root causes, make final recommendations, and develop improvement plans. Capture what you know as *you discover it*, and document

- Important results from any analysis.
- What was learned.
- Likely impacts to the business.
- Possible root causes.
- Preliminary recommendations.

Table 5.3 on the next page lists examples of analysis and results captured using Template 5.2.

 Best Practice

Tracking Results: Create a spreadsheet for tracking assessment results with the summary level on the first sheet. If additional details are needed, created a separate worksheet for each line item.

Template 5.2 • Tracking Results

No.	Category (e.g., one of the Ten Steps or a Type of Assessment)	Lessons Learned/ Observations/ Issues	Known/ Probable Impact	Initial Recommendations	Comments/ Follow-Up
1					
2					
3					
4					

Table 5.3 • Examples of Tracking Data Quality Assessment Results

No.	Category (e.g., One of the Ten Steps or a Type of Assessment)	Lessons Learned/ Observations/ Issues	Known/ Probable Impact	Initial Recommendations	Comments/ Follow-Up
1	Analyze information environment.	Discovered that a team thought to have read-only access to customer records is actually creating customer records.	Since the team has no training on standards or data entry, quality of customer records is impacted.	• Train teams to enter data consistently and according to standards. • Assess the organizational structure and roles and responsibilities to confirm or eliminate redundant data entry roles.	
2	Understand relevant data and specifications.	Discovered that Legal has well-defined requirements for some of the data being assessed.		• Obtain agreement from Legal to have a subject matter expert (SME) participate in the project. • Have the data analyst look at legal requirements and convert them into data rules that can be tested for compliance.	
3	Understand relevant data and specifications.	Discovered that two project teams are maintaining conflicting data models using the same entities.	The same data being used by the two different applications will be different. This will cause user confusion.	Have data modelers from the two project teams collaborate and use one data model for both projects.	Determine whether the emerging data model can be enterprise-wide.

No.	Category (e.g., One of the Ten Steps or a Type of Assessment)	Lessons Learned/ Observations/ Issues	Known/ Probable Impact	Initial Recommendations	Comments/ Follow-Up
4	Data Integrity Fundamentals— assess for completeness.	The parent organization ID number has a lower fill rate than expected.	Think the fill rate is not low enough to be critical.		Is it really a low fill rate or are they standalone companies that don't have parent organization IDs?
5	Data Integrity Fundamentals— assess for consistency.	Inconsistencies between country code and country name were found in approximately 30% of the records.	What is the impact to reports?		Determine the impact to reports.

Metrics

Metrics are an important part of data quality control and are often a high business priority. However, do not lose sight of the fact that metrics are a means to an end—bringing visibility to data quality issues to prevent data quality problems. They are not the end in themselves.

 Best Practice

Metrics and Business Impact: Include a brief statement about the value of metrics and/or their impact to the business if data quality is poor. This gives context and importance to what the reader sees when reviewing the metrics.

Purpose

Metrics are useful for

- Replacing opinions with facts.
- Determining where to focus resources and efforts.
- Identifying sources of problems.
- Confirming the effectiveness of solutions.
- Encouraging behavior that supports business objectives through information quality.

When planning your metrics, be clear on the goal for using them and on their impact to the business. Here is the way one data quality metrics project expressed impact:

The product master metrics focus on key attributes within the product master. The product master comprises the foundational data for all manufacturing processes within the company. For example, problems with the data quality of revisions create bill of material errors and production issues because engineering change orders cannot be released. The metrics website provides a central location for product data that allows sites to pull information and proactively drive their data quality.

Levels of Detail

Consider three levels of detail for your metrics (as shown in Figure 5.4), with different audiences for each. For example, the summary/dashboard level might show "Synchronization of key product master attributes across the four product systems of record"[4] or "Compliance of key attributes to enterprise data standards." The drilldown might contain the data quality status of the key attributes by system of record. If reporting metrics on a website, the drilldown section might contain

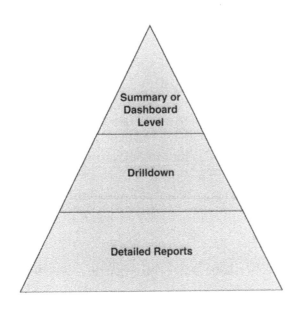

Figure 5.4 • Three levels of detail for metrics.

links to detailed reports that include the actual exception records, the data quality issue, who is working on the report, and the status of the root cause investigation and clean-up efforts.

Summary or dashboard level—Summary-level metrics provide an easy visual glance at and interpretation of metrics such as targets, actual data quality, and status. Status indicates the condition of the metric in easy-to-understand terms. For example, you may use green to equal "results meet or exceed target"; yellow to equal "results fail target or unfavorable trend"; and red to equal "results well outside of tolerance limits or drastic unfavorable change." Some summaries will show a single point in time; others will also include trends and history.

Management is the primary audience for dashboards, so integrate your data quality metrics into other business dashboards for best results. Take advantage of books available to help you design an effective dashboard for your information metrics.[5]

Drilldown—The drilldown is a mid-level view that provides additional information about the dashboard metrics. This is useful to show more about the dashboard numbers —but not in excruciating detail.

Detailed reports—Metrics are based on detailed measurements, which are contained in detailed reports. Detailed reports are not normally viewed by management, but should be available if questions arise about the accuracy of the metrics. They should be used by the project team to monitor and fix data identified as exceptions to the quality assessment and as input to continuous improvement.

---

[4]In an ideal world, there would only be one product master. In reality multiple masters are not uncommon. You may need to use your metrics and associated business impact for a time in order to gather evidence to show that investing in one master will be of benefit to the company.

[5]For example, see Stephen Few, *Information Dashboard Design: The Effective Visual Communication of Data* (O'Reilly, 2006) and Wayne W. Eckerson, *Performance Dashboards: Measuring, Monitoring, and Managing Your Business* (Wiley, 2006).

Key Points

Following are important points to keep in mind as you get started with metrics:

- Make sure your metrics track and act as a clear indicator of what needs to be improved. They should relate to goals and organization strategy.
- Define the desired behavior first.
- Then determine the metrics needed to understand and encourage the desired behavior. If you don't do this, you may get what you ask for but not what you want.
- Focusing on any single piece of data can result in its improvement at the expense of other data. You may want to track some general metrics so that they can act as a check and balance.
- Metrics can change behavior. Make sure they change the behavior you want.
- Measure those things that make a difference.

See *Step 9—Implement Controls* for Template 3.12, Metrics and RACI, to help you get started with your metrics.

Data Quality Tools

The focus of The Ten Steps process is not on tools. The data quality approach in this book is not specific to, nor does it require, any particular data quality software. It is important to understand that any tool used should serve legitimate business needs. In and of themselves tools have no merit unless they are useful and effective, and they can only be useful and effective if you understand what you need first.

Purchasing a data quality tool without knowing why and how you will use it will not give you data quality any more than buying a power saw will give you custom-made cabinets. Still, while The Ten Steps process is tool neutral, it is good to know there *are* tools available to help with many data quality tasks.

Michael Scofield, Manager of Data Asset Development at ESRI in Redlands, California, emphasizes the importance of understanding data quality needs first and then finding the tool to match. He lists three general data quality needs:

- **Data understanding**—Being aware of and comprehending the meaning and behavior of data.
- **Data fixing or improving**—Correcting or updating data, such as name and address updates and specialized find-and-replace functions.
- **Data monitoring**—Checking data as they flow or while at rest by applying tests that draw attention to new anomalies or highlight continuing problems you thought were solved.

Any of the tools soon to be discussed can be used in various ways to meet these needs.

The market for data quality tools is constantly changing, so I have avoided mentioning specific tools or vendors. Be aware that the functionality described next can be found in stand-alone versions or as modules of other tools—for example, tools focused on data integration. Expect new functionality, as well as vendors, to appear over time.

Once again, as helpful as tools can be, they produce no miracles. Meaningful results will only be obtained if people with the appropriate knowledge of business needs, processes, and data work with those who have the skills to implement and use the technology. If you already have data quality tools but are not sure how to use them effectively, The Ten Steps process can help.

Data Profiling/Analysis Tools

Tools used for understanding your data are often referred to as data profiling or analysis tools. I will refer to them as profiling tools since that term has become fairly well known and accepted.

Data Integrity Fundamentals is a dimension of quality that measures the existence, validity, structure, content, and other basic characteristics of data. Profiling tools are very helpful in understanding this dimension because they discover the data's structure, content, and quality. They are used for analysis, but do not change the data. (See more on data profiling in *Step 3.2 —Data Integrity Fundamentals.*)

As mentioned in Step 3.2, profiling can be carried out with a commercial tool or via other means such as the use of SQL to write queries, a report writer to create ad hoc reports, or a statistical analysis tool. Even if you are not using a purchased data profiling product, use its functionality and output to guide the queries or reports you write so you can examine your data from the perspective of data integrity fundamentals.

The specific capabilities and results you derive from data profiling will vary depending on the particular tool you are using, but could include all or some of the following:

Column or content profiling or analysis—Analyzes each column in a record, surveying all of the records in the data set. Column profiling will provide results such as completeness/fill rates, data type, size/length, list of unique values and frequency distribution, patterns, and maximum and minimum ranges. (This may also be referred to as domain analysis.)

Intra-table or intra-file or dependency profiling or analysis—Discovers relationships between attributes (data elements/columns/fields) within a table or file. This enables you to discover the table's or file's actual data structures, functional dependencies, primary keys, and data structure quality problems.

Cross-table or cross-file or redundancy profiling or analysis—Compares data between tables or files, determines overlapping or identical sets of values, identifies duplicate values, or indicates foreign keys. Profiling results can help a data modeler build a third normal form data model, where unwanted redundancies are eliminated. The model can be used to design a staging area that will facilitate the movement and transformation of data from one source to a target database such as an operational data store or data warehouse. Cross-table or cross-file analysis can be extremely powerful when used properly.

Most profiling tools provide the option of profiling against a flat file or connecting directly to a database. They complement the Extract–Transform–Load (ETL) processes and tools because the profiling results help create better source-to-target mappings in a shorter time than the traditional method of producing mappings, which is based only on column headings without knowledge of actual content. Creating correct source-to-target mappings is a good reason for using a data profiling tool.

Data Cleansing Tools

Data cleansing tools are often referred to simply as data quality tools. So even though I use the term "data quality" to refer to any tool that improves data quality, often that term is used to mean just data cleansing. A more descriptive phrase for such tools might be "data improvement," but that usage is uncommon.

Historically, data cleansing tools performed name and address cleansing, such as for customer and vendor records. However, the same functionality can also be used for product or item records and the like. A frequent trigger for data cleansing is the need to link related records (e.g., all people living in a particular household) or to identify duplicates (e.g., multiple records that represent the same company).

The various uses of data cleansing tools include preparing data for record matching and de-duplication, for consolidation, or before moving data from a source to a target. They can be used in batch mode (useful for initial assessments) or online in real time (useful for preventing data quality problems when built into an application). The development of master data efforts has brought with it the increased popularity of data cleansing tools since the tools are used to create valid, clean elements of master data.

Typical functionalities provided by data cleansing tools are described next. (The descriptive terms listed for the various functionalities are not consistent from tool to tool, so synonyms for many are included.)

Investigation or analysis—Data cleansing tools perform similar functions to those offered in data profiling tools, but they are not as thorough.

Standardization—Changes data into standard formats (e.g., Avenue in all addresses to Ave., Corporation in business names to Corp., or variations of a particular company name to the same version). Standardizing facilitates better parsing. In many tools, both standardization and parsing are used to facilitate better matching, linking, and de-duplication.

Parsing—Separates character strings or free-form text fields into their component parts, meaningful patterns, or attributes, and moves the parts into clearly labeled and distinct fields (e.g., the separation of a product description into height, weight, etc.; or a name into first, middle, and last fields; or an address into house number and street name).

Transformation—A general term that can mean any changes to the data such as during parsing and standardization.

Validation or verification or augmentation or enhancing—Updates or corrects data or adds new information to existing data (e.g., compares a U.S. address against the Postal Service file and adds the zip+4 data to zip code fields where that information is missing; adds longitude and latitude to a record of physical location).

Matching or linking—Links associated records through a user-defined or common algorithm. For instance, householding links all records associated with a particular household so that, for example, a young adult with a new checking account is linked to his or her parents, who may have a number of accounts with the bank.

Matching or de-duplication—Identifies multiple records that represent the same real-world object. This is often used to find duplicate name and address records (for customers, vendors, and employees) or non-name and address records such as product or item masters. Note that "matching" is sometimes used to mean linking and/or de-duplication.

Survivorship or merge or consolidation—Combines duplicate records, determining which records, or which fields from duplicate records, should be included in the final record. This often includes the ability to build "best-of-breed" records from multiple sources and/or instances of the same entity. The merge process can be carried out automatically by the tool, or manually by a person reviewing a list of possible duplicates and completing the consolidation.

Match-merge—A commonly used phrase that can mean de-duplication and/or consolidation.

Cleansing or scrubbing—A general term for any updates to the data (e.g., by validation, augmentation, or de-duplication).

Note that data profiling and data cleansing functionalities as described *do not* address the data quality dimension of Accuracy (see *Step 3.4—Accuracy*), which compares the data to the real-world object they represent (the authoritative source of reference). Sometimes it is not possible to access that real-world object and in those cases a carefully chosen substitute may be used as the authoritative source of reference.

The assessment of accuracy is often a manual and time-consuming process. For example, a data profiling tool can show if an item number record contains a valid code indicating a make or buy part, but there is no tool that can answer whether item 123 is a make part or a buy part—only someone familiar with it can make that determination.

Likewise, a data cleansing tool can tell you whether a particular U.S. state–city–zip code combination is valid by comparing it to a Postal Service file, but only your contact can tell you whether that is his or her address. Finally, a data profiling tool can give you the completeness or fill rate of a field containing inventory levels, but only someone counting the inventory on the shelf and comparing it to what is in the record can determine whether the inventory count is accurate.

Other Data Quality Tools

Look for other tools that, although not labeled as data quality, if used properly can enhance the quality of your data, create an environment and system design that enables higher quality data, or address some other quality issue.

Data modeling tools—Provide the ability to create diagrams with text and symbols that represent the data and their definitions, structure, and relationships. Data models define how a business works so that they can be turned into applications and systems that process information. They allow you to understand an existing application (through "reverse engineering") in order to perform impact analysis (the impact of adding or modifying structures for an application already in production), understand a business area, and facilitate training (to understand requirements).[6]

All of these are useful for understanding and better managing data quality. Since these tools provide a place to capture definitions, the data models they construct are a good way to find and capture metadata.

Application development tools—May contain developer tool kits or components that contribute to good data quality that are already part of or available for the application being used, such as a development component for easily verifying and standardizing addresses.

Metadata management tools—Any tools that capture and document metadata (e.g., ETL, spreadsheets, metadata repositories). Use the metadata as input to your assessment process.

ETL tools—The Extract–Transform–Load process extracts data from a source system, transforms and aggregates them to meet target system requirements, and loads them into a target database. ETL tools can be used during development and implementation of a project and throughout production for data that need to be moved periodically, such as when being

---

[6]See Steve Hoberman, *Data Modeling Made Simple* (Technics Publications, 2005), p. 11.

loaded to a warehouse on a regular schedule. Some ETL tools include a module that performs basic data profiling. The careful use of ETL tools can have a positive impact on data quality.

Data relationship discovery or business rule discovery—This is software that looks at multiple data sets, identifies the data available, finds relationships and transformations based on the business rules hidden in the data, and automates the mapping process. Data profiling tools can be used after the discovery tools to look in-depth at the data quality.

Screen emulator—Used for updating data by automating use of the standard interface in an application through replication of keystrokes as if done manually. This is sometimes referred to as screen scraping. A screen emulator tool can be helpful if there are too many records to be updated manually but the updates do not require the functionality of a data cleansing tool.

Tools and the Ten Steps

It has already been mentioned that The Ten Steps process is tool independent. However, it does support effective use of tools to enhance your data quality work.[7]

It is not unusual to find that a company has already purchased a data quality tool, but is not sure how to use it effectively. The Ten Steps process will help you make better use of the data quality tools you may already have. By first understanding your business needs (*Step 1—Define Business Need and Approach*) and analyzing the associated data, processes, people/organizations, and technology (*Step 2—Analyze Information Environment*), you will be able to better apply the tool to solve your data quality issues.

Table 5.4 shows various data quality tool functionality and where they may be used in The Ten Steps process.

---

[7]If you determine the need for a tool, remember to account for the software selection process in your project activities, timeline, and budget (identify tools with funtionality that meet your needs; compare the tools and vendors through documentation and demonstrations; choose, purchase, and implement the tools and obtain training).

Table 5.4 • Data Quality Tools and The Ten Steps Process

TOOL FUNCTIONALITY	THE TEN STEPS PROCESS
Data Profiling and/or Cleansing	Use for applicable data quality dimensions: *Step 3—Assess Data Quality*, for example: • *Step 3.2—Data Integrity Fundamentals* • *Step 3.3—Duplication* • *Step 3.4—Accuracy* (Caution: Only if comparison to the authoritative source of reference can be done with tools) • *Step 3.5—Consistency and Synchronization* Use results as input to: *Step 5—Identify Root Causes* *Step 6—Develop Improvement Plans* Use to prevent and/or correct errors and as part of ongoing controls: *Step 7—Prevent Future Data Errors* *Step 8—Correct Current Data Errors* *Step 9—Implement Controls*
Screen Emulator	*Step 8—Correct Current Data Errors*
Data Modeling Metadata Management Business Rule Discovery or Data Relationship Discovery	Use as input to: *Step 2—Analyze Information Environment* *Step 3—Assess Data Quality* *Step 7—Prevent Future Data Errors* Any good use of data modeling and metadata management tools provides the foundation for avoiding data quality issues. They also provide documentation of data specifications.
Application Development Tools	*Step 7—Prevent Future Data Errors* Use to prevent data quality issues right from initial development.

The Ten Steps and Six Sigma

For those who are familiar with Six Sigma, the Ten Steps can also be easily understood using DMAIC. The DMAIC process comprises five steps that begin with stating the problem and work through to implementing a solution:

- **Define**—Define the problem.
- **Measure**—Gather data to validate and quantify the problem or opportunity.
- **Analyze**—Analyze details, enhance understanding of the problem, and find root cause.

- **Improve**—Implement solutions.
- **Control**—Measure and monitor results.

Figure 5.5 maps the Information and Data Quality Improvement Cycle (Assessment–Awareness–Action) to DMAIC and then to The Ten Steps process.

The Ten Steps process is a way of dealing specifically with information and data quality improvement. The information found in this book can supplement a Six Sigma project if you want more help with its data and information aspects. As with any improvements, it is important to consciously manage information in the same way as business processes are addressed.

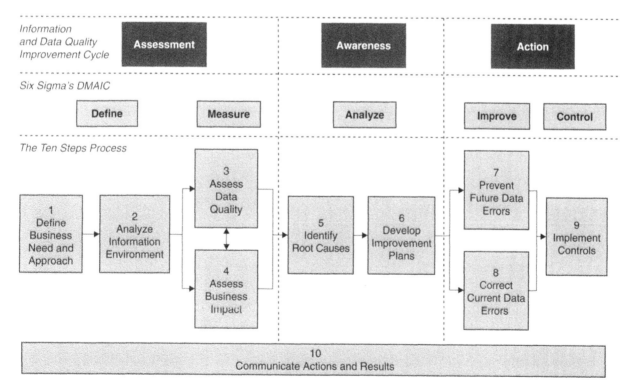

Figure 5.5 • The Ten Steps process and Six Sigma's DMAIC.

Chapter 6

A Few Final Words

Start where you are
Use what you have
Do what you can.

– Arthur Ashe

From this book you have learned key concepts related to information quality, such as the Framework for Information Quality, the Information Life Cycle POSMAD, and the data quality dimensions. You have learned about The Ten Steps process, seen examples, and been provided templates to help you get started. Other techniques and tools to help with your information quality work and ideas for including data quality in your projects have been discussed as well.

If you really understand what has been presented here, your thinking about what information quality entails and its importance to your business has expanded. You will never see data quality in your organization quite the same way as you did before. Now you will be able to quickly assess a situation at a high level and yet be better able to dive into the detail when necessary. You will pick up new clues not noticed before and really understand the connections between data, processes, people and organizations, and technology.

    Key Concept

Sustaining information and data quality requires management support. It requires persistence, commitment, ongoing effort, and attention. It is not just a one-time project.

You will see the importance of including communications every step of the way, and you will understand that information is not trusted just because the application code is working correctly. You will recognize the perception of those utilizing the information, build their awareness, and earn their confidence. You will see that you can't do it alone and so must communicate in order to continue to build support and increase your chances for success.

You will be better able to show business impact because you have seen that there are many different methods for addressing an issue; and you *can* find a way to articulate impact within the time, and with the resources, you have available.

If you are new to information quality, what you have learned here is a starting point. If you already have experience in this arena, your new knowledge will supplement your current information quality work. You will be able to take your previous data and information experience, pull in successful methods and techniques that worked for you in the past, and apply all of this to the many situations that will benefit from your efforts. You will take the ideas here, expand on them, and find new ways to apply them to benefit your organization. I hope this book has motivated you to explore and to continue to educate yourself in the many areas related to information quality.

I'll borrow Michael Spendolini's words in his preface to *The Benchmarking Book*[1] because they apply here also:

> As you gain experience with the process, many of the preparatory steps and technicalities become routine. What's left is the process of discovery and learning, of developing networks of interesting people, of bringing new ideas into your own work and organization. It can be a very rewarding experience for people who are motivated to listen and learn.

The practical concepts, processes, and techniques presented here can be applied to any data or information that supports any part of your organization. And whether your organization is a for-profit business, a government agency, a nonprofit or charity, or an educational institution, all of the ideas apply—because every organization depends on information to support its goals and to deliver on its commitments.

I truly believe that, no matter where you are, there is something you can do to help your organization. I also recognize the fact that true sustainability of any data quality effort requires management support. But don't be discouraged if you don't have the ear of the CEO (of course that would be nice, but don't let it stop you if you don't). Let me suggest the following dos and don'ts:

- You DON'T have to have the CEO's support to begin, but . . .
- You DO have to have the appropriate level of management support to get started while continuing to obtain additional support from as high up the chain as possible.
- You DON'T have to have all the answers, but . . .
- You DO need to do your homework and be willing to ask questions.
- You DON'T need to do everything all at once, but . . .
- You DO need to have a plan of action and get started!

So what are you waiting for? Get going: build on your experience, continue to learn, bring value to your organization, have fun, and enjoy the journey!

---

[1]Used with permission of AMACOM Books. From Michael J. Spendolini, *The Benchmarking Book* (1992, p. xii); permission conveyed through Copyright Clearance Center, Inc.

Quick References

Facts do not cease to exist because they are ignored.

– Anonymous

In This Appendix

The Framework for Information Quality   284

The POSMAD Interaction Matrix in Detail   286

POSMAD Phases and Activities   288

Data Quality Dimensions   289

Business Impact Techniques   290

Overview of The Ten Steps Process   291

Definitions of Data Categories   293

This appendix presents some of the key ideas from the methodology in an at-a-glance format. They are perfect for hanging on your cube or office wall or putting in a notebook when you need a fast reminder of ideas presented in more detail elsewhere in this book. See website at *www.books. elsevier.com/companions/9780123743695* for downloads of printable versions of these items.

The Framework for Information Quality

1. **Business Goals/Strategy/Issues/Opportunities.** The "Why." Anything done with information should help the business meet its goals.

2. **Information Life Cycle.** Use POSMAD to help remember the information life cycle:
   - **P**lan—Identify objectives, plan information architecture, and develop standards and definitions; many activities associated with modeling, designing, and developing applications, databases, processes, organizations, and the like.
   - **O**btain—Data or information is acquired in some way; for example, by creating records, purchasing data, or loading external files.
   - **S**tore and Share—Data are stored and made available for use.
   - **M**aintain—Update, change, manipulate data; cleanse and transform data, match and merge records; and so forth.
   - **A**pply—Retrieve data; use information. Includes all information usage such as completing a transaction, writing a report, making a management decision, and completing automated processes.
   - **D**ispose—Archive information or delete data or records.

3. **Key Components.** Four key components affect information quality.
   - **Data (What)**—Known facts or other items of interest to the business.
   - **Processes (How)**—Functions, activities, actions, tasks, or procedures that touch the data or information (business processes, data management processes, processes external to the company, etc.).
   - **People and Organizations (Who)**—Organizations, teams, roles, responsibilities, or individuals.
   - **Technology (How)**—Forms, applications, databases, files, programs, code, or media that store, share, or manipulate the data are involved with the processes, or are used by the people and organizations.

4. **Interaction Matrix.** Interaction between the Information Life Cycle phases (POSMAD) and the four Key Components.

5. **Location (Where) and Time (When and How Long)**
   Note: The top half of the framework, along with the first long bar, answers the interrogatives of who, what, how, why, where, when, and how long.

6. **Broad-Impact Components.** Additional factors that affect information quality. Lower your risk by ensuring that components have been discussed and appropriately addressed. If they are *not* addressed, you are still at risk (RRISCC) as far as information quality is concerned.
   - **R**equirements and Constraints
   - **R**esponsibility
   - **I**mprovement and Prevention
   - **S**tructure and Meaning
   - **C**ommunication
   - **C**hange

7. **Culture and Environment.** Take into account to better accomplish your goals.

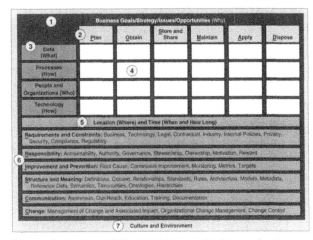

Source: Copyright © 2005–2008 Danette McGilvray, Granite Falls Consulting, Inc.

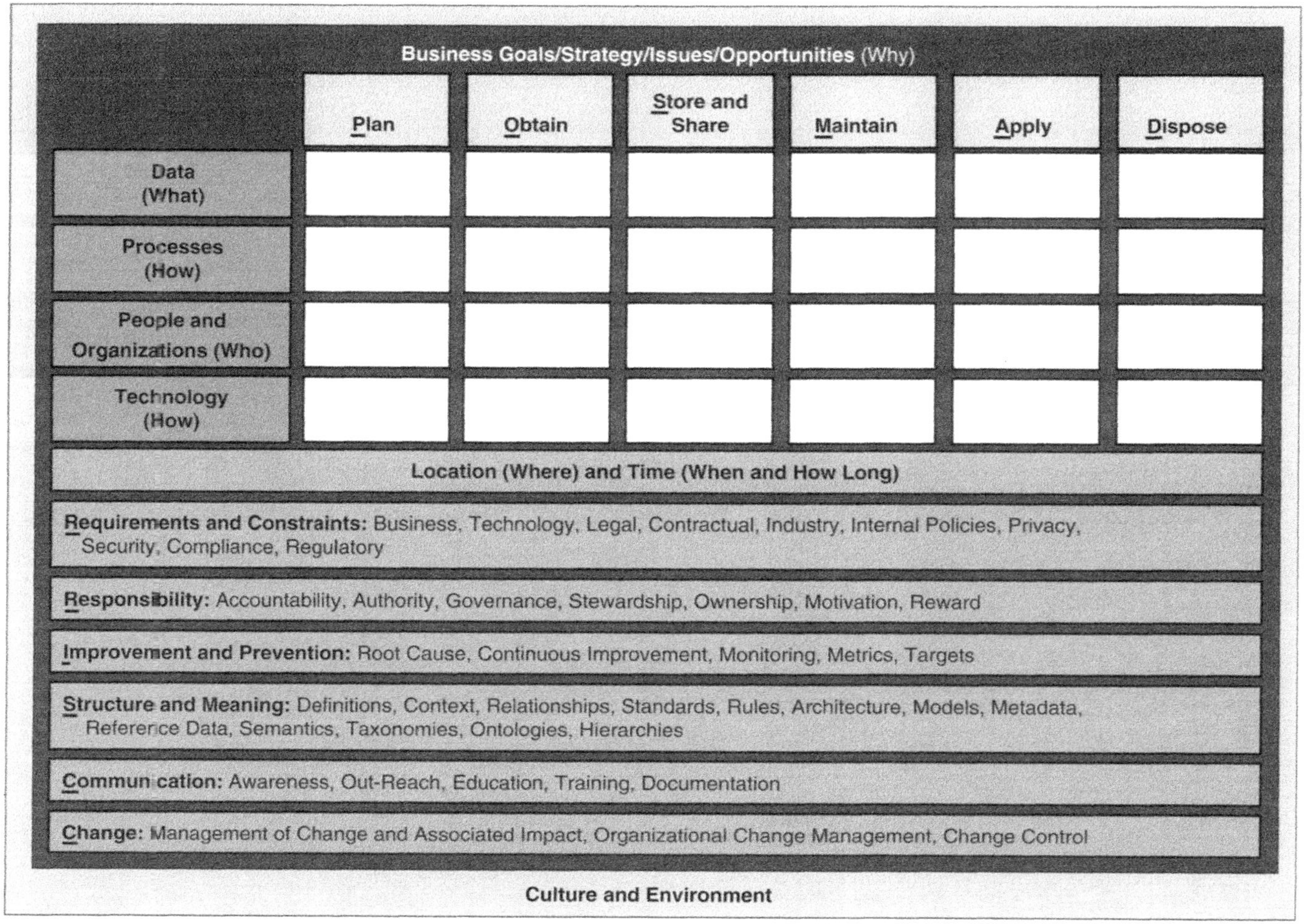

	Plan	Obtain	Store and Share	Maintain	Apply	Dispose
Data (What)						
Processes (How)						
People and Organizations (Who)						
Technology (How)						

Business Goals/Strategy/Issues/Opportunities (Why)

Location (Where) and Time (When and How Long)

Requirements and Constraints: Business, Technology, Legal, Contractual, Industry, Internal Policies, Privacy, Security, Compliance, Regulatory

Responsibility: Accountability, Authority, Governance, Stewardship, Ownership, Motivation, Reward

Improvement and Prevention: Root Cause, Continuous Improvement, Monitoring, Metrics, Targets

Structure and Meaning: Definitions, Context, Relationships, Standards, Rules, Architecture, Models, Metadata, Reference Data, Semantics, Taxonomies, Ontologies, Hierarchies

Communication: Awareness, Out-Reach, Education, Training, Documentation

Change: Management of Change and Associated Impact, Organizational Change Management, Change Control

Culture and Environment

Figure A.1 • The Framework for Information Quality (FIQ).

Source: Copyright © 2005–2008 Danette McGilvray, Granite Falls Consulting, Inc.

The POSMAD Interaction Matrix in Detail

The POSMAD Interaction Matrix is part of the Framework for Information Quality. Figure A.2 contains sample questions in each cell of the matrix to indicate the interaction between the phases of the POSMAD Information Life Cycle and the four Key Components—data, processes, people/organizations, and technology—that impact information quality.

	Plan	Obtain	Store and Share	Maintain	Apply	Dispose
Data (What)	What are the business objectives? Which data supports the business needs? What are the business rules? What are the data standards?	Which data are acquired? Which data are entered into the system—individual data elements or new records?	Which data are stored? Which data are shared? What is the key data to be backed up for rapid recovery?	Which data are updated and changed in the system? Which data will be transformed prior to migration, integration, or sharing? Which data are aggregated to support metrics or reporting?	What information is needed by the business to support transactions, metrics, compliance, requirements, decision making, automated processes, and other objectives? What information is available for use by the business?	Which data need to be archived? Which data need to be deleted?
Processes (How)	What are the high-level processes? What is the training and communication strategy?	How are data acquired from sources (internal and external)? How are data entered into the system? What are the triggers for creating new records?	What is the process for storing data? What is the process for sharing data?	How are data updated? How are data monitored to detect change? How are standards maintained? How are data change managed and impact assessed? Triggers for maintenance?	How are data used? How is information accessed and secured? How is information made available for those using it? What are the triggers for use?	How are data archived? How are data deleted? How are archive locations and processes managed? Triggers for archival? For disposition?
People and Organizations (Who)	Who identifies business objectives and assigns priorities and resources? Who develops processes, business rules, and standards? Who manages those involved in this phase?	Who acquires information from sources? Who enters new data and creates records in the system? Who manages those involved in this phase?	Who supports the storing technology? Who supports the sharing technology? Who manages those involved in this phase?	Who decides what should be updated? Who makes actual changes in the system? Who is responsible for quality? Who needs to know about changes? Who manages those involved in this phase?	Who directly accesses the data? Who uses the information? Who manages those involved in this phase?	Who sets the retention policy? Who archives the data? Who deletes the data? Who needs to be informed? Who manages those involved?
Technology (How)	What is the high-level architecture and the technology that support the business?	How is the application used to create new information and create records in the system?	What is the technology for storing the data? What is the technology for sharing the data?	How are data maintained and updated in the system?	How is information accessed to meet various business needs? How are business rules applied in the application architecture?	How are information and records deleted from system and/or archived? How are information and records archived from system?

Figure A.2 • POSMAD interaction matrix detail—sample questions.

POSMAD Phases and Activities

The acronym POSMAD is used to help remember the six phases—Plan, Obtain, Store and Share, Maintain, Apply, Dispose—in the Information Life Cycle. Table A.1 describes the activities and provides examples of them within each of the life cycle's phases as they apply to information.

Table A.1 • POSMAD Information Life Cycle Phases and Activities

INFORMATION LIFE CYCLE* PHASE (POSMAD)	DEFINITION	EXAMPLE ACTIVITIES FOR INFORMATION
Plan	Prepare for the resource.	Identify objectives, plan information architecture, develop standards and definitions. When modeling, designing, and developing applications, databases, processes, organizations, etc., many activities could be considered part of the Plan phase for information.
Obtain	Acquire the resource.	Create records, purchase data, load external files, etc.
Store and Share	Hold information about the resource electronically or in hardcopy, and make it available for use through a distribution method.	Store data electronically in databases or some type of file, or store as hardcopy such as a paper application form. Share information about the resource through networks, an enterprise service bus, or email.
Maintain	Ensure that the resource continues to work properly.	Update, change, manipulate, parse, standardize, validate, or verify data; enhance or augment data; cleanse, scrub, or transform data; de-duplicate, link, or match records; merge or consolidate records, etc.
Apply	Use the resource to accomplish your goals.	Retrieve data; use information. This includes all information usage: completing a transaction, writing a report, making a management decision from information in those reports, running automated processes, etc.
Dispose	Discard the resource when it is no longer of use.	Archive information; delete data or records.

*Note: The Information Life Cycle may also be referred to as the Information Resource Life Cycle, the Data Life Cycle, the Information Value Chain, or the Information Chain.

Data Quality Dimensions

A Data Quality Dimension is an aspect or feature of information and a way to classify information and data quality needs. Dimensions are used to define, measure, and manage the quality of the data and information. Table A.2 contains a quick reference list of the 12 data quality dimensions used in The Ten Step process.

Table A.2 • Data Quality Dimensions

No.	DIMENSION	DEFINITION
1	Data Specifications	A measure of the existence, completeness, quality, and documentation of data standards, data models, business rules, metadata, and reference data
2	Data Integrity Fundamentals	A measure of the existence, validity, structure, content, and other basic characteristics of the data
3	Duplication	A measure of unwanted duplication existing within or across systems for a particular field, record, or data set
4	Accuracy	A measure of the correctness of the content of the data (which requires an authoritative source of reference to be identified and accessible)
5	Consistency and Synchronization	A measure of the equivalence of information stored or used in various data stores, applications, and systems, and the processes for making data equivalent
6	Timeliness and Availability	A measure of the degree to which data are current and available for use as specified and in the time frame in which they are expected
7	Ease of Use and Maintainability	A measure of the degree to which data can be accessed and used and the degree to which data can be updated, maintained, and managed
8	Data Coverage	A measure of the availability and comprehensiveness of data compared to the total data universe or population of interest
9	Presentation Quality	A measure of how information is presented to and collected from those who utilize it. Format and appearance support appropriate use of information.
10	Perception, Relevance, and Trust	A measure of the perception of and confidence in the quality of the data; the importance, value, and relevance of the data to business needs
11	Data Decay	A measure of the rate of negative change to the data
12	Transactability	A measure of the degree to which data will produce the desired business transaction or outcome

Business Impact Techniques

Business Impact Techniques use qualitative and quantitative measures for determining the effects of data quality on the business. Table A.3 contains a quick reference list of the eight Business Impact Techniques used in the methodology—Ten Steps to Quality Data and Trusted Information™.

Figure A.3 shows a continuum of the relative time and effort to determine business impact for each technique from generally less complex and taking less time (technique 1) to more complex and taking more time (technique 8).

Table A.3 • Business Impact Techniques

No.	BUSINESS IMPACT TECHNIQUE	DEFINITION
1	Anecdotes	Collect examples or stories about the impact of poor data quality.
2	Usage	Inventory the current and/or future uses of the data.
3	Five "Whys" for Business Impact	Ask "Why" five times to get to the real business impact.
4	Benefit versus Cost Matrix	Analyze and rate the relationship between benefits and costs of issues, recommendations, or improvements.
5	Ranking and Prioritization	Rank the impact of missing and incorrect data on specific business processes.
6	Process Impact	Illustrate the effects of poor-quality data on business processes.
7	Cost of Low-Quality Data	Quantify the costs and revenue impact of poor-quality data.
8	Cost–Benefit Analysis	Compare potential benefits of investing in data quality with anticipated costs, through an in-depth evaluation. Includes return on investment (ROI)*—profit from an investment as a percentage of the amount invested.

*The phrases ROI or return on investment are often used in a general sense to indicate any means of showing some type of return on an investment. ROI in technique 8 refers to the formula for calculating return on investment.

Less Time/Less Complex   More Time/More Complex

1 2 3   4   5 6   7   8

Figure A.3 • Business impact techniques relative to time and effort.

Overview of The Ten Steps Process

The Ten Steps process is the approach for assessing, improving, and creating information and data quality. The steps that need to be used are shown in Figure A.4 and described in the box on the next page.

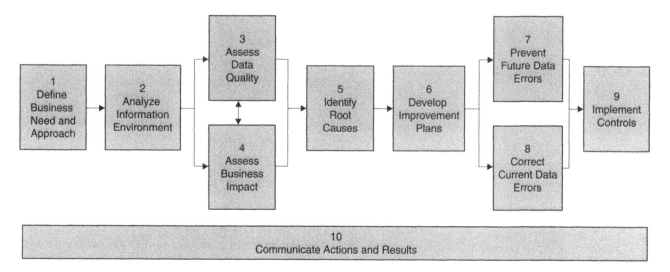

Figure A.4 • The Ten Steps process.

Source: Copyright © 2005–2008 Danette McGilvray, Granite Falls Consulting, Inc.

The Ten Steps Process—Assessing, Improving, and Creating Information and Data Quality

1. **Define Business Need and Approach**—Define and agree on the issue, the opportunity, or the goal to guide all work done throughout the project. Refer to this step throughout the other steps in order to keep the goal at the forefront of all activities.

2. **Analyze Information Environment**—Gather, compile, and analyze information about the current situation and the information environment. Document and verify the information life cycle, which provides a basis for future steps, ensures that relevant data are being assessed, and helps discover root causes. Design the data capture and assessment plan.

3. **Assess Data Quality**—Evaluate data quality for the data quality dimensions applicable to the issue. The assessment results provide a basis for future steps, such as identifying root causes and needed improvements and data corrections.

4. **Assess Business Impact**—Using a variety of techniques, determine the impact of poor-quality data on the business. This step provides input to establish the business case for improvement, to gain support for information quality, and to determine appropriate investments in your information resource.

5. **Identify Root Causes**—Identify and prioritize the true causes of the data quality problems and develop specific recommendations for addressing them.

6. **Develop Improvement Plans**—Finalize specific recommendations for action. Develop and execute improvement plans based on recommendations.

7. **Prevent Future Data Errors**—Implement solutions that address the root causes of the data quality problems.

8. **Correct Current Data Errors**—Implement steps to make appropriate data corrections.

9. **Implement Controls**—Monitor and verify the improvements that were implemented. Maintain improved results by standardizing, documenting, and continuously monitoring successful improvements.

10. **Communicate Actions and Results**—Document and communicate the results of quality tests, improvements made, and results of those improvements. Communication is so important that it is part of every step.

Definitions of Data Categories

Data categories are groupings of data with common characteristics or features. Table A.4 includes definitions and examples for major data categories. These definitions were jointly created by Danette McGilvray, author of *Executing Data Quality: Ten Steps to Quality Data and Trusted Information*™ and Gwen Thomas, president of the Data Governance Institute.

Table A.4 • Definitions of Data Categories

DATA CATEGORY	DEFINITION
Master Data	Master data describe the people, places, and things that are involved in an organization's business. *Examples* include people (e.g., customers, employees, vendors, suppliers), places (e.g., locations, sales territories, offices), and things (e.g., accounts, products, assets, document sets). Because these data tend to be used by multiple business processes and IT systems, standardizing master data formats and synchronizing values are critical for successful system integration. Master data tend to be grouped into master records, which may include associated reference data. An example of associated reference data is a state field within an address in a customer master record.
Transactional Data	Transactional data describe an internal or external event or transaction that takes place as an organization conducts its business. *Examples* include sales orders, invoices, purchase orders, shipping documents, passport applications, credit card payments, and insurance claims. These data are typically grouped into transactional records, which include associated master and reference data.
Reference Data	Reference data are sets of values or classification schemas that are referred to by systems, applications, data stores, processes, and reports, as well as by transactional and master records. *Examples* include lists of valid values, code lists, status codes, state abbreviations, demographic fields, flags, product types, gender, chart of accounts, and product hierarchy. Standardized reference data are key to data integration and interoperability and facilitate the sharing and reporting of information. Reference data may be used to differentiate one type of record from another for categorization and analysis, or they may be a significant fact such as country, which appears within a larger information set such as address. Organizations often create internal reference data to characterize or standardize their own information. Reference data sets are also defined by external groups, such as government or regulatory bodies, to be used by multiple organizations. For example, currency codes are defined and maintained by ISO.

(Continued)

Table A.4 • Definitions of Data Categories (Continued)

Data Category	Definition
Metadata	Metadata literally means "data about data." Metadata label, describe, or characterize other data and make it easier to retrieve, interpret, or use information. Technical metadata are metadata used to describe technology and data structures. Examples of technical metadata are field names, length, type, lineage, and database table layouts. Business metadata describe the nontechnical aspects of data and their usage. Examples are field definitions, report names, headings in reports and on Web pages, application screen names, data quality statistics, and the parties accountable for data quality for a particular field. Some organizations would classify ETL (Extract–Transform–Load) transformations as business metadata. Audit trail metadata are a specific type of metadata, typically stored in a record and protected from alteration, that capture how, when, and by whom the data were created, accessed, updated, or deleted. Audit trail metadata are used for security, compliance, or forensic purposes. Examples include timestamp, creator, create date, and update date. Although audit trail metadata are typically stored in a record, technical metadata and business metadata are usually stored separately from the data they describe. These are the most common types of metadata, but it could be argued that there are other types of metadata that make it easier to retrieve, interpret, or use information. The label for any metadata may not be as important as the fact that it is being deliberately used to support data goals. Any discipline or activity that uses data is likely to have associated metadata.

Additional data categories that impact how systems and databases are designed and data are used:

Data Category	Definition
Historical Data	Historical data contain significant facts, as of a certain point in time, that should not be altered except to correct an error. They are important to security and compliance. Operational systems can also contain history tables for reporting or analysis purposes. Examples include point-in-time reports, database snapshots, and version information.
Temporary Data	Temporary data are kept in memory to speed up processing. They are not viewed by humans and are used for technical purposes. Examples include a copy of a table that is created during a processing session to speed up lookups.

Glossary

Accessibility The degree to which data can be obtained and used. *See Ease of Use and Maintainability*.

Accuracy A data quality dimension that measures the correctness of the content of the data (which requires an authoritative source of reference to be identified and accessible).

Action The third high-level step in the Information and Data Quality Improvement Cycle. In this context, it refers to activities resulting from *Assessment* and *Awareness*, such as preventing data quality problems, implementing controls, correcting current data errors, and verifying by periodic assessments.

Anecdotes A business impact technique in which examples or stories of the impact of poor data quality are collected to garner support for information and data quality activities.

Apply A phase of the Information Life Cycle POSMAD in which data and information are retrieved and used to accomplish goals. Includes all information usage: completing a transaction, writing a report, making a management decision, running automated processes, and so forth.

Appropriateness A standard for choosing and implementing the applicable concepts and steps in The Ten Steps methodology, at a suitable level of detail to meet business and project needs.

Assessment (1) The comparison of the actual environment and data to requirements and expectations. (2) The first high-level step in the Information and Data Quality Improvement Cycle.

Attribute A characteristic, quality, or property of an entity class. For example, the properties "First Name" and "Last Name" are attributes of entity class "Person." *See Entity, Entity Class*.

Audit trail metadata A specific type of metadata, typically stored within a record and protected from alteration, that captures how, when, and by whom the data were created, accessed, updated, or deleted. Used for security, compliance, or forensic purposes. Examples include timestamp, creator, create date, and update date. *See also Metadata*.

Augmentation *See Enhancement*.

Awareness An understanding of the true state of data and information, impact to the business, and root causes. The second high-level step in the Information and Data Quality Improvement Cycle.

Benefit versus Cost Matrix A business impact technique for analyzing and rating the relationship between the benefits and costs of issues, recommendations, or improvements.

Business Impact Techniques In The Ten Steps methodology, qualitative and quantitative methods for determining the effects of data quality on the business.

Business metadata Data that describe the nontechnical aspects of data and their usage. Examples are field definitions, report names, headings in reports and on Web pages, application screen names, data quality statistics, and the parties accountable for data quality in a particular field. In some organizations ETL (Extract–Transform–Load) transformations are classified as business metadata. *See also Metadata*.

Business rules ". . . Guides for conduct or action . . . [that] provide criteria for making decisions." (*Source:* Ron Ross.) As it applies to data quality, a business rule is an authoritative principle or guideline that describes business interactions and establishes rules for actions and resulting data behavior and integrity. An authoritative principle is mandatory; a guideline is optional. (*Source:* Danette McGilvray.)

Cardinality   A relationship in a data model denoting how many instances of one entity class can be related to an instance of another entity class—zero, one, or many.

Cause-and-Effect/Fishbone Diagram   A root cause approach to identifying, exploring, and graphically displaying all possible causes of an issue using a standard quality technique. Also known as *Fishbone Diagram.*

Change   A RRISCC broad-impact component in the Framework for Information Quality that encompasses management of change and associated impact, organizational change management, and change control. See *RRISCC, Framework for Information Quality.*

Cleansing   Generally, any updates to the data (e.g., validation, augmentation, de-duplication). Also known as *scrubbing.*

Communication   (1) A RRISCC broad-impact component in the Framework for Information Quality that encompasses awareness, outreach, education, training, and documentation. (2) An important part of *Step 10— Communicate Actions and Results.*

Completeness   A characteristic of information quality that measures the degree to which there is a value in a field; synonymous with *fill rate.* Assessed in the data quality dimension of Data Integrity Fundamentals.

Comprehensiveness   A measure of the degree to which the scope of the information covers a topic to the satisfaction of its user. See also *Data Coverage.*

Consistency and Synchronization   (1) A data quality dimension that measures the equivalence of information stored or used in various data stores, applications, and systems. (2) The processes for making data equivalent. See also *Equivalence.*

Consolidation   A feature of data cleansing tools. See *Survivorship.*

Cost–Benefit Analysis   A business impact technique using in-depth evaluation to compare the potential benefits of an investment in data quality against its anticipated costs.

Cost of Low-Quality Data   A business impact technique for quantifying the costs and lost-revenue impact of poor-quality data.

Coverage   See *Data Coverage.*

Culture   In the Framework for Information Quality, a company's attitudes, values, customs, practices, and social behavior, including both official policies and unofficial "ways of doing things," "how things get done," and "how decisions get made."

Data   (1) Known facts or other items of interest to the business. (2) A key component in the Framework for Information Quality.

Data capture   Extraction or access of data.

Data categories   Groupings of data with common characteristics or features that determine how the data are treated or used. Major categories include master data, transactional data, reference data, and metadata.

Data Coverage   A data quality dimension that measures the availability and comprehensiveness of data compared to the total data universe or population of interest.

Data Decay   A data quality dimension that measures the rate of negative change to the data.

Data governance   The organization and implementation of policies, procedures, structure, roles, and responsibilities that outline and enforce rules of engagement, decision rights, and accountabilities for the effective management of information assets. (*Source:* John Ladley, Danette McGilvray, Anne-Marie Smith, and Gwen Thomas.)

Data integration The gathering and combining of data from two or more sources in such a way that new and better uses can be made of the resulting information.

Data Integrity Fundamentals A data quality dimension that measures the existence, validity, structure, content, and other basic characteristics of data.

Data mapping (1) The process of associating one data element, field, or idea with another data element, field, or idea. (2) In source-to-target mapping, the process of determining (and the resulting documentation of) where the data in a source data store will be moved to another (target) data store.

Data model A means of visually representing the structure of an organization's data. It is also a specification of how data will be represented in a database.

Data profiling See *Profiling.*

Data quality See *Information quality.*

Data Quality Dimension An aspect or feature of information and a way to classify information and data quality needs. Dimensions are used to define, measure, and manage the quality of the data and information.

Data rule "A condition that must hold true across one or more columns [of data] at any point in time." (*Source:* Jack Olson.) See *Business rules.*

Data specifications (1) A data quality dimension that measures the existence, completeness, quality, and documentation of data standards, data models, business rules, metadata, and reference data. (2) Generally, data standards, data models, business rules, metadata, and reference data.

Data standards ". . . Rules and guidelines that govern how to name data, how to define it, how to establish valid values, and how to establish business rules." (*Source:* Larry English.)

Data stewardship An approach to data governance that formalizes accountability for managing information resources on behalf of others and in the best interests of the organization.

Data store A repository for data—for example, relational databases, XML documents, files and file repositories, and hierarchical databases (LDAP, IMS).

De-duplication A feature of data cleansing tools or processes that identifies multiple records representing the same real-world object—for example, duplicate name-and-address records (for customers, vendors, and employees) or non–name-and-address records such as product or item masters. See *Matching.*

Dispose A phase of the Information Life Cycle POSMAD in which the information resource is discarded when it is no longer of use—for example, through archiving information or deleting data or records.

Duplication A data quality dimension that measures unwanted duplication existing within or across systems for a particular field, record, or data set.

Ease of Use and Maintainability A data quality dimension that measures the degree to which data can be accessed and used, and the degree to which data can be updated, maintained, and managed.

Enhancement A feature of data cleansing tools that updates or corrects data or adds new information to existing data. Also known as *validation, verification,* or *augmentation.*

Entity A person, place, event, thing, or concept that is of interest to the business—for example, "John Doe" or "Smith Corporation." See also *Entity class, Attribute.*

Entity class A set of things whose instances are uniquely identifiable—for example, "Person" or "Organization." Often loosely referred to as an *entity.* See *Entity, Attribute.*

Environment   In the Framework for Information Quality, the conditions within a company that affect the way employees work and act. For example, financial services, pharmaceutical, and government represent different environments.

Equivalence   The degree to which data stored in multiple places are conceptually equal; that is, they have equal values and meanings or are in essence the same. See *Consistency and Synchronization*.

Extract–Transform–Load (ETL)   A process that extracts data from a source system, transforms and aggregates them to meet target system requirements, and loads them into a target database. ETL tools can be used during a project and in ongoing production for data that must be moved regularly, such as when being loaded to a data warehouse on a scheduled basis.

Fill rate   See *Completeness*.

Fishbone Diagram   See *Cause-and-Effect Diagram*.

Five "Whys" for Business Impact   A business impact technique that asks "Why" five times to get to real business impact.

Five "Whys" for Root Cause   A quality technique often used in manufacturing, and also used with information quality, that asks "Why" five times to get to the real root causes of a problem.

Framework for Information Quality (FIQ)   An illustration of the logical structure of the components that contribute to information quality.

Historical data   Significant facts that exist as of a certain point in time and that should not be altered except to correct an error. They are important to security and compliance. In operational systems, significant facts contained in history tables required for reporting or analysis purposes. Examples include point-in-time reports, database snapshots, and version information.

Improvement and Prevention   A RRISCC broad-impact component in the Framework for Infor-

mation Quality that encompasses root cause, continuous improvement, monitoring, metrics, targets, and so forth.

Information and Data Quality Improvement Cycle   A simple method for thinking about and discussing data quality improvement through three high-level steps: assessment, awareness, and action. A modification of the familiar "Plan-Do-Check-Act" (PDCA) approach. See *Assessment*, *Awareness*, *Action*.

Information Life Cycle   The processes required to manage the information resource throughout its life. The six high-level phases in the life cycle are referred to as POSMAD: Plan, Obtain, Store and Share, Maintain, Apply, Dispose. (See the definitions for the individual phases.) Also referred to as Information Resource Life Cycle, Data Life Cycle, Information Value Chain, or Information Chain.

Information quality   In The Ten Steps methodology, the degree to which information and data can be a trusted source for any and/or all required uses—the right set of correct information, at the right time, in the right place, for the right people to make decisions, run the business, serve customers, and achieve company goals. Also referred to as *Data quality*.

Interaction matrix   A section of the Framework for Information Quality that shows the interaction between the Information Life Cycle phases (POSMAD) and the key components affecting information quality (data, processes, people/organizations, and technology).

Interoperability   "The ability of multiple systems with different hardware and software platforms, data structures, and interfaces to exchange data with minimal loss of content and functionality." (*Source*: National Information Standards Organization.)

Knowledge worker   One who uses data or information to perform his or her work or to complete job responsibilities. Also known as information producer, information consumer, or information customer.

Life cycle   The process of change and development throughout the useful life of something. See *Information Life Cycle* and *Resource Life Cycle*.

Linking   A feature of data cleansing tools. See *Matching*.

Maintain   A phase of the Information Life Cycle POSMAD that ensures that the information resource continues to work properly—for example, through updates, changes, manipulation, standardization, validation, verification, cleansing, enhancement, de-duplication, transformation, and so forth.

Maintainability   See *Ease of Use and Maintainability*.

Master data   Data describing the people, places, and things involved in an organization's business. Examples include people (e.g., customers, employees, vendors, suppliers), places (e.g., locations, sales territories, offices), and things (e.g., accounts, products, assets, document sets). Master data tend to be grouped into master records, which may include associated reference data.

Matching   A feature of data cleansing tools or the process that matches, or links, associated records through a user-defined or common algorithm. See *De-duplication*.

Match–Merge   A feature of data cleansing tools. See *De-duplication*.

Media   The various means of communication, such as user guides, Web surveys, hardcopy forms, and database entry interfaces.

Merge   See *Survivorship*.

Metadata   Data about data that label, describe, or characterize other data, and make it easier to retrieve, interpret, or use information. Major types include technical, business, and audit trail metadata. (See the definitions for the individual types.)

Metadata repository   A database where metadata are stored as structured data that can be easily accessed and queried by business and technology workers. See *Metadata*.

Obtain   A phase in the Information Life Cycle POSMAD in which the information resource is acquired—for example, through creating records, purchasing data, loading external files, and so forth.

Parsing   The separation of character strings or free-form text fields into component parts, meaningful patterns, or attributes, which are then moved into clearly labeled and distinct fields (e.g., product description into fields for height and weight; name into fields for first, middle and last; address into fields for house number and street name).

People and Organizations   A key component in the Framework for Information Quality that comprises organizations, teams, roles, responsibilities, or individuals who affect or use the data or who are involved with processes in any of the phases of the Information Life Cycle.

Perception, Relevance, and Trust   A data quality dimension that measures (1) the perception of and confidence in data quality and (2) the importance, value, and relevance of the data to business needs.

Plan   A phase in the Information Life Cycle POSMAD that encompasses preparation for the information resource (e.g., identifying objectives, planning information architecture, developing standards and definitions). Many activities when modeling, designing, and developing applications, databases, processes, and organizations can also be considered part of the plan phase for information.

Plan-Do-Check-Act (PDCA)   A basic technique for improving processes, created by Walter Shewhart. Also known as the Shewhart cycle or the Deming cycle (for W. Edwards Deming, who introduced the technique in Japan).

POSMAD   An acronym for the six high-level phases of the Information Life Cycle—Plan,

Obtain, Store and Share, Maintain, Apply, Dispose. (See *Information Life Cycle* and the definitions for the individual phases.)

Presentation Quality A data quality dimension that measures how effectively information is presented to and collected from those who utilize it. The degree to which format and appearance support the appropriate use of the information.

Process A key component in the Framework for Information Quality that comprises any functions, activities, actions, tasks, or procedures that touch the data or information (business processes, processes external to company, data management processes, etc.).

Process Impact A business impact technique for illustrating the effects of poor-quality data on business processes.

Profiling (1) "The use of analytical techniques to discover the structure, content, and quality of data." (*Source:* Jack Olson.) (2) In this book, a method for assessing the Data Integrity Fundamentals data quality dimension. Also referred to as *data profiling*.

Project In this book, any significant effort that makes use of The Ten Steps methodology.

Ranking and Prioritization A business impact technique that ranks the impact of missing and incorrect data on specific business processes.

Reference data Sets of values or classification schemas referred to by systems, applications, data stores, processes, and reports, as well as by transactional and master records. Examples include lists of valid values, code lists, status codes, flags, product types, charts of accounts, product hierarchy.

Relevance A standard for determining if what is being considered in the project is associated with and meaningful to the business issue to be resolved. See *Perception, Relevance, and Trust.*

Requirements A RRISCC broad-impact component in the Framework for Information Quality

referring to obligations the company must meet and to the information that must support the ability of the company to meet them. Examples are business, technology, legal, contractual, industry, internal policy, privacy, security, compliance, and regulatory requirements.

Resource Life Cycle The processes required to manage any resource—people, money, facilities and equipment, materials and products, and information. Also known as the Universal Resource Life Cycle. See *Information Life Cycle.*

Responsibility A RRISCC broad-impact component in the Framework for Information Quality that encompasses accountability, authority, governance, stewardship, ownership, motivation, and reward.

Return on Investment (ROI) (1) A business impact technique that measures profit from an investment as a percentage of the amount invested. (2) Generally, any means of showing benefit from investing in data quality.

Root Cause Analysis The study of all possible causes of a problem, issue, or condition to determine its actual cause.

RRISCC The acronym for the broad-impact components in the Framework for Information Quality: Requirements, Responsibility, Improvement and Prevention, Structure and Meaning, Communication, Change. (See the definitions of the individual components.)

Rules See *Business rules* and *Data rule.*

Scrubbing See *Cleansing.*

Semantics ". . . The study of meaning (often the meaning of words). In business systems we are concerned with making the meaning of data explicit (structuring unstructured data), as well as making it explicit enough that an agent could reason about it." (*Source:* Dave McComb.)

Stakeholders The people or groups with a direct interest, involvement, or investment in the information quality work—"those actively involved in the project, or whose interests may be positively or negatively affected by execution or completion of the project. [They] may also exert influence over the project and its deliverables." (*Source:* Project Management Institute.) For example, a manufacturing manager is a stakeholder in any data quality improvements that impact the supply chain. Other examples of stakeholders include customers, project sponsors, the public, or organizations whose personnel are most directly involved in the work of the project.

Standardization   Converting data into standard formats to facilitate parsing and thus matching, linking, and de-duplication. Examples include: "Avenue" as "Ave." in addresses; "Corporation" as "Corp." in business names; and variations of a specific company name as one version.

Store and Share   A phase in the Information Life Cycle POSMAD in which information is held electronically or in hardcopy and made available for use through a distribution method. Store examples include electronically, in a database or some type of file, or as hardcopy such as a paper application form. Share examples include networks, enterprise service buses, and email.

Structure and Meaning   A RRISCC broad-impact component in the Framework for Information Quality, referring to anything that provides context for data so that their meanings are known and therefore their best use can be determined. Examples include definitions, relationships, standards, *rules*, architecture, models, *metadata*, *reference data*, *semantics*, taxonomies, ontologies, and hierarchies.

Survivorship   A feature of data cleansing tools that combines duplicate records and determines which records or which fields from the duplicate records should be included in the final record. Survivorship often entails the ability to build "best of breed" records from multiple sources and/or instances of the same entity. Also known as *merging* or *consolidation*.

Synchronization   See *Consistency and Synchronization.*

Technical metadata   Metadata that describe technology and data structures. Examples include field names, length, type, lineage, and database table layouts. See also *Metadata.*

Technology   A key component in the Framework for Information Quality that includes the forms, applications, databases, files, programs, code, or media that store, share, or manipulate the data, are involved in the processes, or are used by the people and organizations.

Temporary data   Data kept in memory to speed processing, not viewed by humans and used only for technical purposes. An example of technical data is a copy of a table created during a processing session to speed lookups.

Timeliness and Availability   A data quality dimension that measures the degree to which data are current and available for use as specified, and in the time frame in which they are expected.

Track and Trace   A root cause technique that locates a problem by tracking the data through the Information Life Cycle, and determines root cause where the problem first appears.

Transactability   A data quality dimension that measures how well the data produce the desired business transaction or outcome.

Transactional data   Data that describe an internal or external event or transaction that takes place as an organization conducts its business. Examples include sales orders, invoices, purchase orders, shipping documents, passport applications, credit card payments, and insurance claims. Transactional data are typically grouped into transactional records, which include associated master and reference data.

Transformation   Any change to the data, such as during parsing and standardization.

Trust   Confidence in data quality. See *Perception, Relevance, and Trust.*

Usage   A business impact technique that inventories the current and/or future uses of the data.

User   See *Knowledge worker.*

Validation   (1) To confirm the validity of data. (2) A feature of data cleansing tools. See *Enhancement.*

Validity   The determination that values in the field are or are not within a set of allowed or valid values. Measured as part of the Data Integrity Fundamentals data quality dimension.

Verification   See *Validation.*

XML   Abbreviation for Extensible Markup Language. XML is a mechanism for identifying structures in a document and is used to aid sharing data across different information systems.

Bibliography

Adelman, Sid, Moss, Larissa, and Abai, Majid (2005). *Data Strategy*. Addison-Wesley.

Adelman, Sid, and Moss, Larissa (2000). *Data Warehouse Project Management*. Addison-Wesley.

Al-Hakim, L. (2007). *Challenges of Managing Information Quality in Service Organizations*. Idea Group Publishing.

Batini, Carlo, and Scannapieco, Monica (2006). *Data Quality: Concepts, Methodologies, and Techniques*. Springer.

Biere, Mike (2003). *Business Intelligence for the Enterprise*. IBM Press/Pearson.

Brackett, Michael H. (2000). *Data Resource Quality: Turning Bad Habits into Good Practices*. Addison-Wesley.

Brandon, Joel, and Morris, Daniel (1997). *Just Don't Do It! Challenging Assumptions in Business*. McGraw-Hill.

Brassard, Michael, and Ritter, Diane (1994). *The Memory Jogger II—A Pocket Guide of Tools for Continuous Improvement and Effective Planning*. GOAL/QPC.

Brooks, R. B., and Wilson, L. W. (1995). *Inventory Record Accuracy: Unleashing the Power of Cycle Counting*. John Wiley & Sons.

Brue, Greg (2003). *Design for Six Sigma*. McGraw-Hill.

Burton, E. James (1999). *Total Business Planning*, 3rd ed. John Wiley & Sons.

Chang, R. Y., and Morgan, M. W. (2000). *Performance Scorecards: Measuring the Right Things in the Real World*. Jossey-Bass.

Chapin, Donald (2008). "MDA Foundational Model Applied to Both the Organization and Business Application Software," Object Management Group (OMG) Working Paper.

Chisholm, Malcom (2004). *How to Build a Business Rules Engine: Extending Application Functionality Through Metadata Engineering*. Morgan Kaufmann.

Chisholm, Malcom (2001). *Managing Reference Data in Enterprise Databases: Binding Corporate Data to the Wider World*. Morgan Kaufmann.

Conley, Chip (2007). *Peak: How Great Companies Get Their Mojo from Maslow*. Jossey-Bass.

Crosby, Philip (1996). *Philip Crosby's Reflections on Quality*. McGraw-Hill.

Cuzzort, R. P., and Vrettos, James S. (1996). *The Elementary Forms of Statistical Reason*. St. Martin's Press.

Data Integration, Data Mapping, Data Model, Data Store, Data Transformation, Wikipedia (2007). Retrieved individually on 1/18/2007; available at *http://en.wikipedia.org/wiki/Main_Page*.

Deming, W. Edwards (2000). *Out of the Crisis*. MIT Press.

Eckerson, Wayne W. (2006). *Performance Dashboards: Measuring, Monitoring, and Managing Your Business*. John Wiley & Sons.

English, Larry P. (1999). *Improving Data Warehouse and Business Information Quality*. John Wiley & Sons.

Eppler, Martin J. (2003). *Managing Information Quality: Increasing the Value of Information in Knowledge-intensive Products and Processes*. Springer.

Few, Stephen (2006). *Information Dashboard Design: The Effective Visual Communication of Data*. O'Reilly.

Gonick, Larry, and Smith, Woollcott (1993). *The Cartoon Guide to Statistics*. HarperCollins.

Grady, Robert B. (1992). *Practical Software Metrics for Project Management and Process Improvement*. Prentice Hall.

Grady, Robert B., and Caswell, Deborah L. (1987). *Software Metrics: Establishing a Company-Wide Program*. Prentice Hall.

Guaspari, J. (1991). *I Know It When I See It: A Modern Fable about Quality*. American Management Association.

Harvard Business Essentials. (2002). *Finance for Managers*. Harvard Business School Press.

Hay, David C. (2006). *Data Model Patterns: A Metadata Map*. Morgan Kaufmann.

Hay, David C. (2003). *Requirements Analysis: From Business Views to Architecture*. Prentice Hall PTR.

Hay, David (2003). "What Exactly Is a Data Model?" *DM Review* 13(2); available at *www.dmreview.com/issues/20030201/6281-1.html*.

Hay, David C. (1996). *Data Model Patterns: Conventions of Thought*. Dorset House Publishing.

Herzog, Thomas N., Scheuren, Fritz J., and Winkler, William E. (2007). *Data Quality and Record Linkage Techniques*. Springer.

Hoberman, Steve (2007). "Leveraging the Industry Logical Data Model as Your Enterprise Data Model," Teradata White Paper, p. 7; available at *www.teradata.com/t/pdf.aspx?a=83673&b=162511*.

Hoberman, Steve (2005). *Data Modeling Made Simple: A Practical Guide for Business and Information Technology Professionals*. Technics Publications.

Hoff, Ron (1992). *"I Can See You Naked": A Fearless Guide to Making Great Presentations*. Andrews and McMeel.

Huang, Kuan-Tsae, Lee, Yang W. and Wang, Richard Y. (1999). *Quality Information and Knowledge*. Prentice Hall PTR.

"IBM Rational Unified Process," Wikipedia (2007). Retrieved 5/31/2007; available at *http://en.wikipedia.org/wiki/Rational_Unified_Process*.

Imai, Masaaki (1997). *Gemba Kaizen: A Commonsense, Low-Cost Approach to Management*. McGraw-Hill.

Inmon, William, O'Neil, Bonnie, and Fryman, Lowell (2008). *Business Metadata: Capturing Enterprise Knowledge*. Morgan Kaufmann.

"IQ/DQ Glossary," IAIDQ (2007). Retrieved 1/18/2007; available at *http://www.iaidq.org/main/glossary.shtml*.

Juran, J. M. (1995). *Managerial Breakthrough: The Classic Book on Improving Management Performance*. McGraw-Hill.

Juran, J. M. (1988). *Juran's Quality Control Handbook*, 4th ed. McGraw-Hill.

Kincaid, Judith W. (2003). *Customer Relationship Management: Getting It Right!* Hewlett-Packard and Prentice Hall PTR.

Lee, Y. W., Pipino, L. L., Funk, J. D., and Wang, R. Y. (2006). *Journey to Data Quality*. MIT Press.

"Legislation Addressing Data Privacy, Security, and Governance," Data Governance Institute (2006). Retrieved 10/01/2006 from *http://www.datagovernance.com/data_laws_center.html*.

Loshin, David (2006). "The Data Quality Business Case: Projecting Return on Investment," Informatica White Paper.

Loshin, David (2003). *Business Intelligence: The Savvy Manager's Guide*. Morgan Kaufmann.

Loshin, David (2001). *Enterprise Knowledge Management: The Data Quality Approach*. Morgan Kaufmann.

Maydanchik, Arkady (2007). *Data Quality Assessment*. Technics Publications.

McComb, David (2004). *Semantics in Business Systems: The Savvy Manager's Guide*. Morgan Kaufmann.

Moss, Larissa T., and Atre, Shaku (2003). *Business Intelligence Roadmap: The Complete Project Lifecycle for Decision-Support Applications*. Addison-Wesley.

NAICS Association (2008). "Frequently Asked Questions"; available at *http://www.naics.com/faq.htm#q1*.

Olson, Jack E. (2003). *Data Quality: The Accuracy Dimension*. Morgan Kaufmann.

O'Rourke, Carol, Fishman, Neal, and Selkow, Warren (2003). *Enterprise Architecture: Using the Zachman Framework*. Thomson Course Technology.

Pande, Peter S., and Holpp, Larry (2002). *What Is Six Sigma?* McGraw-Hill.

Pande, Peter S., Neuman, Robert P., and Cavanagh, Roland R. (2002). *The Six Sigma Way: Team Fieldbook*. McGraw-Hill.

Pande, Peter S., Neuman, Robert P., and Cavanagh, Roland R. (2000). *The Six Sigma Way*. McGraw-Hill.

Parker, Marilyn M., Benson, Roger J., and Trainor, H. E. (1988). *Information Economics: Linking Business Performance to Information Technology*. Prentice Hall.

Project Management Institute (2007). *Combined Standards Glossary*, 3rd ed. Project Management Institute, Inc.

Project Management Institute (2006). Information retrieved 1/18/2007 from *http://www.pmi.org/info/default.asp*.

"Rational Unified Process," IBM (2007). Retrieved 5/31/2007; available at *http://www-306.ibm.com/software/awdtools/rup/*.

Redman, Thomas C. (2001). *Data Quality: The Field Guide*. Digital Press.

Redman, Thomas C. (1996). *Data Quality for the Information Age*. Artech House.

Redman, Thomas C. (1992). *Data Quality: Management and Technology*. Bantam.

"Root Cause Analysis," 12Manage (2008). Retrieved 1/2008; available at *http://www.12manage.com/methods_root_cause_analysis.html*.

Ross, Ronald G. (2005). *Business Rule Concepts: Getting to the Point of Knowledge*, 2nd ed. Business Rule Solutions, LLC.

Ross, Ronald G. (2003). *Principles of the Business Rule Approach*. Addison-Wesley.

Rummler, Geary A., and Brache, Alan P. (1990). *Improving Performance: How to Manage the White Space on the Organization Chart*. Jossey-Bass.

"SAP Best Practices for Mining," SAP (2007). Retrieved 5/31/2007; available at *http://www.sap.com/usa/industries/mining/pdf/SAPBestPracticesforMining.pdf*.

Scofield, Michael (2008). "Fundamentals of Data Quality," *NoCOUG Journal*, February.

Shiba, Shoji, Graham, Alan, and Walden, David (1993). *A New American TQM: Four Practical Revolutions in Management*. Productivity Press and Center for Quality Management.

Shillito, M. Larry, and De Marle, David J. (1992). *Value: Its Measurement, Design & Management*. John Wiley & Sons.

"Siebel eRoadmap Implementation Methodology," PeopleSoft (2007). Information retrieved 5/31/2007 from *http://www.peoplesoftcity.com/siebel78/books/TestGuide/TestGuide_Overview6.html*.

Silverman, Lori (2006). *Wake Me Up When the Data Is Over: How Organizations Use Stories to Drive Results*. Jossey-Bass.

Silverston, Len (2001). *The Data Model Resource Book: A Library of Universal Data Models for All Enterprises*, Volume 1, Revised ed. John Wiley & Sons.

Simsion, Graeme C., and Witt, Graham C. (2005). *Data Modeling Essentials*, 3rd ed. Morgan Kaufmann.

Spendolini, M. J. (1992). *The Benchmarking Book*. AMACOM Books.

Spewak, Steven H. (1992). *Enterprise Architecture Planning: Developing a Blueprint for Data, Applications and Technology*. John Wiley & Sons.

Stephens, R. Todd (2003). *Marketing and Selling Data Management*. Conference session, DAMA International Symposium/Wilshire Meta-Data Conference, Orlando.

Swanson, Roger C. (1995). *The Quality Improvement Handbook: Team Guide to Tools and Techniques*. St. Lucie Press.

Tannenbaum, Adrienne (2002). *Metadata Solutions*. Addison-Wesley.

Thomas, Gwen (2008). Poem (used in chapter 2). Retrieved 3/1/2008; available at *http://datagovernance.com/dh3_song_parodies.html*.

Thomas, Gwen (2006). *Alpha Males and Data Disasters: The Case for Data Governance*. Brass Cannon Press.

Tufte, Edward R. (1983). *The Visual Display of Quantitative Information*. Graphics Press.

"Understanding Metadata," NISO (2006). Retrieved 1/18/2007; available at *http://www.niso.org/publications/press/UnderstandingMetadata.pdf*.

U.S. Department of Agriculture (2008). "The Food Pyramid," developed by the Center for Nutrition Policy and Promotion; available at *http://www.mypyramid.gov/*.

"Using Oracle Tutor with AIM 3.0 and the Oracle Business Models," Oracle White Paper (June 1999). Retrieved 6/1/2007; available at *http://www.oracle.com/applications/human_resources/tutor-aim.pdf*.

Wacker, Mary B., and Silverman, Lori L. (2003). *Stories Trainers Tell: 55 Ready-to-Use Stories to Make Training Stick*. Jossey-Bass/Pfeiffer.

Walsh, Norman (2008). "A Technical Introduction to XML." Retrieved 2/1/2008; available at *http://www.xml.com/pub/a/98/10/guide0.html?page-2#AEN58*.

Wang, Richard Y., Pierce, Elizabeth M., Madnick, Stuart E., and Fisher, Craig W. (Eds.) (2005). *Information Quality*. Advances in Information Systems and M. E. Sharpe.

Wiefling, Kimberly (2007). *Scrappy Project Management™: The 12 Predictable and Avoidable Pitfalls Every Project Faces*. Scrappy About.

Woods, John A., and Cortada, James W. (1996). *QualiTrends: 7 Quality Secrets That Will Change Your Life*. McGraw-Hill.

"What Is GMP?" GMP1st. Retrieved 1/24/2008; available at *http://www.gmp1st.com/gmpinst.htm*.

Wight, Oliver International Inc. (2000). *The Oliver Wight ABCD Checklist for Operational Excellence*, 5th ed. John Wiley & Sons.

Zachman Institute for Framework Advancement (2007). "Zachman Framework for Information Architecture"; available at *http://www.zifa.com/*.

List of Figures, Tables, and Templates

Chapter 2 Key Concepts

Figure 2.1	Visualizing a plan for help: the Food Pyramid and the Framework for Information Quality	17
Figure 2.2	The Framework for Information Quality	18
Figure 2.3	POSMAD interaction matrix detail—sample questions	21
Table 2.1	POSMAD Information Life Cycle Phases and Activities	24
Figure 2.4	Value, cost, and quality and the Information Life Cycle	25
Figure 2.5	The Information Life Cycle is not a linear process	26
Figure 2.6	Organization and the POSMAD life cycle	27
Figure 2.7	Interactions with customers and the POSMAD life cycle	28
Figure 2.8	Roles and the Information Life Cycle	29
Table 2.2	Data Quality Dimensions	31
Table 2.3	Business Impact Techniques Defined	36
Figure 2.9	Relative time and effort of business impact techniques	38
Figure 2.10	An example of data categories	40
Table 2.4	Definitions of Data Categories	42
Figure 2.11	Relationships between data categories	44
Table 2.5	Data Model Comparison	48
Table 2.6	Business Rules and Data Quality Checks	50
Figure 2.12	The Information and Data Quality Improvement Cycle	55
Figure 2.13	The Information and Data Quality Improvement Cycle and The Ten Steps process	56
Figure 2.14	The Ten Steps process	57

Chapter 3 The Ten Steps Process

Figure 3.1	The Ten Steps process	64
Table 3.1	Step Summary Table Explained	65
Table 3.2	Step 1—Define Business Need and Approach	68
Template 3.1	Issue Capture Worksheet	71
Template 3.2	Project Charter	73
Template 3.3	Tracking Issues/Action Items	74
Table 3.3	Step 2—Analyze Information Environment	78
Table 3.4	Learning to Scope	80

Figure 3.2	Process flow for *Step 2—Analyze Information Environment*	80
Template 3.4	Requirements Gathering	83
Figure 3.3	Levels of detail—data	85
Figure 3.4	Context model	86
Template 3.5	Detailed Data List	87
Table 3.5	Collecting Data Specifications	88
Template 3.6	Data Mapping	89
Figure 3.5	Levels of detail—technology	90
Table 3.6	Mapping the POSMAD Life Cycle to CRUD Data Operations	91
Figure 3.6	Levels of detail—processes	94
Table 3.7	High-Level Function/Data Interaction Matrix: Business Functions That Use Customer Information	96
Table 3.8	Detailed Process/Data Interaction Matrix: Account Management Processes That Obtain, Maintain, or Apply Customer Information	97
Figure 3.7	Levels of detail for people and organizations	98
Table 3.9	Information Quality Roles and POSMAD	99
Table 3.10	Role/Data Interaction Matrix	101
Table 3.11	Step 3—Assess Data Quality	110
Table 3.12	Data Quality Dimensions	111
Table 3.13	Data Specification Quality	116
Table 3.14	Documentation Quality	117
Template 3.7	Data Specifications Scope	117
Figure 3.8	Typical profiling functionality	122
Table 3.15	Data Integrity Fundamentals—Tests, Analysis, and Action	123
Figure 3.9	Matching results: Matches, nonmatches, and the gray area	130
Figure 3.10	Matching: False negatives and false positives	130
Table 3.16	Consistency Results	142
Table 3.17	Tracking and Recording Timeliness	145
Table 3.18	Timeliness Results and Initial Recommendations	146
Table 3.19	Presentation Quality Comparison	153
Table 3.20	Presentation Quality—Collecting Credit Card Information	154
Figure 3.11	Use of Customer Contact Validation Date field to analyze data decay	160
Table 3.21	Step 4—Assess Business Impact	164
Table 3.22	Business Impact Techniques	165
Figure 3.12	Business impact techniques relative to time and effort	165
Table 3.23	Information Anecdote—Example 1	169

Template 3.8	Information Anecdote	169
Table 3.24	Information Anecdote—Example 2	170
Figure 3.13	Benefit versus Cost Matrix	178
Figure 3.14	Benefit versus Cost Matrix—evaluating the results	179
Figure 3.15	Example 1—project recommendation results	179
Table 3.25	Example 2—Prioritized Data Quality Tests	180
Table 3.26	Scale for Ranking Data	182
Table 3.27	Example—Ranking Results	184
Table 3.28	Ranking Analysis	185
Figure 3.16	Information Life Cycle with high-quality data	187
Figure 3.17	Information Life Cycle with poor-quality data	188
Table 3.29	Loshin's Poor-Quality Data Types of Costs—Categories 1 and 2	190
Table 3.30	Loshin's Poor-Quality Data Types of Costs—Categories 3 to 6	191
Table 3.31	English's Poor-Quality Data Types of Costs	192
Template 3.9	Direct Costs	193
Template 3.10	Missed Revenue	194
Table 3.32	Step 5—Identify Root Causes	199
Table 3.33	Root Cause Techniques	200
Table 3.34	Common Categories of Root Causes	206
Figure 3.18	Example Cause-and-Effect diagram	206
Table 3.35	Step 6—Develop Improvement Plans	209
Template 3.11	Recommendations for Action	211
Table 3.36	Step 7—Prevent Future Data Errors	214
Table 3.37	RRISCC Questions for Prevention	215
Table 3.38	Step 8—Correct Current Data Errors	219
Table 3.39	Step 9—Implement Controls	223
Template 3.12	Metrics and RACI	226
Table 3.40	Step 10—Communicate Actions and Results	228
Table 3.41	RACI	229
Table 3.42	30-3-30-3 of Selling Data Quality	230
Template 3.13	Communication Plan	231
Table 3.43	Mapping The Ten Steps Process to the Framework	233
Table 3.44	Mapping the Framework to The Ten Steps Process	236

Chapter 4 Structuring Your Project

Figure 4.1	Approaches to data quality in projects and The Ten Steps process	241

Table 4.1   Estimated Time to Spend on Step 2   243

Figure 4.2   Project life cycle comparison   247

Table 4.2   Data Quality Activities in the Project Life Cycle   248

Table 4.3   Data Quality Dimensions and Requirements Gathering   251

Figure 4.3   Areas of knowledge a project team needs   252

Table 4.4   Project Roles and Skills and Knowledge   254

Chapter 5 Other Techniques and Tools

Figure 5.1   Swim lane template   259

Figure 5.2   Common flowchart symbols   259

Figure 5.3   Example of the swim lane approach   260

Template 5.1   Table Approach   261

Table 5.1   Example of the Table Approach   262

Table 5.2   Data to Be Captured   264

Template 5.2   Tracking Results   267

Table 5.3   Examples of Tracking Data Quality Assessment Results   268

Figure 5.4   Three levels of detail for metrics   270

Table 5.4   Data Quality Tools and The Ten Steps Process   276

Figure 5.5   The Ten Steps process and Six Sigma's DMAIC   277

Appendix Quick References

Figure A.1   The Framework for Information Quality (FIQ)   285

Figure A.2   POSMAD interaction matrix detail—sample questions   287

Table A.1   POSMAD Information Life Cycle Phases and Activities   288

Table A.2   Data Quality Dimensions   289

Table A.3   Business Impact Techniques   290

Figure A.3   Business impact techniques relative to time and effort   290

Figure A.4   The Ten Steps process   291

Table A.4   Definitions of Data Categories   293

Index

A

Accessibility, of data, 32, 147–148, 295
Accountability
  Communicate Actions and Results, Step 10, 229
  data governance for, 52, 54
  data stewardship for, 53
  Develop Improvement Plans, Step 6, 210
  RACI, 229
  RRISCC, 20, 215
Accuracy, Step 3.4, and data quality dimension
  approach, 135–139
  business benefit and context, 134–135
  defined, 31–32, 111, 289, 295
  with other data quality dimensions, 35
Actions, 295
  Communicate Actions and Results, Step 10, 227–232
  Data Integrity Fundamentals, Step 3.2, 123–127
  effective, 4
  Information and Data Quality Improvement Cycle, 55
  Plan the Project, Step 1.2, 74
Address Data Quality as an Individual approach,
  245–246
Advocates and allies, identifying, 100
Aera Energy, 157–158, 171–172
Analysis, 61, 263, 265–269
  Accuracy, Step 3.4, surveys, 138
  cost–benefit, 37, 195–196
  data cleansing tools, 273
  Data Coverage, Step 3.8, 149
  Data Decay, Step 3.11, 160
  Data Integrity Fundamentals, Step 3.2, 122–127
  Define the Information Life Cycle, Step 2.6, 103
  Duplication, Step 3.3, 131–133
  mapping to FIQ, 233–234
  Perception, Relevance, and Trust, Step 3.10,
    surveys, 157
  root cause, 120, 198–199, 211, 243–244
  Six Sigma DMAIC process, 277
  Understand Relevant People/Organizations,
    Step 2.5, 100
  Understand Relevant Processes, Step 2.4, 94–95
Analyze Information Environment, Step 2, 76–81
  Define the Information Life Cycle, Step 2.6, 102–104
  Design Data Capture and Assessment Plan,
    Step 2.7, 105
  mapping to FIQ, 233
  step summary table, 78–79
  summary, 105–107
  Understand Relevant Data and Specifications,
    Step 2.2, 84–89
  Understand Relevant People/Organizations,
    Step 2.5, 98–101
  Understand Relevant Processes, Step 2.4, 93–97
  Understand Relevant Requirements, Step 2.1, 82–83
  Understand Relevant Technology, Step 2.3, 90–92
Analyze step, in DMAIC process, 277
Anecdotes, Step 4.1, and business impact technique
  approach, 167–168
  business benefit and context, 167
  defined, 36, 165, 290, 295
  sample output and templates, 168–172
Application development tools, 274, 276
Apply phase, 295
  FIQ POSMAD, 19, 21, 284–285, 287
  Information Life Cycle, 23–24, 288
  Understand Relevant Technology, Step 2.3, 91
Approach, 9–12, 65
  Accuracy, Step 3.4, 135–139
  analyze and document results techniques, 265–269
  Anecdotes, Step 4.1, 167–168
  Assess Business Impact, Step 4, 166
  Assess Data Quality, Step 3, 108–112
  Benefit versus Cost Matrix, Step 4.4, 177–178
  Cause-and-Effect/Fishbone Diagram, Step 5.3,
    204–205
  Communicate Actions and Results, Step 10, 227–230
  Consistency and Synchronization, Step 3.5, 140–141
  Correct Current Data Errors, Step 8, 218–220
  Cost–Benefit Analysis, Step 4.8, 195–196
  Cost of Low-Quality Data, Step 4.7, 189–192
  Data Coverage, Step 3.8, 149–150
  Data Decay, Step 3.11, 159–160
  Data Integrity Fundamentals, Step 3.2, 122–127
  Data Specifications, Step 3.1, 114–115
  Define the Information Life Cycle, Step 2.6, 102–104
  Design Data Capture and Assessment Plan,
    Step 2.7, 105
  Develop Improvement Plans, Step 6, 208–210
  Duplication, Step 3.3, 130–133
  Ease of Use and Maintainability, Step 3.7, 147–148
  Five "Whys" for Business Impact, Step 4.3, 175

Approach (cont'd)
    Five "Whys" for Root Cause, Step 5.1, 201
    Implement Controls, Step 9, 222–224
    Perception, Relevance, and Trust, Step 3.10, 155–157
    Plan the Project, Step 1.2, 72
    Presentation Quality, Step 3.9, 151–152
    Prevent Future Data Errors, Step 7, 213–216
    Prioritize the Business Issue, Step 1.1, 69–70
    Process Impact, Step 4.6, 186
    Ranking and Prioritization, Step 4.5, 181–183
    Root Cause Analysis, 198–200
    swim lane technique, 258–260
    table technique, 260–262
    Timeliness and Availability, Step 3.6, 143–144
    Track and Trace, Step 5.2, 203
    Transactability, Step 3.12, 161
    Understand Relevant Data and Specifications,
        Step 2.2, 84–87
    Understand Relevant People/Organizations,
        Step 2.5, 98–101
    Understand Relevant Processes, Step 2.4, 93–95
    Understand Relevant Requirements, Step 2.1, 82–83
    Understand Relevant Technology, Step 2.3, 90–91
    Usage, Step 4.2, 173–174
Appropriateness, 80, 295
Ashe, Arthur, 278
Assess Business Impact, Step 4, 163–166
    Anecdotes, Step 4.1, 167–172
    Benefit versus Cost Matrix, Step 4.4, 177–180
    Cost–Benefit Analysis, Step 4.8, 195–196
    Cost of Low-Quality Data, Step 4.7, 189–194
    Five "Whys" for Business Impact, Step 4.3,
        175–176
    mapping to FIQ, 234
    Process Impact, Step 4.6, 186–188
    Ranking and Prioritization, Step 4.5, 181–185
    step summary table, 164
    summary, 196–197
    Usage, Step 4.2, 173–174
Assess Data Quality, Step 3, 108–113
    Accuracy, Step 3.4, 134–139
    Consistency and Synchronization, Step 3.5, 140–142
    Data Coverage, Step 3.8, 149–150
    Data Decay, Step 3.11, 159–160
    Data Integrity Fundamentals, Step 3.2, 118–127
    Data Specifications, Step 3.1, 114–117
    Duplication, Step 3.3, 128–133
    Ease of Use and Maintainability, Step 3.7, 147–148
    frequently asked questions, 112–113
    mapping to FIQ, 234
    Perception, Relevance, and Trust, Step 3.10, 155–158
    Presentation Quality, Step 3.9, 151–154

    step summary table, 110–111, 164
    summary, 161–162
    Timeliness and Availability, Step 3.6, 143–146
    Transactability, Step 3.12, 161
Assessment, 295
    Accuracy, Step 3.4, 135–136
    business impact techniques, 166
    Data Specifications, Step 3.1, 117
    Duplication, Step 3.3, 132
    Information and Data Quality Improvement Cycle,
        55
    in project timing, 253
    root cause analysis for, 198–199
Associated data
    Prioritize the Business Issue, Step 1.1, 70
    quality checks, 49
    relevant requirements, 82
    relevant technology, 90
Attribute, in data models, 46, 295
Audience
    Communicate Actions and Results, Step 10,
        228–232
    levels of detail, 270
    for management support, 12
Audit trail metadata
    defined, 43, 294, 295
Augmentation, of data, 273, 295
Authoritative sources of reference, 134–135
Availability. See Timeliness and Availability, Step 3.6,
        and data quality dimension
Awareness, in Information and Data Quality Improve-
        ment Cycle, 8, 55, 295
Axis, in Benefit versus Cost Matrix, Step 4.4, 177–178

B

Background, in Data Specifications, Step 3.1, 117
Bases of issues, in Prioritize the Business Issue,
        Step 1.1, 70
Benefit versus Cost Matrix, Step 4.4, and business
        impact technique
    approach, 177–178
    business benefit and context, 177
    defined, 36, 165, 290, 295
    sample output and templates, 178–180
Best-case scenarios, 12
Best practices and guidelines, 59–61
Brache, Alan, 258, 305
Broad data management perspective, 61
Broad-impact components section, in FIQ, 20, 22, 284
Burton, Bruce, 40

Business benefit and context, 65
    Accuracy, Step 3.4, 134–135
    Anecdotes, Step 4.1, 167
    Benefit versus Cost Matrix, Step 4.4, 177
    Cause-and-Effect/Fishbone Diagram, Step 5.3, 204
    Communicate Actions and Results, Step 10, 227
    Consistency and Synchronization, Step 3.5, 140
    Correct Current Data Errors, Step 8, 218
    Cost–Benefit Analysis, Step 4.8, 195
    Cost of Low-Quality Data, Step 4.7, 189
    Data Coverage, Step 3.8, 149
    Data Decay, Step 3.11, 159
    Data Integrity Fundamentals, Step 3.2, 118–122
    Data Specifications, Step 3.1, 114
    Define the Information Life Cycle, Step 2.6, 102
    Design Data Capture and Assessment Plan,
        Step 2.7, 105
    Develop Improvement Plans, Step 6, 208
    Duplication, Step 3.3, 128–130
    Ease of Use and Maintainability, Step 3.7, 147
    Five "Whys" for Business Impact, Step 4.3, 175
    Five "Whys" for Root Cause, Step 5.1, 201
    Implement Controls, Step 9, 222
    Perception, Relevance, and Trust, Step 3.10, 155
    Plan the Project, Step 1.2, 72
    Presentation Quality, Step 3.9, 151
    Prevent Future Data Errors, Step 7, 213
    Prioritize the Business Issue, Step 1.1, 69
    Process Impact, Step 4.6, 186
    Ranking and Prioritization, Step 4.5, 181
    Timeliness and Availability, Step 3.6, 143
    Track and Trace, Step 5.2, 203
    Transactability, Step 3.12, 161
    Understand Relevant Data and Specifications,
        Step 2.2, 84
    Understand Relevant People/Organizations,
        Step 2.5, 98
    Understand Relevant Processes, Step 2.4, 93
    Understand Relevant Requirements, Step 2.1, 82
    Understand Relevant Technology, Step 2.3, 90
    Usage, Step 4.2, 173
Business Goals/Strategy/Issues/Opportunities section,
    in FIQ, 19, 284
Business impact techniques, 35
    Assess Business Impact, Step 4, 163–166
    choosing, 38–39
    Define the Information Life Cycle, Step 2.6, 102
    defined, 35–37, 165, 290, 295
    Implement Controls, Step 9, 224
    reasons, 36–37
    working together, 37–38
Business metadata, defined, 42, 294, 295

Business rules
    data definitions and conventions for, 45
    Data Integrity Fundamentals, Step 3.2, 127
    data quality checks, 50
    data specifications, 47, 49–50, 116–117
    defined, 47, 295–296
    discovery, 275–276
    Duplication, Step 3.3, 129, 131
    Understand Relevant Data and Specifications,
        Step 2.2, 88
Business terms, in Understand Relevant Data and
        Specifications, Step 2.2, 84–85
Buy-in, in Implement Controls, Step 9, 224

C

Capturing data
    Analyze Information Environment, Step 2, 105
    technique, 263–265
Cardinality, 46, 296
Catastrophes, in Prioritize the Business Issue,
        Step 1.1, 70
Categories
    Cause-and-Effect diagrams, 204
    data, 39–44
    reference values for, 45
Cause-and-Effect/Fishbone Diagram, Step 5.3, and
        root cause technique, 204–206
    defined, 200, 296
Celebrate strategy, 253
Change, 296
    FIQ RRISCC, 22, 284
    mapping to The Ten Steps process, 236
    Prevent Future Data Errors, Step 7, 215
Chapin, Donald, 49, 303
Checkpoint guidelines
    Analyze Information Environment, Step 2, 79,
        107
    Assess Business Impact, Step 4, 164, 197
    Assess Data Quality, Step 3, 111, 162
    Communicate Actions and Results, Step 10, 228,
        232
    Correct Current Data Errors, Step 8, 219, 221
    Define Business Need and Approach, Step 1, 68,
        75
    Develop Improvement Plans, Step 6, 209, 212
    Identify Root Causes, Step 5, 199, 207
    Implement Controls, Step 9, 223, 225
    Prevent Future Data Errors, Step 7, 214, 217
    step summary table, 65
Classification, reference values for, 45

Cleansing, 296
    Correct Current Data Errors, Step 8, 219
    working with tools, 272–274, 276
Column profiling and analysis, 121, 272
Communicate Actions and Results, Step 10
    approach, 227–230
    business benefit and context, 227
    mapping to FIQ, 235
    sample output and templates, 230–231
    step summary table, 228
    summary, 231–232
Communication, 296
    Address Data Quality as an Individual
        approach, 246
    Analyze Information Environment, Step 2, 106
    Assess Business Impact, Step 4, 196
    Assess Data Quality, Step 3, 162
    Communicate Actions and Results, Step 10,
        227–232
    Correct Current Data Errors, Step 8, 220–221
    Define Business Need and Approach, Step 1, 75
    Determine Root Causes approach, 244
    Develop Improvement Plans, Step 6, 212
    Establish Business Case approach, 242
    Establish Data Quality Baseline approach, 243
    FIQ RRISCC, 18, 22, 284
    Identify Root Causes, Step 5, 207
    Implement Controls, Step 9, 224–225
    Implement Improvements approach, 245
    Implement Ongoing Monitoring and Metrics
        approach, 245
    Integrate Data Quality Activities into Other
        Projects and Methodologies approach, 246
    for management support, 12
    Prevent Future Data Errors, Step 7, 215, 217
    RRISCC, 22, 215, 236
Communication plan
    template, 231
Completeness of tests, 123, 296
Completion dates, 231
Complexity issues, 219
Components, FIQ, 18–22
Comprehensiveness, 296. See Data Coverage
Computation business rules, 50
Conceptual models, 47
Concurrency tests, 127
Conley, Chip, 229, 303
Consistency and Synchronization, Step 3.5, and
        data quality dimension
    approach, 140–141
    business benefit and context, 140
    Data Integrity Fundamentals, Step 3.2, 126

    defined, 32, 111, 289, 296
    sample output and templates, 141–142
    with other data quality dimensions, 35
Consolidation, of data, 273, 296. See Surviorship
Constraints
    RRISCC, 20, 22, 236
    Understand Relevant Requirements,
        Step 2.1, 82
Consulting, in RACI, 229
Content profiling and analysis, 272
Content tests, 125
Context model, 86
Control step, in DMAIC process, 277
Correct Current Data Errors, Step 8
    approach, 218–220
    business benefit and context, 218
    mapping to FIQ, 235
    step summary table, 219
    summary, 221
Cost–Benefit Analysis, Step 4.8, and business
        impact technique, 195–196
    defined, 37, 165, 290, 296
Cost, in Information Life Cycle, 25
Cost of Low-Quality Data, Step 4.7, and business
        impact technique
    approach, 189–192
    business benefit and context, 189
    defined, 37, 165, 290, 296
    sample output and templates, 192–194
Coverage, in Data Coverage, Step 3.8, 149–150. See
        also Data Coverage
Create, Read, Update, and Delete (CRUD)
        operations, 90–91
Critical business decisions in anecdotes, 167
Cross-table and cross-file profiling and analysis,
        272
Culture, defined, 296
Culture and Environment section
    in FIQ, 22, 284
    mapping to The Ten Steps process, 236
Current uses, 173
Custom interface programs, 219

D

Dashboard level metrics, 270
Data, 5, 19, 296
    in FIQ, 22, 284–285, 287
    of interest, 84–86
Data Analyst role, 254
Data Architect role, 255

Data capture, 296
  Analyze Information Environment, Step 2, 105
  technique, 263–265
Data categories, 39
  defined, 41–43, 296
  example, 39–41
  importance, 44
  relationships between, 43–44
Data cleansing tools
  Correct Current Data Errors, Step 8, 219
  working with, 272–273, 276
Data components, in FIQ, 19, 21
Data correction
  Correct Current Data Errors, Step 8, 218–221
  Develop Improvement Plans, Step 6, 211
Data Coverage, Step 3.8, and data quality dimension, 149–150
  defined, 33, 111, 289, 296
  with other data quality dimensions, 35
Data Decay, Step 3.11, and data quality dimension, 159–160
  defined, 33, 111, 289, 296
  with other data quality dimensions, 35
Data definitions and conventions for business rules, 45
Data Expert role, 255
Data flow, 102
Data governance, 52–54
  and data stewardship, 52–54,
  defined, 52, 296
Data integration, 297
Data Integrity Fundamentals, Step 3.2, and data quality dimension
  approach, 122–127
  business benefit and context, 118–122
  data profiling, 118–122
  data quality tools, 272
  defined, 31, 111, 289, 297
  with other data quality dimensions, 34–35
Data Mapping, 297. See also Source-to-target mapping
  template, 89
Data Modeler role, 255
Data models, 46–49, 276, 297
  data profiling for, 120
  Data Specifications, Step 3.1, 116–117
  tools, 274
  Understand Relevant Data and Specifications, Step 2.2, 88
Data profiling, 32, 276, 297. See also Profiling
  Data Integrity Fundamentals, Step 3.2, 118–122
  tools, 272

Data quality. See also Information Quality
  Assess Data Quality step. See Assess Data Quality, Step 3
  Data Integrity Fundamentals, Step 3.2, 118–122
  Define the Information Life Cycle, Step 2.6, 102
  defined, 5, 297
  Information Life Cycle, 25–26
  in project life cycle, 247–249
  project roles, 252, 254–255
  requirements gathering, 249–251
  tools, 271–275
  Understand Relevant Technology, Step 2.3, 92
Data quality dimensions, 30–33
  Assess Data Quality, Step 3, 108–113
  choosing, 35
  defined, 32–33, 111, 289, 297
  reasons, 30–31
  working together, 34–35
Data Quality Tools section, 258
Data relationship discovery, 275–276
Data rule, 297. See also Business rules
Data Specifications, Key Concept, 297
  business rules, 47, 49–50
  data models, 46–49
  data standards, 45–46
  importance of, 52
  metadata, 51
  reference data, 51–52
Data Specifications, Step 3.1, and data quality dimension
  approach, 114–115
  business benefit and context, 114
  defined, 31, 111, 289, 297
  sample output and templates, 116–117
  template, scope, 117
  with other data quality dimensions, 34
Data standards, 45–46, 273, 297
  Data Specifications, Step 3.1, 116–117
  Understand Relevant Data and Specifications, Step 2.2, 88
Data Stewardship, 52–54
  and data governance, 52–54
  defined, 52, 297
Data store, 90, 297
Data type tests, 126
Database Administrator (DBA) role, 255
De-duplication, 273, 297
Default values, 45, 124
Define Business Need and Approach, Step 1, 66–67
  mapping to FIQ, 233
  Plan the Project, Step 1.2, 72–74
  Prioritize the Business Issue, Step 1.1, 69–71

Define Business Need and Approach, Step 1 (cont'd)
  step summary table, 68
  summary, 74–75
Define step, in DMAIC process, 277
Define the Information Life Cycle, Step 2.6, 102–104
Delivery section, in Communication Plan, 231
Deming, W. Edwards, 55, 303
Dependencies
  Correct Current Data Errors, Step 8, 220
  data profiling, 121, 126
  Define the Information Life Cycle, Step 2.6, 103
  Detailed Data List template, 88
  profiling and analysis, 272
  project charter, 73
Deployment activities, in project life cycle, 249
Description, for data capture, 264
Design activities, in project life cycle, 248
Design Data Capture and Assessment Plan, Step 2.7, 105
Detailed Data List, 87–89
  template, 87
Detailed reports for metrics, 270
Determine Root Causes approach, 10, 243–244
Develop Improvement Plans, Step 6
  approach, 208–210
  business benefit and context, 208
  mapping to FIQ, 234
  sample output and templates, 211
  step summary table, 209
  summary, 212
Developers
  skill and knowledge, 255
  Understand Relevant People/Organizations, Step 2.5, 99
Development activities
  Communicate Actions and Results, Step 10, 231
  project life cycle, 248–249
Diagnosis, FIQ for, 18
Dimensions, for data quality assessment, 109, 111–112
Direct costs
  template, 193
Dispose phase, 297
  FIQ POSMAD, 19, 21, 284–285, 287
  Information Life Cycle, 23–24, 288
  Understand Relevant Technology, Step 2.3, 91
Distinct values
  Data Integrity Fundamentals, Step 3.2, 125
  data quality, 31
  Duplication, Step 3.3, 128–133
  redundancy profiling and analysis, 272
  tests, 123–124
Divide and conquer strategy, 253

DMAIC process, 277
Documentation, 61, 263–269
  Accuracy, Step 3.4, 139
  Address Data Quality as an Individual approach, 246
  anecdotes, 168
  Benefit versus Cost Matrix, Step 4.4, 178
  Cause-and-Effect/Fishbone Diagram, Step 5.3, 205
  Consistency and Synchronization, Step 3.5, 141
  Correct Current Data Errors, Step 8, 220
  Cost of Low-Quality Data, Step 4.7, 191
  Data Coverage, Step 3.8, 150
  Data Decay, Step 3.11, 160
  Data Integrity Fundamentals, Step 3.2, 122
  data specifications, 45, 115
  Define the Information Life Cycle, Step 2.6, 103–104
  Determine Root Causes approach, 244
  Duplication, Step 3.3, 133
  Ease of Use and Maintainability, Step 3.7, 148
  Establish Business Case approach, 242
  Establish Data Quality Baseline approach, 243
  Five "Whys" for Business Impact, Step 4.3, 175
  Five "Whys" for Root Cause, Step 5.1, 201
  Implement Improvements approach, 244
  Implement Ongoing Monitoring and Metrics approach, 245
  Integrate Data Quality Activities into Other Projects and Methodologies approach, 246
  ongoing, 109
  Perception, Relevance, and Trust, Step 3.10, 157
  Presentation Quality, Step 3.9, 152
  Process Impact, Step 4.6, 186
  Ranking and Prioritization, Step 4.5, 183
  root causes, 205
  Timeliness and Availability, Step 3.6, 144
  Track and Trace, Step 5.2, 203
  Transactability, Step 3.12, 161
  Understand Relevant People/Organizations, Step 2.5, 100
  Understand Relevant Processes, Step 2.4, 94–95
  Understand Relevant Requirements, Step 2.1, 82–83
  Understand Relevant Technology, Step 2.3, 92
  Usage, Step 4.2, 173
Drilldown into metrics, 270
Duplication, Step 3.3, and data quality dimension approach, 130–133
  business benefit and context, 128–130
  Data Integrity Fundamentals, Step 3.2, 125
  defined, 31, 111, 289, 297
  redundancy profiling and analysis, 272

tests, 123–124
with other data quality dimensions, 34

E

Early victories strategy, 253
Ease of Use and Maintainability, Step 3.7, and data
    quality dimension, 147–148
  defined, 32, 111, 289, 297
  with other data quality dimensions, 35
Eckerson, Wayne W., 270, 303
Effective business decisions and actions, 4
Engaging management, 12–13
English, Larry, 2, 23, 25–26, 45, 140, 190–193, 218,
    303
Enhancing data, 273
Enhancement, 297
Enterprise Architect role, 255
Entities, in data models, 46
Entity, 46, 297
Entity class, 46, 297
Environment, in FIQ, 22, 298
Equivalence, of data, 140, 298
Errors
  Correct Current Data Errors, Step 8, 218–221
  Prevent Future Data Errors, Step 7, 213–217
Establish Business Case approach, 9–10, 242
Establish Data Quality Baseline approach, 10, 242–243
ETL (Extract–Transform–Load) tools, 274–275, 298
Evaluation
  Benefit versus Cost Matrix, Step 4.4, results, 178
  data specifications, 115
  Implement Controls, Step 9, 224
Examples as starting points, 60
Excessive costs, 70
Execution
  Accuracy, Step 3.4, 138
  Perception, Relevance, and Trust, Step 3.10,
    surveys, 157
EXtensible Markup Language (XML), 90, 302
External data sources, 120
Extracting records, 137

F

Few, Stephen, 265, 270, 303
Field level uniqueness, 131
Fields, naming conventions for, 45
Files, profiling within, 121
Fill rate test, 123. *See* Completeness

FIQ. *See* Framework for Information Quality
Fishbone diagrams. *See* Cause-and-Effect/Fishbone
    Diagram
Fisher, Craig W., 263, 306
Five "Whys" for Business Impact, Step 4.3, and business
    impact technique, 175–176
  defined, 36, 165, 290, 298
Five "Whys" for Root Cause, Step 5.1, and root cause
    technique, 201–202
  defined, 200, 298
Fixing data, 271
Flexibility, 60
Float, information, 143
Flowchart symbols, in swim lane approach, 258–260
Focus strategy, 253
Food Pyramid, 16–17
Framework for Information Quality (FIQ), 8, 16–18,
    298
  mapping The Ten Steps process to, 233–236
  Prevent Future Data Errors, Step 7, 215
  quick-assessment parameters, 22–23
  sections, 19–22
Frequency distribution tests, 124–125
Frequently asked questions, 112–113
Functions, business, 94
Future issues
  Prevent Future Data Errors, Step 7, 213–217
  uses, 173

G

Generalizing anecdote impact, 168
Good judgment, 59
Graph section, 65
Guidelines
  best practices, 59–61
  business rules, 50

H

Hard impacts, 190
Haverstick, Rachel, 12, 253
Hay, David, 46, 49, 304
Historical data category, 43, 294, 298
Hoberman, Steve, 49, 274, 304
Hoff, Ron, 229, 304
Huang, Kuan-Tsae, 4, 304
Human element
  business issues, 80
  Prevent Future Data Errors, Step 7, 213

I

Identify Root Causes, Step 5, 198–200
  Cause-and-Effect/Fishbone Diagram,
    Step 5.3, 204–206
  Five "Whys" for Root Cause, Step 5.1, 201–202
  mapping to FIQ, 234
  step summary table, 199
  summary, 205, 207
  Track and Trace, Step 5.2, 203
Impact of information and data quality, 4–6
  engaging management, 12–13
  methodology, 6–9
  project approaches, 9–12
Implement Controls, Step 9
  approach, 222–224
  business benefit and context, 222
  mapping to FIQ, 235
  sample output and templates, 225
  step summary table, 223
  summary, 225–226
Implement Improvements approach, 10–11,
    244–245
Implement Ongoing Monitoring and Metrics
    approach, 11, 245
Improve step, in DMAIC process, 277
Improvement and Prevention, 20, 298
  activities, 61, 271
  FIQ RRISCC, 20, 284
    mapping to The Ten Steps process, 236
    Prevent Future Data Errors, Step 7, 215
Individuals, data quality addressed by, 11
Inference business rules, 50
Information and Data Quality Improvement Cycle,
    54–55, 298
  example, 55–56
  and The Ten Steps process, 56
Information anecdotes, 168–171
Information float, 143
Information Life Cycle, 23, 298
  Analyze Information Environment, Step 2,
    102–104
  Cost of Low-Quality Data, Step 4.7, 189
  levels of thinking, 27–30
  nonlinear process, 26
  phases, 24–25
  reusable resources, 25–26
  swim lane, 258–260
  table approach, 260–262
  Timeliness and Availability, Step 3.6, 143
  universal resource life cycle, 23–24
  value, cost, and quality, 25

Information Life Cycle section, in FIQ, 19, 284
Information Product Maps (IP Maps), 263
Information quality. See also Data quality
  challenges, 6
  defined, 5, 298
  problem sources, 5–6
  Ten Steps process, The, 57–58
Information scrap and rework costs, 190
Information Technology (IT) resources, 90–91
Informing, in RACI, 229
Inputs step
  Analyze Information Environment, Step 2, 78
  Assess Business Impact, Step 4, 164
  Assess Data Quality, Step 3, 110
  Communicate Actions and Results, Step 10, 228
  Correct Current Data Errors, Step 8, 219
  Define Business Need and Approach, Step 1, 68
  Develop Improvement Plans, Step 6, 209
  Identify Root Causes, Step 5, 199
  Implement Controls, Step 9, 223
  Prevent Future Data Errors, Step 7, 214
  step summary table, 65
Integrating data quality activities, 11–12, 246–247
Integrity. See Data Integrity Fundamentals, Step 3.2,
    and data quality dimension
Interaction matrix, 298
  in FIQ, 20–21, 284, 286–287
  roles and data, 98, 100–101
Interoperability, 42, 44, 293, 298
Intra-table and intra-file profiling, 272
Inventory of data assets, 120
Investigation of data, 273
Ishikawa, Kaoru, 204
Issue Capture Worksheet, 70–71
  template, 71
IT Support role, 255
Iterative approach, 60

J

Juran, Joseph, 222, 224, 304
Justification activities, 248

K

Key Components section in FIQ, 19–20, 284
Key concepts, 7–8, 16
  Analyze Information Environment, Step 2, 76
  best practices and guidelines, 59–61
  business impact techniques, 35–39

data categories, 39–44
data governance and stewardship, 52–54
data quality dimensions, 30–35
data specifications, 45–52
Framework for Information Quality, 16–23
Information and Data Quality Improvement Cycle,
    54–56
Information Life Cycle, 23–30
metrics, 271
Ten Steps process, The, 57–58
Key indicators for data quality, 189
Key processes, in anecdotes, 167
Knowledge worker, 20, 298
    Implement Controls, Step 9, 224
    surveying, 34
    Understand Relevant People/Organizations,
        Step 2.5, 99–100

L

Lee, Yang W., 4, 304
Legal data quality requirements, 6, 20
Length tests, 126
Levels of detail, 60, 80
    Define the Information Life Cycle, Step 2.6, 103
    metrics, 270
    people and organizations, 98
    Relevant Data and Specifications Step 2.2, 85
    Understand Relevant Processes, Step 2.4, 93–94
Levels of management, 12
Levels of thinking, 27–30
Life cycle, 299. *See* Information Life Cycle
Life of solutions, 220
Linking, 299. *See also* Matching
    data, 128–129, 273
Location and Time section, in FIQ, 20, 284
Logical models, 47
Loshin, David, 190–191, 205, 304
Lost revenue and missed opportunities
    Cost of Low-Quality Data, Step 4.7, 190
    Prioritize the Business Issue, Step 1.1, 69

M

Madnick, Stuart E., 263, 306
Maintain phase, 299
    FIQ POSMAD, 19, 21, 284–285, 287
    Information Life Cycle, 23–24, 288
    Understand Relevant Technology, Step 2.3, 91
Maintainability, 32, 147–148, 299

Manageability, 80
Management
    engaging, 12–13
    perspective, 61
    tools, 274
Managers as resource, 13
Master data category, 42, 293, 299
Master data, in anecdotes, 167
Master reference data (MRD), 43
Match–merge data, 273, 299. *See also* De-duplication
Matching data, 129–130, 273, 299
Maximum value tests, 125
Maydanchik, Arkady, 159, 305
Measure step, in DMAIC, 277
Media, defined, 151, 299
Merge data, 273. *See* Surviorship
Messages
    Communicate Actions and Results, Step 10,
        230
    for management support, 12
Metadata, 51, 299
    Audit trail, 43, 294, 295
    business, 42, 294, 295
    category, 42–43, 294
    Data Specifications, Step 3.1, 116–117
    management tools, 274
    technical, 42, 294, 301
    Understand Relevant Data and Specifications,
        Step 2.2, 88
Metadata repository, 299
Methodology
    concepts and steps, 6–9
    for management support, 12
Metrics, 269
    Implement Controls, Step 9, 223
    key points, 271
    levels of detail, 270
    purpose, 269–270
    and RACI, template, 226
Minimum value tests, 125
Misinformation checks, 266
Missed opportunities
    Cost of Low-Quality Data, Step 4.7, 190
    Prioritize the Business Issue, Step 1.1, 69
Missed revenue
    template, 194
Monitoring
    Accuracy, Step 3.4, surveys, 138
    data, 271
    Implement Controls, Step 9, 223
    Implement Ongoing Monitoring and Metrics
        approach, 11, 245

N

NAICS standards, 45–46
Naming conventions, 45
Notation and modeling methods, 46
Nulls tests, 123
Number, of records test, 123
Number of tables and records, in data capture, 265

O

Objective step
    Analyze Information Environment, Step 2, 78
    Assess Business Impact, Step 4, 164
    Assess Data Quality, Step 3, 110
    Communicate Actions and Results, Step 10, 228
    Correct Current Data Errors, Step 8, 219
    Define Business Need and Approach, Step 1, 68
    Develop Improvement Plans, Step 6, 209
    Identify Root Causes, Step 5, 199
    Implement Controls, Step 9, 223
    Prevent Future Data Errors, Step 7, 214
    step summary table, 65
Obtain phase, 299
    FIQ POSMAD, 19, 284–285, 287
    Information Life Cycle, 23–24, 288
    Understand Relevant Technology, Step 2.3, 91
Olson, Jack E., 5, 82, 118, 305
Omissions, identifying, 266
Organizations. *See* People and organizations.
Orun, Mehmet, 2, 249–251
Out-of-place information, 266
Outputs step
    Analyze Information Environment, Step 2, 78–79
    Assess Business Impact, Step 4, 164
    Assess Data Quality, Step 3, 111
    Communicate Actions and Results, Step 10, 228
    Correct Current Data Errors, Step 8, 219
    Define Business Need and Approach, Step 1, 68
    Develop Improvement Plans, Step 6, 209
    Identify Root Causes, Step 5, 199
    Implement Controls, Step 9, 223
    Prevent Future Data Errors, Step 7, 214
    step summary table, 65
Owners vs. stewards, 53

P

Parsing data, 273, 299
Patterns and trends
    analyze and document results techniques, 266
    tests, 126

People and organizations, 299
    Analyze Information Environment, Step 2, 98–101
    in FIQ, 19–21, 284–285, 287
Perception, Relevance, and Trust, Step 3.10, and data quality dimension
    approach, 155–157
    business benefit and context, 155
    defined, 33, 111, 289, 299
    sample output and templates, 157–158
    with other data quality dimensions, 34
Periodic assessments, 55
Phases, in Information Life Cycle, 24–25
Physical models, 47
Pierce, Elizabeth, 263, 306
Plan-Do-Check-Act (PDCA) approach, 55, 299
Plan phase, 299
    FIQ POSMAD, 19, 21, 284–285, 287
    Information Life Cycle, 23–24, 288
    Understand Relevant Technology, Step 2.3, 91
Plan the Project, Step 1.2
    action items, 74
    approach, 72
    business benefit and context, 72
    sample output and templates, 72–74
Planners, 99
Plans
    communication, 228–229
    data capture, 105
    Develop Improvement Plans, Step 6, 208–212
    FIQ for, 18
    project life cycle, 248
Population
    data capture, 264
    Data Coverage, Step 3.8, 149
    Design Data Capture and Assessment Plan, Step 2.7, 105
POSMAD acronym, 19, 21, 299–300
    Information Life Cycle, 24–25
    Understand Relevant People/Organizations, Step 2.5, 98–100
    Understand Relevant Technology, Step 2.3, 91
Postproduction support activities, 249
Practice, 61
Precision tests, 126
Preparation
    Accuracy, Step 3.4, 135–138
    Communicate Actions and Results, Step 10, 231
Prepare the path strategy, 253
Presentation Quality, Step 3.9, and data quality dimension
    approach, 151–152

business benefit and context, 151
defined, 33, 111, 289, 300
sample output and templates, 152–154
with other data quality dimensions, 35
Prevent Future Data Errors, Step 7
approach, 213–216
business benefit and context, 213
mapping to FIQ, 235
step summary table, 214
summary, 217
Prioritize the Business Issue, Step 1.1
approach, 69–70
business benefit and context, 69
sample output and templates, 70–71
Prioritizing
Accuracy substep survey weighting, 137
Benefit versus Cost Matrix, Step 4.4, 177–178, 180
Design Data Capture and Assessment Plan, Step 2.7, 105
Develop Improvement Plans, Step 6, 209–210
Prioritize the Business Issue, Step 1.1, 69–71
Ranking and Prioritization, Step 4.5, 181–185
Process, in FIQ, 300
Process Impact, Step 4.6, and business impact technique, 186–188
defined, 37, 165, 290, 300
Processes
Analyze Information Environment, Step 2, 93–97
DMAIC, 277
failure costs, 190
in FIQ, 18–19, 21, 284–285, 287
Producers, 99
Profiling data, 32, 276, 300. See also Data profiling
Data Integrity Fundamentals, Step 3.2, 118–122
tools, 272
Project charter
template, 73
Project Manager role, 254
Project, defined, 9, 300
Project Sponsor role, 254
Project Stakeholders role, 254
Project structure, 240–242
Address Data Quality as an Individual approach, 245–246
data quality activities, 247–249
data quality overview, 249–251
data quality roles, 252, 254–255
Determine Root Causes approach, 243–244
Establish Business Case approach, 242
Establish Data Quality Baseline approach, 242–243
Implement Improvements approach, 244–245
Implement Ongoing Monitoring and Metrics approach, 245

Integrate Data Quality Activities into Other Projects and Methodologies approach, 246–247
timing, 253
Project teams, 211
Projects
approaches, 9–12
data quality roles, 252, 254–255
life cycles, 246–247
management, 59
Plan the Project, Step 1.2, 72–74
timing strategy, 253
Publish-and-subscribe technology, 250
Purpose step
Analyze Information Environment, Step 2, 78
Assess Business Impact, Step 4, 164
Assess Data Quality, Step 3, 110
Communicate Actions and Results, Step 10, 228
Correct Current Data Errors, Step 8, 219
Define Business Need and Approach, Step 1, 68
Develop Improvement Plans, Step 6, 209
Identify Root Causes, Step 5, 199
Implement Controls, Step 9, 223
Prevent Future Data Errors, Step 7, 214
step summary table, 65

Q

Quality. See Data quality
Quantifying anecdote impact, 168
Questions
analyze and document results techniques, 266
frequently asked questions, 112–113
Quick-assessment parameters, 22–23

R

RACI technique, 224–229
Random sampling, 136
Range of values tests, 125
Ranking and Prioritization, Step 4.5, and business impact technique
approach, 181–183
Benefit versus Cost Matrix, Step 4.4, 178
business benefit and context, 181
defined, 37, 165, 290, 300
sample output and templates, 183–185
Real-world usage, 4, 89
Recommendations, for action template, 211
Recency tests, 125

Record dispositions, 136
Record level uniqueness, 131
Records managers, 100
Redman, Tom, 4, 143, 224, 305
Redundancy. *See* Consistency and Synchronization, Step 3.5, and data quality dimension; Duplication, Step 3.3, and data quality dimension
Reference data, 51–52, 300
    category, 42, 293
    for classification and categorization, 45
    Data Specifications, Step 3.1, 116–117
    sources, 134–135
    Understand Relevant Data and Specifications, Step 2.2, 88
Regulatory data quality requirements, 6
Relevance, defined, 300
Relevant data and specifications, 80
    Perception, Relevance, and Trust, Step 3.10, 155–158
    Understand Relevant Data and Specifications, Step 2.2, 84–89
    Understand Relevant People/Organizations, Step 2.5, 98–101
    Understand Relevant Processes, Step 2.4, 93–97
    Understand Relevant Requirements, Step 2.1, 82–83
    Understand Relevant Technology, Step 2.3, 90–92
Repetition for management support, 13
Reports and reporting process
    Accuracy, Step 3.4, surveys, 137
    metrics, 270
Requirements, 6, 300
    anecdote fields, 167–168
    FIQ RRISCC, 20, 22, 284
    gathering, 82–83, 249–251
    mapping to The Ten Steps process, 236
    Prevent Future Data Errors, Step 7, 215
    project life cycle, 248
    relevant, 82–83
    template, gathering, 83
Resource Life Cycle, defined, 300
Responsibility
    data capture, 264
    FIQ RRISCC, 20, 284, 300
    mapping to The Ten Steps process, 236
    Prevent Future Data Errors, Step 7, 215
    RACI, 229
Restriction business rules, 50
Return on investment (ROI), 195–196, 300
Reusable resources, information as, 25–26

Reuse (80/20 Rule), 60
Revenue
    Cost of Low-Quality Data, Step 4.7, 190–194
    Prioritize the Business Issue, Step 1.1, 69
Right-sizing messages, 12
Risk factors
    Cost of Low-Quality Data, Step 4.7, 191
    Prioritize the Business Issue, Step 1.1, 70
Roles
    Analyze Information Environment, Step 2, 98–101
    data quality, 252, 254–255
Root cause analysis, 300
    data profiling for, 120
    Determine Root Causes approach, 10, 243–244
    Develop Improvement Plans, Step 6, 211
    Identify Root Causes, Step 5. *See* Identify Root Causes, Step 5
Ross, Ron, 47, 49, 50, 305
RRISCC, 300
    FIQ, 20, 22, 284
    mapping to The Ten Steps process, 236
    Prevent Future Data Errors, Step 7, 215
Rules. *See* Business rules; Data rule
Rummler, Geary, 258, 305

S

Sample output and templates, 65
    Anecdotes, Step 4.1, 168–172
    Benefit versus Cost Matrix, Step 4.4 results, 178–180
    Cause-and-Effect/Fishbone Diagram, Step 5.3, 205–206
    Communicate Actions and Results, Step 10, 230–231
    Consistency and Synchronization, Step 3.5, 141–142
    Cost of Low-Quality Data, Step 4.7, 192–194
    Data Decay, Step 3.11, 160
    Data Specifications, Step 3.1, 116–117
    Define the Information Life Cycle, Step 2.6, 104
    Develop Improvement Plans, Step 6, 211
    Five "Whys" for Business Impact, Step 4.3, 175–176
    Five "Whys" for Root Cause, Step 5.1, 201–202
    Implement Controls, Step 9, 225
    Perception, Relevance, and Trust, Step 3.10, 157–158
    Plan the Project, Step 1.2, 72–74
    Presentation Quality, Step 3.9, 152–154
    Prioritize the Business Issue, Step 1.1, 70–71
    Process Impact, Step 4.6, 186–188
    Ranking and Prioritization, Step 4.5, 183–185
    Timeliness and Availability, Step 3.6, 144–146

Understand Relevant Data and Specifications,
    Step 2.2, 87–89
Understand Relevant Processes, Step 2.4, 95–97
Understand Relevant Requirements, Step 2.1, 83
Usage, Step 4.2, 174
Sampling methods
    Accuracy, Step 3.4, 135–136
    data capture, 265
Sarbanes–Oxley Act, 4
Scalability, 60
Scales, for ranking data, 182
Scofield, Michael, 271, 305
Scope, for management support, 13
Scoring guidelines, for surveys, 137–138
Screen emulators, 218–219, 275–276
Scrubbing data, 273–274, 300. *See also* Cleansing
Selection criteria
    data capture, 105, 264
    data profiling for, 120
Semantics, 20, 300
Shared processes and data, 70
Shewhart, Walter, 224, 299
Silverman, Lori, 168, 305, 306
Similarities and differences, patterns of, 94–95
Simsion, Graeme, 46, 49, 306
SIPOC (Supplier-Input-Process-Output-Customer)
    approach, 261, 263
Six Sigma process, 56, 277
Size
    field, 126
    sampling, 136
Soft impacts, 190
Source-to-target mappings, 87, 120. *See also* Data
    mapping
Sources, reference, 134–135
Specificity, in anecdotes, 167–168
Spendolini, Michael, 266, 280, 306
Spewak, Stephen H., 168, 306
Spread the word strategy, 253
Stability, sampling, 136
Stakeholders, 300–301
    Prioritize the Business Issue, Step 1.1, 69
    role, 254
Standards, data, 45–46, 273
    Data Specifications, Step 3.1, 116–117
    Understand Relevant Data and Specifications,
        Step 2.2, 88
Standardization, defined, 273, 301
Statistical quality control (SQC), 224
Status, in Communicate Plan template, 231
Stephens, R. Todd, 51, 230, 306
Stewardship, data, 52–54

Store and Share phase, 301
    FIQ POSMAD, 19, 21, 284–285, 287
    Information Life Cycle, 23–24, 288
    Understand Relevant Technology, Step 2.3, 91
Structure and Meaning
    FIQ RRISCC, 20, 284, 301
    mapping to The Ten Steps process, 236
    Prevent Future Data Errors, Step 7, 215
    project. *See* Project structure
Subject Matter Expert (SME) role, 254–255
Summary level for metrics, 270
Surveys
    Accuracy, Step 3.4, 135–138
    Implement Controls, Step 9, 224
    Perception, Relevance, and Trust, Step 3.10,
        155–157
Survivorship, 129, 131–132, 273, 301
Swim lane approach, 258–260
Synchronization. *See also* Consistency and
    Synchronization
    Assess Data Quality, Step 3, 140–142
    business impact assessment results, 166
    Data Integrity Fundamentals, Step 3.2, tests, 127
    quality assessment results, 109
System performance, 219

T

Table approach, 260–262
    template, 261
Tables
    naming conventions for, 45
    profiling within, 121
Target date, in Communicate Plan template, 231
Technical metadata, defined, 42, 294, 301
Techniques. *See* Tools and techniques
Technology, 301
    in FIQ, 20–21, 284–285, 287
    Understand Relevant Technology, Step 2.3, 90–92
Templates. *See also* Sample output and templates
    Communication Plan, 231
    Data Specifications Scope, 117
    Data Mapping, 89
    Detailed Data List, 87
    Direct Costs, 193
    Information Anecdote, 169
    Issue Capture Worksheet, 71
    Metrics and RACI, 226
    Missed Revenue, 194
    Recommendations for Action, 211
    Requirements Gathering, 83

Templates (cont'd)
  Project Charter, 73
  Table Approach, 261
  Tracking Issues/Action Items, 74
  Tracking Results, 267
Temporary data category, 43, 294, 301
Ten Steps process, The, 7, 9, 57–58, 64–65
  Information and Data Quality Improvement
      Cycle in, 56
  mapping to FIQ, 233–236
  and Six Sigma, 277
  Step 1—Define Business Need and Approach,
      66–75
  Step 2. See Analyze Information Environment step
  Step 3. See Assess Data Quality step
  Step 4. See Assess Business Impact step
  Step 5—Identify Root Causes, 198–207
  Step 6—Develop Improvement Plans, 208–212
  Step 7—Prevent Future Data Errors step,
      213–217
  Step 8—Correct Current Data Errors, 218–221
  Step 9—Implement Controls, 222–226
  Step 10—Communicate Actions and Results,
      227–232
  tools, 275–276
Terminology, 8
Tests
  Data Integrity Fundamentals, Step 3.2,
      123–127
  data profiling for, 120
  Duplication, Step 3.3, 132–133
Thinking levels, in Information Life Cycle, 27–30
30-3-30-3 communication strategy, 230
Thomas, Gwen, 41, 293, 306
Time. See Location and time
Timeliness and Availability, Step 3.6, and data
      quality dimension
  approach, 143–144
  business benefit and context, 143
  Data Integrity Fundamentals, Step 3.2, tests, 127
  defined, 32, 111, 289, 301
  sample output and templates, 144–146
  with other data quality dimensions, 35
Timing
  Address Data Quality as an Individual
      approach, 246
  business rules, 50
  data capture, 265
  Determine Root Causes approach, 244
  Establish Business Case approach, 242
  Establish Data Quality Baseline approach, 243
  Implement Improvements approach, 245

Implement Ongoing Monitoring and Metrics
      approach, 245
Integrate Data Quality Activities into Other
      Projects and Methodologies approach, 246
  project, 253
Tools and techniques, 258
  analyze and document results, 263,
      265–269
  Analyze Information Environment, Step 2, 78
  Assess Business Impact, Step 4, 164
  Assess Data Quality, Step 3, 110
  business impact. See Business impact techniques
  capture data, 263–265
  Communicate Actions and Results, Step 10, 228
  Correct Current Data Errors, Step 8, 219
  data quality, 271–275
  Define Business Need and Approach, Step 1, 68
  Develop Improvement Plans, Step 6, 209
  Identify Root Causes, Step 5, 199
  Implement Controls, Step 9, 223
  independent, 61
  information life cycle approaches, 258–263
  for matches, 129
  metrics, 269–271
  Prevent Future Data Errors, Step 7, 214
  step summary table, 65
  and The Ten Steps, 275–276
Track and Trace, Step 5.2, and root cause
      technique, 201
  defined, 200, 301
Tracking
  data specifications gathering, 115
  results, 267–269
  template, results, 267
Training Accuracy substep surveys, 137
Transactability dimension, for data quality, 33
Transactability, Step 3.12, and data quality
      dimension, 161
  defined, 33, 111, 289, 301
Transactional data
  in anecdotes, 167
  category, 42, 293, 301
Transformation, 301
  data, 273
  data profiling for, 120
Triggers
  business rules, 50
  Communicate Actions and Results, Step 10,
      230
Trust, 155–158, 302
Tufte, Edward R., 265–266, 306
Type of access or extract, in data capture, 264

U

Understand Relevant Data and Specifications, Step 2.2
approach, 84–87
business benefit and context, 84
sample output and templates, 87–89
Understand Relevant People/Organizations, Step 2.5, 98–101
Understand Relevant Processes, Step 2.4
approach, 93–95
business benefit and context, 93
sample output and templates, 95–97
Understand Relevant Requirements, Step 2.1, 82–83
Understand Relevant Technology, Step 2.3, 90–92
Understanding data, 271
Unique values, 128
Data Integrity Fundamentals, Step 3.2, 125
data quality, 31
Duplication, Step 3.3, 128–133
redundancy profiling and analysis, 272
tests, 123–124
Unnecessary and excessive costs, 70
Updating
Accuracy, Step 3.4, survey reasons, 137
Correct Current Data Errors, Step 8, 219
Usage, Step 4.2, and business impact technique, 173–174
defined, 36, 165, 290, 302
User. *See* Knowledge worker

V

Valid values
Data Integrity Fundamentals, Step 3.2, tests, 124
establishing, documenting, and updating lists of, 45
validating, 273
Validation, defined, 273, 302
Validity, defined, 302
Value, in Information Life Cycle, 25
Verification, of data, 273, 302
Volume criteria, 219

W

Wacker, Mary B., 306
Wang, Richard Y., 4, 263, 304, 306
Weighting data, 137
"Whys"
Business Impact, Step 4.3, 175–176
business impact techniques, 36
Root Cause, Step 5.1, 201–202
Wiefling, Kimberly, 67, 306
Winchester Mystery House, 171–172
Witt, Graham, 46, 49, 306

X

XML, 90, 302

Y

Yonke, C. Lwanga, 157

Z

Zachman, John, 238
Zachman Framework for Enterprise Architecture, 20, 306

About the Author

Danette McGilvray is president and principal of Granite Falls Consulting, Inc., a firm specializing in information quality management and data governance to support key business processes around customer satisfaction, decision support, supply chain management, and operational excellence.

For more than ten years she led information quality initiatives at Hewlett-Packard and Agilent Technologies. In her roles as practitioner, program and project manager, and internal consultant, she gained firsthand experience in implementing data quality in projects. She saw the benefits resulting from a focus on information quality in addition to the challenges and opportunities. Her initial work with customer information that supported sales and marketing functions expanded to include all types of information and the integration of data into ERPs and data warehouses.

As principal consultant for Granite Falls, she continues to use her expertise to help clients in many industries. She has seen how organizations, once they understand the benefits of information quality, still face difficulties in implementing data quality-focused projects and integrating important information quality activities into other projects and methodologies. She also recognized those ideas common to all data and all types and sizes of organizations. This, along with her previous experience, led her to develop The Ten Steps methodology—a practical and flexible approach that combines concepts with realistic how-to advice.

Danette is an invited speaker at conferences throughout the United States and Europe. She has been profiled in *PC Week* and *HP Measure Magazine* and was an invited delegate to the People's Republic of China to discuss roles and opportunities for women in the computer field. She is a faculty member for The Data Warehousing Institute (TDWI) and a member of DMReview.com's Ask the Expert panel; here business intelligence and data warehousing professionals can ask questions of industry leaders. Danette is a founding member of the International Association for Information and Data Quality Professionals (IAIDQ) and an active member of DAMA International. She authored best practices highlighted in Larry P. English's *Improving Data Warehouse and Business Information Quality*, which is a highly regarded book about information quality and value.

Danette graduated with honors from Utah State University in Logan, Utah, with a B.S. in Business Information Systems and minored in Business Administration.

Currently, Danette resides in the San Francisco Bay area with her husband, Jeff. You can contact her at *www.gfalls.com*.

Printed and bound by CPI Group (UK) Ltd, Croydon, CR0 4YY

03/10/2024

01040315-0012